Evolution of

A

"This is a very thoughtful and an insightful book by Murali Patibandla, which fills up a big void in blending business management, international perspectives, global marketing from an interdisciplinary context. A must read for professionals and a must textbook for business students who want to have a global vision. An excellent book."

Bala Balachandran
J. L. Kellogg Distinguished Professor
Kellogg School of Management
Northwestern University

"Patibandla provides an insightful analysis of how economic reforms are transforming firms and industries in India. A most worthwhile read for anyone interested in the institutional foundations of development."

Amar Bhidé
Lawrence D. Glaubinger Professor of Business
Columbia University
Author of *The Origin of Evolution of New Businesses*

# Evolution of Markets and Institutions

The rich and growing field of the new institutional economics has been one of the most influential schools of thought to emerge in the past quarter-century. Taking its roots in the transaction cost theory of the firm as an economic organization rather than purely a production function, it has been developed further by scholars such as Oliver Williamson, Douglas North and their followers. This branch of economics stresses the importance of institutions in the functioning of free markets, which include elaborately defined and effectively enforced property rights in the presence of transaction costs, large corporate organizations with agency and hierarchical controls, formal contracts, bankruptcy laws, and regulatory institutions. In this timely volume, Murali Patibandla applies some of the precepts of the new institutional economics to India – one of the world's most promising economies.

**Murali Patibandla** is Professor of Economics and Corporate Strategy at the Indian Institute of Management Bangalore, India. Prior to this, he was a faculty member of the Copenhagen Business School, Denmark, the Indian Institute of Management, Ahmedabad, India and the Fulbright Scholar at the University of California, Berkeley. He has published extensively in the areas of international economics, applied industrial organization, development and the new institutional economics in journals such as *World Development*, the *Journal of Economic Behavior and Organization*, the *Journal of Development Studies*, the *Review of Applied Economics*, the *International Journal of Management and Decision Making*, *Economic and Political Weekly*, the *Indian Economic Journal* and *IIMB Management Review*. He serves on the editorial board of *Industry and Innovation*.

# Routledge studies in development economics

# Evolution of Markets and Institutions

## A study of an emerging economy

## Murali Patibandla

Routledge
Taylor & Francis Group

LONDON AND NEW YORK

First published 2006
by Routledge
2 Park Square, Milton Park, Abingdon, Oxon OX14 4RN

Simultaneously published in the USA and Canada
by Routledge
270 Madison Ave, New York, NY 10016

*Routledge is an imprint of the Taylor & Francis Group, an informa business*

© 2006 Murali Patibandla

Typeset in Baskerville by Wearset Ltd, Boldon, Tyne and Wear

Printed and bound in Great Britain by TJ Digital, Padstow, Cornwall

*British Library Cataloguing in Publication Data*
A catalogue record for this book is available from the British Library

*Library of Congress Cataloging in Publication Data*
A catalog record for this book has been requested

ISBN10: 0-415-33967-7 (hbk)
ISBN10: 0-203-02277-7 (ebk)

ISBN13: 978-0-415-33967-4 (hbk)
ISBN13: 798-0-203-02277-1 (ebk)

To my mother,
Indira Devi,
Who, when I was very young, said
I should find my own way in this world.
I chose my journeys to make their paths.

# Contents

# Figures

# Tables

# Preface

"One life, many stories" is what a common man may say about making a living by dealing with institutions at different levels in India. My interest in the new institutional economics originated from my struggles as a doctoral student and a participant in the labor markets in India during the late 1980s and the early 1990s. Around the same time, India embarked on a program of policy reforms towards a liberal market economy. I submitted my doctoral thesis in economics to one of the leading universities in India, Jawaharlal Nehru University (JNU), in January 1991, and had to wait almost four years to get the degree. The university sent the thesis to two external examiners in India. One of the examiners gave the evaluation reports promptly within three months, while the other refused to send the report for three years, despite numerous reminders from the university. During this period, I did not have a job. Our daughter Pratyusha was born in February 1992. As I could not afford to support the family, I had to leave them at my wife's parents' home in Hyderabad in the south. Barely surviving with borrowed funds, I had to make numerous thirty-hour train trips from Hyderabad to New Delhi, stay in cheap motels, and run around the university officials, pleading with them to do something. They would say that the best they could do was to send reminders to the examiner, and the examiner did not care to reply. In the labor market, I attended a few job interviews, for which I had to incur high transaction costs. In several instances, the experience of the interview process was humiliating because they were basically a farce, with insider trading. I felt that there was something drastically wrong with the way the free market mechanism was understood and propagated in several circles in India. If people in powerful and responsible positions could break contracts and impose high transaction costs on common people with impunity, there was something drastically wrong with the institutions. With these kinds of institutional conditions, the free market mechanism would be a highly distorted process. My interest in the new institutional economics (NIE) began to germinate.

In October 1993, I was invited for a job interview to the best management school in India, the Indian Institute of Management, Ahmedabad

(IIMA). As I did a good seminar and interview, the selection committee offered me an assistant professor position, subject to my obtaining my doctoral degree. I took the letter of conditional offer and in desperation I met the vice-chancellor of JNU, who happened to be a leading economist in the country and a very kind person. He withdrew the thesis from the examiner and appointed a new one. I had my thesis defense on 15 April, 1994 and immediately afterwards I took a train to Ahmedabad to take up the position at IIMA. The four years I spent at IIMA as a faculty member were the most gratifying professionally. During this period, I published two papers from my doctoral thesis in the leading international journals, the *Journal of Development Studies* and the *Journal of Economic Behavior and Organization*, and three papers on institutional economics in *Economic and Political Weekly.*

In 1998, I was awarded the Fulbright Fellowship. Prof. Oliver Williamson, the father of the new institutional economics, offered me an invitation to the University of California, Berkeley (UCB). I spent one year at the UCB reading extensively on NIE and closely interacting with Oliver Williamson. He showed me that great scholarship and humaneness are inclusive. During this time, I received an offer of tenured associate professorship from the Copenhagen Business School of Denmark. I took it, as I wanted to see how capitalist institutions function in Europe. I had the opportunity of first-hand experience of the functioning of institutions of capitalism in the three continents.

Amal Sanyal read the first versions of all the chapters in this book and gave very valuable comments. I benefited from my discussions with Amar Bhide, Rahul De, Deepak Sinha and Bent Petersen. Several arguments and the underlying evidences are drawn from my papers, published over the years in the following journals: *Journal of Development Studies, Journal of Economic Behavior and Organization, World Development, International Journal of Management and Decision Making, Review of Applied Economics, Economic and Political Weekly, Indian Economic Journal* and *IIMB Management Review.*

On the personal front, when our father died at our very young age, my brother, Narasimha Rao, took the responsibility of the family so that I could pursue academics by trial and error. My uncle, Siva Ramakrishnaiah, inspired my childhood with stories about great poets, philosophers and scientists. My wife, Aruna, and daughters, Pratyusha and Nikhita, put up with my difficult times, and my broodiness when I was working on this book. As the Upanishads of India say, 'wondering of a tiny bubble on the great ocean'.

Murali Patibandla
Indian Institute of Management, Bangalore, India

# Abbreviations

| | |
|---|---|
| ADR | American Depository Receipts |
| BPO | business process operations |
| DFI | Development Financial Institution |
| CII | Confederation of Indian Industries |
| CMIE | Center for Monitoring the Indian Economy |
| CSIR | Center for Scientific and Industrial Research |
| FDI | foreign direct investment |
| GDR | Global Depository Receipts |
| GE | General Electric |
| HP | Hewlett-Packard |
| IMF | International Monetary Fund |
| IPRs | intellectual property rights |
| IT | information technology |
| JIT | just in time |
| MS | Maruti-Suzuki |
| NASSCOM | National Association of Software and Services Companies |
| NIS | National Innovative System |
| NSE | National Stock Exchange |
| RBI | Reserve Bank of India |
| SBI | State Bank of India |
| SEBI | Securities Exchange Board of India |
| TNC | transnational corporation |
| WTO | World Trade Organization |

# 1 Introduction

The 1980s and 1990s witnessed extraordinary changes in the world economy. Several socialist and developing economies made a dramatic move towards free markets and outward orientation after pursuing decades of the socialistic economic system as activist states. At the same time, a general reduction in barriers to international trade and investment and rapid technological progress in information and communication technology contributed to increasing globalization of the economic activity of nations. At the beginning of the millennium, China and India are the two fastest-growing developing economies, with important implications in the world economy as they are also the two most populous countries.[1] One of the dominant reasons for their growth is the unleashing of the free market forces of capitalism. While China remains politically a communist state, it started to open its economy to free market forces and the outside world in the late 1970s. On the other hand, economic reforms in India relate to the reduction in excessive intervention in the economy by the state, which took up a developmental role under a democratic polity. Internal reforms were initiated in the middle of the 1980s and major internal and external reforms began in 1991, necessitated by the balance of payments crisis, with the help of the World Bank and International Monetary Fund (IMF) structural adjustment and stabilization program. India achieved an average annual growth rate of 6 percent throughout the 1990s, and about 7 percent in the early 2000s, which is a success story compared to a 3 percent Hindu growth rate in the 1970s and the early 1980s.

The structural adjustment and stabilization program is basically a package deal based on a textbook case of a free market mechanism in which markets are the central institutions and others do not matter. As the outcome of the reforms in India is fundamentally a success story, why should we talk of institutions? If one examines India's growth pattern, a major part of growth benefits have accrued mostly to the urban middle class and there are significant regional differences in growth levels. While the states in the western and southern part of India have been growing at a rapid pace, the large states in the north and some in the east remain stagnant. Even after fifteen years since the initiation of the reforms, close to 300 million people remain below the poverty line and illiterate, outside the market mechanism.

The international and intranational differences in the growth outcomes of the reforms towards the free market economy can be traced from differences in the initial endowments of capitalist institutions, apart from technological and capital endowments at the onset of the reforms.[2] The new institutional economics emphasizes the importance of the institutions of capitalism, such as the rule of law, social and economic norms, property and contractual rights and transaction costs of enforcement in determining the economic prosperity of societies.

Ronald Coase (1992) in his Nobel lecture commented:

> The value of including ... institutional factors in the corpus of mainstream economics is made clear by recent events in Eastern Europe. These ex-communist countries are advised to move to a market economy, and their leaders wish to do so, but without the appropriate institutions no market economy of any significance is possible. If we knew more about our own economy, we would be in better position to advise them.

The free market mechanism of the Western advanced capitalist nations functions on the basis of underlying economic and political institutions that have evolved through painstaking process over time. The following illustration shows the importance of institutions in the efficient functioning of capitalism. One of the indicators of economic development of nations is the productivity of the workforce. In the mainstream neoclassical economics, productivity is determined by capital and technology. A worker who has access to capital and better technology is more productive than the one who works with inferior technology and less capital. However, this is only a partial explanation. A worker with similar skills and access to similar technology in India may still turn out to be less productive than one in the US because of the inefficient market institutions he or she operates in. Let us take three basic elements of economic institutions to discuss this issue – property rights, incentives and transaction costs. A person refrains from investing his/her efforts in a particular activity (durable asset) if he or she is not sure of receiving the returns on the investment, particularly if there is fear of appropriation by the state and other private agents. A productive worker is not motivated if rewards within an organization are not based on performance relative to peers, that is, organizations (and societies) fail to adopt incentive-compatible practices. A worker will be less productive in a given activity if he or she has to divert her time and resources in dealing with transaction costs (searching, information processing, paper work, long queues, etc.).

In analyzing the evolution of markets and institutions in response to policy reforms, this book takes the following approach. From the neoclassical economics, the evolution of markets can be viewed in terms of the emergence of non-existing markets and of prices approaching long-run marginal (opportunity) costs. The new institutional economics shows that the presence of transaction costs due to information search and contracts makes the costs of operating competitive markets non-zero. The efficiency of markets is determined by minimizing transaction costs, but it is impossible to eliminate them, which leads to the issue of comparative economic organization, elaborated on later. The new institutional economics makes a distinction between the institutional environment (North, 1990) and the institutions of governance (Williamson, 1985, 1998). The institutional environment is defined jointly by the rules of the game (the formal constraints: constitutions, laws, and property rights) and the conditions of embeddedness (the informal constraints: sanctions, taboos, customs, traditions, and codes of conduct). The institutions of governance are market, quasi-market, and hierarchical modes of contracting, more generally of managing transactions and seeing economic activity through to completion (Williamson, 1998). The interaction between the institutional environment and governance mechanisms determines the economic efficiency of exchange and incentives for investments in durable assets, both physical and human (skills). Policy reforms refer to changes in certain elements of institutional environment, which, in turn, influence micro-level governance mechanisms with feedback effects on the institutional environment.

Policy reforms in the east European (transition) economies relate to shifting from a socialist to a capitalist system. Shifts within the paradigm imply that there exists a broad framework of capitalism, but with inefficient institutions, and that policy changes are necessary to improve these institutional elements. This distinction is important because the fundamental paradigm shifts from communism to capitalism involve complex issues and this book's focus is on the development of institutions. I approach the evolution of institutions under the condition that there is a critical minimum level of capitalist institutions at the onset of economic reforms, on the basis of which further evolution takes place.[3] The initial institutional endowments are existence of a certain level of property rights, and commercial laws (the rules of the game) so that there are privately owned firms with functioning product and input markets.[4]

Economic reforms are taken as exogenous shifts in certain elements of the institutional environment which trigger an endogenous process of evolution of markets and institutions. I make a distiction between parameter and qualitative shifts. The former refer to quantitative changes in taxes, exchange rates, tariffs, and licensing fees, etc., while the latter refer to changes in the rules of the game between different players. To illustrate the qualitative shifts, removal of licensing policies changes the rules of the game between producers, consumers and government agents, for example by increasing competition. The shifts change absolute and relative prices in an economy (between different sectors and economic actors), as well as the transaction costs of doing business in different spheres. This, in turn, determines structural changes in terms of growth and the relative importance of different sectors, and micro-level governance of technology and organization through increased competitive dynamics. The direction of the endogenous process is determined by initial institutional and market endowments.

The changing economic interests of different agents and groups determine whether the reforms progress, and there will be cohesive bargaining for effciency-enhancing institutional change. The importance of the initial conditions is that they determine how soon the positive gains of the reforms are realized, so that political interests become entrenched for further efficiency-enhancing institutional change.[5]

To illustrate the above point, in applying transaction-costs logic to political aspects of the reform process, Dixit (1999) characterizes three phases in the formation of interest groups under information asymmetry: ex ante, interim, and ex post. At the ex ante stage, each individual is uncertain about his own type (preferences) as well as the types of others because there is no private information. At the interim stage, each individual knows his own type, but not the types of others. The ex post stage is when all players' types are publicly revealed. In the case of countries such as India, unlike Eastern Europe and China, one might start from the interim stage because of the existence of powerful incumbents, both private firms and the policy-makers, with their interests known at least for the short term. Policy reforms would mean a fall in monopoly rents to dominant incumbent firms and a decline in the control and rent-seeking powers of government agents. To illustrate this with an example of industrialists in India, when reforms initiated the process of liberalizing the entry of transnational corporations (TNCs) in the mid-1980s, a few dominant incumbent industrialists organized themselves into what was then called 'the Bombay Club'. They put forward the argument of a level playing field to lobby against the entry of TNCs. However, the reforms continued in a slow process. By the early 2000s, two main benefits of the increasing presence of TNCs in the Indian economy became apparent. The competitive dynamics between TNCs and local firms resulted in several incumbent local firms becoming efficient. Local firms started to derive gains through the expansion of markets, a part of it caused by increased competition (fall in prices). Second, the case of software and service industries has shown the employment and export benefits of TNCs' operations in India, which altered both the public and policy perceptions about TNCs. Consequently, both the policy-makers and the main industry body, the Confederation of Indian Industry, now want to attract more foreign direct investment (FDI). Several companies who lobbied against the entry of TNCs, have become multinational firms themselves by investing in green-field ventures and acquiring firms abroad by the early 2000s. The argument is that the reforms may make everybody better off in the long run, but in the interim period the myopic interests of incumbents can block or distort the process. If the initial conditions are such that the benefits of the reforms are realized quickly, then institutional evolution may not be blocked

## India: a brief background

A major part of the reason for the positive outcome of economic reforms is that India possessed a critical level of markets and capitalist institutions on the basis of which policy reforms were undertaken. Several of the initial endowment conditions were acquired both from the free market mechanism of British rule and the import substitution policies of the post-independence period since 1947.

India's economy in the early part of the twentieth century under the British rule was basically a free market economy, which declined economically (Clark and Wolcott, 2001). However, British rule established a critical level of infrastructure conditions for free markets in terms of railroads and telegraphs, which reduced the transaction costs of trade both internally and internationally, and certain elements of capitalist institutions of contract and property laws through the adoption of Common Law, which continued after independence. At the time of independence in 1947, the Indian leadership bestowed on the government the responsibility of overcoming India's poverty and achieving economic prosperity. In order to achieve this objective, the government adopted a highly interventionist planning system for rapid industrialization, with relative success, accelerating the aggregate growth rate to about 6 percent in the 1950s and early 1960s. In the following decades, the growth rate declined to a 'Hindu growth rate' of 3 percent as the state started to impose several controls and transaction costs on economic actors in the name of socialism and eradicating poverty.

The dominant philosophy in development economics in the 1950s was that developing economies, most of which were victims of colonial rule, required a 'big push' by the state taking up the developmental role. The basic concern was that the private sector would be unable to save enough, and government was seen to be in a position to lift the saving rate through budgetary manipulations (Nurske, 1953). Apart from this, there was the concept of 'development externalities' drawn from Hirschman's (1958) theory of sectoral linkages, namely that private investments in individual products were unprofitable unless there were a concerted program of investment in a number of complementary sectors, each providing demand and reducing costs for the other. This required massive investments simultaneously in different sectors such as railroads, power, roads, banking, mining, and heavy industry. At that time, government alone was in a position to undertake the investment because, singly, private investors would have found it unprofitable. These investments by the government reduced several types of transaction costs by generating developmental externalities, contributing to increased growth rates in the 1950s and early 1960s. Similarly, the active policy intervention in the agriculture sector in the late 1960s contributed to the Green Revolution, which made India self-sufficient in food grain production within a short period. However, as the policy intervention increased over time, creating vested interest groups with rent-seeking interests (bureaucracy, politicians, and the monopoly businesses), the government started to impose new types of transaction costs on private activity, thereby stunting growth.

In several areas, the stock of the previous government investments made it easy for private sector and markets to take over and reduce transaction costs significantly in the post-reform era. One example is the communication sector. Another is the government's massive investment in higher education for facilitating import substitution, which became the basis for high-tech industries such as the software and pharmaceutical industries to expand significantly in the post-reform period (Patibandla *et al.*, 2000). The other side of the story is that the government intervention took on a life of its own as it became a major source of rents to government agents and powerful incumbents, imposing efficiency-curtailing transaction costs at every level of economic activity. This trapped the economy into distributional politics at the cost of wealth-generation (Sanyal, 1984; Bardhan, 1984). As mentioned before, India's growth in the post-reform period remains fragmented, with close to 300 million people below the poverty line and outside the market economy. One possible explanation is that, in the pursuit of heavy industrialization, the previous government ignored the generation of universal primary and secondary education and the generation of social security systems (or land reforms), and thereby failed to create conditions of 'equality of opportunity' for its people.

As is well known in the literature on India, the major economic reforms of 1991 were made possible by the balance of payments crisis, a crisis driven reform in a complex democratic polity. Although the reforms of 1991 can be considered a major policy shock, they were only a partial reduction in government intervention, and the subsequent reform process continues in a slow process owing to the complex web of interactions of the different interest groups. To exemplify this observation, the Indian economy averaged about 7 percent growth rate, its foreign exchange reserves crossed $100 billion and the country came to be known globally as a software superpower in the early 2000s. The then ruling NDA (National Democratic Alliance) government went to the elections in 2004 with the slogan of 'India Shining', but lost. The Congress party in coalition with the communist parties formed the government at the center. One of the explanations given for the fall of the NDA government by

several writers in the popular press (including Salman Rushdie) was that
the economic reforms and growth benefited only the rich and the middle
class, while a large section of the rural poor were left behind. The reforms
process continues slowly with a complex interaction between the coalition
members, the Communist Party, which wants to block market-friendly
reforms, and the Prime Minister, Dr Manmohan Singh, an eminent economist, who favours reforms and was the major architect of the 1991
reforms as the then finance minister.

India is probably the most interesting case among the emerging
economies with which to study the evolution of markets and institutions in
response to economic reforms, owing to its democratic polity, which is
characterized as 'one polity and many countries' (Clark and Wolcott,
2001). India as a nation-state is like putting all of Europe into one
country. When the East Asian economies and China were growing at a
rapid pace in the 1980s, they were called 'Tigers' in the popular press. In
view of her slow growth rate and the presence of a large section of poor
and illiterate people, India is generally referred to as a 'lumbering ele-
phant'. A few attribute this to the way in which democracy functions in
India, while the East Asian countries and China have been able to implement policy changes quickly because of their totalitarian systems. As mentioned before, India, unlike the Eastern European countries and China,
has a critical level of markets and capitalist institutions acquired both
from British rule and under the Fabian socialist policies of the pre-
reforms period. The institutional evolution in response to the policy
reforms operates from the basis of the initial conditions under a complex
democratic process. These factors make India an interesting case and at
the same time render the task at hand a very difficult one. Just to give an
example, the striking duality of India is that in the early 2000s, India has
come to be known as a great destination for outsourcing of high-tech jobs
in the areas of software and services, pharmaceutical, and biotechnology
industries. One of the results of the reforms is by the early 2000s India had
started to produce a few indigenous, world-class companies both in the
service and manufacturing industries. There has been a rapid increase in
the incomes of especially the urban middle class. At the same time, she
houses the largest number of poor and illiterate people in the world.

## A few conceptual issues

Does evolution of markets and institutions refer to movements towards an
optimum? Arrow-Debreu's general equilibrium theory of the neo-classical
economics is basically a formalization of Adam Smith's idea of the 'invisible hand' of free markets, which shows the efficiency of free markets
through the lens of the Pareto optimality conditions. In the presence of a
complete set of markets, prices in equilibrium reflect their true opportunity costs in space and time. With a large number of perfectly rational

anonymous agents with perfect foresight under an assumed perfect set of markets, the model shows how free markets lead to Pareto optimal outcomes of welfare. If one goes by the optimality criteria, policy reforms should be aimed at letting these conditions prevail either by withdrawing government controls or by public policy intervention in specific spheres, depending on the nature of the market failure. Market failure refers to the presence of externalities and non-convexities. Any student of economics knows that it is literally impossible to meet all the conditions necessary for Arrow-Debreu general equilibrium in the real world, which, in turn, can be used to justify selective policy intervention in correcting for market failures. If government intervened as a result of market failure considerations in the first place, where is the need for reforms eliminating government intervention? The question leads to the notion of 'government failure'. Ronald Coase envisaged the notion of government failure as early as 1964 through his conceptualization of comparative economic organization.[6] Commenting on the obsession of the economics profession with the frictionless free markets, he observed,

> It has led economists to derive conclusions for economic policy from a study of an abstract of a market situation. It is no accident that in the literature . . . we find a category of market failure but no category of government failure. Until we realize that we are choosing between social arrangements which are more or less failures, we are not likely to make much headway.

The Arrow-Debreu general equilibrium theory helps in identifying different conditions necessary for the efficient functioning of markets under the equilibrium criteria of collective economic welfare of societies (Arrow, 1964). Where does the notion of economic institutions of capitalism become germane? One of the fundamental assumptions of the neo-classical economics is that people participate in economic activity as anonymous and autonomous agents acting in a large group context. We all know that a major part of economic activity is organized with more than one agent as a group or an organization. For several reasons of indivisibility of economic tasks, collective action results in higher surplus than individual action, and economic activity by organizations instead of by single individuals reduces the transaction costs of markets – 'Robinson Crusoe gets married'. The rules and norms at the micro level of firms, bureaus, and societies at large are a result of collective action of the public and private order institutions.

When economic exchange moves from small-group to large-group exchange, it results in a high degree of uncertainty for economic agents in figuring out the attributes, and ownership rights of what is exchanged (North, 1990). High uncertainty reduces gains through specialization and expansion of markets and number of transactions, thereby stunting economic progress. This is where government, which can be viewed as a public order institutional arrangement, has to define and enforce the rules of the game so that uncertainty of exchange is minimized. Countries that are able to arrive at governance mechanisms that bring out a fine balance between individual incentives and the formal and informal rules formed by collective action are the ones that facilitate free markets to generate material prosperity at large. But there is no theory of this 'thin red line' of fine balance or its optimality, which makes the logic of comparative economics logical. To exemplify this, the US can be considered the most advanced capitalist economy at present. The major corporate failures in the early 2000s, which destroyed savings worth billions of dollars through corporate misgovernance, illustrate the institutional failures. Another example is the East Asian financial crisis of 1997. Until the crisis, the high economic growth rate of these economies was termed the East Asian miracle. The financial crisis was seen as a result of institutional failures. Countries such as South Korea, which were able to undertake institutional reforms, recovered relatively quickly from the after-effects of the financial crisis, in contrast to the other East Asian economies.

The new institutional economics takes the approach that an institutional framework for efficiency considerations should be examined in a comparative economic organization perspective. At a given point of time, a configuration of institutional elements may result in relatively high economic efficiency in comparison to the past and in relation to other societies. However, a similar configuration may result in relative inefficiency in the future when certain external factors change or when a new set of goals and benchmarks come into play for judging efficiency. The institutional evolution (or change) in this context implies the ability of societies to realign economic organization in accordance with the external changes or in relation to emergence of superior forms of institutional configuration for benchmarking.

The new institutional economics took its roots in the transaction cost theory of the firm as an economic organization rather than purely a production function, following the seminal paper of Ronald Coase on 'The Nature of the Firm' (1937). Later, scholars such as Oliver Williamson, Douglas North and others developed and extended the basic idea into the field of the new institutional economics. Williamson's main focus is on the issue of devising economic organizations that mitigate transaction costs of market exchange from a science of contract perspective. The main motivation behind his work was to understand vertical integration strategies of firms, which led to his seminal book, *Markets and Hierarchies* (1975), with the basic idea that firms adopt vertical integration for economizing on transaction costs of contracts and their enforcement. Once production is internally organized, individual choices and incentives are governed by hierarchical organizational structure in which incentives become low-powered, as compared to high-powered incentives of markets. Once we bring in the contractual aspect of economic activity, the issue becomes the ability of agents in a transaction to align incentives and to devise governance structures that are better attuned to their exchange needs. By this reasoning, Williamson brings forth a comparative economic organization approach to institutional aspects of economies. When superior feasible forms of organizing economic activity can be described and implemented, one has to find what the underlying governing factors are and how they can be achieved. In other words, this approach of comparative economic organization observes economic efficiency in terms of choices among alternative arrangements that show their relative economic merits. A similar economic activity under different institutional environments may exhibit different levels of economic efficiency.

Williamson's approach to organizational economics can be extended to a broader level of looking at an economy as an organization. In an economy, individual choices are constrained by scarcity of economic resources and also economic, social, and political institutions. In other words, economic activity is organized in an economy by balancing trade-offs between high-powered incentives of individual choices and low-powered incentives of institutional constraints. For example, in the Western capitalist societies, complex institutional structures at the constitutional and corporate level have been devised and implemented over time in order to constrain economic agents, so as to reduce the uncertainty of social interaction and prevent transactions from being too costly. Following from this, one can take the view that one of the major sources of development of the Western capitalist societies is their ability to find a fine balance between high- and low-powered incentives in economic organization.

The essential issue here is that comparative economic organizational approach implies understanding and analysing feasible forms of relative efficiency in both space and time, and nothing can be called an optimum institution. For example, economists have not yet developed a theory to say a particular organizational structure is the optimum. Organization of economic activity internally involves several elements, such as teamwork and monitoring (Alchian and Demsetz, 1972), hierarchy versus high-powered incentives of individuals (Williamson, 1975), agency relations, and incentives (Holmstrom, 1979) within an organization. There is no such thing as an optimal combination of these factors. At best, one can benchmark one form of organization against another to understand relative efficiency.

## The international context: comparative economic organization

In terms of human and physical capital and natural resource endowments, Russia can be termed one of the richest nations in the world. The country has 100 percent literacy, a large number of highly trained technical personnel and a large base of natural resources. However, Russia's sudden move from a socialist to a capitalist economy in the absence of minimum capitalist institutions resulted in disastrous consequences. This also led to the emergence of perverse institutions of the politically powerful Communist Party members confiscating a major part of the stock of government assets, and the emergence of the mafia in determining and enforcing property rights. Similarly, Nigeria was termed a middle-income country about twenty years ago, with a large natural-resource base. Despite its free market policies and openness to international trade and investment, it declined economically over the years, with erosion of institutional conditions caused by the emergence of a series of military dictators, who destroyed property rights and the conditions necessary for productive investment.

During the last 200 years, the Western capitalist economies have presented the case of capitalism with democracy, except in the case of Germany for a brief period between the First and Second World Wars under Hitler (of course, Hitler came into power through democratic elections). Japan and South Korea present the case of remarkable growth in the post-Second World War era. Japan's rapid growth was under democratic polity.

One of the dramatic economic stories of the 1980s and 1990s is the rapid growth and subsequent financial crisis (of 1997) of the East Asian economies. Among these economies, South Korea presents a highly successful story. The country achieved spectacular economic growth from the early part of 1960s under the polity of dictatorship of President Park. Under the hard-state system, the state implemented significant institutional reforms such as land reforms, the breaking-up of the trade union power and the forcing of the rich to convert assets to productive activities. The political system implemented an incentive mechanism of 'carrot and stick'. Industrial groups that were identified as potential winners in international markets were provided with preferential access to capital and resources and were made to perform in accordance with the objectives set by the government. The forced cooperation between the state and the private sector also facilitated periodic assessment of the possible strategies to be adopted in accordance with changing market conditions. This model transformed South Korea from a poor country to an advanced economy by the early part of the 1990s, within twenty years of the implementation of the development strategy. South Korea's industrialization strategy, that of activist state, was similar to that of Japan, with the main difference in the polity (Amsden, 1989; Pack and Westphal, 1986). The 'follower' East Asian countries, such as Malaysia, Indonesia and Thailand, adopted market economies open to international trade and investment under authoritarian political systems. These countries experienced rapid economic growth rates until the financial crisis of 1997 slowed them down.

After a prolonged period of rapid expansion, the Japanese economy started stagnating in the 1990s. The East Asian financial crisis involving

South Korea, Malaysia, Thailand and Indonesia put a brake on the rapid growth rates. These outcomes are generally explained as a result of macro-economic policy mismanagement and institutional deficiencies of the market economy models adopted by these countries. Krugman (1994) termed the market economy model of the East Asian Economies 'Crony Capitalism' – an institutional arrangement of insider dealings of powerful industrialists, bankers, and government agents. In assessing the East Asian financial crisis of 1997, the editorial of the *Far Eastern Economic Review* (8 January 1998) observed,

> The skid-marks all point to one source: the lack of accountability, gener-ally stemming from the too-cozy relationship between government and business. In South Korea, banks acted as investment arms of the govern-ment, with risk analysis almost unheard of. In Indonesia, the first family lavished preferential licenses for everything from cellular phones to the ill-starred Timor national car on presidential kin and cronies. In Thai-land, financial institutions, which fed a real-estate bubble, could count on political connections to keep the problem hidden until the pressures became too great. And in Japan, each time a company goes belly up we learn that its bad debts are many times higher than the official figure. This, of course, is just what we might expect from systems where capital is diverted from its most efficient uses and whose opacity allows players to hide the costs of these diversions.

In other words, the institutional arrangements of the market mechanism played a very important role for both the rapid growth rates and sub-sequent financial crisis in these economies (Patibandla and Prusti, 1998). South Korea, which implemented certain institutional reforms in corpor-ate governance mechanisms and functioning of the banking system, recov-ered quite quickly from the financial crisis.

The Japanese institutional mechanism of lifetime employment practice, close relations between banks and big business, and organizational prac-tices which were different from the Western capitalist practices was glori-fied during its rapid growth of 1950–90. However, the prolonged recession of Japan since the early 1990s is generally attributed to its insti-tutional deficiencies. Some observers of Japan attribute the slow process of institutional reforms to the functioning of the Japanese social system.

The importance of political elements in shaping capitalist institutions comes out strikingly in the context of emerging economies of the present from the comparative analysis of China and India. In the early part of the 2000s, China and India are considered the two-fastest growing developing economies, with highly divergent political institutions. China is able to achieve rapid economic growth rates by combining its communist political institutions of party dictatorship with capitalist market forces. On the other hand, India's transition from a highly-state interventionist model to freer markets has been done under democracy. India's economic growth and institutional evolution take place under a complex web of political equations of a federal democracy.

Until 1978, China was one of the most autarkic economies in the world. The economic stagnation under communism, the high economic and social costs of the Cultural Revolution under Mao and the changes in the geopolitical equations prompted the Chinese government to open up its economy to the outside world in 1978 under the leadership of Deng Xiaoping. The Chinese state, in its attempts to retain the communist philosophy of state ownership of capital, undertook external reforms of opening up to foreign capital first and kept the basic internal structure unreformed. In the process, it created a peculiar institutional framework. In order to utilize foreign capital and technology for economic growth, the state bestowed property rights and free mobility within the country to foreign capital, but not to local private agents. Limited property rights given to local agents are termed ambiguous property rights (Li, 1996). The Chinese state created a political pecking order in which at the top were the state-owned enterprises (SOEs) and at the bottom were the private firms (Huang, 2002). The major component of the non-state sector (private) was collective enterprises – rural enterprises and the Township and Village Enterprises. The collective enterprises were not totally private because local government involvement in the provision of production and services allowed the government agents to exercise a degree of control rights on the enterprises. The government agents were involved in several spheres of investment decisions, profit-sharing, bargaining and the issue of local taxes. The decentralized nature of the Chinese state provided a certain degree of alignment of incentives of local government agents with the private agents of the collective enterprises for profit generation instead of pure predation.

Private agents in the industrial sector were denied private property rights until 1998. Moreover, access to capital was made very difficult for them. However, the state used foreign capital to bring about a peculiar system of capitalist incentives. Under China's decentralized economic system, local governments restricted trade and capital flows to other regions: domestic firms were not allowed to invest outside their regional jurisdiction, while there were no similar restrictions on foreign firms. This created peculiar incentives for local private firms to convert their businesses to foreign ones: one reason was to get access to capital, and the other was to obtain legal property rights. The private firms, therefore, took their limited capital out to neighboring countries such as Hong Kong, Taiwan and Singapore and brought it back as foreign capital in order to be recognized as foreign-owned firms. Private firms also got into equity arrangements with foreign firms mostly from neighboring countries in order to get access to capital and achieve formal recognition as foreign firms (Huang, 2002).

On the other hand, SOEs had generous access to capital from the state, but most of them were operationally highly inefficient. In order to overcome the operational inefficiencies of SOEs, the state used foreign capital to privatize them, as local private agents were not allowed to acquire private property. With this valuable asset base, SOEs became profitable targets for acquisition by multinational firms. Despite high domestic savings rates in China, Chinese institutional mechanisms caused large flows of foreign capital, which became a major source for economic growth. However, it is at the cost of economic efficiency – if the local agents were given property rights and allowed to bid and compete with transnational corporations (TNCs), it could have resulted in higher growth benefits through competitive dynamics (Patibandla, 2002b).

The other side of this success story is that of China's Township and Village Enterprises (TVEs). TVEs are cooperative institutional arrangements with common ownership of capital of local people. Their economic performance has been highly remarkable. In 1991, there were about nineteen million TVEs, which made up about 67 percent of the rural industrial sector. As Levi and Pellegrin-Rescia (1997) observe,

> The TVEs have been characterized as organizations where there is no owner according to the traditional property rights theory: there is no residual claimant in the traditional sense and the assets are non-sellable, nontransferable and non-inheritable. Ownership and control are mainly collective and community based.

Membership is not voluntary but all local residents have automatic membership, an institutional arrangement initiated (or imposed) by the government. Unlike the SOEs, which were provided with large sums of capital under soft budget constraints, TVEs were subject to hard budget constraints and to competitive market conditions. Their total factor productivity during 1979–91 grew three times faster than that of SOEs, comparable to the private firms. What explains their success?

One way it can be interpreted is that it is a combination of capitalist incentives of hard budget constraints and competitive markets and a cooperative institutional arrangement under commitment, not in terms of membership (as it is involuntary), but in terms of restraining free-riding. When each TVE is able to realize high productivity and compete effectively, it generates surplus for all members. All members, being local residents, have a social commitment to the small communities and TVEs are an economic extension of the social commitment. A free-rider may face social stigma similar to that which can occur in a small society in which cheating in economic exchange results in social boycott. Furthermore, as long as an individual is better off being a member of the cooperative than defecting, he or she has the incentive to develop commitment.

In China, the centralization of power in the hands of the Communist

Party, with limited legal rights to local agents, allows government to undertake policy changes that suit its interests without much resistance. India, on the other hand, is a federal democratic polity under the parliamentarian system with diffused powers and three autonomous branches of state – the legislative, the executive and the judiciary. The government donned the mantle of a development state with pervasive intervention in economic activity from 1950 to 1991, which led to a large presence of the public sector and numerous commands and controls on the private sector (Mohan and Aggarwal, 1990). Under democracy and the semblance of a mixed economy, private agents were given property rights, but these were modified by several controls. The property rights led to the emergence of a large base of private sector firms in the organized and non-organized sectors. However, the pervasive government intervention also led to the emergence of a few organized vested interest groups – the politicians and bureaucrats, the organized industrialists, organized labor, and the large landholders. The distributional politics and rent-seeking behavior of these powerful groups generated economic inefficiencies and stunted the growth rate to an annual average rate of 3 percent from 1960 till the early 1980s. The government of India initiated a slow process of economic reforms in the mid-1980s and major reforms were implemented in 1991. Since 1991, the reforms process in several spheres continues slowly with a complex web of calculations, as mentioned before.

Unlike China, India moved on the internal front first and external reforms were undertaken later in a slow and gradual fashion. Under democracy, the political equations favor domestic capital – removing the controls on the domestic capital first and introducing competition from foreign capital at a later stage. In the case of communist China, private property rights were perceived as a threat to the state and it therefore used foreign capital to bring about the incentives of capitalism for augmenting economic growth. India's Fabian socialist policies of the previous policy regime under democracy, in spite of generating pervasive inefficiencies with institutional controls on the markets, did not destroy the capitalist forces of private property. Consequently, it led to the emergence of a strong local entrepreneurial class, which became the basis for rapid industrial growth in the post-reform era. The policies also generated a reasonably well-functioning institutional infrastructure for private capital – the well-developed capital markets, local managerial talent, endowment of skilled workers, and a functioning legal system, although with high transaction costs. When the gradual elimination of controls on markets was initiated from the mid-1980s, it led to growth of a significant number of indigenously born companies that could compete internationally. Furthermore, the reforms also led to rapid growth of internationally competitive knowledge-based industries such as the software, business processing and pharmaceutical industries.

In essence, while India is considered to have evolved its capitalist forces from the ground up, China has been pursuing a top-down approach, which is attributed to their contrasting political systems of democracy and totalitarian communism (Huang and Khanna, 2003; Patibandla, 2002b). China has been experiencing a faster economic growth rate than India, one of the reasons being a higher savings rate, and large inflows of foreign capital. India's savings and gross domestic capital formation have been much lower but the ground-up approach to free markets has resulted in better utilization of capital (Sutton, 2004).

Table 1 shows some of the indices of economic freedom in India and China. On most counts of the measures of economic freedom, China and India are on equal footing, but one has to go into micro level details to understand the differences in the functioning of the institutions. This is illustrated by a comparative analysis of the clearance and operation of large infrastructure projects in China and India. In the case of India's federal democracy, clearance of large projects is more complex, involving the federal government at the center, the state government and several other regulatory agencies such as the environmental regulators. The regulatory decisions governing issues such as zoning, land use, and environment vary from one state to the other. The investment approval in India is made at the central level, while implementation is left to state governments. The regulatory system allows for bureaucratic discretion. Apart from this, if corrupt practices are suspected, government clearances of projects can be politicized by the independent press, which can delay projects. Furthermore, the independent judiciary can also be a source of high transaction costs. For example, the Enron Corporation, in its involvement with the Dabhol Power Company (DPC), had to fight about twenty-seven court cases filed by private parties under public interest litigation and environmental grounds.

On the other hand, the centralized nature of the decision-making on the clearance of large foreign direct investment (FDI) projects in communist China provides a clearer signal for the target of negotiation and fast-track clearances for investors. Moreover, government contracts are not subject to litigation by private parties. The centralized decision-making, however, increases the contractual hazards of cancellation as the judiciary and different layers of government do not provide safeguards to contracts. Centralization of power with regard to clearing of large projects makes this process subject to lower transaction costs in China than in India. At the operational level, China poses higher transaction costs as a result of predation by local government agents since the local governments hold significant regulatory powers and powers of enforcement. As the rules are not transparent, the regulation is subject to a high degree of discretion by the local agents (Ahlstrom, Bruton and Lui, 2000).[7] The question that follows is, if contractual hazards are very high in China, why is it attracting large amounts of foreign capital in the infrastructure projects with a lot of sunk costs? A probable explanation could be the investors who show risk-

Table 1 Index of economic freedom

| Overall rank | Country | Overall score | Trade | Fiscal burden | Government intervention | Monetary policy | Foreign investment | Banking/ finance | Wages/ prices | Property rights | Regulation | Black market |
|---|---|---|---|---|---|---|---|---|---|---|---|---|
| 6 | United States | 1.80 | 2.0 | 3.5 | 2.0 | 1.0 | 2.0 | 1.0 | 2.0 | 1.0 | 2.0 | 1.5 |
| 119 | India | 3.50 | 5.0 | 4.0 | 3.0 | 2.0 | 3.0 | 4.0 | 3.0 | 3.0 | 4.0 | 4.0 |
| 127 | China | 3.55 | 5.0 | 3.0 | 4.0 | 1.0 | 4.0 | 4.0 | 3.0 | 4.0 | 4.0 | 3.5 |

Source: The Heritage Foundation – *Wall Street Journal*.

Note
The Index of Economic Freedom (IEF) has offered the international community an annual in-depth examination of the factors that contribute most directly to economic freedom and prosperity. The IEF includes the broadest array of institutional factors determining economic freedom:

• Corruption in the judiciary, customs, and government bureaucracy;
• Non-tariff barriers to trade, such as import bans and quotas, as well as strict labeling and licensing requirements;
• The fiscal burden of government, which encompasses income tax rates, corporate tax rates, and government expenditures as a percentage of output;
• The rule of law, reliability, impartiality, and efficiency of the judiciary, and the ability to enforce contracts;
• Regulatory burdens on business, including health, safety, and environmental regulation;
• Restrictions on banks regarding financial services, such as selling securities and insurance;
• Labor market regulations, such as established work weeks and mandatory separation pay; and
• Black market activities, including smuggling, piracy of intellectual property rights, and the underground provision of labor and other services.

taking behavior – gains from a large market might be worth the risk. One of the main factors for China's higher growth is that it built a good infrastructure, while the corresponding infrastructure investment in India, both by the private and foreign investors, has been low, owing to high market transaction costs of the government clearances (Patibandla, 2005b).

The comparative economic organization approach to economic efficiency is quite useful in understanding evolution of markets and institutions in developing economies. One can benchmark the institutional change by comparing it across developed and developing economies and also in terms of improvements over time in the efficiency of economic organizations. The approach helps us to test the proposition of convergence of best practices. Economic reforms increase global integration through trade and multinational investment, which make it possible for local firms to imitate global best practices through competition, and through the demonstration effect. In this context, where does the neoclassical price theory become germane? It helps in getting some of the market conditions right. For example, the theory of contestable markets shows that monopoly power can be curtailed when markets are contestable, which requires entry and exit costs to be zero. One of the conditions for entry costs to be zero is a perfect capital market, which means that a new entrant with a good project can raise capital without collateral and compete with incumbents. Although it may not be possible to have something called a perfect capital market in the real world, government policies can be aimed at reducing capital market imperfections by reducing transaction costs and informational asymmetries. For example, one of the underlying reasons for the East Asian financial crisis was the collusion between big banks and conglomerates under poor disclosure (corporate governance) practices, which led to misuse of capital. Government, by establishing legal conditions that improve disclosures and curtail collusion, can improve the functioning of the markets. As mentioned before, South Korea recovered quickly from the financial crisis because of the government reforms on these fronts.

## Methodological issues

The main notion of the new institutional economics is that of the transaction costs of the exchange mechanism of capitalism. The growing literature in the new institutional economics has extended its implications to larger issues both at the micro level of governance and macro level of the institutional environment. In several instances, it is criticized that everything can be called transaction costs. Williamson, in a series of influential papers which I discuss in Chapter 2, formalized the notion of transaction costs systematically. However, it is difficult to measure and capture several dimensions of transaction costs empirically in a precise way, which obliges us to work with proxies. I make use of both quantitative and qualitative information in deriving inferences on macro level issues relating to structural changes and evolution of public and private order institutions, and micro level issues relating to competitive dynamics and technological and organizational changes.

It is pertinent to mention here that if one looks at the improvements in the institutions in terms of the reduction in transaction costs of exchange mechanisms, it is not a straightforward issue to understand the effect of reforms on economic activity. This is because on one hand the reforms will reduce transaction costs of dealing with governments, and on the other hand, they could result in increases in other forms of transaction costs if economic growth increases complexity, uncertainty and frequency of exchange. This varies in different activities depending on the complexity of contracts and investments in durable and specific assets. In some spheres, transaction costs can go up as a result of increasing complexity of exchange and technology. The overall efficiency of economic activity can increase because it is determined by the combination of transformation (technology and organization) and transaction costs, if technological progress and economies of specialization outweigh increase in transaction costs. Apart from this, as growth takes place, aggregate transaction costs increase, but the average cost to the individual declines, which is an indication of improvements in market exchange. With the changing nature of transaction costs, organizations (firms and governments) have to alter governance structures for reducing the transaction costs of the exchange mechanism over time. This can take place at different levels, both at the micro level of firms and individuals, and at the collective (macro) level. I examine these issues from the analysis of structural dynamics and from the micro level analysis of firms and industries.

The evolution of markets and institutions involves a gamut of complex issues and different spheres of economic organization in an economy. This book confines itself mostly to the study of the industrial sector. It draws a simple analytical framework in Chapter 2, which serves as the basic structure for the analysis of the rest of the book. The framework brings forth the definitions of markets and economic institutions and mechanisms of their evolution in response to the policy reforms. Chapter 3 characterizes the initial endowments of markets and institutions and the policy reforms implemented in India. Chapter 4 examines the structural changes of the economy in response to the reforms. Chapter 5 analyses competitive dynamics, especially among incumbent firms and new entrant TNCs, and tests the proposition that competition causes convergence of best practices. The focus of Chapter 6 is on technological change at firm and industry level and on the evolution of the National Innovative System (NIS) and their implications on the evolution of markets and institutions. Chapter 7 examines organizational change at firm and industry level, which covers issues such as ownership, decentralization of organization, corporate governance, and standalone companies, and finally evolution of market structure. Chapter 8 examines the evolution of public and private order institutions and Chapter 9 provides concluding remarks.

The empirical analysis is based on both quantitative econometric analysis of industry and firm level data pertaining to the post-reform period and qualitative analysis of case studies of firms and industries. Given the limitations in capturing the evolutionary dynamics empirically, in several instances the inferences are drawn indirectly with underlying conceptual constructs. To illustrate this point, if we find a positive empirical association between firms' market share in an industry with relative production efficiency, it implies that prices are approaching long-run marginal costs based on the oligopoly theory. Decline in prices implies increase in real incomes, which results in increased consumption and savings, and which, in turn, is analyzed for its implications on the evolution of markets and institutions.

# 2 The conceptual framework

The analytical framework of this chapter serves as a basic conceptual structure for the discussion of the following chapters in tracing the evolution of markets and institutions. To recall, I take the approach that policy reforms are parameter and qualitative shifts in certain elements of the institutional environment which change prices and transaction costs in different spheres of economic activity. This has implications on structural changes of aggregate growth of different industries and micro level governance mechanisms. Structural changes and improvements in micro level governance mechanisms, in turn, engender evolution of markets and institutions.

I briefly discuss what I mean by policy reforms as parameter and qualitative shifts in elements of the institutional environment. More detailed discussion of this issue comes in the following chapters. Parameter shifts refer to quantitative changes in spheres such as taxes, licensing fees, tariffs, and exchange and interest rates. Qualitative changes refer to changes in the policy framework such as the removal of licensing, reservation for small-scale industry and quantitative restrictions on imports. Parameter shifts change relative and absolute prices and transaction costs in different spheres and facilitate resource mobilization for productive use. For example, reductions in import tariffs and exchange rate movements change the relative prices faced by different industries.

Qualitative shifts in the institutional environment eliminate some transaction costs once and for all and change the rules of the game between different economic agents. For example, the removal of licensing policies eliminates the transaction costs of acquiring licenses and hence the need for special organizational forms of firms set up for lobbying with the government. The removal of licensing and capacity restriction policies increases competition between incumbents and new entrants. It also causes a reduction in the predatory powers of government agents with respect to producers, and an increase in the bargaining power of consumers and workers with respect to producers. The evolution of markets and institutions is an outcome of the repeated play by all participants – firms, consumers, workers, investors and governments – in the various decision games, after the initial changes in the rules of the game.

In the following paragraphs, I discuss the definition of markets and economic institutions and trace the mechanism of their evolution.

## Markets

In the neoclassical theory, markets are central institutions in which individual actions interact. An economy can be seen broadly as consisting of two markets: product and factor markets (labor, capital and land). Under frictionless exchange, individual interactions through demand and supply result in market clearing prices in a general equilibrium of all markets. The Arrow-Debreu general equilibrium approach lists out all the conditions required for the equilibrium to meet the Pareto efficiency criteria. Since markets in the real world generally fail to meet all the conditions required for equilibrium, they are generally termed as market failures. Policy interventions in the market are therefore theoretically justified because of market failures. Reforms are aimed at withdrawal of government intervention either because the costs of government failure are more than those of market failure or because the dynamics of markets in terms of technological change and the emergence of new markets reduce the need for the government's intervention. An example of the latter aspect is deregulation when technological change reduces the natural monopoly (global economies of scale) properties of certain industries.

On the basis of Pareto optimality conditions, policy changes are supposed to meet both efficiency and distributional criteria. On efficiency grounds, policy changes should drive product and factor market prices to reflect their true opportunity costs (long-run marginal costs and productivity). On distributional grounds, policy changes that make some agents in the economy better off should not be at the cost of others. However, by their definition, the fundamental objectives of the policy shifts in developing and transition economies are not supposed to meet the distributional criteria at least in the short and medium term. This is because the policy shifts are made on the assumption that the previous policy regimes generated monopolies and inefficiency in the allocation of resources in an economy. The policy reforms are aimed at shifting economic activity to competitive mode to eliminate monopoly rents so that consumers gain at the cost of monopoly producers. Furthermore, the policy reforms also aim at improving the allocative efficiency of resources. This means that some sectors gain at the cost of others in an economy. The basic theory of comparative advantage shows, for example, that opening to international trade makes protected industries contract and industries with comparative advantage expand. Therefore, people engaged in the protected industries lose out as a result of policy shifts. The distributional outcomes have implications on the changing bargaining position of different groups, which, in turn, determines the direction of institutional change.

When one goes by the pure neoclassical approach of markets as institutions, the Pareto efficiency criteria can result in awkward results under certain conditions. Consider, for example, the textbook case of a perfectly discriminating monopolist. He can be shown to be Pareto-efficient because he charges different prices from different consumers depending on their willingness and ability to pay. The total market is served, and the last and poorest consumer pays a price equal to marginal cost. However, the monopolist takes away the consumer surplus. By the same logic, the institutional arrangement of slavery or bonded labor is Pareto-efficient because a landlord pays a wage to a worker on the basis of his/her bargaining power. Some ways in which these institutional arrangements can change in a normative way are the emergence of new (or previously non-existent) markets and a reduction in transaction costs of exchange which improve the bargaining power of workers and consumers; for example, there can be an increase in the number of producers, or improvements in capital markets, which reduce the power of access to capital as a monopoly source. To illustrate, bonded labor, an institutional arrangement quite prevalent in rural India till recently, came about as a result of the interlocking of capital and labor markets, which slowly disappeared in several parts of south India as a result of the commercialization of agriculture and improvements in capital markets.

Drawing from the above example, efficiency outcomes are the primary focus from a purely positivist approach and in normative terms distributional considerations become germane for the analysis. In the short term, the policy reforms may result in adverse outcomes to certain sections of the society on distributional grounds. In the long run, however, as markets and institutions evolve, some of these adverse outcomes of distribution may be rectified and it is possible that productivity increases may result in improvement for everyone.

The evolution of markets in response to economic reforms involves two interrelated elements: prices (in the product and input markets) approaching their opportunity costs, and the emergence of new markets which were non-existent prior to the reforms. These two elements are interrelated because Arrow-Debreu general equilibrium requires the existence of a complete set of markets for prices to reflect their true opportunity costs in space and time. Absence of one market may block emergence or development of other necessary markets, whereas the emergence of a new market leads to emergence of other markets. If markets for information emerge, it leads to greater participation of agents and expansion or emergence of other markets. For example, the entry of large institutional investors in India's capital markets led to the emergence of markets for information about India's corporations, which, in turn, saw further development of financial markets.

## Economic institutions

The main concept of the new institutional economics is transaction costs of exchange, which implies that market exchange is subject to friction, in contrast to the neoclassical definition of markets. As discussed in the previous chapter, from Coase's idea of transaction costs, two streams of analysis came about in the discipline of economics. One is the economics of organization, that a significant level of economic activity in a free market economy is governed not only by individual free choice but also by hierarchy of organization in order to economize on market transaction costs. Second, the Coasian theorem of property rights (1960) shows that the presence of transaction costs in market exchange necessitates collective action through social arrangements of public (governments) and private ordering to rectify the social costs of individual rational choices. Collective action is an institutional arrangement of the governance mechanism. To recapitulate from the previous chapter, the analytical developments in transaction costs economics led to two interrelated issues of analyzing institutions of capitalism – one that deals with the institutional environment (the rules of the game) (North, 1990), and the other dealing with the institutions of governance (the playing of the game) (Williamson, 1975, 1985). The institutional environment deals with the issues of the rules of the game, such as the property rights (polity, constitution, judiciary, bureaucracy), embeddedness conditions of customs, traditions, and norms. Economics of organization concentrates on the issues of contracts and governance structures, with the notion of the playing of the game under the given rules. The interplay of these two aspects determines the economic institutions of capitalism and their evolution.

In Coase's theory of property rights, collective action is required when individual actions cause costs to a society at large owing to negative externalities. Collective action is socially more efficient than individuals acting in isolation. For example, a negative externality resulting out of a single individual's action affects a group of individuals. The sum of costs of individual actions in isolation could be higher than the costs of collective action in rectifying the negative externality. Collective action can take two forms – private ordering of individuals getting together for bargaining, and public ordering of government enforcing property rights. In the presence of high transaction costs and a high degree of individual free-riding, individuals forming into an effective bargaining group may fail to be effective. In this context, the emergence of public ordering through government and legal bodies becomes pertinent. However, the issue is not so simple in terms of understanding institutions, because there could be several situations where transaction costs associated with the courts and governments may be higher than private ordering solutions. In this context, private ordering institutions may become more efficient than the public ordering institutions of governments.

Apart from people forming into associations for repeated interactions, social norms and trust are important elements of private ordering, which determine relative efficiency of institutions of different societies or nations. For example, throwing garbage on the streets is illegal in most countries, but enforcing it by government is highly costly. Societies that have developed the norm of individuals not throwing garbage end up with lower collective costs, while societies which could not develop the norm end up with high social costs, both in terms of the costs of the negative externalities and the costs of monitoring and enforcing by government.

What are the boundaries of collective action of a group through social capital? A family keeps its home very clean and throws garbage into the streets, or a nation throws polluting industries on to other nations. In other words, when one group can get into effective collective action it generates surplus for the group, the surplus generation could be purely owing to collective production (indivisibilities and specialization) or on distributional grounds of redistributing wealth from other groups. The latter outcome need not be monetary or direct transfers: it can take the form that the collective action of a group results in negative externalities to outsiders. The countervailing collective action of the outside agents depends on the transaction costs of organizing and cohesiveness of the group. If outside agents are diffused, their ability for collective action will be low. In other words, in Coasian theory, individuals forming into a group can bring out socially efficient outcome through bargaining with the polluter. In the above example, a powerful group could redistribute wealth in their favor or impose costs of negative externalities on the less organized, who could not undertake transaction costs of their own group formation. This may not be socially efficient.

North (1990) in his analysis of institutional environment observes that institutions are "the humanly devised constraints that structure political, economic, and social interactions. They consist of both informal constraints (sanctions, taboos, customs, traditions, and codes of conduct), and formal rules (constitutions, laws, property rights)." These institutional factors determine the extent of transaction costs of an economy both at micro and aggregate levels. Societies that are able to realize lower transaction costs for any specific economic activity realize higher material value for any given resources than those societies with higher transaction costs. In other words, the relative efficiency of the institutional environment across nations and over time can be seen in terms of the extent of transaction costs in individual and collective economic activity. To illustrate this with simple examples, one can compare the transaction costs incurred by an individual in different spheres of economic activity, say in India and the US: for example, transaction costs to obtain a driver's license (in India, someone who can bribe the relevant officer may obtain the license with zero 'search costs' by incurring transaction costs of the bribe); or the transaction costs a job-seeker has to incur and a firm incurs in hiring a specific skilled worker in the labor market. The higher the opportunity costs of an economic agent, the higher is the loss of value to a society in the presence of high market transaction costs – 'the search costs'. As a matter of fact, the opportunity cost of skilled labor is dampened because of inefficient institutions.

The institutional environment determines micro-level governance choices of private agents, which, in turn, determine the economic efficiency of a society. For example, if property rights and enforcement of contracts are weak, and information is highly imperfect, transaction costs will be high and the magnitude of transactions will be low, resulting in inefficient governance choices. As Coase's paper on 'The Nature of the Firm' suggested, one of the ways of mitigating transaction costs of market exchange is to internalize economic activity into an organization, and internalization has its costs of bureaucracy. High transaction costs of markets result in excess integration, which means economic loss through the costs of bureaucracy, apart from loss of benefits through division of labor.

Here, the issue is what are the differential transaction costs. Although Coase put forward powerful arguments for the relevance of transaction costs in two of his famous papers, he did not bring forth specific elements of transaction costs, which, in turn, led to the criticism by mainstream economists that everything can be termed a transaction cost. Williamson, in a series of influential papers, formalized different elements and the nature of transaction costs and their implications for governance choices.

Williamson conceptualizes differential transaction costs through the lens of the science of contracts and shows how they result in differential governance structures. In his schema, transaction costs differ in three critical dimensions – frequency, uncertainty, and asset specificity. Asset specificity has a strong contractual dimension. All contracts are incomplete: it is literally impossible for agents to foresee all possible contingencies and incorporate them into contracts. Williamson makes two main behavioral assumptions – bounded rationality and opportunistic behavior. Bounded rationality, following Simon (1957), refers to behavior intendedly rational, but limitedly so owing to both informational asymmetry and cognitive abilities. This makes the notion of incomplete contracts logically consistent. The opportunistic behavior is seen in terms of self-interest with guile. Guile, basically, implies that, when contracts are incomplete, agents renege on promises when it suits their purposes.[1] In the ex ante contractual stage, the market is competitive. Once two agents get into a contract for an economic activity, it becomes a bilateral monopoly (bargaining). In the context of incomplete contracts, agents can behave opportunistically when the environment changes in their favor in the ex post contractual stage. The costs of the opportunistic behavior are high when the agents have to invest in assets with low redeployable properties – these are assets that are very specific to an economic activity but have low economic value in other uses.

The behavioral assumption of opportunism is effective to understand the generation of institutional conditions that mitigate the costs of opportunistic behavior of economic agents. At the micro level, it refers to incorporation of contractual safeguards at the ex ante stage, and at the macro level, it refers to adoption of formal laws and regulation that protect the larger section of society from the costs of the opportunism of powerful agents. To illustrate the latter point, in the case of stock markets, managers and large investors may have more inside information than a large number of dispersed investors. In the absence of effective laws and regulation, the powerful agents can behave opportunistically, resulting in heavy costs to the larger sections. This was the case in the early and the mid-1990s in India, when a couple of stock market scams took place. Several bogus companies raised capital in the equity market and vanished.

Given the differential transaction costs of different economic activities, economic agents choose among different governance structures – markets, firms, hybrids, and public bureaus. They represent different costs and benefits in relation to the transaction costs of contracts and exchange under uncertainty. The alignment of property rights and their enforcement by government agencies or by private ordering is determined by transaction costs. If enforcement of property rights involves high transaction costs to individuals, the public bureaus are more efficient. However, enforcement through public bureaus like courts and government bodies also involves transaction costs to individuals and the additional costs of the bureaucracy of the public bureaus. Here, one has to examine the trade-offs between the two governance structures (public bureau and private ordering) for economic efficiency considerations. For example, a contractual dispute can be settled through courts or through mutual negotiations by weighing legal costs to the concerned parties. This logic can be extended to explain the functioning of government, and even the mafia, as a forced social arrangement by an organized group.

What is the difference between the mafia and government as institutions of public or private ordering? In the advanced capitalist societies of the West, government is seen as a result of democratic collective action. Arrows (1951) 'impossibility theorem' in the social choice literature has shown us that however hard we try, it is not possible for the collective-action-based rules to reflect each individual's preferences perfectly. The larger the group, the more difficult it is. Individuals whose preferences are not reflected in the formal rules either accept their being worse off or find ways to break the rules. Thus, imposition of prohibition of consumption of alcohol in the US in the 1920s and 1930s and the black market for gold in India in the pre-reform period both led to emergence of the mafia. This is one form of the mafia as a private ordering that caters to those individuals whose preferences are left out of the rules of the public ordering. While individuals can operate a black market, the mafia is an organization. A mafia is a small, organized group imposing rules on the unorganized, in a manner similar to dictatorships. They are de facto governments of forced governance, whose internal organization, rules and methods of deriving revenues depend on a given social and economic environment, discussion of which is beyond the scope of the present work.

One of the possible ways to increase the degree of individuals' choices reflected in collective-action-based rules is to build governance of public ordering institutions from the bottom up of decentralized government structure.[2] In other words, smaller groups' participation has a higher probability of each individual's preferences getting a higher degree of reflection in the policy formulation than large groups' participation. I briefly discuss the issues related to formal rules (public ordering) in the following.

## Formal rules and laws

In small societies in which everybody knows everybody else, with a dense network of interaction, transaction costs are low as most economic exchanges do not need formal contracts. Cheating and opportunistic behaviour are restrained because of the penalties of social stigma. However, in these societies production costs are high because of the small-scale organization of production. Once economic activity becomes large-scale and complex through division of labor, it results in the emergence of large group and anonymous (one-shot) interactions. Taking from Adam Smith, North (1989) observes, "Increasing specialization and division of labor necessitates the development of institutional structures that permit individuals to take actions involving complex relationships with other individuals far removed from any personal knowledge and extending over a long period of time." This results in the increased need for formal rules and contracts to enable large group interactions to reduce costs of cheating and opportunism. This is when the importance of the rules defined and enforced by the governments becomes imperative for the economic efficiency of the exchange mechanism. Countries that have developed better definition of the rules and better mechanisms of enforcement by the state will have lower transaction costs for a similar transaction.

There are two dimensions to formal rules: one is the definition of the rules (the laws), and the other is enforcement, with the two being interrelated in determining the efficiency of an outcome. The definition of the rules is similar to designing an organization (they can be copied from other societies). Enforcement of rules involves institutional effectiveness (embeddedness). The transaction costs of enforcement determine the efficiency of the outcome. When laws are poorly defined, they give discretionary powers to government and government agents to change and enforce them at will. This discourages private agents from investing in durable assets for fear of appropriation. Furthermore, government agents can act as predators, extracting bribes. This again results in both high transaction costs and uncertainty for investors. Even if the laws are well defined, mechanisms of enforcement can be weak: the enforcement mechanism involves the costs of monitoring and information, delegation under agency relations, and the transaction costs of courts. India, for example, has one of the finest and most elaborately defined laws for protecting the environment but their enforcement has been quite weak. On the other hand, the US, despite having fewer laws, has effective enforcement with the end result of better protection of the environment. Enforcement may involve monitoring and initiation of legal cases, both by government and private agents. A private agent can go to the court if the laws are broken either by government or other private agents. The latter aspect stems from the ability of private agents to incur transaction costs and undertake collective action.

Although the Western capitalist countries have a broadly similar legal framework of capitalism, the underlying features of emergence and enforcement of laws are different in different countries, which is partly traceable to their economic history. The differences in the legal framework have implications for the economic efficiency of the rules, especially in their enforcement. In the common-law countries, laws emanate from judicial decisions. In the civil-law countries, they emanate from the center. Although, several elements among the two are similar – for example the limited liability system in the financial markets emerged in the common-law countries first and was later copied by the civil-law countries – the processes differ. It is easier for new laws to be enacted by the civil-law countries because of the centralization of powers. The capture of the government by the vested interest groups is higher in the civil-law countries than in the common-law countries (Rajan and Zingales, 2003). This issue is, however, rather blurred because when courts in the US implemented the regulation in the nineteenth century, it was subverted by big business, which obliged government to usurp the main role in regulation (Glaeser and Shleifer, 2003).

Similarly, the centralized versus decentralized governance structures determine the effectiveness of enforcement of laws. Under the centralized structure, there could be a higher amount of informational imperfections, which may give a high degree of discretionary powers to the government agents at the bottom. Furthermore, there could be a high degree of moral hazard behavior on the part of public agents under centralization because of the distance between the governed and the government.

Credible commitments of government actions to given rules and laws, such that the government does not have too many discretionary powers to change rules, depend on the extent of centralization of legislative and executive powers. For example, under the parliamentarian system of the UK and India, the government (executive) controls the legislative process. In the presidential system of the US, the president does not have full control over the legislative process. Here, the legislature tends to impose much stronger procedural burdens on the executive branch to limit the deviations from legislators' interests. The discretionary powers of government are higher under the parliamentarian system than in the presidential system. Low credible commitments of governments discourage private agents from investing in durable and sunk-cost intensive assets, which is basically a form of mitigation of property rights (Levy and Spiller, 1996; Williamson, 1998).

## Formal rules of property rights

Under capitalism, private property right is an important institutional condition based on the premise that private ownership provides the right incentives in utilizing resources efficiently, while common ownership can result in the tragedy of commons-people free-riding and causing degradation of resources. The issue of property rights under capitalism is subject to complex definitions because several resources have common property properties. To give a simple example, a private agent can own a piece of land but groundwater is basically a common property. A single person's misuse of groundwater can result in negative externalities to others and everybody becomes worse off. The management of private and public property in different spheres is done both by elaborately defined and enforced rules of governments and by evolved social norms of societies.

A well-defined property rights system reflects a set of entitlements that define owners' privileges and obligations regarding the use of a resource. It is expected to have the following general features:

- Comprehensively assigned – all resources are either collectively or privately owned and all entitlements are known and enforced.
- Exclusive – owners internalize all benefits and costs from the use of a resource.
- Transferable – all property rights should be transferable in voluntary exchange with minimum transaction costs.
- Secure – property rights should be safeguarded/protected from involuntary seizure or encroachment by other private agents and governments.

The modern property rights approach of Grossman and Hart (1986) and Hart and Moore (1990), which draws from Williamson's theory of incomplete contracts, refers to the organization of collective effort and incentives of economic agents. This approach looks at the firm as a set of property rights and focuses on the role of physical assets in contractual relationship. Two agents, say *A* and *B*, with human and physical capital have the incentive to enter into a contract for joint production if combining their assets results in higher surplus value than each working independently of the other. In other words, the assets in consideration have complementarity properties. As contracts are invariably incomplete, each one has residual rights in using his or her own physical assets arising out of the conditions not specified in the contract. Ownership of physical assets is the source of control rights. The incentive for $A$ to buy $B$ is to take over the residual rights of $B$ when $A$ needs $B$ to increase investments in the relationship specific assets but $B$ has low incentives in undertaking the investment. Merger gives $A$ full control over all the physical assets for production. The merging outcome is determined by the incentives of agents before and after the merger in undertaking investments and sharing the surplus value. $A$'s having full control rights after the merger is the source of higher surplus to $A$, which, in turn, reduces the surplus and alters the incentives of $B$ within the merged firm. The control rights of $A$ give him or her power in assigning tasks to workers and firing them (denying them the opportunity to work with the physical assets of the firm).

Some of the possible disputes and the issue of control rights under incomplete contracts can be illustrated by the following story from India's Panchatantra (children's story book):

> On a hot summer day a traveler hired a donkey to carry him across a dusty road to the next town. The owner of the donkey walked along to bring the donkey back after the journey. In the middle of the day, the traveler wanted to shelter from the heat. As there was no other shade, he sat under the shadow of the donkey. The donkey's owner also wanted to rest and had the same idea of using the shade provided by the donkey. He said to the traveler, "The donkey is mine and you hired only the donkey but said nothing about the shadow of the donkey. So let me sit in the shade of the donkey." The traveler replied, "I hired the donkey for the day and you cannot separate the shadow from the donkey." As the two men quarreled, the donkey ran off. The moral of the story is that if one fights over the shadow, one may lose the substance.

In the present context, the story is an illustration of the hazards inherent in incomplete contracts.

According to modern property rights literature, establishing property rights means enforcing the contracts through which economic agents try to arrive at efficient control structures or finding ways to improve the efficiency of control rights. As implicit in the previous observations, efficiency of control rights involves incentives of agents in a contract to undertake investments and efficient utilization of physical assets. The issue of control rights can be applied to a broad spectrum of economic activity, such as the separation of ownership and control of capital of public limited companies, financial institutions, and government policies. For example, if there is imperfect or asymmetric information under agency relations between managers and stock-investors, the investors lose control rights on their investments. This could make managers exercise undue control rights, which, in turn, can result in misutilization of capital. Governments can impose policies which increase their control rights of capital: for example, tax and regulatory policies that impose high costs on transferability of assets imply loss of control rights by private agents. Furthermore, government might exercise high control rights by retaining discretionary powers in changing the rules. This can also arise out of the absence of regulatory predictability and procedural transparency. If the rules are unclear and non-transparent and judicial enforcement costs are high, government agents can prey on private agents for extracting bribes. The administrative discretion not only places those who have already invested at great hazard, but also forces those who are contemplating investment to think again. These possibilities relate to the concept of the credible commitment of government policies by Williamson (1998).

When property rights are inefficiently defined and enforced, it results in predation by both private agents and the governments, which, in turn, discourages investments in durable assets. An inefficient property rights system also prompts agents to adopt inefficient ownership structures. Where property rights protection is greater, the ownership mode is less important, as the risk of asset appropriation is less. Under a weak property rights system, private agents might have to make large investments in bribing government agents, co-opting government agents into the ownership structure, and undertaking high costs of contractual safe guards.

The above observations can be extended to the issue of intellectual property rights of the modern economies, in which knowledge and human capital constitute an important source of productivity gains. When the value of knowledge assets protected by copyrights, patents and trademarks cannot be fully realized by owners, the incentive to invest in these technological and marketing-based assets is reduced. The complexity of technological change in knowledge-intensive industries magnifies the hazards associated with incomplete contracts. This, in turn, requires effective legal mechanisms that minimize transaction costs in the formulation and enforcement of contracts. In the absence of such mechanisms, investments in these industries will be low and if some investments take place, firms choose high levels of internalization of governance to protect intellectual property, dissipating social benefits through linkages.

Investment levels and governance modes in high-tech industries have implications for investment in human capital by private agents. If there are large investments in knowledge-intensive industries, it will generate incentives for the acquisition of human capital by providing higher wages for higher skills. Furthermore, improvements in property rights and contract enforcement encourage high-tech firms to build backward and forward linkages with other firms and industries to take advantage of the division of labor, which can result in significant technological and pecuniary externalities for human capital accumulation. An increase in investment in human capital contributes to improvements in institutions by reducing informational asymmetries and enhancing perceptions of economic opportunities. In other words, institutional protection of intellectual property results in investment in high-tech industries, which contribute to investment in human capital with implications for the further evolution of institutions through enhancements in social capability.

Capitalist institutions work efficiently when there is a fine balance between defining private and common property and enforcing the rules with minimum transaction costs. Efficient management of common property requires individual rights and obligations regarding how common property can be shared. Similarly, in the case of intellectual property, there has to be a fine balance between private and public stock of knowledge. This is because, if private intellectual property is not protected, it provides low individual incentives for innovation and if public stock of knowledge is turned into a private good, it reduces the potential for technological innovation at the larger level.

## Informal rules and norms

Societies with embedded norms of trust incur low transaction costs. Qualitative empirics show that formal rules and norms that shape the behavior of economic agents evolve through repeated interactions (North, 1990). Some norms are a result of the learning and cooperation that take place through such interactions. These help in avoidance of prisoners' dilemma outcomes of myopic competitive behavior. Some norms could be such that they perpetuate prisoners' dilemma interactions, resulting in societies being trapped in a low level of development. Several feudal norms and institutions belong to the latter category, for example the behavior of landlords and tenants not investing in productivity-enhancing practices, even though they both could benefit from these practices.

Although norms and informal rules refer to small societies in which there is repeated interaction of economic agents, certain norms of economic exchange of large group anonymous interactions may evolve and take root at larger country level. The differences in Japan and the US are an illustration of country differences; India and the US also vary greatly. In the US, the interactions between government agents and the public may be more trust based than in India, where there is high degree of corruption in the lower level bureaucracy. Similarly, the transaction costs of the labor market in the US are lower than in India. In the labor market, an employer who trusts the information given by a jobseeker does not incur costs of verifying the information in detail. Trust comes into existence if past experience shows that incidences of cheating are few.

## Organization

Organizational economics involves a gamut of issues for understanding the economic efficiency of the organization – transaction costs, hierarchy, team production and incentives, agency relations, and informational structure. I briefly discuss a few streams of literature in this field to develop insights for the present task of understanding organizational change in response to policy reforms. Coase–Williamson showed that the firm develops as an organization to economize on transaction costs of the market. The organization resolves the problem of coordination of economic activity through hierarchy. Alchian and Demsetz (1972) rejected the relevance of hierarchy and argued that the firm evolves into an organization to resolve the issue of measurement of effort and assignment of rewards under team production (with indivisibilities of tasks) by employing a monitor with claims on the residual output and decision rights. In their conceptualization, there is no power and hierarchy in the organization because the firm does not own all the inputs. In the principal agency literature of Jensen and Meckling (1976), the firm is basically a result of a nexus of (complete) contracts under the agency problem of separation of ownership and control of capital. In the incomplete contract framework of Grossman, Hart and Moore, the theory of property rights defines the firm on the basis of residual decision rights arising owing to asset ownership under incomplete contracts. Internalization takes place when contracting agents face asymmetric incentives for undertaking relation-specific investments. Organization results when one party takes over all the physical assets with full residual rights.

The information economics (Arrow, 1974) shows that internalization of information or knowledge is a solution to market failure, which takes place when knowledge can be easily appropriated. When knowledge or information can be easily transferred, the market for that information will not take place, so that internalization into a firm could be a solution. Further extending the information logic, Arrow, following Hayek (1945), argues that the elements of the firm are agents among whom both decision-making and information are dispersed. Hence, the economic problem is to allocate information and decision correctly to optimize pay-offs. Pay-offs will depend on some factors that the firm has control over and some that it does not control. Arrow explicitly assumes that incentive problems do not exist in order to focus on the coordination of information. In this framework, the firm is a communication network designed to minimize both the costs of processing new information and the costs of communicating this information among agents. Information economies can be achieved by the introduction of a central party with all the information who allocates resources to agents who do not need all information. The firm is basically an information-economizing response to market failure.

Although different streams of literature in the organizational economics emphasize a specific issue or a set of issues, in the real world there is a simultaneous operation of different elements in determining organizational boundaries and efficiency. The importance or degree of significance of these elements will be different in different contexts. Furthermore, organizational economists usually ignore technological factors for the sake of analytical tractability of organizational issues. In practice, technology and organization are interlinked in determining the economic efficiency of organizations. For example, in human-capital-intensive industries, power through ownership of physical assets is negligible, and hierarchy is less important and profit-sharing practices are more important. Technology also determines the importance of teamwork and monitoring the agency problem of teams (Milgrom and Roberts, 1992; Patibandla and Chandra, 1998).

To illustrate the above point of simultaneous operation of different factors in organization, I examine the empirical example given in Alchian and Demsetz a little further. In their attempt to emphasize the importance of teamwork, Alchian and Demsetz show that sometimes technological development lowers the cost of a market transaction, while at the same time it expands the role of the firm. They give the example of the changes in the organization of weaving, in which the advent of centralized power increased the importance of teamwork. The firm expanded as an organization even though transaction costs declined. If we examine this more closely, it is not that transaction costs were not relevant, but that the trade-offs among simultaneous factors were more relevant; that is, the costs saved by internalizing to take advantage of the residual output of teamwork were more than the costs that could be saved by resorting to the market exchange when transaction costs went down.

Clark and Wolcott (2001) show that the industrial revolution in the West brought in not only technological change and greater division of labor but also a complex hierarchy of employees supervising employees. In the pre-industrial period, most industrial workers were subcontractors. The arrival of steam-powered factories in the 1770s brought with it the new employment concept of 'factory discipline' and the complex hierarchical organization of production through division of labor. These issues are germane to the present task of examination of the evolution of institutions and markets in response to policy reforms, which involves simultaneous operation of a gamut of factors in determining organizational choices and efficiency.

The other important issue is the internal organization in terms of centralization versus decentralization. Chandler (1977) and Williamson (1975) show that when firms grow large, one way in which the internal coordination of information burden at the top can be resolved is by adopting a multi-divisional form (M-form) of organization. M-form can also facilitate internal capital and labor markets with a combination of low-powered incentives of hierarchy and high-powered incentives of competition among different divisions. In many industries, one observes both decentralized M-form firms and also centralized L-form firms. The question is, if M-form is better at internal coordination, why do all large firms not adopt M-form instead of L-form? Stylized empirics show that L-form firms tend to be family-owned and M-form firms tend to be professionally run companies – the examples being Ford Motors and General Motors in the US. The efficiency objectives of the two forms could be different, with the professional companies driven by short-term profits and shareholder interests, while the family-owned firms concentrate on long-term ownership objectives, under which short-term efficiency considerations could be suppressed.

Aoki (1990) characterizes a T-form – that is, temporary or transitional – organization. Joint ventures and alliances fall into this category. These arrangements are important for the success or failure of firms operating in developing markets where technology and rivalry are undergoing rapid change. This issue is quite relevant in the present effort of understanding the evolution of markets and institutions in a developing economy.

One of the important dimensions of organization is the diversification behavior of firms. The theory of the firm explains vertical integration, but there is no systematic theory to explain horizontal mergers and firms' diversification into unrelated businesses. A plausible explanation from the new institutional economics is that in the presence of capital and labor market imperfections, diversification helps firms to generate internal markets, which can be spread over multi-level activities. In other words, well-developed capital markets make firms adopt focused organization, and imperfect markets lead to diversification (Rajan and Zingales; 2003, Khanna and Palepu, 1997). In the managerial tradition, Penrose (1959) argues that firms end up with excess resources because of indivisibilities and learning over time through increase in productivity. Firms can deploy these resources in three ways: they sell the services in the market if they are not subject to market failure, they can diversify, or, if the resources are cash, they can return it to shareholders.

## The evolution of economic institutions

In the following, I discuss the mechanisms of evolution of the different elements of institutions in response to policy reforms. To recapitulate, policy reforms are treated as parameter and qualitative shifts in certain elements of the institutional environment, which change absolute and relative prices and transaction costs in different spheres of economic activity and the rules of the game between different economic players. Parameter and qualitative elements are not exclusive of each other. For example, quantitative changes such as in exchange rates change the rules of the game between local and international players. Changes in relative prices cause a differential growth rate of industries and rules of the game between the players engaged in different industries and government agents. To give a simple example, the devaluation of the rupee in 1991 caused rapid growth in India's software industry through exports and has become a major source of employment of skilled people coming from the upper and lower middle class. This became a basis for further opening up of the Indian economy to international trade and multinational investment. Changes in the rules of the game in terms of increasing competition, especially between local firms and new-entrant TNCs, have significant implications for micro-level governance choices and economic efficiency. Improvement in economic efficiency reduces prices and increases real incomes and surplus for investment.

An increase in the number of people participating in the market increases the number of transactions. Elimination of monopolies on efficiency grounds reduces dead-weight losses and thereby increases aggregate economic surplus (incomes). On distributional grounds, there is a transfer of surplus from monopoly producers to a larger number of consumers in the system. This, in turn, engenders forces for change in the institutional environment. An increase in the number of people in the market may lead them to make attempts at reducing uncertainty and transaction costs in the market through lobbying with government or finding private order solutions. An increase in the surplus in the system may prompt people to search for avenues to invest in durable assets, which requires improvements in property rights.

Improvements in the efficiency of governance choices, in turn, will influence the evolution of the institutional environment by causing growth dynamics. If policy reforms enhance competition, from North's (1993) proposition, "Competition forces organizations to continually invest in skills and knowledge to survive. The kinds of skills and knowledge individuals and their organizations acquire will shape evolving perceptions about opportunities and hence choices that will incrementally alter institutions." However, for competition to result in efficient outcomes it should be based on certain (given) rules of the game, and how the rules of the game come about endogenously is a complex and difficult issue. To recapitulate, the outcome of the reforms through its effect on structural and micro level factors depends on the initial endowments of markets and institutions at the onset of the reforms.

North (1990) shows that government regulation of the market through anti-trust policies in terms of defining and enforcing the rules of competition came about in the US because the destructive competitive behavior of capitalists resulted in everyone being worse off. The capitalists needed a neutral body to define and enforce the rules of competition. Similarly, destructive competition can make a larger section of people, including those who are not participants in the specific market, worse off. For example, the high degree of price competition in the chemical and leather industries in India led to negative externalities of land degradation in several parts of west and south India, destroying the livelihood of millions. In other words, for North's proposition to hold, competition should be based on certain underlying rules for positive outcomes, and I take the approach that there are certain initial conditions of the rules, instead of dealing with the endogenous process from scratch.

The parameter and qualitative shifts in the institutional environment can be one at a time (piecemeal) or through a related set of changes made simultaneously. In several cases, piecemeal shifts may not result in the desired outcomes, and may lead to perverse ones. For example, the privatization of public monopolies without establishing property rights with credible commitments by the state, and without a transparent bidding process, is doomed to fail, as witnessed in Russia. Similarly, the removal of policy-based entry barriers to enhance competition is ineffective if capital markets are imperfect – only powerful incumbents have privileged access to capital.

As mentioned in the previous chapter, a change in the nature of transaction costs in response to the above characterization of the growth process is not a straightforward issue, because the reforms on one hand will reduce the transaction costs of dealing with governments, and on the other hand, the reforms could result in an increase in other forms of transaction costs if economic growth increases complexity, uncertainty, and frequency of exchange. If growth led to an increase in the technological sophistication of firms, an increase in the number of firms, and the emergence of new markets, it would increase complexity of contracts. This would require an effective legal mechanism for contractual formulation and enforcement. If the growth process of the post-reforms period created economic agents who could undertake effective collective action, they could bargain with governments to improve the formal laws for enhancing the economic efficiency of transactions.[3]

Policy reforms, as qualitative shifts in the institutional environment, are basically changes in certain formal laws of the government. The subsequent issue would be effective enforcement of the changes in the laws and further improvements in the laws as a dynamic process. In the case of the first aspect, in discussing shifts in the institutional environment in transition and developing economies, Williamson (1998) observes, "A noteworthy feature of this privatisation literature is that nominal changes in contract and property laws do not necessarily imply effective changes. There is a need to go beyond the (nominal) laws in books to consider the de facto laws, which bring in the mechanisms of enforcement."

To illustrate this in the case of India's economic reform process, Khanna and Melito (1997) observe:

> In industries where licenses were still required (for example, private companies that sought entry into formerly public sector industries),

the rights to projects and new businesses were allocated by sealed bids. This reform was intended to cut down on venality. However, corrupt officials were still able to make a deal or two in their favour. One way was by extracting 'speed money', that is, delaying the project in question until the winning bidder paid a bribe. Avaricious officials could also declare (or merely intimate) a change in the bidding requirements after the bidding had been completed, thereby leaving bidders scrambling to secure the officials' favour. Officials had also been known to accept monies from the losing bidders to declare that all former bids had been insufficient and start the bidding process again.

Changes in laws should be followed by changes in governance mechanisms, such as reduction in informational imperfections, organizational forms of government (decentralization), and government and private litigation for effective enforcement. The second aspect is changing a few laws, thus triggering a growth process, which may provide further impetus to improve or change other laws. To illustrate this, the policy reforms in India that led to the opening-up of equity markets to institutional investors, both foreign and local, caused the large institutional investors to make demands on the government to change the regulations to protect the investors' interests.

If we take the case of property rights, their evolution involves improvements both in definition and enforcement. As discussed earlier, there are four main dimensions to the traditional definition of property rights. If the laws remain obscure regarding any of these dimensions and impose high costs in enforcement, property rights are mitigated. For example, high costs in transferring property and enforcing contracts reduce the number of potential transactions and investments. A conspicuous example is the case of the Rent Control Act in Bombay, India. Under the Act, it is literally impossible for a landlord who gets into a leasing contract with a tenant for a specific period to enforce the contract and evict the tenant after the completion of the time period. This acts as a disincentive for a landlord to rent out his or her property. It appears that there are more than 200,000 constructed flats vacant and locked up in Bombay alone. The rental price of the few flats that are let out is very high, not only because of the scarcity of flats, but also because of the high costs of contractual safeguards. Bombay's real estate prices are some of the highest in the world, and at the same time, one sees the most underdeveloped real estates in the heart of the city, implying underinvestment (Patibandla, 1997). What are the possible forces that could change these inefficient laws? Under democratic public ordering, the rules should reflect the preferences of the majority. In the present context, it is logical for government to change the laws to suit the interests of the increasing numbers of flat-owners as compared to tenants. However, it depends on the relative effectiveness of these groups in organizing themselves for lobbying the governments. On the other hand, it is likely that, in a developing economy, owners of real estate will be lower in numbers compared to non-owners.

We can take the case of stock markets and corporate governance, as briefly mentioned previously, in illustrating changes in control rights. The main issue of corporate governance is the principal agency relation under the separation of owership and control of capital. The institutional conditions that reduce informational imperfections and facilitate effective monitoring of agents determine the efficiency of the control rights of investors. Apart from the prevailing laws, information and the monitoring of agents' actions are also governed by how investors are organized in terms of the existence of a large number of small investors and a few large players. Large investors invest in information and monitor managers more effectively than a large number of small, dispersed investors (Shleifer and Vishny, 1997). The organization of outside investors also determines the effectiveness of the legal system in protecting investors' interests (La Porta *et al.*, 1997). If the reforms increase the importance of large institutional investors, it can result in improvements in disclosure practices of companies because of the higher ability of large investors to generate economic and political pressure to create financial instruments that improve their control rights (Patibandla, 2005a).

This also can be seen in a different perspective: a few powerful, organized groups could neutralize the negative externalities through governmental action while a larger group, less powerful and organized, pays a heavy price for the negative externalities of growth. To give an example, the harmful effects of pollution through the rapid increase in automobiles in Delhi are rectified by governmental regulation in a relatively quick process because Delhi is the home of powerful politicians, judges and bureaucrats. On the other hand, a large number of small farmers lost their livelihood owing to pollution from the expansion of the leather and garment industries in the southern state of Tamil Nadu.

Changes in the institutional elements of formal rules, as discussed in the previous chapter, can be caused both by gradual changes in the political economy and by sudden changes through crises. To illustrate, the government of India established the SEBI (Securities and Exchange Board of India) and attempted to make it into an effective body for regulating the stock markets at the early stages of the reform process. This was in response to the stock market scandal of 1992, which destroyed billions of rupees of small investors' savings, forcing the government to examine the functioning of the market. However, so far (2005), the government has not adopted a systematic competition policy in India, perhaps because the short- and medium-term benefits of increased competitive conditions are positive enough for both consumers and producers.

# The evolution of norms

As mentioned before, norms evolve and take root through the cooperation of repeated interactions in small societies and, at a larger level, learning through repeated transaction. Some norms cause efficiency of economic exchange and some perpetuate inefficiency. The question is, how do norms change and evolve in response to policy reforms?

When informal rules take root, one way they can be broken up is by exogenous shocks (crises) or outside influences and reduction in informational imperfections. At the level of small societies, the role of an external agent is to facilitate cooperative behavior by fostering institutions that reduce transaction costs and informational imperfections for individuals to get together. This becomes pertinent when local people fail to form into collective action either because of high transaction costs or because of their myopic prisoner's dilemma behavior, which constrains them from realizing the benefits of collective action.

Similarly, as mentioned in the previous section, good norms can be destroyed when one introduces outside agents or freewheeling capital that does not have long-term commitment to local resources or institutions. In several villages in India, common property resources such as irrigation water are managed not by the laws of the government but by evolved norms of social behavior. The commitment to resource management in small societies arises through evolved norms of behavior that result in collective well-being. To give an example, the fishering community of the states of Kerala and Tamil Nadu managed the common resource of sea fishing for centuries through highly evolved norms that preserved the resources. The introduction of large fishing trawlers owned by multinationals and local large firms in the early 1990s led to overfishing and the rapid depletion of fish, eroding the livelihood of thousands of fishermen (Patibandla, 1997).[4] One interpretation could be that the 'norms' maintained by small fishermen or farmers have survived partly because they remained small, and that made it beyond their technical capability to do harm to environment. When producers become large, the historical experience is that conservation norms start disappearing, even in the pre-capitalist formation. In other words, even under capitalism, if capital has no long-term commitment to resources it could result in similar tragic outcomes in common ownership of resources and capital. This is when formal laws and rules should come into play in neutralizing costs of freewheeling big capital.

On the other hand, policy reforms may instill forces for evolution of efficient norms endogenously without any conscious exogenous forces. One example is the formation of industrial clusters for the realization of agglomeration economies. One of the elements of agglomeration (or pecuniary externalities) is a decline in contractual hazards by facilitating repeated interactions, and consequent trust in exchange. In the clusters of the cities of Bombay and Surat in India, diamonds worth millions of rupees change hands among the diamond merchants without any formal contracts. However, the penalities for an invidual of defection or cheating are high, through business and social boycott.

## Organizational change

North makes a distinction between organizations and institutions in terms of forms and substance. Organizations as forms can be engineered or copied, but their effectiveness or enforcement of engineered rules depends on institutional conditions of embeddedness. Organizational change can be induced at two levels: one is quantitative and qualitative shifts in the institutional environment, and the other is engineering organizations in terms of copying superior forms from other societies under a given institutional environment. In the first case, changes in institutional environment should induce changes in micro level governance. In the second case, organizational forms are implanted without changes in the institutional environment. Both have implications for the evolution of overall institutional factors in the long run, depending on the adaptation.

If we take it that the central problem of organization is adaptation to external factors, and the external factors are the institutional environmental factors, different institutional environments elicit different organizational forms and efficiency. In this context, we can look at inducement for organizational change in two ways: one is parameter and qualitative shifts in the institutional environment; the other is that, given the institutional environment, a firm innovates a superior organizational practice which, under comparative organizational logic, induces other firms to benchmark the superior practice and imitate it. In the latter case, the institutional environment is similar for all firms. On the basis of the argument that there is nothing called an optimal organizational form, innovations can bring out superior organizational practices even in the absence of changes in the institutional environment. Micro level entrepreneurial creativity can result in innovations which, in turn, engender feedback effects for changes in the institutional environment. Furthermore, in a developing economy context, superior organizational forms are copied from developed economies and implanted in the home market conditions.

For example, the innovation and adoption of assembly line production by Ford in the early part of the twentieth century revolutionized the organization of production. Similarly, developments in information and communication technology resulted in large-scale outsourcing of service jobs across the globe in the 2000s. These developments, in turn, will have feedback effects on the institutional environment. If technological change engenders economies of specialization, firms have to find ways to induce governments to make laws to improve contractual enforcements, both nationally and internationally, to form alliances with other firms.

An even more interesting aspect of this is the international effect. When American firms adopted outsourcing to India and set up their operations there in the software and services industries in the 1990s and 2000s, they spread American work culture and beliefs among the local skilled workers, which, in turn, influenced the Indian institutional environment. The globalization of the industry also made Indian firms find organizational forms to attain competitiveness; for example the Indian firms mastered the global delivery model of software, which, in turn, is copied by TNCs in India for undertaking software exports. Moreover, in order to cater for the increasing presence of TNCs in outsourcing from India, a few specialized firms came into the market to mitigate transaction costs for TNCs. These firms form contracts with TNCs to build and operate services: local firms build the infrastructure, recruit the people for the operation and transfer them to a TNC.[5]

Williamson examines the choice of organizational forms as responses to the institutional environment in terms of discrete structural choices among markets, hybrids and hierarchies. 'Market' refers to spontaneous adaptation. 'Hierarchy' refers to coordinated adaptation. 'Hybrid' form of organization refers to the negotiated order of credible commitments (Williamson, 1983) of organization and contracting that combines autonomy and cooperation of a variable degree. Institutional environment factors such as contract laws, property rights, and regulation, which determine transaction costs and contractual hazards of market exchange, determine the choices depending on the extent of asset-specificity of transactions. Policy reforms, as mentioned before, are treated as shifts in the institutional conditions, such as property rights and contract laws, etc., which determine the relative efficiency of organizational choices.

I illustrate the above logic by the following example. Under a weak property regime, people shy away from investing in durable assets and invest in mostly generic assets and non-productive activities such as gold and black money (wealth will be disguised, deflected, and consumed). This was very common in the middle class and the rich in the pre-reforms period of India. Let us take the case that policy reforms improve property rights through improvements in definitions and enforcement, reduction in the discretionary powers of governments and increase in credible commitments. This induces economic agents to undertake investments in durable assets, which can be in several forms, such as physical assets, technology-intensive assets, and human capital. This not only improves the productivity of existing firms but also propels the entrepreneurial activity of new entrants. Furthermore, this also changes the internal organizational practices of firms – hierarchy (low-powered incentives), teamwork, and profit-sharing incentives. For example, in human capital-intensive industries, the power of hierarchy through ownership of physical assets is low and firms may adopt flatter organization and profit-sharing incentives in managing skilled workers. This is especially the case if the capital markets are highly developed in terms of the ability of agents to raise capital on the basis of new ideas rather than collateral (Rajan and Zingales, 1998). An example of this outcome is the case of India's software industry in the post-reforms period, in which there has been a greater degree of entrepreneurial activity and incentive-compatible organizational practices.[6]

As mentioned before, engineering organizations can be treated as copying a form from other societies or countries and implanting them under the local institutional environment. These could be political and economic organizations. To give an example of the political, after independence from the British in 1947, India copied a major part of the parliamentarian democratic institutions from the Britain and adapted them to local conditions with a fair degree of success. In the case of economic organization, examples could be transnational corporations' operations in different nations and local firms in developing economies copying the superior practices of firms of developed economies. TNCs develop organizational practices in response to the home institutional environment and adopt these practices in the host country institutional environment. The result of adaptation could be a mutation. A good example is Toyota's plant, NUMMI (New United Motor Manufacturing Inc.) in the US. When Toyota set up its plant, it faced difficulty in adopting Japanese organizational practices because of the differences in the institutional environments of the US and Japan. The long-term success of the Toyota plant in the US depended on its ability to combine some of its Japanese organizational practices with the organizational culture of the US in general (Adler, 1999). It is observed that NUMMI successfully implemented its practices in the areas of work organization, learning and human resource policy, while they made some adaptation in the area of employment relations and associated methods, which were influenced by US institutional factors. This, in turn, resulted in the competitive advantage of higher productivity at NUMMI in comparison to the American firms within the US. Toyota's superior performance in the US invoked imitation of some of its practices by local firms, which, in turn, engendered marginal changes in elements of the institutional environment.

Another dimension of engineering of organizational forms is the emergence of 'islands of competitiveness'. An example is India's software industry, which became internationally competitive by reducing its dependence on domestic infrastructure, the hardware industry, and domestic product demand, by drawing upon the large pool of low-cost skilled manpower. The organizational and technological practices adopted by firms in this industry have been quite different from firms in the rest of the industries. The high degree of export orientation towards the US market made Indian firms adopt organizational and technological practices that were responsive to US market conditions, rather than local markets. The success of this industry generated forces for imitation of some of the practices by firms in other industries, which, in the long run, could contribute to the evolution of the institutional environment (Patibandla *et al.*, 2000).

To recapitulate, Williamson looks at shifts in organizational forms in response to change in the institutional environment as discrete structural choices under the logic that larger parameter changes are required to induce a shift from market to hierarchy than are required to induce shift from market to hybrid or from hybrid to hierarchy. However, organizational change may not be discrete and firms may not be able to move from one form to another easily in response to changes in the institutional environment owing to inertia and path dependence (Hannan and Freeman, 1984). This is more relevant to incumbent firms that have to face a sudden change in certain elements of the institutional environment as a result of policy reforms than to newer firms. Even when the institutional environment changes, firms with a certain organizational culture may not adopt more efficient structures. Organizational theorists of sociology argue that "institutionalized products, services, techniques, policies, and programs function as powerful myths, and many organizations adopt them ceremonially" (Meyer and Rowen, 1977). The myths may legitimize particular bureaucratic forms as rational and socially accepted. The inefficient forms will change only when they are challenged by superior forms, which will cause high disturbance in the markets, and which can take place by the emergence of new firms (entrepreneurs) or through the international interactions of economic agents.

When path dependency effects arising out of organizational inertia and network externalities of interdependence among existing practices and rules are strong, changes in the institutional environment will not immediately bring about changes in the prevailing micro level governance. Let us take the case that changes in the institutional environment bring in new agents, and superior organizational forms come into play along with the existing incumbents. The practices of the new agents should be far superior to those of incumbents to generate significant disturbance for the incumbents to get rid of inferior practices. Otherwise they face extinction. An example is the entry of TNCs with far superior technology and organizational practices in the post-reforms period of India, which drove many incumbent large firms to adopt changes in their technological and organizational behavior. In contrast to the case of islands of competitiveness, the policy reforms generate conditions for the entry of new entrepreneurs and entrants, who, in turn, can generate feedback effects for changes in the institutional environment.

Another dimension that can induce organizational change, irrespective of changes in the institutional environment, is technological change. Organization economists, as discussed earlier, assume technology as given in order to track the analytical issues regarding the organizational efficiency of firms. However, technology and organization of production are interlinked in determining overall efficiency of firms. To recapitulate, the adoption of assembly line production and realization of economies of scale by Ford in the early twentieth century led to the emergence of large firms, with significant implications for internal organization. Similarly, the technological changes in information technology had dramatic effects on the global organization of production of several services. As an illustration, Mexico, being in geographical proximity with the US, benefited from the relocation of some of the production activities from the US. Mexico started to lose this geographical advantage to India and China in the late 1990s, owing to developments in information technology – 'Death of Distance' (Cairncross, 1997). Here, there can be several linkage effects between technological change and institutional change. Technological change requires changes in the institutional environment, which, in turn, can have implications for organization, in either direction. For example, changes in the institutional environment may reduce transaction costs and make firms reduce integration. On the other hand, technological change may increase economies of scale and scope, thereby causing firms to increase integration.

## Feedback effects on the institutional environment

The feedback effects refer to the effect of changes in structural factors and micro level governance on the elements of markets and institutional environment. I have mentioned before that if parameter and qualitative shifts in elements of the institutional environment engender forces towards micro level activities of enhancing productivity, it results in growth dynamics, which, in turn, may provide incentives for economic agents to work towards further improvements in the institutional environment. When we talk of feedback effects, we need to talk of the evolution of institutions that are subject to further improvements, rather than reversal of the policies, which implies improvements in the credible commitments of the government to the reform process. The second issue is the conscious efforts of economic agents to change informal constraints to improve the efficiency of economic activity. Let us take the case that initial policy changes send signals for investment in durable assets and human capital (formal education and new technologies). If it improves the productivity and incomes of economic agents, it will increase the pay-offs of further improvements in the formal and informal constraints of the previous institutional regime. To give an example, India's policy reforms in 1991, which devalued the currency and liberalized the external sector, gave a substantial boost to the exports of the software industry. This, in turn, increased the demand for skilled labor, which gave incentives for young people to acquire industry-specific skills. This outcome gave impetus for further liberalization of the external sector. This depends on the outcome of the initial reforms – whether they increase the pay-offs to, and cause emergence of, politically powerful groups or not, which again depends on the initial conditions at the onset of policy changes and how fast the positive gains are perceived and realized. The initial policy shifts could result in increasing demands for improvements in the elements of specific formal laws or policies and also for a particular policy reform to be followed by other, complementary policy changes. The latter aspect implies that a policy change causes certain positive outcomes, which can be further enhanced by complementary policy changes.

# 3 Initial conditions and economic policy reforms

Clark and Wolcott (2001), in their paper titled 'One Polity and Many Countries', observe that India is perhaps the most interesting of all economies for those interested in development economics. What makes it so interesting? India's diversity is like putting all of Europe into one country. Despite its diversity and prolonged period of poverty it has remained a democracy, with its flaws, since independence in 1947. Clark and Wolcott observe that India declined economically under the British and after independence, in spite of a long period of relative political stability, while the economic decline of countries in Africa and Latin America was associated with social and political instability. They attribute this to the decline in the relative efficiency of utilization of technology in India as compared to Britain and the US. This can be traced to the market institutions under British rule and the import substitution regime that was in existence from 1950 to 1991, after independence from the British.

Although the British were responsible for generating a critical level of modern infrastructure of railroads and the telegraph network, and capitalist institutions of property rights that suited the prevailing ruling class in some pockets of India, they were primarily motivated to serve Britain's colonial interests. Thus they built railroads in India, which facilitated both internal and international commerce. But the cost of building these railroads was three times higher than in Britain, as the British used the Indian taxpayer's money to generate supernormal rents both to the British contractors and to the Queen.

The economic policy reforms of 1991, driven by the balance of payments crisis, were initiated through a democratic process, without much political and social turmoil. As mentioned in the previous chapters, the reforms led to an increase in the economic growth rate, with the economy experiencing about 6 percent annual growth throughout the nineties. Most of the growth benefits, however, were concentrated in a few regional pockets, mostly in the western and southern states, while the central and northern states remained stagnant. Furthermore, the growth benefits accrued mostly to the rich and middle class, who could participate in the market mechanism with durable physical and human capital endowments while close to 300 million remained illiterate and outside the market mechanism. The initial conditions of duality and fragmentation of the markets at the time of the policy reforms shaped the direction of structural change and growth.

## Definition of fragmentation of markets and institutions

I define the fragmentation of institutions and markets in terms of the institutional environment of capitalism being different for different sections of the people within a country. Marx's dialectic interpretation of history shows how capitalism evolved from primitive communism to feudalism and from feudalism to capitalism. This characterization refers to the different stages of evolution but not the coexistence of the different systems in any given period. In developing economies, fragmentation of markets is characterized in terms of economic duality – coexistence of feudalism, capitalism and socialist institutions of public ownership of capital. The economic duality can also be seen in terms of the coexistence of different choices of techniques in performing a specific activity. For example, in the city of Bangalore, which has come to be known as the Silicon Valley of India, one finds the most sophisticated high-tech firms, and one also sees several instances of bullock carts transporting goods.

Another dimension of the fragmentation is that the elements of the institutional environment may work in different manner for different agents within the system. For example, the formal laws of property rights, as defined in the constitution, emphasize equality of all agents in the state. In the Coasian theorem of property rights, all agents face similar transaction costs. However, the transaction costs of enforcement could be different for different agents depending on, to use the terminology of Dreze and Sen (1996), 'social capability'. If there were a weak legal system and a corrupt bureaucracy, an agent who could invest in transaction costs, owing to differential social capability, would be in a better position to protect his or her rights than one who could not undertake transaction costs.

An example of fragmentation of markets in the Indian context is the segmentation of labor and capital markets into the organized and the unorganized. Fragmentation, here, means that a worker with similar skills would be able to get a higher wage and benefits if he or she were able to break into the organized labor markets than if he or she were to remain in the unorganised markets. When we talk of labor market segmentation, the unorganised labor markets present the crude form of capitalist forces where workers are hired and fired without minimum social benefits. On the contrary, in the organized labor markets, workers are provided with social security benefits but regulations on employment security block the operation of free market forces. Similarly, capital cost is higher in the unorganised capital markets than for those operating in the organized capital markets (Patibandla, 1994). A part of the explanation can be drawn from information economics: when property rights are ill defined and poorly enforced and high informational imperfections exist, agents who cannot provide collateral end up taking loans with high interest rates. The high interest rates are also a result of high default incidence (Akerlof, 1970; Stiglitz and Weiss, 1981).

Several pockets of India have well-functioning capitalist institutions and markets, with property rights enforced and low information and transaction costs of exchange in the product and input markets. However, as mentioned before, 30 percent of India's population are outside the market mechanism owing to illiteracy and poverty. About 65 percent of the population live in rural areas, engaged in agriculture. Within the rural economy, there are areas of well-developed, commercialised agricultural markets and also underdeveloped markets. In the latter, output, capital and labor markets are interlocked, resulting in a poverty trap for marginal farmers and also the institutional arrangement of bonded labor (Patibandla and Sastry, 2004). A high degree of informational imperfections, transaction costs, and poor property rights of land force small farmers to acquire capital at high interest rates and undertake distress sales of the output. The buyers are mostly the middlemen, who, in most cases, are the moneylenders themselves.

Illiteracy can be a major source of fragmentation of institutions. In the advanced capitalist economies, under the notion of 'equality of opportunity and incentives of higher rewards for higher effort', institutions of universal primary and secondary education were established. A minimum social security net was also provided. An illiterate agent's ability to participate in the markets is restricted because he or she incurs higher transaction costs than a literate agent. Moreover, while an educated and well-informed agent sees to it that government agents enforce his or her rights, an illiterate agent could be subjected to high costs and bribes when the government agents are corrupt.[1] In the Indian context, there is neither universal primary education nor a social security net for the majority of population and therefore there is no 'equality of opportunity'. When one combines this with distorted incentives of 'equality of rewards' (insensitivity to effort levels and talent) under pseudo-socialism and 'crony capitalism', the institutional framework becomes skewed.

Given the degree of fragmentation of the markets and institutional conditions, the policy reforms aimed at shifting the institutional environment towards freer markets benefit only those who are able to participate in the markets. Therefore, a major element of the evolution of markets and institutions is a reduction in fragmentation. This can take place in two ways. One is that the policy reforms towards freer markets should be complemented by investment and improvements in primary and secondary education and health. A simple increase in investment alone may not be effective unless there are effective institutional improvements of the services reaching the targeted groups. Second, if the policy reforms result in expansion of the markets, this may reduce fragmentation. A simple qualitative example is that of the poor investing in (private primary) education for their children when they perceive expanding markets providing opportunities to the skilled workers. I discuss this issue in detail in Chapter 8.

I trace the historical outcome of fragmented markets starting from the conditions of British rule to the import substitution regime of the post-independence era.

## British India and the capitalist institutions

From the discussion of the previous chapter, the essential features of the capitalist system are efficiently defined and well-enforced property rights, low transaction costs and a low incidence of informational imperfections of market exchange. The British rule in India first amalgamated several princely states and then built railroads and a telegraph infrastructure, which reduced the domestic and international transaction costs of commodity trade.[2] Second, the British adopted the Anglo-Saxon common law, which facilitated the emergence of Indian industrialists in the latter half of the nineteenth century. However, in several parts of India they purposely kept the property rights of agricultural land ill defined for the collection of land revenue. They adopted and extended the Zamindari system of the Mughal period, in which a large landlord was responsible for the collection of land revenue and property rights of farmers for specified rural regions. The adverse consequences of the institutional arrangement of feudal conditions continued into the post-independence era. I briefly sketch out the historical process in the following.

In 1750, when the East India Company was making its presence felt in India, India's craftsmen accounted for about a quarter of the world's production of manufactured goods, with most of it in the handicrafts sector. By 1850, the East India Company came to govern most of India by amalgamating several princely states. After the 1857 mutiny by Indian soldiers, the British Crown took over the governance of India. India became a major source of capital for funding Britain's industrialization and a major market for her manufactured goods. The transportation costs of shipping goods to and from the Indian ports of Bombay, Calcutta and Madras to England reduced drastically following the cutting of the Suez Canal by the French in 1869. In order to develop the inland transport of raw materials and manufactured goods, the British developed the railroads in 1850. Roy (2001) shows that the major economic impact of colonialism was India's integration into the world economy, thanks to the railroad network. Furthermore, the political integration of the different princely states also led to economic integration by eliminating taxes on movements of goods within the country and the adoption of a common currency (Tripathi, 2004). Around the same time, the telegraph network linking major cities was developed. These factors significantly reduced transaction and transportation costs and thereby contributed to a substantial increase in the commodity trade.

By 1870, India became a large exporter of primary products (cotton, opium, rice, oil seeds, jute, and wheat) and a large importer of manufactured goods (cotton textiles and yarn, iron and steel, brass and copper, railway equipment) (Collins, 1999). Consequently, the necessary infrastructure for capitalist institutions to develop took root mostly in the coastal cities of Bombay, Calcutta and Madras. In order to govern the large country, they generated local bureaucracy. For this purpose they adopted English-based higher education, mostly in the major centers of Calcutta, Bombay and Madras.

The bureaucracy was also used to collect taxes, particularly land revenue, a major source of income for the British. They were assisted in this task by the Zamindari system of the native landed nobility, who functioned as a class of intermediary revenue collectors. The Indian industrialists came into existence in the early nineteenth century not from the Zamindari class but from the ethnic group of Parsis of the western part of India, and later from the Gujaratis and Marwaris. As a consequence of the institutional conditions created by the British, the coastal areas of Bombay, Surat (in the west), Calcutta (east) and Madras (south) became industrialized and developed a critical level of capitalist institutions, while the interior part remained feudal and backward.

On the capital market side, the Bank of Calcutta was established in 1806, the Bank of Bombay in 1840 and the Bank of Madras in 1843. In 1921, all three banks were amalgamated to form the Imperial Bank of India. The Bombay stock exchange was established as early as 1875. It was owned and controlled by a small group of brokers, mostly coming from the state of Gujarat. Trading was in a limited amount of debentures and equity with high control resting with the brokers. The Indian industrial houses were managed by the 'managing agency system', legalized by the British in 1936, in which the managing agency (joint families) controlled large numbers of companies across a range of industries, with limited liability to the agency.[3]

At the time of independence in 1947, as Desai (2002) observes, India had one of the oldest modern industries in the Third World. The country had the largest group of native modern capitalist entrepreneurs, the largest jute industry, and a cotton textile industry which was globally competitive. There was a modern legal system, which recognized property rights, independent courts and a well-trained legal profession (Williamson and Zagha, 2002). However, the industrialization was concentrated in small pockets of the coastal districts and the rest of the country remained highly feudal, with a large number of illiterate peasants outside the capitalist system. At the time of independence, about 70 percent of the population were engaged in agriculture, which accounted for 50 percent of GDP, and only about 18 percent of the population were literate (Krueger and Chinoy, 2002).

One more important institutional outcome of British rule was the civil service, which on the one hand contributed to the political and administrative stability of the large country, and on the other hand, contributed to dirigisme of independent India's economy. In post-independent India, the bureaucracy of the civil administration and management of the public sector grew at a phenomenal rate. This later became a source of rent-seeking activity by imposing high transaction costs on economic activity.

## Independent India

At the time of independence, there were three ideologies regarding India's development strategy within the National Congress. One was that of the father of the nation, Mahatma Gandhi, who opined that the development efforts of the state should operate on a decentralized basis of focusing on the villages where most people in India lived. Another was that of Nehru, the first Indian prime minister, who adopted Fabian socialism. There was also a third ideology regarding free markets and enterprises, which was outside the National Congress and hence was marginalized. Nehru's Fabian socialism prevailed, by which large-scale industrialization was undertaken under an import substitution strategy. This was, however, carried out in the absence of land reforms and there was a benign neglect of agriculture, the rural economy and universal primary education. Thus, whatever little growth took place affected only a small minority.

On the political institutional front, India copied and adopted the British parliamentarian system of democracy. Under the parliamentarian system, the government (executive) controls the legislative process. It also has higher discretionary powers. The consequence of this was that the government at the center wielded strong powers. Nehru was able to impose his ideology of Fabian socialism on the country without much resistance. He also had the support of the property-owning classes of the time, who saw the import-substituting, government-led industrialization as the most politically feasible economic strategy (Sanyal, 1984). Later, Indira Gandhi, Nehru's daughter, who became the third prime minister of India, adopted a pervasive command-and-control regime in the name of socialism and the eradication of poverty.

However, Myrdal (1968) described the Indian state as a 'soft state' where the government had to work consensually, dealing with myriad interest groups across different regions, and exert control sparingly.[4] On the economic front, the federal democracy under Nehru functioned in such a way that public sector investments were made to serve the interests of regional leaders. Weiner (1999, 271) observes, "If West Bengal was given an oil refinery to process oil from Assam, then Assam too had to be given a refinery though economically it was more efficient to build a single refinery near a port and railway." In other words, it is not possible to define India's polity and institutions in a simple or unidirectional way, given the complexity of its democracy, which can be termed 'the Hindu Democracy' – Hinduism consists of multiple gods and different ways of living, all coexisting rather peacefully. This issue is pertinent to the present task, because institutional change under Indian democracy is subject to a complex gamut of political and economic calculations, in contrast to a totalitarian system such as China's (Desai, 2003).

The Soviet model of industrialization through five year plans inspired Nehru's Fabian socialism. However, India adopted a hybrid model of coexistence of the public and private sectors, which was termed a 'mixed economy'. The commanding heights reserved for the public sector had their intellectual foundations in the development economics theories of the 1950s and 1960s, such as Ragner Nurske's theory of vicious circle of poverty and Hirschman's theory of sectoral linkages. As discussed in chapter 1, at that time the basic concern was that the private sector would be unable to save enough and invest in projects with long gestation periods. The government was seen to be in a position to lift the saving rate through budgetary manipulations. Additionally, Hirschman's theory of linkages showed that government's concerted large-scale investments in a number of complementary sectors, each providing demand and reducing the cost of another, led to 'developmental externalities' which benefit both private and public sector firms. This required massive simultaneous investments in different sectors (like roads, power, railways, banking, mining, and so on), which at that time governments alone were in a position to undertake.

However, as mentioned before, the Indian parliamentary system gave discretionary powers to the politicians in office and to bureaucrats, which, over time, led to the degeneration of the system due to excessive regulation, dirigisme and vested interest groups capturing the policies. This resulted in inefficient institutions imposing high transaction costs and widespread corruption, and consequently inefficient use of capital and technology. This leads to the question of whether the dirigisme of the past regime was a result of political institutions or bad economic policies, or perhaps a combination of both. If the political factors are important ones, the reforms should encompass both the political and economic factors for efficient outcomes.[5]

There are several studies that have analyzed the policy regime of import substitution in detail (Srinivasan, 2000; Bhagawati and Srinivansan, 1975 and 1993; Joshi and Little, 1994, Williamson and Zagha, 2002). Therefore, I refrain from replicating the discussion of the policies. I briefly list the major policies and outline their implications on the markets, institutions, and qualitative behavior of economic agents in the product, labor, and capital markets.

**Product markets**

The product market refers to production of final goods, intermediate inputs and raw materials. There were five components of the policies in the product markets: commanding heights given to the public sector; regulation of the private sector through licensing and MRTP (monopoly restrictive trade practices) policies; reservation of about 830 products for production by small-scale firms; price controls imposed on certain sectors especially in those where there was coexistence of the public and private sectors; and a closed-door policy towards international trade and investment under import substitution.

The industrial policy resolutions of 1948, 1954 and 1956 reserved the commanding heights of the economy for the public sector by including a large number of industries for the sole participation of the public sector. These sectors included power, telecommunications, coal, oil, railroads, airlines, heavy machinery, etc. Apart from this, in several areas such as steel, fertilizers, and electronics, public sector firms were established, while simultaneously a limited number of private sector firms were set up subject to regulations on capacity and also pricing. In the late 1960s and the early 1970s, the banks were nationalized. The public sector's share in GDP and in employment of the organized sector increased significantly over the years. In other words, the role of the public sector was extended far beyond the market failure considerations of the growth theory. In those areas where there was coexistence of the public and private sector, such as steel and fertilizers, the government determined the prices based on the costs of the public sector firms. Consequently, the private sector firms, who were able to utilize capital more efficiently than the public sector firms, were able to reap supernormal profits.

In the case of the private sector, the industrial licensing and MRTP policies directed at capacity restrictions controlled the investment and operations of the private sector firms. The regulations of the private sector in one area interacted with those in another, multiplying the transaction costs (Williamson and Zagha, 2002). For example, without an industrial license from the Ministry of Industry, the Ministry of Commerce would not provide a license to import capital goods, and the Reserve Bank of India (RBI) would not authorize the sale of foreign currency to buy them. These highly restrictive trade policies, which imposed both high tariffs and quantitative restrictions on imports, made the private sector dependent on the public sector for the provision of raw materials and intermediate inputs.

With the objective of promoting employment, 830 products were reserved for exclusive production by small-scale firms. Apart from this, fiscal incentives in terms of tax (excise duty) concessions were directed at the small-scale sector. Most of the reserved products were intermediate-input products such as bicycle components, automobile components, engineering products such as hand tools, diesel engines, and a few finished products such as garments. The consequence of these policies was that there was a large entry of small firms into these segments to utilize the fiscal benefits. Most of the intermediate-producer small firms became dependent on a few final-product producer large firms, which, in turn, engendered a high degree of monopsony power to the final producers. Furthermore, there was a disincentive for the relatively efficient small firms to grow in size. This resulted in a premature diversification into the setting-up of multiple plants within an industry, and also across different segments. It also resulted in accentuation of negative externalities. Take the example of industries such as dyestuffs and chemicals and leather products, which cause a lot of water pollution. These industries were characterized by the presence of a large number of small firms which could not afford to set up effluent treatment plants, while it was economically viable for a few large firms to undertake investments in pollution prevention measures.

In the pre-independence period of the early twentieth century, the colonial government used tariffs as a source of revenue. In 1933, textile and sugar imports faced duties of up to 75 percent and 190 percent respectively. Post-independence governments, which wanted to protect domestic enterprises, further increased the import barriers. Under the import substitution policies, India's product markets were cut off from international trade. High tariffs and quantitative restrictions blocked competition from imports. Apart from this, imports were subjected to the license regime based on twenty-six lists of all importable products, and each had its own approval procedure imposing high transaction costs. The highly overvalued exchange rate discouraged exports even in those areas where India had comparative advantage. For example, India's textile industry, which was more competitive than that of South Korea in the early 1960s, lost out to South Korea in the international market because of adverse trade and industrial policies which restricted the scale of the firms. However, there were a few traditional export sectors, such as cut and polished diamonds, and garments, which were export-oriented under a gamut of export incentive policies. Nevertheless, these export incentives, such as duty draw-backs, were subject to high transaction costs in taking advantage of them.

An even worse feature of the policies had been restrictions on the internal mobility of goods. India's internal market remained highly fragmented, with varying excise duties and commodity taxes across different states and restrictions on the mobility of goods, especially agricultural commodities across state borders. This resulted in underdevelopment of internal commodity markets. The Green Revolution in agriculture was made possible in the late 1960s with the combination of new agricultural seeds, subsidies and product price incentives, which made India self-sufficient in food production. This led to commercialization of agriculture in a few regions, especially in the northern states of Punjab and Haryana. However, the myriad controls and regulations at the central and the state level, restrictions on the mobility of agricultural goods across different states, and virtual banning of futures and forward trading kept the product markets underdeveloped.

On the foreign direct investment front, at the time of independence, foreign capital dominated a narrow industrial base mostly in the extractive industries and trade. After independence, government policy was friendly to FDI until the late 1960s. In the early 1970s, foreign oil majors were nationalized. The Foreign Exchange Regulation Act (FERA) of 1973 imposed several controls on foreign capital. It forced foreign firms to reduce their equity stakes to 26 percent, but allowed them to have higher than 40 percent equity in 'export intensive' sectors. Furthermore, the policy imposed restrictions on technology imports and royalty payments. As a consequence, the presence of TNCs remained marginal and was mostly restricted to the manufacturing industries.

The extent of transaction costs imposed on private entrepreneurial activity can be seen from the number of permissions one had to acquire from government bodies, whose internal organization consisted of numerous layers of bureaucratic controls. The following list by Mohan and Aggarwal (1990) is illustrative. These are: a letter of intent to start an industrial firm; capital goods imports clearances; foreign technology collaboration clearances; capital issue clearances; raw material import clearances; essentiality clearances; indigenous non-availability of equipment and material clearances; monopolies clearances; small-scale sector clearances; and clearances for locating in non-municipal areas (Majumdar, 2004). After these stages of clearances, there were also transaction costs imposed by the predatory bureaucracy, which were high. For example, frequent visits by the government agents of the regulatory bodies such as labor and environmental standards for extraction of bribes entailed high transaction costs, especially to small- and medium-scale firms (Forbes, 2002).

## Labor markets

One major consequence of the labor market policies is the segmentation of the market into the organized and unorganized. The organized market refers to the people employed in the public sector, government services, and private sector firms employing more than 100 employees. The workers of the organized sector are provided with job security and employee benefits such as pension, leave and other entitlements. In the private sector, the firms are not allowed to replace workers without permission from the government. Even the bankruptcy laws, which prevented non-performing companies from closing down, were directed at protecting the organized labor. On the other hand, the unorganized labor markets are characterized by extreme flexibility of hire and fire, and absence of employee benefits. The institutional factors are such that the workers of given skill levels get higher wages in the organized markets with lower productivity than those in the unorganized market.

There are forty-five labor laws in operation dealing with a range of issues with respect to minimum wages, job security, benefits, industrial safety, and trade unions. These laws were observed to have introduced uncertainty and ambiguity regarding key legal concepts, thus increasing the scope for conflicting interpretations (Zagha, 1999). The unorganized sector developed because the laws such as reporting requirements were waived for firms with less than twenty employees. Mandatory health insurance was waived for firms with less than fifty employees. These laws combined with the policies pertaining to the small-scale sector, as Zagha observed, provided incentives for firms to remain small. Apart from this, they encouraged large firms to find indirect ways of overcoming the inflexibility of organized labor markets. For example, the laws about firing workers and stringent bankruptcy laws made several large textile firms in Ahmedabad (of Gujarat state) declare lockouts. As a result, the workers ended up losing their jobs without any benefits (Anant and Goswami, 1997; Patibandla, 1997).

Organized labor includes government bureaucracy, employment in the public sector and large-scale private sector firms. On the supply side, most of it was drawn from higher education, which was heavily subsidized by the government at the cost of universal primary education. In other words, the organized sector had access to skilled labor without having to invest in the generation of skills. Second, wages in this sector were protected from inflation and employment security was provided, which meant that the wage rate could be above productivity in the absence of employment adjustment. For the period 1971 to 1989, gross capital investment in the public sector grew at 5.86 percent and in the private organized sector at 3.32 percent, with the corresponding figures for employment at 3.03 and 0.68 respectively. In other words, capital growth in the organized sector was higher than employment, which meant that the sectors became more capital-intensive or just paid higher wages to employees. With low growth in employment in the organized sector and an annual population growth of 2.1 percent during the period, unorganized labor increased over the years.

In 1991, the share of the organized sector accounted for 7.49 percent of total employment, which declined to 6.38 percent in 1999. India's labor force consisted of 350 million – 67 percent were in the agriculture sector, 13 percent in manufacturing and the rest in service industries. Half the labor force was illiterate (Zagha, 1999). At the time of independence the literacy rate was about 18 percent, which increased to 62 percent in 1996–7 (Ahluwalia, 1999). On the other hand, under the import substitution regime, the government of India greatly subsidized higher education.

It established half a dozen Indian Institutes of Technology (IIT) of high-standard engineering education, and several regional engineering colleges all over the country. The government set up four world-standard management schools (Indian Institutes of Management). The government also set up numerous universities that charged nominal fees to students. Apart from this, the government set up several research institutions. All these generated a significant pool of English-speaking skilled labor, which became a major factor that facilitated the emergence of internationally competitive high-tech industries such as the software, pharmaceutical and nascent biotechnology industries in the post-reform period. Furthermore, the base of engineering skills also contributed to the increasing international competitiveness of a few manufacturing industries, such as the two-wheelers, automobiles and auto-component industries in the post-reform era. These cases will be discussed in more detail in the following chapters.

**Capital markets**

India's capital markets could be the most prominent example of the costs of institutional failures both before and after the reforms. At the time of independence, India had a string of banks, and the Life Insurance Corporation in the private sector. They used to lend to their shareholders and directors, which were large business and trading houses. They also used to lend for commodity speculation. At that time, the cost of capital was low for these business houses, and for smaller borrowers either loans were not available or the cost was very high. In the pre-reforms period, the government of India took a major role in mobilizing capital for heavy industrialization. This domineering role of the government in addition to several controls resulted in high transaction costs, which restricted the development of the markets. In the sixties the government nationalised all large banks and the Life Insurance Corporation. Soon, other public sector financial institutions were created. The bank nationalisation mobilized small savers in the country by reaching out to remote parts and by accepting deposits, which were risk-free investments. These measures reduced the cost of capital for the economy as a whole and for small industries, the farm sector and other small-to-medium-size borrowers, though the cost increased for the preferred borrowers of the earlier private banks. However, there was mismanagement, bad debts, wastage, and interest rates fixed by fiat, and thus not reflecting the true costs of anything. I discuss this later in detail.

Immediately after the reforms of 1991, there was a series of major stock market scandals and corrupt practices by both the public and private financial institutions. Although these outcomes destroyed (or redistributed) billions of rupees of public savings (mostly small investors'), none of the culprits were punished or convicted. Government failed in two ways.

First, the government-generated institutional infrastructure for transferring public savings for its objectives of development resulted in a high degree of moral hazard on the part of the public agents and the capturing of the institutions by powerful vested interest groups, leading to inefficient use and redistribution of capital in favor of these groups. Second, the movement towards freer markets in the absence of effective regulatory and legal institutions resulted in the criminalization of the capital markets through a series of financial scandals.

The fundamental institutional arrangement of the financial markets is the relationship of principal and agent. According to the famous Modigliani-Miller (1958) theorem, financial institutions do not matter under the assumption of perfect and costless information and zero transaction costs of contracts. The importance of financial institutions in determining the costs of capital and efficiency in the utilization of capital becomes prominent because of informational asymmetry and costs, and the presence of transaction costs. The financial institutions on the one hand are a means for reducing information and transaction costs to individual investors, and for the expansion of markets. On the other hand, they themselves can be a source of high agency costs, depending on the institutional arrangements of formal laws and regulations of the country. In the following discussion, I trace out the public financial institutional arrangements under the previous policy regime.

The major feature of India's financial institutions is the central bank, the Reserve Bank of India. It was assigned two roles: the role of macro policy management of the internal and external sectors, and also that of acting as an instrument of growth through its direction of the banks and public financial institutions. The public ownership of central banks is essentially a post-Second World War phenomenon – both the Bank of England and the Reserve Bank of India were nationalized in the late 1940s. The issue that follows is the autonomy of the bank from the government, and its politicization. The autonomy of the central bank and the regulatory institutions becomes an important institutional issue for retaining the long-term public interests free from the short-run political interests of politicians in power. Reddy (2002, 12) observes,

> While discussing the issue of autonomy, it is necessary to recognize that the function of debt management is performed by a central bank essentially as an agent of government and the issue of autonomy in such a case becomes nebulous. In fact, this function could be in conflict with autonomy in the conduct of monetary policy.

As the government intervention in the economy increased, the RBI's autonomy was systematically eroded. In 1969, fourteen major national banks were nationalized, followed by six more banks in 1980. This engendered the institutional condition that the government became the owner of a large number of banks, and the RBI, which was also owned by the government, became responsible for the supervision of these banks. Consequently, the government used the banking sector as a captive source of funds for deficit financing and allocation of capital both for the public and private sectors. However, one of the important outcomes of the bank nationalization was the major expansion in the coverage of the banking system: bank branches increased from 8,262 in 1969 to 60,190 in 1991, with about 60 percent of them being located in rural areas. This also led to a rapid increase in bank deposits and credits and mobilization of savings across the country. India in this period realized one of the highest savings rates in the world for its current level of development – about 20 percent of GDP (Joshi and Little, 1994; Sen and Vaidya, 1997). The growth theory tells us that at that rate of capital accumulation, the economy should grow at a rapid pace. In India's case, however, the institutional arrangements led to inefficient utilization of capital, which stunted the growth rate.

In the 1950s and 1960s, the government of India established three all-India development finance institutions (DFIs): the Industrial Finance Corporation of India (IFCI), the Industrial Development Bank of India (IDBI), and the Industrial Credit and Investment Corporation of India (ICICI). Later on, the government also set up the public sector mutual fund, the Unit Trust of India (UTI), which used small investors' savings to provide loans to the corporate sector and also to invest in the equity markets. The objective of these public sector financial institutions was to foster industrialization by providing long-term loans for setting up plant and machinery at low, often subsidized, real interest rates (Goswami, 2001). These institutions were judged by the amount of loans sanctioned rather than by their asset quality under soft budget constraints, which led to moral hazard behaviour on the part of the agents of these institutions. As a consequence, lending took place with inadequate project appraisals and loans were not based on perceived risks and expected returns. Furthermore, there was no uniform system of accounting practices. The accounting and disclosure practices of Indian firms were in general poor. Consequently, these institutions were saddled with a huge amount of bad loans and non-performing assets. In the year 2002, the government of India had earmarked over Rs 200,000 million of taxpayers' money to bail out just three of the public financial institutions.

Furthermore, the laws and regulations with regard to bankruptcy (exit) of firms resulted in misutilization of capital. The laws dealing with bankruptcy were: the Industrial Disputes Act, according to which large firms were not allowed to retrench workers or close down; the Urban Land Act, which prevented firms from selling land without permission from state governments; and the Sick Industrial Companies Act. The Sick Industrial Companies Act imposed large transaction costs on sick firms for closing or for rehabilitation. In 1992, there were 1,599 large and medium units and

223,441 small units that were declared sick, with capital amounting to Rs 101,510 million locked in (Sen and Vaidya, 1997).

An important feature of India's capital market is the large presence of unorganized capital markets in which the interest rates are a lot higher than those of the organized markets. The unorganized capital markets can be broadly defined as those in which borrowers do not get access to formal banks and financial institutions, and therefore they resort to the traditional moneylenders. In India, this market covers mostly the rural economy of small and marginal farmers and small-scale firms. In the case of small-scale firms, although they are provided with fiscal incentives such as excise duty wavers, they have limited access to formal credit owing to high market transaction costs.

Information economics shows that interest rates in rural credit markets tend to be high because of adverse selection and high loan defaults. This is accentuated when there is high risk in production due to environmental uncertainty, high transaction costs of small loans and underdeveloped output markets (Stiglitz and Weiss, 1981). In India's case, the uncertainty is high because agricultural productivity is dependent on monsoons. Under these conditions, collateral is the means of obtaining loans from the formal markets. However, property rights being poorly defined and enforced, especially in the case of small farmers, who cannot undertake transaction costs of enforcement, the collateral becomes ineffective. Apart from this, commodity and futures markets are not developed in rural areas, which results in small farmers realizing low prices or even distress sales at the time of harvest. One of the institutional outcomes of this is the interlocking of capital, labor, and output markets. A small farmer gets access to loans from moneylenders, to whom the output or even labor services are sold at low prices. The government of India and the RBI built up extensive credit institutions, such as the Rural Credit Cooperatives, and mandatory quota loans imposed on the government banks to cater to the rural economy. However, this had little impact on solving the problem, because these benefits are availed of by larger farmers, who are able to incur the transaction costs of dealing with government agents, and also because of loan arbitrage by those who can incur the transaction costs (Patibandla and Sastry, 2004).

## Structural outcomes of the policies

The interventionist policies followed by the Indian government from the onset of independence till the middle of 1980s meant that the active role of the state in development reduced transaction costs over the decades through investment in railways, roads, insurance, and telecommunications, and later in banking. From 1947 to the 1990s, steel production increased from 1.5 million tons a year to 14.7 million, and the number of kilowatt-hours of electricity generated increased more than fiftyfold. In the 1990s, India developed space satellites and set up nuclear power plants. Life expectancy rose from twenty-seven years to fifty-nine. The per capita availability of food grains increased from 395 grams per day in 1950 to 466 grams in 1992. However, increased government controls over the years blocked the expansion of these sectors and markets. Weiner (1999) observes, "India's political elite chose to limit investments in telecommunications, television, and computers, mistakenly believing that the new technologies would reduce employment and only benefit the wealthy, a decision that had perverse consequences for the economy and limited the expansion of the country's knowledge base."

The import substitution policies resulted in a diverse industrial base and structure, although far below international technological frontiers. They generated a large, matured private sector with managerial endowments. At the same time, the discretionary powers of government agents, politicians, and bureaucrats led to excessive market intervention for rent-seeking. This, in turn, imposed high transaction costs in different spheres and saw the emergence of powerful vested interest groups.

Certain elements of import substitution policies, such as subsidization of higher education and creation of public sector R&D institutions, generated a considerable pool of scientific base and skilled labor. These, in turn, became the nodal point for the emergence of pockets of internationally competitive high-tech industries such as the software and pharmaceutical industries in the post-reform era. However, the neglect of universal primary education and creation of social capital on a decentralized basis resulted in a segmented economy and an institutional framework of capitalism, with close to 300 million illiterate people below the poverty line and outside the market system by the early part of the millennium. Dreze and Sen (1996) observe:

> the abysmal inequalities in India's education system represent a real barrier against widely sharing the fruits of economic progress, in general, and of industrialization, in particular, in the way it has happened in economies like South Korea and China – economies which have succeeded in flooding the world market with goods the making of which requires no great university training, but is helped by widespread basic education that enables people to follow precise guidelines and maintain standards of quality.

The market institutions that provided the right incentives to private agents with an appropriate government institutional role generated an institutional framework for Western-style capitalism to succeed better than socialist economies in achieving sustained long-run economic growth. For example, Russia's achievement in space technology and also India's success in certain high-technology areas such as satellite technology were made possible by public sector investment. However, poor incentives for private agents to make use of the stock of technology and knowledge created by the public sector investment led to a downward drag on growth. Government investment in the defense industry in the US led to the generation of new technologies. Combining this investment with private incentives for using the stock of knowledge led to effective commercialization and use of technology for the private and public good. In India's case, government investment in higher education and public sector firms worked as the basis for the birth of the country's software industry. The subsequent entry of private firms and open trade policies provided incentives for its rapid growth in the post-reform era (Patibandla *et al.*, 2000). However, the high agency costs of moral hazard of the public agents of the government sector sucked in a lot of capital, but with low efficiency, which dragged down growth.

The economic history of developed capitalist economies since the industrial revolution in the UK shows that structural transformation led to the majority of the workforce moving from agriculture to industry and from industry to service sectors as technological change and capital accumulation improved productivity in agriculture and industry. At the advanced stage, the service sector employs a major part of the workforce (Kuznet, 1966). In India's case, the structural evolution has been different: while the share of agriculture in the total employment remained the same, decreasing slightly from 70 percent to 65 percent in the last 100 years (from the beginning to the end of the twentieth century), the share of the service sector in the GDP increased rapidly since independence. In 1991, at the time of the reforms, the primary sector (agriculture, fishing, mining, and forestry) accounted for 32.8 percent of GDP, industry accounted for 27.4 percent and the service sector accounted for 39.8 percent. By 2004, the service sector share had increased to 50 percent of GDP.

A major reason for the expansion of the service sector is the government policies that led to the massive expansion of bureaucracy and public sector employment, and greatly subsidized higher education, which was to the benefit of the bureaucracy. In 1977, in the formal service sector, the public sector employed 9.8 million and the private sector 1.6 million, which increased to fourteen million and 2.2 million respectively in 1994. The share of government in the net domestic product was 17.5 percent in 1981, which increased to 24 percent in 1991, while the figures for the private organized sector were 12.5 percent and 12.3 percent respectively. The government sector accounted for 67 percent of employment in the organized sector in 1991. In 1971, the public sector accounted for 45.8 percent of the total paid-up capital, while the private sector had 54.2 percent, and these figures changed to 71.6 percent and 28.4 percent in 1992.

The gross investment in the public sector increased phenomenally in this period as a part of the heavy industrialization strategy, which resulted in high capital intensity and low employment generation in the formal sector. Most of the increase in the working population had to be absorbed by the informal and unorganized sectors of the economy. As mentioned before, the share of the organized sector in the total employment was only 6.3 percent, while the rest were employed in the unorganized agricultural and industrial sectors in the later part of the 1990s.

Table 2 shows that while there was a 5-percentage-point decline in the share of the primary sector in employment, its contribution in GDP declined close to 8 points. The per capita output (income) was much lower and grew at a lower pace in the primary sector than in the secondary and tertiary sectors. This is despite the Green Revolution of the 1970s, which increased agricultural output significantly.

## Regional inequalities

As discussed before, under British India a few regions, especially the coastal cities of Bombay, Madras and Calcutta, developed industrially, with a critical level of capitalist institutions, while interior India remained feudal and backward. After independence, one of the important objectives of government policies was to foster equality in regional development. Decisions regarding where to locate the public sector were based on regional distribution objectives rather than on pure economic efficiency considerations. Moreover, the private sector was offered a set of fiscal incentives to locate in backward areas. Despite all this, the regional inequalities increased modestly under the pre-reforms policy regime, and rapidly in the post-reform period.

Ahluwalia (2002) constructs Gini coefficient measure of inequality with Gross State Domestic Product (GSDP) across fourteen major states in India. The Gini coefficient was 0.15 in 1980–1, increased to 0.17 in 1990–1, and then increased rapidly to 0.23 by 1998–91. It has interesting implications: the increase in regional disparities can be attributed to differences in the initial endowment of market institutional conditions. The inequality increased steeply in the post-reforms period, which supports my previous arguments that the reforms resulted in positive gains in those areas which were endowed with a critical level of initial market and institutional conditions. Ahluwalia shows that annual growth rates in per capita GSDP for the interior (landlocked) northern states such as Bihar, Uttar Pradesh and Rajasthan declined, while it increased significantly for the states of Maharashtra, Tamil Nadu, West Bengal and Gujarat from the period 1980–91 to 1991–9. As discussed before, the northern states remained feudal both under the British and later, in independent India, while the coastal areas such as Maharashtra and Tamil Nadu developed a critical level of capitalist institutions and industrial endowments under British rule.

To understand the importance of institutions, take the case of the state

*Table 2* Percentage share of three major sectors in employment and GDP

| Year | Employment (E) | | | GDP (G) | | | G/E | | |
|---|---|---|---|---|---|---|---|---|---|
| | 1983 | 1988 | 1994 | 1983 | 1988 | 1994 | 1983 | 1988 | 1994 |
| Primary sector | 68.25 | 64.89 | 63.98 | 37.09 | 31.39 | 29.49 | 2,563 | 2,584 | 2,995 |
| Secondary sector | 13.76 | 15.84 | 14.98 | 27.01 | 28.98 | 29.28 | 9,260 | 9,774 | 12,700 |
| Tertiary sector | 17.55 | 18.78 | 21.02 | 35.89 | 39.61 | 41.21 | 9,647 | 11,268 | 12,739 |
| Total | 305.9 | 318.8 | 367.6 | 1,443,100 | 1,703,220 | 2,388,640 | 4,717 | 5,342 | 6,497 |

Source: National Accounts Statistics.

Note
The total figures are in millions.

of Orissa, a coastal state in the south-east of India. This should actually give it an advantage for growth over landlocked regions. However, Orissa also declined economically during this period. One reason was that the state was never a base for the British and hence was not chosen for industrialization and commerce. It thus remained dominated by feudal institutions. One of the interesting aspects of the figures is that the northern states of Punjab and Haryana, which are rich as a result of agricultural produce, thanks to the Green Revolution, showed lower growth rates in the post-reforms period. One conjecture could be that, in the post-reform era, private investment in the industry and service sectors was the major source of growth, and this was concentrated mostly in the west and south of India.

The state of West Bengal has been under the rule of the Communist Party since the late 1970s. Its growth is primarily due to the benefits of land reforms, despite its industrial decline in the post-independence period. In the case of Kerala, a state in the south which also had Communist rule for a long period, there is historically high social capital in terms of literacy and decentralized governance within the state. However, despite high levels of development indices there is low economic growth. Whatever growth that took place in Kerala could be attributed to the multiplier and investment effect of repatriation from the earnings sent back by emigrants from overseas. Kerala is a counter-example to the observation of Dreze and Sen, cited earlier, that primary and secondary education can be a source of employment for the masses in the manufacturing sector, as in China. The reason that Kerala does not conform to this observation is that other institutions need to support high literacy for industrialization to take place and expand. In the case of Kerala, heavy protection of organized labor by the state discouraged industrialization and investments in technology.

## Market structure and qualitative behavior of agents

### The public sector

As discussed earlier, the policies gave a prominent role to the public sector in industry. In terms of market structure, industries such as railways, telecommunications, aircraft, and defense were public sector monopolies. In industries such as steel, electronics, heavy chemicals, fertilizers, etc., there was both public and private sector participation, but it was mostly dominated by the large public sector and a few large private sector firms. In 1989–90, the share of the public sector in national GDP was 27 percent, and its share in the gross capital formation was around 40 percent from 1960 to 1990. In 1960, the number of public sector companies was 142 and that of private companies 26,007, and their paid-up capitals were Rs 5,470 million and Rs 12,715 million respectively. In 1991, these figures were 1,180 and 249,181, and Rs 564,814 million and Rs 224,158 million respectively (Sarma, 1997). While the private sector firms increased tenfold compared to the public sector, the public sector sucked in almost double the amount of capital for this period.

Several studies on the Indian economy documented the extent of inefficient utilization of capital in the industrial sector (Goldar, 1986). This can be explained by the qualitative behavior of economic agents in response to the market structure and the institutional arrangements. One of the prominent elements of the institutional arrangement is the principal–agency relation of the ownership of capital and its management. In the case of the public sector, the owners of capital are the taxpayers or the public (households who pay taxes and invest their savings), and the managers of capital are the government agents – the politicians in power and the bureaucrats. In the case of the private sector, the owners are the shareholders and the public and private financial institutions. The agents, in this case, are the managers (or promoters in India) of companies. The agency costs of moral hazard behavior on the part of the agents were high both in the public and private sector in Indian industry, but more accentuated in the case of the public sector, owing to complex institutional arrangements which bestowed a high degree of informational imperfection on the owners. A simple example of informational manipulation is that the government protects a public bank's depositors. When the bank fails with non-performing loans, the taxpayer's money is used to save the bank and its depositors. If we assume that the majority of depositors are also the taxpayers (the larger public), the public pays up for the banking failure and there is redistribution of wealth from them to the loan defaulters. An even worse feature, which applies to the institutional arrangements in India, would be the case where the major part of tax revenues are from indirect taxes, which are highly regressive, when the poor (with no savings) subsidize the well-off.

In the case of the public sector, apart from the issue of agency costs, the other institutional issues are autonomy and soft-budget constraint in determining the utilization of capital. Autonomy refers to the freedom of managers from political interference from the government agents – the politicians and bureaucrats. The government undertakings were organized into two main categories – departmental and non-departmental – the former being owned and run by central government and covering public goods such as railways and telecommunications. The central and state governments owned the non-departmental public sector firms. The organization of management was based on a three-tier system: at the top was the concerned ministry (the center or the state), followed by the board of directors, in which the government was represented by a civil servant and at the bottom was the CEO of the company, who again would be a civil servant. The CEO of the company was appointed or removed by the ministry and subject to frequent political interference. The concerned ministries directly interfered in decisions concerning pricing, diversification, modernization, and employment. The interferences were not only based on the political objectives of the ministries but also catered to the interests of the private sector firms if they existed in specific industries. The latter aspect was especially prominent when the ministries and government bureaucrats were captured by the powerful private sector firms. For example, pricing policies in industries such as steel and fertilizers caused private sector firms to make supernormal profits as the government set prices on the basis of the cost structure of public sector firms. One of my colleagues who worked for a public sector firm observed that most of the reports of the public sector units reached the private sector firms before they evolved into policies of public sector pricing and supply.

On the other hand, in the case of South Korea, public sector undertakings were observed to be more efficient than the private sector because the undertakings were given total autonomy, subjected to the profit motive with hard budget constraints (Pack and Westphal, 1986). In India, too, there are a few efficient and profit-making public sector firms, such as Bharat Heavy Electricals and the Oil and Natural Gas Commission. The case of Maruti-Suzuki in the automobile industry presents a highly successful public sector undertaking. It was set up as a joint venture between the Indian government and the Japanese Suzuki Company in the early 1980s. The only political interference was in the location of the plant. Although the economic efficiency criteria showed its location to be best in a coastal area, the plant was set up in northern India, in a landlocked area in the city of Gurgaon, on the basis of interference by one of the central ministers. The company was given autonomy in its operations, with the Japanese company stake at 50 percent. Japanese management and production practices were adopted. Later on, Maruti's management and subcontracting practices became a role model for private sector firms for realizing efficiency. Another example of an efficient government undertaking is the National Stock Exchange (NSE), which was set up in the early 1990s. The NSE has expanded and increased the transparency of Indian stock markets all over the nation and has also contributed to the decline of the monopoly grip of the privately owned Bombay stock exchange, controlled by a set of brokers. Its success should be attributed to the autonomy bestowed upon it, free from political interferences.

### The private sector

The organization of large business houses in India can be traced from British times. As discussed before, the first seeds of Indian entrepreneurship were sown in the later part of the nineteenth century. A few traders belonging to specific ethnic communities in the west (Bombay, Surat) set up textile mills and later branched into steel in 1910. The predominant name at this time was that of the Tatas. Later on, similar developments took place in Calcutta in the east, and Madras in the south. Most industries were textiles, textile machinery, jute, sugar, steel, and construction, and later, light engineering products. In 1950, all industries were in the hands of eighteen Indian families, with Tatas and Birlas in the lead, and two British houses (Hazari, 1966). Almost all of them were organized by the managing agency system on the lines of the joint family system of India's social structure. For undertaking industrial investments with a long gestation period, the promoting families enlisted the cooperation of relatives and close friends for raising capital, with the management remaining with the promoting family. The promoting families were called managing agents. A family with direct control over a number of companies could have a minority hold in other units held by a different family, the organization of which is called business groups or houses. The large houses, such as Tatas and Birlas, created charitable trusts to control their companies (Tripathi, 2004). Tripathi observes that most business houses never adopted workers' welfare schemes except under pressure from trade unions and treated the shareholders with similar disdain, without much regard for protecting their interests. Although the managing agency system was abolished in 1970, the business group organization continues even at present.

An interesting outcome in the post-independence era was that while the business families expanded by using joint family funds in British India, they built family empires after independence with the taxpayers' money, without staking a single rupee of their own. The powerful industrial houses could influence the politicians and the bureaucrats and secured industrial licenses, which automatically gave them access to funding from government financial institutions. Although the company boards had some government-appointed directors, the promoting families usually captured them – dummy directors. Consequently, the families retained high control rights with no investment of their own.

As mentioned earlier, while, on the one hand, the industrial policies of licensing and MRTP restricted the expansion of industries by imposing high transaction costs and entry barriers for new entry, on the other hand, they worked in favor of the powerful business houses who could capture the relevant ministries. Several houses adopted the practices of cornering licenses to pre-empt new entrants and consequently derived a high degree of long-run monopoly power in several industries (Hazari, 1986; Patibandla, 1998). Even in those industries in which there was large-scale coexistence of the public and private sector, such as steel and fertilizers, it worked in the favor of the private sector to derive large monopoly rents as the market prices were determined by the public sector firms.

Contrary to the widely held view that licensing policies put all kinds of restrictions on the private sector, Tripathi (2004, 304) observes, "Barring a few exceptions, practically all the major houses that dominated Indian business before independence underwent substantial expansion and consolidation." To give an example, at the end of 1950 the Tata house had the largest private sector presence in steel, engineering, power generation, trading, insurance, and cotton mills (Hazari, 1966). Later on, they diversified into the production and sale of tea, watches, consulting, and software and several other activities. A similar pattern of diversification took place for other dominant business houses. This type of expansion was primarily motivated by monopoly rent-seeking under the command and control regime of the policy. Most industries in which large scale private sector was allowed were characterized by high concentration ratios. Combined with a high degree of protection from imports, the large corporations derived long-run market power, which brought them supernormal profits. To give an example, the average rate of profits of large firms in India was around 30 percent, while it was around 4 percent in South Korea in the early part of the 1980s (Patibandla, 1994).

The diversification behavior of firms was on both horizontal and vertical lines, in the first case, firms diversifying into a whole variety of related and unrelated activities, and in the second, into producing a range of products from raw materials to the final goods. As far as horizontal diversification is concerned, there is no systematic theory for its explanation in the theory of the firm, except factors such as economies of scope in related activities. As discussed in the previous chapter, Penrose's theory explains multi-products as a result of excess capacity arising out of growth of the firm. Under the highly protected markets characterized by pervasive capital market imperfections, diversification can be motivated by monopoly profits under the import substitution cycles, especially when large oligopolists collude. Instead of expanding output in one single industry, which would depress prices and monopoly profits, the large houses diversify into several areas. Additionally, as mentioned before, the social explanation of joint family businesses is that as families expand with sons and daughters, family businesses may diversify their operations, especially when they have access to licenses and finance from the public financial institutions. This behavior of empire-building by family business houses can be motivated by two reasons – rent-seeking, and also what sociologists call 'power' considerations (Pfeffer, 1996), when the prevailing institutional environment does not force firms to search for economic efficiency.

In the pre-reforms era, large Indian firms adopted a high degree of vertical integration. Vertical integration taken as value-added/production[6] was about 48 percent for the top fifty firms in the Indian industry in the early 1980s (Patibandla, 1994). As discussed in the previous section, vertical integration behavior could be motivated by efficiency considerations of economizing on transaction costs, especially if local institutions in product and factor markets are inefficient. On the other hand, under the import-substituting regime, vertical integration could be undertaken in the monopoly practices of final-goods producers for monopolizing the supply of critical inputs, especially when imports were subjected to high protection. For example, the Reliance textile firm monopolized the production of polyester filament yarn, which gave it a significant advantage in upstream competition in textiles, as other textile producers had to depend on it for their input. Another example was the engineering tools industry. Three large firms controlled the production of a critical input of carbide, and a large number of medium- and small-scale firms had to depend on these three large firms for the supply of the input. To prove the argument of rent-seeking vertical integration behavior qualitatively, the prices of several of the intermediate inputs produced domestically declined within a short period when tariffs on them were reduced in the early 1990s. To give an example, when the tariffs on the imports of textile yarn were reduced in the early 1990s, the Reliance textile firm reduced the price of yarn significantly, which, in turn, led to the generation of a large market for synthetic fabrics (Ghemawat and Patibandla, 1999). Had the prices of the inputs been based on long-run marginal costs in the pre-reforms period, it would not have been possible to reduce the prices immediately when tariffs were reduced, unless firms were willing to take short-run losses or undertake cross-product subsidization.

As discussed before, about 853 industrial products were reserved for small-scale firms. Combining this with the institutional conditions of factor and product segmentation resulted in a market structure termed 'long-tailed' in quite a few broadly defined industries in which the fixed costs of technology were not high. In these industries, a few large firms catered to a major part of the market share and a large number of small firms catered to the rest (Patibandla, 1998). The examples are hand tools, small and cutting tools, diesel engines and parts, steel tubes and pipes, and shoes, etc. Large firms generally concentrated on those industries where effective rates of protection (ERP) were high and small firms concentrated on those areas where ERPs were low. For example, in the automobile industry small firms concentrated on the production of components while large firms were in the final product (Bruch and Hiemenz, 1983). In other words, small firms faced higher competition from imports than large firms. The above structural distribution of large and small firms resulted in two qualitative behavioral outcomes: mobility barriers on efficient small firms, and subcontracting activity between the large and small firms.

On the issue of firm size and production efficiency, Little *et al.* (1987) showed that there was no statistically significant relation between firm size and efficiency in three out of the four industries that they studied, which implies that large and small firms realize similar levels of efficiency in production. Patibandla (1998) showed that in the case of the hand tools and small and cutting tools industry, very small and very large firms were relatively inefficient compared to firms in the middle. Why were large firms, which had better access to capital and imported technologies, not more efficient? An explanation can be drawn from the organizational behavior of large and small firms in response to the differential structural and institutional conditions they faced. As mentioned earlier, large firms operate in the organized, and the small in the unorganized, input markets, which gives large firms better access to capital at lower cost, while small firms tend to pay lower wages to labor. The pervasive regulatory policies of the government, capital market imperfections and inefficient contractual enforcements in general imposed high transaction costs, which functioned as a source of long-run market power to incumbent large houses and as an entry and mobility barrier to efficient small or new-entrant firms. It is generally argued that under the import substitution policy regime, X-inefficiency owing to the lack of competitive markets was high and it could be more prominent for large firms with long-run market power than for small firms. Under the structural conditions, while large firms were able to derive supernormal profits despite organizational slack, small firms that could survive were those that operated with a high degree of (internal) organizational efficiency.

Despite better access to imported technologies, access to capital below its shadow price and lack of competitive market conditions might have prevented most large firms from undertaking systematic organizational efforts in adapting imported technologies efficiently. Lall (1987) observed that most large firms in India underutilized capital and were weak in labor management. A significant part of the organizational X-inefficiency of large firms stemmed from poor coordination between different departments, which was magnified by a large number of layers of hierarchy. In a typical large Indian firm, hierarchy levels ranged between fifteen and twenty categories. Within five or six broad categories, there were three or four subcategories.

In contrast, small firms faced two interlinked structural constraints: capital market imperfections and high transaction costs. To illustrate this, small firms had to wait long periods for payments on domestic deliveries, which, in turn, raised the costs of working capital, especially since they had to pay higher costs to capital. This is an important factor because most small firms tended to have a higher percentage of bought-in inputs than did large firms, which were generally more vertically integrated. Working capital constraints, in a highly inefficient institutional environment of high transaction costs, was one of the major reasons for the high incidence of sickness among small firms. Given these institutional factors, a successful small firm could be one that adopted organizational behavior which minimized fixed and working capital requirements at all stages of operation. This is illustrated on the basis of my fieldwork for my doctoral thesis (1994, 1998).

The first stage was the choice of product line on a narrow specialization. The second stage was the minimization of costs in buying and installing machinery. In one of the cases, the machinery cost was reduced substantially by second-hand machinery and renovating it with new components secured both domestically and overseas. The third stage was the minimization of variable costs (working capital) in raw material procurement and labor management. The inventory costs of raw materials were managed efficiently by maintaining consistent relations with the suppliers. In the case of labor, as the small firms operated in the unorganized labor markets they had higher flexibility. They employed a small amount of permanent labor and temporary semi- and unskilled labor. The temporary workers could be fired in times of low demand conditions. When a small firm realized higher efficiency than a large firm in a particular product segment, large multi-product firms targeted the efficient small firms to impose mobility barriers through cross-product subsidization.

One of the structural outcomes of the institutional conditions characterized above was the increasing practice of subcontracting between large and small firms since the late 1970s. One of the primary motives behind it was the large firms' attempts at overcoming the labor market rigidities of the organized labor markets (Nagaraj, 1984). Apart from this, the reservation policies and excise duty concession directed at small-scale industry led to the entry of a large number of small firms into the intermediate goods industries such as bicycle and auto components. Small firms became dependent on a few large final producers to sell their products, which, in turn, provided a degree of monopsony power to the large final-product producers. An outcome of this was unequal bargaining between the large and small producers. Small firms were generally made to wait long periods to get payments for their deliveries, as mentioned before. The final-goods producers used to pass the losses of market fluctuations on to intermediate suppliers. To give an example from my field work, a few small firms in the auto component industry were made to expand their capacities when the market for automobiles was booming (in the mid- and late 1980s), and when the market declined the small firms were left in the dock. One of the qualitative outcomes of this was increasing export presence by small firms, even though exports were in general not a profitable activity in the overvalued exchange regime. Under the prevailing domestic institutional conditions, a small firm which reached a critical level of size and efficiency and had access to information would perceive doing business with overseas buyers as less costly than in the domestic market. One simple example is the prompt payments on deliveries through letters of credit for exports, which made a big difference, given the high cost of capital and working capital constraints of small firms (Patibandla, 1995). For the period 1981–4, small firms accounted for about 30 percent of the total exports of the engineering industry.

The large-scale organized sector played an insignificant role in exports, mostly as a residual activity to get access to import licenses and foreign exchange under the import policies of the previous policy regime. Given the captive domestic market with monopoly profits and their operations in the areas with high ERPs, exports were not profitable for the large firms. It is possible to show theoretically that there was systematic wealth transfer from the labor-intensive unorganized sector to the organized large-scale sector under the import substitution policies.

Let us take two sectors in the economy: capital-intensive (organized) manufacturing ($M$) and labor-intensive agriculture or unorganized manufacturing ($A$); and two inputs: capital ($K$) and labor ($L$). $A$ has comparative advantage for exports owing to its labor-intensity. In the capital-scarce Indian economy, $K$ is fully employed but there is surplus labor (unemployment). Let us take the case that $M$ was protected from imports either through overvalued exchange or high tariffs (or both). It results in expansion of $M$ at the cost of $A$. Expansion of $M$ requires more capital than labor. Contraction of $A$ releases more labor than that which can be absorbed by $M$, as $A$ is labor-intensive. As $M$ is capital intensive, it draws capital from $A$, and every unit of capital released from $A$ results in proportionately more labor discharge. Adjustment of employment through depression in wages is not possible as there is surplus labor, which means that labor would be paid a wage close to subsistence. This, in turn, worsens unemployment in the economy.

Apart from this, there would be a net transfer of wealth from sector $A$ to sector $M$. Let us assume that $A$ is an intermediate input, consumed by $M$. Figure 1 represents sector $A$ in a partial equilibrium framework. $D$ is the domestic demand curve and $S$ is the supply curve of the sector. Under the assumption of a price-taking small country in the world market, $P_w$ is the world market price for $A$. Under free trade, $0g$ will be supplied to the domestic market, $gd$ will be exported and the producer surplus of $A$ is $P_w bS$. Let us take the case that the government restricts the exports of $A$ or depresses its price realization by adopting an overvalued exchange rate. Consequently the domestic price is at $P$ and output contracts to the extent of $df$. Consequently, $P_w acP$ amount of the producer surplus of $A$ will be transferred to $M$ and there would be a dead-weight loss to the extent of $abc$. If the market structure of $M$ is monopoly or collusive oligopoly, all of the surplus transferred from $A$ to $M$ will not be passed to the consumers of $M$, but a major part of it will be appropriated by the producers of $M$. The output contraction of $A$ to the extent of $fd$ can be simplified to the extent of labor released from $A$.

The theoretical argument for the protection of $M$ can be based on the infant-industry argument that, under temporary protection, $M$ can realize both static and dynamic (learning) economies, which makes the industry internationally competitive over a period of time. However, this depends on the technology adopted and the technological efforts of the producers of $M$, which, in turn, depends on whether the domestic market structure is competitive or a monopoly with several possibilities.

In the case of South Korea's industrialization strategy, temporary protection was combined with licensing policies of restricting entry to a few

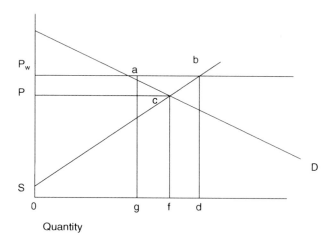

*Figure 1* Trade policy and distribution outcomes: partial equilibrium.

large players to realize economies of scale with positive outcomes. However, the producers were given a clear policy signal that import protection would be removed after a period of time, which caused protected firms to make systematic technological efforts at arriving at international frontiers to be able to compete with imports (Jacobsson and Alam, 1994). However, the results were not the same in India for several reasons: licenses imposed entry barriers, but MRTP policies restricted firm size to realize economies of scale. Moreover, the protected firms were given a policy signal amounting to indefinite protection. This, in turn, resulted in long-run monopoly power to the firms and provided incentives for premature diversification into multiple areas by large houses. Additionally, a captive local market with supernormal profits did not provide sufficient incentives for collusive oligopolists to adopt the latest technologies, which could be imported from developed economies without actually having to undertake risky R&D.

In addition, Parente and Prescott (1999) show that when monopolies are protected by state regulation, it makes it costly for a group of potential adopters to enter the industry with superior technology, as the non-adopters force the potential adopters to spend large resources for adoption of superior technology. This is because a superior technology could result in higher productivity and output, and steep decline in prices and monopoly rents. Apart from the non-adopters, organized labor could also block the adoption of superior technology out of fear of labor-replacement, which was the case in several industries in India, especially in the public sector.

The nature of the technological activity that took place in the Indian industry of the pre-reforms era was diverse. There were a few cases of efficient adoption of imported technologies to local market conditions in industries such as the tractor and boiler industries (Desai, 1988). India's bicycle industry, which had the largest local market in the world, generated indigenous technological activity in congruence with local demand conditions of price-sensitive poor consumers and rough road conditions. However, a major part of the technological activity in the Indian industry in general consisted of the importation of older technologies under the import substitution cycles. There was little effort to enhance technological capabilities. According to Desai (1988), many industries that expanded in India were either insignificant or declining in industrialized countries. For example, in the early 1980s India produced a large volume of sturdy machine tools and other industrial equipment which were passing out of use in the industrialized countries twenty years earlier.

Lall (1987) observed that when capital-intensive technologies were imported from advanced countries, Indian firms did not make systematic efforts at adapting them in accordance with local product and factor market conditions. An even more interesting aspect of this was that the thrust of the process engineering efforts was towards greater capital intensity – which was inconsistent with the relative prices of factors of production of the capital-scarce and labor-surplus economy. This can be explained by two institutional factors. One was that, for most of the large houses (the promoters), who were able to capture the public financial institutions, the cost of capital was low in relation to the high monopoly profits of the protected markets. The other was that increasing capital intensity was a means of overcoming the labor market rigidities of the organized labor markets.

One germane issue is to what extent the large firms were able to realize economies of scale. Conceptually, economies of scale can be seen in terms of static and dynamic economies. The former implies that as more output is produced, average costs keep declining; and the latter that dynamic learning economies takes place over time through cumulative output expansion. The learning economies are generally more prominent in high-technology industries. The static and dynamic economies can take place both internal and external to a firm, but internal to an industry. The latter aspect of external economies implies that as an industry's output expands, it supports production of a larger base of intermediate inputs, which results in downward shifts in an individual firm's cost curves. "Division of labor is limited by the extent of the market": the famous words of Adam Smith emphasize the importance of market size for the realization of economies of scale. Market size is determined by income levels and the distribution of households in the economy, and also access to export markets. In the case of the industrialization strategies of Japan and South Korea and, at present, China, economies of scale were realized from two dimensions: prior to undertaking industrialization, land reforms were implemented, which generated a critical level of local demand for manufactured goods; and the high degree of export orientation extended the market size for manufactured goods. Both these factors were missing in India's industrialization strategy. India's income distribution remained skewed, segmenting the market for industrial goods. Furthermore, inward orientation restricted the realization of economies of scale.

The qualitative behavior of large-scale firms in relation to the policy institutions and domestic demand factors restricted the realization of both static and dynamic economies in Indian industry. As discussed before, it was more profitable for large houses to diversify into multiple areas rather than to expand in closely related activities under the import substitution cycles. Premature diversification dissipates both static and dynamic economies. Moreover, when a firm had the choice to make monopoly rents in different areas through diversification, its choice of technology in each specific area would be such that there would be no efforts at extending the market size by exports. Although MRTP policies restricted the expansion of firms within a single line, firms were nevertheless allowed to expand capacity for exports. By taking this policy relaxation, I illustrate the point by a simple theoretical argument through Figure 2.

$D$ is the domestic demand curve and $P_w$ is the world price. $MC_1$ and $MC_2$ can be taken to be marginal cost curves representing two different technologies. They also can be treated as downward shifts in cost curves owing to dynamic learning economies. If a monopolist chooses technology $MC_1$, it rules itself out from exporting and primarily derives monopoly rents in the domestic market, and there will be excess capacity or dead-weight loss in the system to the extent of $ab$ – under utilized capacity. When a firm

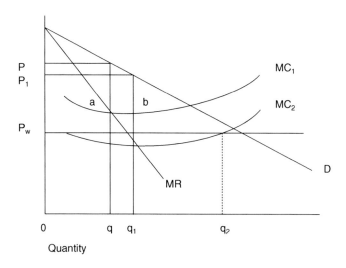

*Figure 2* Markets and technology adoption.

adopts $MC_2$, the firm will undertake exports by operating price discrimination in which the domestic quantity and price will be determined by the condition of $MC_2 = MR = P_w$. Consequently, the firm realizes full capacity utilization (efficient scales), the domestic price goes down from $P$ to $P_1$, and the quantity supplied in the domestic market increases from $q$ to $q_1$, increasing the domestic consumer surplus industry exports to the extent of $q_1 q_2$. As mentioned before, the firm would adopt the inferior technology $MC_1$ because the domestic market structure and institutional conditions make adoption of superior technology costly. Additionally, when the firm had opportunities to diversify into multiple areas with monopoly power, it would not have sufficient incentive to adopt superior technology in each area. A simple proof that the large firms did not adopt superior technology was the very low export orientation of large firms in the pre-reforms period.[7]

The issue that follows is the realization of dynamic economies with the adoption of $MC_1$ through technological behavior in response to the prevailing market structure and institutions that shifts $MC_1$ down to $MC_2$. The extent and ability to realize dynamic economies can be a function of the X-efficiency levels of firms. The concept of X-(in)efficiency developed by Lebenstein (1966) is similar to John Hicks' observation, "The best of all monopoly profit is a quiet life." When competition is low the degree of involvement of managers and skilled workers in technological activity would be low, and there could also be a high incidence of organizational slack. Realization of learning-by-doing economies depends on organizational conditions in terms of coordination between different departments, layers of hierarchy and flow of information. As mentioned before, most large firms in Indian industries derived long-run market power and adopted inefficient organizations, in that these were too many hierarchies and a high degree of centralization, dissipating the realization of dynamic economies.

Furthermore, diversification behavior with centralization of control and management, which was very common among most large Indian business houses, could dissipate the potential for dynamic economies. There are fixed costs for workers and managers in learning to perform a task well in terms of absorbing new information about a new technology and ways of performing specialized tasks and their coordination. As a result of the fixed costs, there are 'switching costs'. If a firm switches to a new product or technology or diversifies into producing many products with different technologies, the switching costs will be high and the learning effects will be low (Stiglitz, 1987). The empirical study of Ferrantino (1992) found that the purchasers of imported technology in Indian industry in the 1980s were less efficient than the non-purchasers, which suggests two points: one, that there were additional costs of transferring technology, and if technology was not adapted to local conditions, it would cause inefficiency; and second, it also suggests that the firms were not able to realize the dynamic economies associated with capital-intensive imported technologies.

At the macro level, the Kaldor-Verdoorn law (Kaldor, 1966) shows that learning economies will be significant if industry grows at a sustained growth rate, thereby augmenting cumulative output and learning by workers and managers. A two-way relation between demand and supply side factors determines industrial growth. On the demand side, sustained industrial growth requires growth in effective demand, which is determined by growth in income levels and the number of people with purchasing power. Productivity growth determines income (wage) levels and employment growth determines the increase in the number of people with purchasing power. Low industrial productivity depresses wage levels and also results in high product prices, which, in turn, reduces real incomes. Apart from this, monopoly pricing reduces consumer surplus and results in dead-weight loss in the system, which, in turn, reduces incomes and also employment generation.

The previous discussion suggests that one of the reasons for low economic growth could be the income distributional outcome of the pre-reform policy regime. The income redistribution in favor of organized groups at the cost of the unorganized was a result of the political economy outcomes of the policy regime and the prevailing institutional arrangements. Sanyal (1984) and Bardhan (1984) illustrate the emergence of three powerful interest groups under the interventionist regime: the politicians and bureaucrats whose powers of patronage and rent-seeking increased as intervention was increased; the large industrial houses, who captured the industrial licenses and public financial institutions, and derived monopoly rents; and organized labor, which was partially responsible for blocking the adoption of superior technologies.

An interesting aspect of the policy intervention was that it was a relative failure in the industrial sector as compared to the agriculture sector. As mentioned before, policy intervention in agriculture in terms of the generation and supply of new seeds, price support, and fertilizer provision led to the spectacular results of the Green Revolution, which made India self-sufficient in food grain production within a very short period. The government investments in agriculture in the areas of irrigation, the generation of new seeds and other infrastructure resulted in high productivity gains, in contrast to the situation in industry (Dholakia and Dholakia, 1993). One possible explanation for the relative success of the agriculture policy is that the agriculture sector is characterized by atomistic producers, spread across the country with little possibility of collusive behavior, unlike the case of the oligopolistic industrial sector. Consequently, the agriculture sector was more responsive to policy incentives to expand output than the monopolistic industrial sector. The argument that the agriculture sector was pampered and highly subsidized with income tax exemptions and large fertilizer subsidies was rather tenuous. The terms of trade remained in favor of the organized industrial sector because agricultural output prices were kept below international prices, while organized industry realized prices much above international prices through protection. Furthermore, public and private sector producers appropriated a major part of the fertilizer subsidies, rather than farmers. Putting these factors together, Gulati (1990) shows that the agriculture sector actually paid a net tax.

Following from the discussion, the germane issue would be whether the structural outcomes of the policies reduced or increased the fragmentation of the markets and institutions and, if there was a reduction, whether the reduction was less than it could have been with an alternative institutional environment. The latter question refers to the economic system where the state takes the role of providing public goods, universal primary education, and social security with no intervention in the market mechanism, and I refrain from dealing with it. The reason is that the increased growth rate of the post-reform period could be attributed to freer market forces but they operate on the basis of market and institutional endowments acquired in the past.

The previous discussion qualitatively shows that there was a systematic redistribution of wealth and income in favor of the organized sector from the unorganized. The qualitative argument is summarized in the following. The large Indian business houses, which were able to capture industrial licenses, were also able to raise capital from the public financial institutions by retaining high control rights, which meant that the cost of capital to the promoters was negligible. The finance of the public financial institutions was raised from households through taxes and mobilization of savings. A major part of the tax revenue of the government was indirect taxes and it is well established in the public finance literature that indirect taxes are highly regressive, with the major part of the burden falling on the poor. Apart from this, in the 1980s the government borrowed from the market to meet the budget deficit, which arose in the first place because of transfer payments to various classes of property owners. Thus, in the name of socialism, the taxpayers' money was not only redistributed to the rich, but they were offered an interest earning on what they got as transfer (Sanyal, 1986).

Government protected the public savings deposited in the public banks and institutions, which meant that when these institutions failed with default loans they were bailed out by tax revenues. Until recently, several large business houses did not pay corporate taxes as a result of the manipulation of accounts, and tax laws with loopholes. This, combined with the long-run monopoly power of large firms, meant that there was a transfer of consumer surplus into producer surplus. In other words, there was net transfer of wealth in favor of the promoters of the large industrial houses. A notable feature of the institutions is that the expansion of the public sector banks across the country mobilized savings from the public in a big way, but access to loans remained the preserve of powerful groups, those who could incur the transaction costs of dealing with the government and had the collateral, which was not necessarily putting up a physical property as guarantee in the case of default.

The basic structural outcome of the policy regime at the time of the initiation of the economic reforms in the late 1980s was a large industrial base, below international technological frontiers. A large pool of technical and skilled manpower, generated with the taxpayers' money, was utilized below its potential productivity owing to monopoly and monopsony power in the product and labor markets. The structural outcome generated a sizeable middle class, close to 250 million, mostly concentrated in urban areas, with the major part engaged in the service economy. Close to 300 million people remained illiterate, below the poverty line and outside the market mechanism.

## The policy reforms

I briefly sketch out the main policy reforms undertaken since the mid-1980s. There are several other published studies that list the reforms comprehensively for readers interested in the details (Srinivasan, 2000; Bhagwati, 1993; Ahluwalia, 1999).

There are two phases to the reforms – the first phase was from mid-1980 to 1991, and second has been in progress since 1991. Although the reforms were accelerated from 1991, driven by the balance of payments crisis, they have been gradual and piecemeal, which prompted Yergin (1998) to term the process as 'the Hindu rate of change'. The internal product market reforms in terms of the removal of industrial licensing policies and of restrictions on firm size and capacity expansion of firms were implemented in the mid-1980s. The policies relaxed restrictions on the entry of TNCs through joint ventures and there were considerable reductions in import tariffs, especially on intermediate goods. However, the reforms process was drastically slowed down in the late 1980s as a result of political economy considerations as the government attempted to deal with varied interest groups and ideologies – the followers of Nehruvian socialism, the parties of the left, and the 'nationalist' tones of the Bharatiya Janata Party (Varshney, 1999). The balance of payments crisis of 1991 made Indian policy-makers undertake a major shift in the overall policies backed by the IMF and the World Bank's conditionalities. Although the reforms of 1991 could be seen as a major policy shock compared to the previous forty years of pervasive state intervention and controls, policy reforms in India have been piecemeal and incremental, unlike those in the east European transition economies. Some of the elements of the reforms in the early 1990s were the devaluation of the Indian rupee, a reduction in the number of quantitative restrictions on imports, a reduction in import tariffs, the removal of price and distribution controls, and further liberalization on the entry of foreign direct investment (Ahluwalia, 1999).

The import-weighted average tariff rate for all products was brought down from 87 percent in 1990–1 to 30 percent in 1998–9. However, differential tariff rates on intermediate and final goods still prevail. Quantitative restrictions (QR) on imports have been reduced gradually. In 1998 about 350 items were removed from the QR list. Under the WTO agreement, these restrictions were eliminated by 2000, except on defense-related items. By 2001, import licensing had been completely abolished. In order to promote exports, imports of capital and intermediate goods for exporting firms are allowed duty free. In 2001, the government of India announced the setting-up of Special Economic Zones (SEZs) to promote exports. In these zones, 100 percent foreign firms are permitted automatically and imports are allowed duty-free.

Over the period of 1991 to 2001, controls on multinational investment were reduced significantly. The industrial policy reform eliminated industrial licensing requirements for FDI, except for a select list of hazardous and environmentally sensitive industries. In 1991 investment proposals in a specified list of high-technology and high-priority industries received automatic approvals. The hiring of foreign technicians and the testing of indigenously developed and imported technology no longer required permission. It is possible for transnational firms intending to take over a domestic firm to buy stock through the market. However, such investments cannot be translated into control unless they follow an approval route. In 1993–4, conditions prohibiting the use of foreign brand names and trademarks in goods sold domestically were removed. All restrictions on foreign companies borrowing funds or raising deposits in India, as well as taking over or creating any interest in business in Indian companies, were eliminated. They were also exempted from restrictions on the establishment of liaison offices and acquisition of the whole or part of any undertaking in all businesses in India (trade, commerce, and industry), except in the areas of agriculture and plantations.

In 1995–6, India's policy was made more attractive for FDI. The list of industries eligible for automatic approval was expanded. Basic telecommunications were opened up for FDI investment. Industrial licensing for almost all bulk drugs was abolished. FDI investment up to 51 percent was made automatic. Several incentives for investment in infrastructure projects were initiated in 1996–7. The Infrastructure Development Finance Corporation was registered for innovative financing to address the needs of infrastructure projects. A five-year tax holiday was made available to companies developing, maintaining, and operating infrastructure facilities such as roads, bridges, new airports, ports, railway projects, water supply, sanitation and sewerage projects, power, telecommunications, industrial parks, and oil exploration. In 1996–7, the Foreign Investment Promotion Board (FIPB) was set up, which was directed at promoting FDI in

infrastructure, export-potential industries, employment-intensive industries, social sector projects like hospitals, healthcare and medicines, and
proposals that led to the introduction of technology and the infusion of
capital.

However, some sectors were still subject to equity caps: 20 percent in
banking; 51 percent in non-banking financial companies; 51 percent in
the pharmaceutical industry for bulk drugs; 40 percent for domestic airlines; and 50 percent in mining, except for gold, silver, diamonds, and
precious stones. In 1998–9, the credit card and money changing businesses were included in FDI-permissible undertakings, under Non-
banking Financial Services. Remittances of dividends are freely permitted
and remittance of principal and interest on foreign loans is also freely
allowed, subject to a priori approval from the Reserve Bank of India. The
remittance of royalties, technical fees, and salaries to foreign employees is
allowed according to the terms and conditions of specific collaboration
agreements.

By the year 2000, almost all the sectors were opened to TNCs and 100
percent ownership was allowed. Most investment proposals were to be
given automatic clearance, subject only to central bank scrutiny of the
foreign exchange details. Foreign equity ceilings in some sectors have
been raised: in pharmaceuticals from 51 to 74 percent, in mining from 74
to 100 percent. Sectors such as advertising and the film industry are
opened up for FDI. In 2001, even defense-related production was opened
up for private investment. However, the retail sector is still not open to
FDI.

The reservations for the small-scale sector still persist, with about 700
items reserved for them. In 1997–8, the investment ceiling for small-scale
firms was increased from Rs 7.5 million to Rs 30 million, and the apparel
sector, with the largest export potential, was removed from the reservation
for small firms and opened to all investors. In 2001, the reservation of
fourteen items for the small-scale sector, such as leather goods, shoes, and
toys, was removed for promoting exports.

The reforms still remain piecemeal and incremental. For example, privatization of public sector firms is still slow. In 2000, government-owned
entities still accounted for 43 percent of India's capital stock. The process
of clearances for FDI investment still remains cumbersome and subject to
high transaction costs. For example, FDI investment approvals in power
projects require about 100 clearances. These especially refer to post-
approval clearances, which escalate the costs of the projects.[8] With the
opening up of the telecommunication sector to private participation, both
local and foreign firms made it a fast-growing sector. However, the regulation of infrastructure sectors such as power and telecommunications with
public good properties is still subject to non-transparency. Sales taxes and
excise duties are not still uniform across products and different regions of
the country, which restricts free movement of goods across the country.

The tax structure is till subject to complexity, which causes high transaction costs and corruption.

On the labor market side, until 2001, large firms with more than 100 employees were required to obtain state permission to lay off workers or to exit. This limit was raised to 1,000 employees in 2001. However, the bankruptcy laws with regard to the closure of firms still remain subject to high transaction costs. The government encouraged the adoption of voluntary retirement schemes in both the public and private sector to bring forth an element of flexibility in the organized labor market. While private sector firms are able to find legal and extra-legal ways of getting around the labor legislation, the public sector is still characterized by gross overmanning.

On the financial sector front, the Capital Issues Control Act 1947 was abolished, giving way to free pricing of capital issues and making equity finance an attractive source for corporations. The Foreign Exchange Regulation Act has been replaced by the Foreign Exchange Management Act to liberalize the operation of firms with foreign equity and for Indian firms doing business abroad. Indian firms are now allowed to raise capital abroad through GDRs (Global Depository Receipts) and ADRs (American Depository Receipts). Policy changes included making the foreign exchange rate market-determined and moving towards current account convertibility. In 1992, the capital market was opened up for foreign portfolio investment, which opened the country's stock markets to direct participation by Foreign Institutional Investors (FII), such as pension funds, mutual funds, investment trusts, and asset management companies. They are permitted to invest in all the securities traded on the primary and secondary markets. These would include shares, debentures, warrants, and schemes floated by domestic mutual funds. This has led to an increasing role for FIIs in the India's equity markets. FIIs' investment increased from $827 million in 1993 to $10.2 billion in 1999. Forbes (2002) observes that FIIs account for fewer than 10 percent of total market capitalization, but account for a disproportionate share of daily trading. Their buying preferences have led to the imposition of a penalty on stock valuations of those firms that have group cross-holding, inadequate disclosure, or are closely held. This has led FIIs to raise their demands steadily for better corporate governance, more transparency, and greater disclosure (Goswami, 2001; Khanna and Palepu, 1999).

The deregulation of interest rates and a gradual weaning-off the historically privileged access to the public financial institutions has led some institutions to reform their operations. For example, the ICICI, which was a government-owned development bank, has shifted into merchant banking and funding of high-technology activities and assisting their listing on the public stock exchange since 1994. The DFIs still continue to play an important role in the debt financing of Indian corporations. However, most public financial institutions continue to be saddled with non-performing assets. For example, one of the institutions, the UTI, was bailed out by the government in 1998 with a sum of Rs 33,000 million of taxpayers' money (Menon, 2001). Some estimates show that the government of India has earmarked over Rs 200,000 million of taxpayers' money in 2002 to bail out just three of the public financial institutions: UTI, IFCI, and IDBI (Dalal, 2002). The financial sector, which is still dominated by the public sector, suffers from several structural problems. The transaction costs associated with legal contractual formation and enforcement are still high, with Indian courts taking a long period to settle disputes. Government's role in capital markets also involves costs due to the existence of a multitude of government audit and law enforcement agencies, high levels of deposit pre-emption through mandated reserves, and directed lending requirements (Bhattacharya and Patel, 2003).

Two main institutional reforms in the early 1990s included the setting up of the Securities and Exchange Board of India (SEBI) and the National Stock Exchange (NSE) by the government of India, prompted by a major stock market scandal in 1992, when a large stockbroker of Bombay Stock Exchange manipulated stock prices and created a bubble by using illegally acquired monies from the public sector banks. The SEBI was started with the intent of forcing firms to adopt better disclosures and restrain them from insider training. However, this body has not been assigned sufficient powers to police violations of regulations (Khanna and Palepu, 1999). Although a takeover code was introduced in 1994, takeovers remain difficult owing to the high transaction costs and paucity of information. The NSE expanded equity markets across the country and reduced the monopoly power of Bombay Stock Exchange. In 2003, with more than 9,000 listed companies and a market capitalization of $125 billion, India has efficient back-office and settlement systems, and the ability to attract international capital. The insurance sector is also opened to private firms, both local and foreign investment, with foreign equity capped at 26 percent, with an additional provision of 14 percent to non-resident Indians. However, about 80 percent of banking and insurance is still in the hands of the public sector. Compared to the pre-reforms period, banks have been given greater freedom in their operations through the abolition of the requirements for credit authorization by the central bank.

In most of the country, except in the state of Tamil Nadu, the urban land market is subject to controls of protected tenancies, rent controls, and zoning laws. This has made urban land prices among the highest in Asia. The Rent Control Act, which restricts the property rights of owners, still prevails in several parts of India, preventing urban development and restructuring. Indian businesses are still subject to high transaction costs imposed by bureaucracy. In the year 2004, nearly two decades after the initiation of the reforms, it is observed that each industrial unit was visited by between forty and sixty inspectors in the course of a month. Indian managers spent close to 16 percent of their time dealing with government officials (*Economist*, 2004). A World Bank study (2004) observes that it takes about eighty-nine days to start a new business and register property in India. It takes about ten years to recover 12.5 cents to a dollar in a case of bankruptcy in India, against five years and 25.8 cents in Nepal, four years and 23.2 cents in Bangladesh, 2.8 years and 38.1 cents in Pakistan, and 2.2 years and 33.1 cents in Sri Lanka. The study observes that India is among the worst countries in the world to do business in, when it comes to employment regulation.

# 4 The direction of structural changes

Douglas North postulated that one of the important elements of institutional evolution is a change in the perceptions and attitudes of economic agents with regard to opportunity sets. Perhaps the most profound effect of the reforms in India since their initiation in the mid-1980s is the change in the attitude and perceptions of the middle class towards industry, business, and investment and their international outlook.[1] This change may have a more influential effect on the evolution of the capitalist institutions than piecemeal changes in policies. Why has this change taken place?

Since the initiation of the reforms, far-reaching structural changes have been taking place in the economy. The most significant are that new industries have emerged and have become important wealth and employment generators, and that old and established industries have reoriented themselves in terms of products and markets. A few entrepreneurs from the middle class have become highly successful and achieved global recognition. Size and composition in many sectors are under change. Management and ownership structures are changing. Important regional changes have taken place in the industrial map. The relationship between agriculture and industry has changed significantly. The relationship with consumers has changed drastically in the service industry, and relations with the rest of the world have changed both quantitatively and qualitatively. These changes have become a major source of employment opportunities for the educated young people of the middle class and have led to increased consumption of the newest products. Several of the positive changes have taken place quickly owing to the initial endowments, which make the reform process continue under credible commitments of the government.

The focus of this chapter is the effect of the policy reforms on the direction of structural change and its implication on the evolution of markets and institutions. Policy reforms induce structural change by releasing resources, and by changing relative prices. The changes in transaction costs and relative prices result in differential growth of different industries and their share in the national income, and consequently their contribution to income distribution. Differences in the relative growth of different sectors and income groups alter the composition of different interest groups in their stake in, and in their ability to further or block, the reforms, which, in turn, determine the direction of institutional change.

## The underlying mechanics of structural change

As discussed in Chapter 2, the policy reforms are treated as parameter and qualitative shifts in partial elements of the institutional environment. The parameter and qualitative shifts have implications on structural factors in two ways: the release and transfer of resources among government and private agents, and among different private agents; and their effect on changes in the relative prices of different sectors and industries. The initial endowments at the onset of the reforms determine the direction of evolution of markets and institutions.

Qualitative changes in the policy framework, such as the removal of industrial licenses, release resources, for example transaction costs and investments incurred for acquiring licenses. Parameter shifts, such as reduction in taxes, cause transfer of resources from the government to the private agents and also distributional transfer in terms of a fall in government investment or spending on certain sectors or groups. Whether reduction in taxes results in the release of resources in terms of a fall in transaction costs depends on several conditions. Suppose a reduction in income tax results in increased compliance; it then results in a fall in the cost of 'bribes', which means a transfer from government agents to private agents under the changed rules of the game. The net gain could be the extent of decline in dead-weight losses in the revenue transfers of taxes and bribes. A decline in transaction costs requires simplification of the rules and paperwork. If the government agents do not simplify the rules in order to safeguard their predatory powers, and impose other conditions along with the reduction in taxes, it may result in higher transaction costs than before.[2] This implies no net gain, or even net losses.

The benefit for economic efficiency depends on the net release of resources from unproductive to productive activities. Hirschman (1958, 5) observed that the critical factor in economic development "was calling forth and enlisting for development purposes resources and abilities that are hidden, scattered, or badly utilized". A simple example is the removal of industrial licenses. This move helped managers of large corporations to close down their lobby offices, cut down on frequent travels to the capital of India, New Delhi, and thereby channel their abilities and resources to productive tasks. A reduction in oppressively high rates of income tax releases black money for productive investments.

A set of policy reforms can be taken as a one-shot change in the rules of the game. The consequent short- and medium-term outcomes of the reforms on the structural factors determine whether the rules of the game will be retracted or change for the better. The structural changes result in gainers and losers in the short and medium term. If there are more gainers than losers, or gainers are powerfully organized, the reforms will progress, and vice versa, similar to the (endogenous) formation of preferences in the analysis of Dixit, as discussed in Chapter 1. Furthermore, the course of the reform process depends on how soon the positive outcomes of the reforms will be realized, which, in turn, depends on the initial conditions at the onset of the reforms. The outcome of the reforms also depends on the credibility of the government. Agents react differently if they believe that the reform is only political window-dressing and most of it will be retracted in the face of opposition. This behavior has a significant effect on the success of the reforms and the time it takes for the reform process.

The credibility of government, especially when governments change through the electoral process, survives if the well-organized groups develop entrenched interests in the continuation of the reform, and, second, when the government agents' interests are entrenched with the changing structural conditions. To give an example, in 2004 the Congress party in coalition with the leftist parties formed the government in the center. When the new government announced further reforms, such as private agents' participation in infrastructure and abiding by the WTO agreement on product patents, the left attempted to negate them. However, as the government remained committed to the process, the left started to soften its stand.

One can simplify the outcome of changes in relative prices in terms of a closed economy opening up to international trade. As a result, product prices are equalized to international prices, which, in turn, changes the prices paid to factors of production, labor, and capital. The theory of comparative advantage shows that opening up to international trade results in contraction of protected industries and expansion of industries with comparative advantage. At the aggregate level, this results in one-shot allocative efficiency gains on the lines of international prices. However, subsequent growth depends on two conditions: first, the initial conditions at the time of reforms, and second, the micro level technological and organizational dynamics in response to reforms. As an illustration of the importance of initial conditions, international trade for a developing economy could lead to specialization in those sectors with limited learning economies on the basis of static comparative advantage, which will result in the economy being stuck at low-level growth. Lucas (1988) shows how a natural (comparative) advantage in specializing can backfire in the long run. He shows a world in which an initial comparative advantage in farming can cause a region to become a food producer. Growth potential may, however, lie not in farming but in industrial goods, goods that people living in regions that do not have good farmland will turn to.

People in these countries will eventually become expert manufacturers, whereas farmers will in the long run lag far behind, because they are specialized in a product with no growth potential.

Following this line of reasoning, the initial endowments in terms of skills and industrial base determine subsequent growth. As discussed in the previous chapter, the previous policies of import substitution generated a large industrial base and skill endowments. If opening up to international trade makes the country realize comparative advantage in its endowment of skilled labor and high-tech industries with potential for learning economies, it results in growth. If these sectors become major wealth generators and a source of employment for a significant portion of people in the country, it could lead to further positive changes in the institutional environment. As mentioned before, educated and skilled people are better at dealing with informational imperfection and organizing themselves effectively, which could bring out institutional changes that suit the interests of the agents engaged in the industries. For example, if protection of intellectual property rights is important for these industries, the industry lobby can bargain with the government to improve them. However, the ability of the industry to succeed in its bargaining with the government depends on how strategically important the industry is for the economy and whether it has resources. An example of this is India's software industry, and a counter-example is the country's movie industry, which despite being the second-largest in the world, has so far failed to reduce pirating of movies.

Similarly, qualitative shifts in policies in terms of the removal of licenses result in one-shot gains in reduction in transaction costs of dealing with government. The subsequent growth depends on to what extent resources are released for productive investments and how the qualitative shifts change the rules of the game among different economic agents – increase in competition, and entry of new players. An increase in competition drives firms to invest in technology and organizational efficiency and results in a decline in the prices of individual sectors, which reduces monopoly rents and augments the real incomes of consumers and the expansion and emergence of new markets. Sum of the effects of individual reform measures may not necessarily describe a reform's total effect. This is because a sequence of favorable announcements by a committed-looking government may dramatically change expectations and free up the imagination of economic agents. Projects, ideas, and investments that were nowhere in sight, or considered wild and impossible, now appear within reach and feasible.

## Policy reforms, government, and transaction costs

One of the propositions is that policy reforms, by reducing transaction costs, release resources, which augments investments by economic agents both in durable and non-durable assets. Let us view how transaction costs in dealing with government have declined in response to the reforms. Forbes (2002, 138) observes the effect of the reforms on the transaction costs of dealing with government:

> Previously, any technology license, foreign investment, or major expansion of capacity required a visit to Delhi and often months of form-filling and pushing, often with bribes to grease the way. In 1991, the need was largely eliminated at a stroke; the importance of this change is difficult to appreciate for those who have not experienced it in the old system.
>
> The reforms that took place at a stroke, though, were largely confined to the finance, commerce and industry Ministries. What did not change was the local Inspector Raj (regime), where several government inspectors could drop in on firms at will, each with absolute power to make firms cease operations first and challenge the order later.

Table 3 is reproduced from Forbes (2002) to illustrate the changes in transaction costs of the Inspector Raj through the reforms.

Forbes observes that the transaction costs in dealing with inspectors and undertaking export and import activities still remain high because processes continue to be complex – 'What is missing is the nitty-gritty of reform, the commitment to drive detailed change through at the local level.' As mentioned in the previous chapter, about 16 percent of a manager's time is still spent in dealing with government bureaucracy. In the same way, high transaction costs in international trade reduce the comparative advantage in trade in relation to other countries that have similar comparative advantage in relative factor endowments but have lower transaction costs.

As stated earlier, decline in transaction costs both in the product and financial markets should release resources and increase investments. Table 4 shows that there has been a substantial increase in private investment in the 1990s as compared to the 1980s, peaking to 13.01 percent for the period of 1992–3 to 1996–7 and declining to 6.71 percent for 1997–8 to 2000–1. Rakshit (2004) attributes this not only to product market liberalizations, but also to financial market reforms and the decline in real interest rates.

The historical pattern of development of developed economies shows that at the higher level of development, a major part of the workforce is employed in the service economy, and a considerable part is in the transaction cost sectors of intermediation – banking, financial intermediaries, and stock markets, etc. Thus, close to 80 percent of the workforce in the US is employed in the service economy. The interesting aspect of the story is that a high share of the transaction cost (service) sector at the aggregate

*Table 3* Transaction costs of the Inspector Raj in May 2000

| Inspector | Powers | Change since 1991 |
|---|---|---|
| Factory | Can halt work at a particular work area where there is a fault and issue penalties | License fee, formerly paid every year, can now be paid in a five-year lump sum |
| Electrical | Can issue a notice and levy penalties | None |
| ESIS | Can levy penalties | None |
| Octroi | In case of default, can collect the difference in amount | None |
| Food | Can close down canteen | None |
| Income tax | Can levy penalties | None |
| Sales tax | Can levy penalties | None |
| Excise | Can stop dispatch of material | Excise records are simplified. Verification/inspection of documents, formerly semi-annual, is now annual |
| Municipal corporation | Can serve notice and demolish unauthorized construction | None |
| Lift | Can stop the operation of the lift | None |
| Customs | Does not clear goods, can impose penalties (pay first and argue later) | Discretionary powers greatly reduced by reducing the number of different classifications and different tax rates. Clearances still take a minimum of two days |

Source: Forbes (2002).

Note
These are the inspector/inspections to which a medium-scale firm (Forbes Marshall, Pune) was subject in 1991 and the changes effected by 2000. The transaction costs would be higher for small firms with imperfect knowledge about the changes in the rules, which allows inspectors to extract 'bribes' at their discretion.

level could be a reflection of both a high and a low level of development. If government bureaucracy has a major share in the service economy, for controls and excess regulation, it is a reflection of low growth. On the other hand, if the major part of the service sector consists of productive services such as banking, financial intermediaries, telecommunications, and software services, etc., it reflects high levels of development in an economy.

Furthermore, economic efficiency requires that a high share of transaction costs at the aggregate level should result in a decline in average transactions to individual agents (economies of scale). This explains why airline and telephone prices in the US are lower than in India. Firms are able to spread fixed costs over a large number of consumers with

Table 4 Performance of the Indian economy, 1970–2001

| | | 1970–1 to 1979–80 | 1980–1 to 1989–90 | 1990–1 to 2000–1 | 1992–3 to 2000–1 | 1992–3 to 1996–7 | 1997–8 to 2000–1 |
|---|---|---|---|---|---|---|---|
| GDP | Growth rate | 2.95 (141.9) | 5.81 (38.9) | 5.61 (32.7) | 6.1 (20.9) | 6.68 (16.9) | 5.35 (21.6) |
| Per capita GDP | Growth rate | 0.73 | 3.67 | 3.68 | 4.17 | 4.75 | 3.42 |
| Investment[2,3] | Growth rate | 4.65 (238.4) | 6.38 (88.2) | 6.93 (136.3) | 8.31 (91.08) | 9.63 (90.89) | 6.68 (99.8) |
| Fixed capital formation | Growth rate | 3.62 (181.2) | 6.72 (33.8) | 6.68 (85.9) | 7.39 (75.7) | 8.47 (84.62) | 6.03 (53.32) |
| Public investment | Growth rate | N/A | 6.89 (151.3) | 3.14 (238.39) | 4.12 (180.7) | 2.28 (343.53) | 6.43 (113.75) |
| Private investment | Growth rate | N/A | 7.60 (251.2) | 8.75 (136.32) | 10.21 (92.2) | 13.01 (81.03) | 6.71 (114.12) |
| Public consumption | Growth rate | 4.42 (120.1) | 6.92 (37.2) | 6.23 (71.38) | 7.31 (55.5) | 4.66 (57.44) | 10.61 (26.8) |
| Investment as % of GDP | | 18.27 | 22.04 | 22.87 | 22.85 | 223.34 | 22.22 |
| Savings as % of GDP | | 18.38 | 19.51 | 23.20 | 23.15 | 23.50 | 22.80 |
| ICOR | | 5.98 | 3.65 | 4.35 | 4.00 | 3.72 | 4.47 |
| WPI inflation | | 9.4 (100.6) | 7.97 (48.8) | 8.04 (42.1) | 7.16 (54.6) | 8.74 (42.9) | 5.18 (70.5) |
| Services | Share in GDP | 34.40 | 38.60 | 44.30 | 44.92 | 43.04 | 47.28 |
| | Growth rate | 4.5 (36.2) | 6.6 (29.9) | 7.6 (24.9) | 8.1 (19.6) | 7.55 (24.4) | 8.82 (11.4) |
| | Contribution to GDP growth | 52.70 | 43.60 | 57.60 | 59.65 | 48.66 | 77.94 |
| Industry | Share in GDP | 22.80 | 25.00 | 27.10 | 27.12 | 27.11 | 27.13 |
| | Growth rate | 3.7 (95.8) | 6.8 (31.3) | 5.9 (56.7) | 6.39 (44.3) | 7.61 (42.6) | 4.86 (26.7) |
| | Contribution to GDP growth | 28.70 | 28.90 | 27.60 | 28.42 | 30.91 | 24.67 |
| Agriculture | Share in GDP | 42.80 | 36.40 | 31.15 | 30.40 | 32.42 | 27.88 |
| | Growth rate | 1.3 (587.7) | 4.67 (125.6) | 2.87 (131.2) | 3.12 (125.1) | 4.64 (80.8) | 1.23 (297.8) |
| | Contribution to GDP growth | 18.60 | 27.50 | 14.80 | 15.55 | 22.54 | 6.38 |

Sources: Reserve Bank of India (2001, 2002); Government of India (2002); Rakshit (2004).

Notes
1 Figures in parentheses indicate coefficient of variation (%).
2 Growth rates of investment may not lie between private and public investment growth rates for some of the periods because they are simple averages of individual annual growth rates.
3 Investment growth rate for the period 1980–1 to 1989–90 is the average from 1981–2 to 1989–90, since data for public investment for 1980–1 are not available.

purchasing power. Average costs go down as more agents participate in the markets. This is similar to an insurance market, which becomes efficient if/when it is able to spread risk to larger number of agents. Similarly, transaction and information costs for an individual agent to participate in the equity markets would be high, since it involves the collection and processing of information about a large number of companies. By pooling a large group of investors, a financial intermediary or a mutual fund realizes economies of scale in its investments in the collection and processing of information, thereby causing a fall in average transaction costs to individual agents. Table 4 shows that India's service or transaction cost economy increased its share in GDP from 38.6 percent in 1980–1 to 1989–90, to 47.28 percent in 1997–8 to 2000–1. The question that follows is whether average transaction costs are going down and, if so, in which spheres.

The government institutional reforms reduce transaction costs in some spheres and increase transaction costs in other spheres. Reforms towards a market economy should lead government to eliminate controls on economic activity and undertake an effective role in regulation and the provision of public goods. The conceptual distinction between controls and regulation is that industrial licenses and restrictions on capacities and entry and exit of firms can be termed as controls on the natural play of economic forces. Regulation is ensuring that markets are competitive, by making sure that firms do not charge monopoly prices through collusion, imposing entry barriers, restraining generation of negative externalities such as pollution, and seeing to it that firms maintain labor standards, etc. In such a case, the transaction costs of controls go down, but new transaction costs of regulation come into existence. If government undertakes the effective provision of public goods, such as the universal provision of primary and secondary education and social security, this should contribute to a fall in transaction costs to the previously illiterate and poor populace.

Table 4 shows growth rates in two components of government expenditures – public investment and public consumption. Public investments in infrastructure such as roads, railroads, education, and telecommunications contribute to a fall in average transaction costs. On the other hand, an increase in certain components of public consumption expenditure, which includes expenditure on public bureaucracy, may increase transaction costs. Table 4 shows that the growth rate in public consumption expenditure is a lot higher than in public investments. The RBI data shows that the gross capital formation (at constant prices of 1993–4) of the public sector was at Rs 806,800 million in 1994–5 and it remained more or less the same in 2002–3 at Rs 808,230 million, while it increased for the private sector from Rs 651,470 million to Rs 863,670 million for the same periods. In the same periods, organized employment in the public sector was 19.45 million and 18.77 million, and for the private sector 7.85 million and 8.43 million. In other words, the government's share in the capital formation and also organized employment has been going down, while it is increasing significantly for the private sector. One possible reason could be that the government has been disengaging from its loss-making investment activities.

If growth in infrastructure and provision of public goods does not match the aggregate economic growth rate, it increases transaction costs, stunting growth. Several infrastructure areas, such as airports, power generation, etc., are dominated by the public sector. Private sector investment in these areas is subject to complex rules and regulations and political interference, which constrain such investment. For example, India has been facing a severe shortage of power supply. In the period from 2000 to January 2003, the shortages in normal and peak demand have been around 8 percent and 12 percent respectively. Because of the shortage of supply and numerous transaction costs, Indian industry is required to pay a significantly higher cost for power than countries like China, dampening productivity gains. One of the institutional responses of the private sector is that a number of power-intensive industries, such as cement, textiles, fertilizers, and software firms, have set up captive power projects, mainly as a back-up source of power to protect themselves against unreliable grid power and to avoid paying a high price for power. This means additional production and transaction costs to the private sector. The current captive power capacity in the country is more than 14,000 MW. Even though the installed generation capacity has increased from 301 billion kWh in 1992–3 to 515 billion kWh in 2001–2, it should be noted that India's annual per capita electricity consumption was 359 kWh from 1996–2000. This is much lower than the consumption in other Asian developing economies, such as China (717 kWh). However, in certain areas, such as telecommunications, in which privatization has been implemented and an appropriate regulatory framework has been put in place, there has been rapid growth – direct telephone connections increased at an annual growth rate of about 30 percent from 1998–9 to 2003–4. In the year 2004, total mobile connections correspond to about 33.7 million lines and is growing at a rapid pace.

The growth of the service sector, such as expansion of banks, employment agencies, and consumer distribution agencies, results in a decline in average transaction costs. Technological change in the service industry can be a major source of reduction in average transaction costs. For example, technological change in the telecommunications industry significantly reduced communication costs both nationally and internationally, further inducing organizational and technological change in other sectors.[3]

Apart from this, technological change in service industries, such as the adoption of information technology, result in a reduction in transaction costs. A few public sector service areas have adopted information technology, demonstrating this decline in transaction costs. To give an example, making a rail reservation in the 1980s involved high transaction costs of standing in long queues at the railway stations. In the early 1990s, the Indian railways adopted extensive information technology, which reduced the transaction costs of rail reservations significantly. Today, one can make online reservations using credit card payment, with tickets delivered at home. Similarly, the public sector banks, despite resistance from workers, adopted IT-enabled banking services, thereby reducing transaction costs. Some of the state governments, such as that of Andhra Pradesh, adopted information technology in governance in the 1990s, which significantly reduced transaction costs in the provision of certain public goods.

## Transaction costs of business organization

It is rather difficult to quantify the extent of reductions in transaction costs and their contribution to investments. The above discussion considers the decline in transaction costs in dealing with government agencies. The next issue is how transaction costs change in market exchange – business to business, and business to consumer, such as information and search costs, contractual costs, and distributional costs. As mentioned before, there is a two-way relation between transaction costs and market expansion. A one-shot reduction in certain transaction costs expands markets, and market expansion reduces average transaction costs further. To illustrate this, information expansion through advertising or distribution expands markets, and expansion of markets further reduces the entry costs of new players, which further expands markets. This process is discussed in detail in Chapter 7. Here, I broadly deal with business transaction cost behavior in the post-reform era, while micro level issues are discussed in detail in the following chapters.

One of the ways of throwing some light on the decline in transaction costs for private firms is to examine the inventory levels of firms over time in the post-reform period (Bussolo and Whalley, 2002). Inventory levels can decline because market transaction costs of information and search decline, and also because firms adopt efficient organizational practices of just in time, and vertical integration (dis-integration). I empirically test for this by a simple econometric estimation, followed by a discussion of the qualitative data of the industries. The technical details are provided in Appendix 1. I briefly summarize the implications of the results in the following.

The results show that the time path of changes in inventories to sales in the post-reform era demonstrates an inverted 'U' shape. The implication is that inventories at the beginning of the reforms increased, but as reforms deepened, inventories started to decline. This suggests that as the reforms deepen the transaction costs of business have been declining.

One of the explanations is that at the beginning of the reforms, firms expanded capacities rapidly, which might have resulted in capacities exceeding demand. But as the reforms and markets deepened, they were able to reduce inventories owing to organizational changes and a general decline in business transaction costs. The results also indicate that higher export orientation and expenditure on technology result in lower inventories to sales.

A study of Indian automobile parts manufacturers found that firms in less-developed regions maintained higher inventories as most inputs could not be sourced locally (Gulyani, 2001). However, in the 1990s several Japanese and South Korean TNCs in the automobile and electronics industries adopted quality controls and just-in-time practices, which led to diffusion of these practices to local firms (Sutton, 2004; Okada, 2004). These aspects of micro-level governance changes are discussed in the next chapter. Structural changes in the business organization and economy-level factors that reduce transaction costs and informational imperfections result in a decline in the inventory/sales ratio by a combination of factors, such as: a fall in the time taken to communicate and transport; a fall in the costs of transport and communication; a decline in uncertainty, i.e. a smaller variance of demand because of the growth of markets; and competition forcing better inventory management. The average of the seventy-eight industries for annual average growth for the fifteen-year period of 1989 to 2003 show that the inventory of raw materials to sales declined by 1.7 percent while the inventory of finished and semi finished goods to sales increased by 1.8 percent.[4]

## Transaction costs, capital and labor markets

The following example illustrates how government investment in infrastructure and the right kind of regulatory bodies can result in the expansion of the markets. As mentioned in the previous chapter, the government of India in response to the stock market scandal of 1992, set up two institutions in the capital market – the NSE and the regulatory body, the SEBI.

Until 1993, the Bombay Stock Exchange was the dominant player in the equity market. It was an institutional arrangement consisting of mutual ownership by a few stockbrokers within a small-group social network of a specific ethnic community of western India. The small-group interaction facilitated mutual monitoring by the group in honoring daily transactions, within themselves. The market was more or less monopolized by the stockbrokers – any outsider investment in the equity market had to go through the brokers, exercising significant powers. As a result, the market remained less liquid. It also suited the interests of the large corporate houses, who had access to debt finance from the public financial institutions. However, the liquidity of equity markets started to increase with the entry of a major player – Reliance Industries, belonging to the Ambani family, in the mid-1980s. Mr Ambani, starting as a small textile merchant, developed Reliance Industries into a large industrial house by innovative manipulation of the prevailing institutional regime. Reliance Industries was the first major corporate house that adopted the strategy of raising a major part of its capital for expansion from the equity markets. This resulted in more shares available in the market and a significant increase in the participation of middle-class investors.

The fall of the Bombay Stock Exchange was precipitated by the entry of a large stockbroker, Harshad Mehta, who created the stock market bubble and the crash of 1992 by using large sums of money secured from banks in dubious deals. The interesting aspect of the story is that the entry of the large player also damaged the social network and mutual monitoring of the Bombay stockbrokers. In other words, the entry of a large player broke the collusive behavior of the brokers.

The stock market crash of 1992 destroyed large sums of small investors' savings, which prompted the government of India to bring about institutional change by setting up the National Stock Exchange and the regulatory body, the SEBI. This institutional reform had a significant effect on equity market evolution in India. The NSE adopted screen-based trading across the country. The autonomy of the institutions led to the adoption of the incentive-compatible practices of its employees, which, in turn, caused human capital accumulation in managing the market across the country (Shah, 1998). The SEBI, on its part, contributed to improvements in the corporate governance and disclosure practices of the registered corporations.

The effective functioning and countrywide expansion of the NSE, with adoption of information technology (electronic trading), and risk management at the clearing, reduced the monopoly power of the stockbrokers of the Bombay Stock Exchange and brought down transaction costs to individual and institutional investors in a significant way. The transition from physical share certificates to depository settlement resulted in the loss of thousands of jobs (middlemen). About a hundred large brokerage firms went bankrupt (Shaw and Thomas, 2002). On the other hand, the regulatory body, the SEBI, imposes a code of conduct of corporate practices. Similarly, in the 1990s, there has been an increasing presence of financial intermediaries such as mutual funds, investment banks, and foreign institutional investors (FIIs). One general impression is that an increase in the number of middlemen increases transaction costs. However, in the case of financial intermediaries, as mentioned before, economies of scale in information collection reduces average transaction costs to individual investors. Regulation improved information and the transparency of corporations; the credit information of financial intermediaries and banks has thereby contributed to the expansion of financial markets.

Since 1993, the Indian capital markets have been opened to FIIs and

*Table 5* Comparative profile of financial intermediaries and markets in India

|  | *1990–1* | *1998–9* | *2002–3* |
|---|---|---|---|
| Gross domestic savings | 1,301 (24.3) | 3,932 (22.3) | 5,500 (24.0) |
| Bank deposits outstanding | 2,078 (38.2) | 7,140 (40.5) | 13,043 (50.1) |
| Small savings deposits, PPFs, outstanding | 1,071 (20.0) | 3,333 (19.1) | 3,810 (15.4) |
| Mutual funds (assets under management) | 253 (4.7) | 858 (4.9) | 1,093 (4.2) |
| Total borrowings by DFI (outstanding) | – | 2,108 (12.0) | 901 (3.5) |
| Annual stock market turnover | 360 (5.6) | 15,241 (79.0) | 9,321 (35.8) |
| Stock market capitalization | 845 (15.8) | 18, 732 (97.1) | 11,093 (35.8) |

Source: Bhattacharya and Patel (2003).

Note
Monetary amounts are in Rs billion; figures in parentheses are the percentage of GDP.

they have started to play an important role in India's equity markets. In the year 2002, FIIs accounted for less than 10 percent of total market capitalization, but for a disproportionately higher share of daily trading. Their buying preferences led to the imposition of a penalty on stock valuations of those firms that had group cross-holding, inadequate disclosure or were closely held. The increasing role of FIIs has contributed to an increase in liquidity and also improvements in disclosure and corporate governance practices of firms in India (Patibandla, 2005a). Apart from this, the importance of the public financial institutions declined in the post-reforms period, as they had been saddled with non-performing assets. Some of these institutions, such as ICICI, have reformed themselves into the merchant bankers and venture capitalists since the mid-1990s. Table 5 presents the profile of the expanding financial intermediaries and markets in India in the 1990s.

## Transaction costs of labor markets

In the labor market, the government policy reforms of relaxing the rules regarding replacement of workers by increasing the upper limit of a large-scale organized-sector firm from 100 to 1,000 employees have reduced transaction costs for firms. Another institutional outcome in the labor markets is the emergence of contract suppliers and employment agencies, especially in the 1990s. Contract labor suppliers recruit unskilled and semi-skilled workers in different parts of the country and supply workers to different organizations all over the country on a temporary and casual basis. As a consequence, several firms employ a few permanent employees and temporary employees for certain services. Additionally, as labor markets deepen, with an increasing need for specialized services and skills (division of labor), there has been a growing presence of employment agencies and human resource consultants offering services to both job seekers and employers. In fact, a search of the Web shows that there were close to 1,000 employment agencies in 2004, serving both job seekers and employers in different fields. The point is that the increasing presence of middleman services at the aggregate level increases the service component of GDP, but reduces average transaction costs to individual agents. It is, however, important to note that the bargaining power of contract labor companies with respect to semi-skilled labor remains high because there is no formal institutional mechanism of certification of semi-skilled labor such as carpenters, plumbers, etc. If the institutional arrangements of contract labor suppliers were to become a dominant practice, it is possible that they could block the emergence of institutions that could provide certification services to semi-skilled labor.

Nagaraj (2004) shows that between 1995–6 and 2000–1, about 1.1 million workers in the organized sector lost their jobs. On the other hand, employment and wage levels of supervisors increased significantly. One of the conjectures he makes is that some of the jobs shed are likely to have reappeared in the unorganized sector with growing subcontracting of production and shedding of auxiliary services, such as transport, security, cleaning, and provision of food at the work place. In other words, the post-reforms period of increased competitive conditions drove large firms to find ways of overcoming the rigidities of the labor policies. One of the ways is by the emergence of specialized contractors supplying workers on temporary basis. Table 6, reproduced from Nagaraj (2004), shows a significant increase in labor productivity in the post-reforms period and a significant decline in wage/capital cost. The increase in labor productivity can be attributed to an increased adoption of capital, micro level technological and organizational change, and a fall in the transaction costs of the labor markets. An increase in productivity means a fall in the labor costs of output. Similarly, labor costs of output can go down owing to organizational changes of the labor market in terms of a reduction in the number of permanent employees and an increase in temporary and unorganized labor. Some of these aspects are discussed in detail in the following chapters.

## Changes in transaction costs and relative prices

The differential growth of industries depends on changes in relative prices and decline in transaction costs. The transaction costs effect of the reforms on the differential growth of sectors depends on which sectors were subjected to controls the most in the previous regime, and how fast or efficiently different industries altered their business organization to changed rules of the game, which, in turn, may depend on the initial conditions at the onset of the reforms. This aspect of changes in transaction

*Table 6* Performance of organized manufacturing sector: some selected indicators, 1980–1 to 2000–1

|  | 1980–1 | 1990–1 | 2000–1 | Percentage change 1981–91 | 1991–2001 |
|---|---|---|---|---|---|
| No of workers (million) | 5.5 | 5.7 | 5.7 | 3.6 | – |
| Real wages/workers (index) | 100 | 118.2 | 134.0 | 18.2 | 13.1 |
| Wage-rental ratio (index) | 100 | 80.6 | 60.6 | −19.4 | −24.8 |
| Product wage/workers (index) | 100 | 165.4 | 210.0 | 65.4 | 27.2 |
| Labor productivity (index) | 100 | 219.1 | 395.7 | 119.1 | 80.6 |
| Capital stock per workers (index) | 100 | 183.3 | 423.8 | 83.3 | 131.2 |
| Memo: per capita net national product | 145.2 | 198.5 | 278.1 | 36.7 | 40.1 |

Source: Nagaraj (2004).

Notes
All relevant variables are at constant prices. Capital stock refers to net fixed capital stock at 1993–4 prices for total manufacturing. Product wage per worker divided by the deflator for machinery and equipment (proxy for cost of capital) is the wage-rental ratio. In principle, it is perhaps a more appropriate measure of the relative cost of labor than the widely used product wage per worker.

costs has been discussed earlier. In the following paragraphs, I briefly discuss the extent of internationalization of the Indian economy to address the argument regarding changes in the relative prices.

### Internationalization of Indian industries

One of the structural outcomes of the Indian economy in the post-reform period is the internationalization of industries. Internationalization of the economy is a many-dimensional process having great consequences – increase in international trade, the presence of multinational firms, technology flows, international mobility (both short- and long-term) of labor, and outward investment by local firms. Internationalization can be viewed as a process of declining transaction costs of securing internationally traded intermediate and capital goods and technology, realization of the external economies of a reduction in the idea gap through the movement of managers and workers, increase in competition, and market expansion through multinational investment. These elements have important implications for production and transaction costs, market expansion, and micro-level governance.

As shown in Table 7, the share of imports in GDP increased from 7.7 percent in 1991–2 to 11.6 percent in 1999–2000, and for this period the share of exports in GDP increased from 7.1 percent to 9.3 percent. Exports grew more rapidly than imports, although they slowed from 1996 onwards. Garments and textiles and jewelry continued to account for

*Table 7* Foreign direct investment and trade in India

| | 1991–2 | 1992–3 | 1993–4 | 1994–5 | 1995–6 | 1996–7 | 1997–8 | 1998–9 | 1999–2000 |
|---|---|---|---|---|---|---|---|---|---|
| Total foreign investment flows | 133 | 559 | 4,153 | 5,138 | 4,881 | 6,008 | 4,798 | 2,401 | 5,181 |
| FDI | 129 | 315 | 586 | 1,314 | 2,133 | 2,696 | 3,197 | 2,462 | 2,155 |
| Foreign institutional investors | 4 | 4 | 2,047 | 1,742 | 2,065 | 1,946 | 956 | −390 | 2,135 |
| Imports | 19,411 | 21,882 | 23,306 | 28,251 | 37,279 | 39,132 | 41,449 | 47,544 | 55,383 |
| | (7.7)* | (8.9) | (9.0) | (9.2) | (10.8) | (10.8) | (11) | (11.1) | (11.6) |
| Exports | 17,868 | 18,501 | 22,237 | 26,233 | 31,831 | 33,470 | 34,976 | 34,298 | 44,145 |
| | (7.1)** | (8.1) | (8.6) | (8.5) | (9.5) | (9.3) | (9.1) | (8.9) | (9.3) |

Source: Reserve Bank of India.

Notes

* Percentage share of imports in GDP at current prices. ** Percentage share of exports in GDP.
Figures are in US$ million.

about half of total exports with software emerging as one of the leading export sectors. On the basis of the industry data of seventy-eight industries from the CMIE as illustrated before, export-intensive industries include both the traditional industries such as textiles, dyes, and pigments, and also high-tech industries such as computer software and drugs and pharmaceuticals. The new, emerging software industry accounted for 12 percent of total exports in 1999–2000. As mentioned before, exports of software and business process outsourcing (BPO) have been growing at a rapid pace through the 1990s and 2000s owing to its comparative advantage in low-cost, English-speaking skilled labor. Apart from this, there are newly emerging, internationally competitive manufacturing industries such as auto components, drawing from the endowment of engineering capabilities and skilled labor which will be discussed in detail in the following chapter.

Annual foreign investment flows, which were about $133 million in 1991–2, increased to $5.1 billion in 1999–2000. Foreign investment, which accounted for 0.1 percent of GDP in 1991, increased to 2.8 percent by 1999, although this compares poorly with China's 12.7 percent and Malaysia's 16.5 percent (Forbes, 2002). In 2000, infrastructure industries such as telecommunications and power generation received 44 percent, manufacturing and mining 28 percent, services 10 percent, and agriculture 5 percent of foreign investment. The manufacturing, mining and metallurgical industries, transportation, electrical equipment and chemicals and telecommunications accounted for a major share of FDI inflows. The nature of investment shifted from an arm's length to an equity form of investment during the period of 1990 to 1997. Furthermore, from the data concerning seventy-eight industries, the average growth rate for the period of 1989 to 2003 in royalties and technical fees payments to sales for all industries was 74 percent, which indicates that there was a significant increase in overseas technology purchases by Indian industries.

In the case of TNCs, there have been gradual improvements in the property rights as a result of the reduction of restrictions on joint ventures and allowing fully owned ventures in several fields. Arm's length licensing comprised 70 percent of collaboration approvals in 1991 and it fell to 30 percent by 1997. This is mainly because of the raising of the upper cap to 51 percent for automatic approval for industry groups such as food processing and textile industries, and up to 74 percent for some others, such as mining services, basic metals, and alloy industries. As mentioned before, in recent years telecommunications, the automobile industry, metallurgical industries, fuels, fertilizers, chemicals, and pharmaceuticals have become major sectors of FDI investment. Nevertheless, non-equity ventures, such as joint ventures, management contracts, marketing agreements, franchising, turnkey operations, international subcontracting, service contracts, production-sharing agreements, compensation arrangements, technical assistance/consultancy agreements and holding companies still play an important part in multinational operations in India. A significant amount of FDI is flowing into the service sector in areas such as call centers, insurance and medical transcript processing, and financial services. A major part of FDI in India has been in the infrastructure sector, such as in telecommunications, transportation, power and fuels, and service sectors such as software, rather than manufacturing. The telecommunications sector, which was a public sector monopoly in the early 1990s, is now a fast-growing industry, with both TNCs and local firms playing an active role.

The presence of a well-developed private sector facilitates FDI through mergers and acquisitions. Between 1997 and 1999, about 40 percent of FDI in India came through mergers and acquisitions. In 1999–2000, M&A deals were worth Rs 369,630 million. Within the M&A segment, acquisitions or takeovers dominate in India as they do in most developed countries. Mergers account for about one-quarter of M&A deals in the country. The sectors that attracted FDI through this route were banking and financial services, advertising and other business services, and travel agencies. Other sectors witnessing a sharp increase in FDI included chemicals, textiles, the electrical and electronic industries, hotels, and pharmaceuticals. Business restructuring through takeovers, acquisitions, mergers and sale of assets has been most pronounced in the financial sector in 1999–2000 (Rosario, 1999; Patibandla, 2005b). The policy reforms improved the property rights of TNCs by gradually allowing them to set up fully owned subsidiaries in several sectors. Another important dimension of internationalization is that of Indian corporations investing abroad, both through acquisitions and green-field ventures which increased significantly in the post-reform era. Thus, Indian corporations acquired about seventy-five international companies in 2003 alone, and there were also several green-field investments. Most of these investments have been in the internationalized industries, such as software and services, pharmaceuticals, paints, polyester yarn, tube manufacturing, and auto component industry.

### Relative growth of different industries

Table 4 shows that the service sector increased its share of GDP from 38.6 percent in 1980–1 to 1989–90, to 47.28 percent in 1997–8 to 2000–1, growing at a high annual average rate of about 7.8 percent. The corresponding figures for the industrial sector are 25.0 percent and 27.13 percent, with an annual average growth rate of about 6.2 percent. For agriculture, the corresponding figures are 36.4 percent and 27.88 percent, with an annual growth rate of about 3 percent. On the employment front, based on the National Sample Survey, the share of the service sector was 21.2 percent in 1993–4, which increased to 22.5 percent, and the corresponding figures for manufacturing were 14.2 percent and 15.8 percent.

For agriculture, the figures were, 64.6 percent and 61.6 percent. Comparing the growth rates in the shares in GDP and employment, this indicates that a major part of the per capita growth benefits went to the service sector, while the agriculture sector derived the least benefit.[5] However, changes in the terms of trade should have benefited the agriculture sector in the 1990s, compared to the previous era. Throughout the import substitution period, the terms of trade were kept in favor of the industrial sector; especially the large-scale capital-intensive sector and the urban sector, as against the agriculture and rural sector. The large industrial sector was protected from imports, so manufactured goods prices were much above the international level, while agricultural prices were kept below international prices. The liberalization of the 1990s reduced the protection of organized industry, which led to a decline in the prices of manufactured goods. These changes should have improved the terms of trade to agriculture. The fall in prices should actually increase real incomes and reduce poverty levels (of course, depending on the basket of consumption of the poor).

Which spheres of the service sector grew faster and why? Gordon and Gupta (2003) show that "almost all service subsectors in India have grown faster than GDP over time, but the pick-up in growth in the 1990s was strongest in business services, communication, and financial services, followed by community services, hotels, and restaurants." As discussed in the previous chapter, the earlier policies of high subsidies to higher education, growth of bureaucracy, and expansion of the public sector banks led to the service sector taking a major share of GDP. The policies generated a large pool of technical manpower which became a basis of comparative advantage for service sectors such as the software and BPO sectors to grow rapidly in the post-reform period through exports. Additionally, the technical manpower of the public sector firms became a source from which the private sector firms could poach high-skilled labor.[6] Table 8 shows interesting figures. The education, research, and scientific and health services component of the service economy grew at a high annual rate of 8.4 percent in the 1990s. The increasing expansion of the service sector provided job opportunities for skilled people, which, in turn, resulted in the emergence of private training institutions to cater to the rapid expansion of demand for skilled workers (Patibandla *et al.*, 2000; Patibandla and Petersen, 2002, 2004). The other high growth area is the communications sector, which grew at 13 percent. In the 1980s, public sector investments in telecommunications through firms such as C-DOT led to the expansion of telephone services across the country. In the latter part of the 1990s, the policy opened up the sector to both local private and foreign players. The rapid growth of communications should be attributed not only to the policy reforms but also to rapid technological changes in this sector. This resulted in a steep decline in average costs of telephone calls, and also made mobile phones affordable to low-income groups. The banking sector increased its growth marginally from the 1980s to the 1990s by about 0.8 percent, partly owing to the entry of foreign banks and the liberalization of the banking sector. The entertainment sector grew at about 7.1 percent in the 1990s, mostly because of the rapid expansion of cable TV. India today has one of the highest numbers of cable TV connections in the world, at fifty million connections in 2004. The monthly cost of a cable connection in India translates to about $1.50–4, which is affordable by low-income groups. Connections are increasing at a rapid pace, along with a steep decline in the average price of televisions. Cable TV has become one of the means of access to information and contributes to the increasing aspirations of the poor, as well as the middle class.

The growth in service sector components such as business services, distribution services, real estate, and hotels and restaurants should be traced to linkage effects with both industry and the service sector. The industrial sector on average achieved about 6–7 percent growth in the 1990s – this growth had to be supported by linkages with service sectors such as business services, distribution, real estate and catering. In other words, when an economy grows and matures, it results in a higher division of labor, which, in turn, leads to rapid growth of the service economy. However, in India's case, it is to be seen in fragmented terms, as a major part of the workforce – close to 61 percent – still remains engaged in agriculture, with low potential for the division of labor.

On the basis of annual average growth rate of value added (nominal) from 1989 to 2000, from the industry data set, the fast-growing industries consist of both capital goods industries, such as storage batteries, plastic tubes; and cement products, and consumer durable goods industries, such as two-wheelers, air-conditioners, refrigerators, bicycles, passenger cars, and consumer electronics. In other words, mostly lower- and upper-middle-class consumers demand these products. As these industries grow and prices decline, lower-middle-class real incomes will increase, further expanding markets. For example, refrigerators were a high-priced luxury item in the early 1980s. Today the lower-middle-class consumer can afford them. The interesting feature of this group of fast-growing industries is that the average annual growth rate in exports to sales, imports to sales, royalties of technology purchases to sales and net profits sales are higher than the total industry sample averages. In other words, the faster-growing industries are more internationalized than the others.[7]

## Industry case studies

As discussed before, some of the fastest-growing industries are the traditional industries, such as cotton and synthetic yarn, but also skill-intensive and modern industries, such as software, auto components, two-wheelers, and pharmaceutical industries. These industries are the most internationally oriented in terms of exports and the presence of TNCs, especially the

*Table 8* Growth rates and sectoral shares of the service industry

| Sector | Activities included | Avg. growth in 50s–70s (Share of GDP in 1980) | Avg. growth in 80s (Share of GDP in 1990) | Avg. growth in 90s (Share of GDP in 2000) |
|---|---|---|---|---|
| **Trade, hotels and restaurant** | | | | |
| Trade (distribution services) | Wholesale and retail trade in commodities both produced at home (including exports) and imported, purchase and selling agents, brokers and auctioneers | 4.8 (11.7) | 5.9 (11.9) | 7.3 (13.7) |
| Hotel and restaurants | Services rendered by hotels and other lodging places, restaurants, cafes, and other eating and drinking places | 4.8 (0.7) | 6.5 (0.7) | 9.3 (1.0) |
| **Transport, storage and communication** | | | | |
| Railways | | 4.2 (1.5) | 4.5 (1.4) | 3.6 (1.1) |
| Transport by other means | Road, water, air transport, services incidental to transport | 6.3 (3.6) | 6.3 (3.8) | 6.9 (4.3) |
| Storage | | 5.5 (0.1) | 2.7 (0.1) | 2 (0.1) |
| Communication | Postal, money orders, telegrams, telephones, overseas communications services, miscellaneous | 6.7 (1.0) | 6.1 (1.0) | 13.6 (2.0) |

**Financing, insurance, real estate and business services**

| | | | | |
|---|---|---|---|---|
| Banking | Banks, banking department of RBI, post office savings bank, non-bank financial institution, cooperative credit societies, employees' provident fund | 7.2 (1.9) | 11.9 (3.4) | 12.7 (6.3) |
| Insurance | Life, postal life, non-life | 7.1 (0.5) | 10.9 (0.8) | 6.7 (0.7) |
| Dwellings, real estate | | 2.6 (4.0) | 7.7 (4.8) | 5.0 (4.5) |
| Business services | | 4.2 (0.2) | 13.5 (0.3) | 19.8 (1.1) |
| Legal services | | 2.6 (0.0) | 8.6 (0.0) | 5.8 (0.0) |

**Community, social and personal services**

| | | | | |
|---|---|---|---|---|
| Public administration, defense | | 6.1 (5.3) | 7.0 (6.0) | 6.0 (6.1) |
| Personal services | Domestic, laundry, barber, beauty shops, tailoring, others | 1.7 (1.6) | 2.4 (1.1) | 5.0 (1.1) |
| Community services | Education, research, scientific, medical, health, religious, and other community | 4.8 (4.0) | 6.5 (4.3) | 8.4 (5.5) |
| Other services | Recreation, entertainment, radio, TV broadcast, sanitary services | 3.4 (1.1) | 5.3 (1.0) | 7.1 (0.7) |

Source: Gordon and Gupta (2003).

software industry. Apart from this, most of the fast-growing industries are regionally concentrated in the south and west, and small pockets of north India. One of the main reasons for this is the initial conditions and endowments. In the following paragraphs, I discuss three industry case studies – software, pharmaceuticals, and textiles and garments – to trace out the initial institutional conditions and implications of their growth on the evolution of markets and institutions.

## India's software industry

India's software industry presents two important dimensions: first, the importance of the initial conditions of the endowment of skilled labor and a critical level of technological and entrepreneurial institutions; and second, given the initial conditions, how openness to international trade can result in positive gains for a developing economy – namely, employment generation, market expansion, and institutional change.

India's software industry was initially labeled 'an island of competitiveness' (Ghemawat and Patibandla, 1999). When it started to export in the mid-1980s, there was no domestic demand base, no input (hardware) industry, and infrastructure, such as telecommunications, was highly inefficient. Its export success in the 1980s depended primarily on its ability to draw on a large pool of local engineering talent and reduce its dependence on other local institutions. The large pool of engineering graduates in India was a result of the government subsidization of higher education under the import substitution regime, under which the government of India established half a dozen Indian Institutes of Technology (IIT) and several regional engineering colleges.[8] This large engineering skill-base became a readily available source for the software industry to draw upon for its export success.

### A brief history

Defense industry research in the US led to the emergence of computers in the 1940s, and their commercial application started in the 1950s. In 1968, the US anti-trust agency forced IBM to stop bundling software with hardware, which gave birth to the software industry. The US government's large-scale procurement of software services from private firms gave an initial boost to the industry. Similarly, the Indian IT industry was born as a result of government spending on defense research and public sector undertakings. The first computer was introduced in India in 1956 for use at the Indian Statistical Institute. Around the mid-1960s, the government of India started a policy towards localizing the production of computers. However, the closed-door policy and licensing controls restricted the growth of the hardware industry. A by-product of this was the birth of the software industry.

In the early 1970s, the Department of Electronics was created. A few private software vendor firms came into the market mainly to serve the public sector. The government also initiated software-related training courses in the Indian Institutes of Technology and universities at around this time. One of the landmarks in this industry was the setting-up of the private sector firm Tata Consultancy Services (TCS) in 1969. In the initial years, TCS did software development for its own group of firms and for public sector firms. IBM's exit from India in 1977 contributed to TCS's growth. The government of India set up the Computer Maintenance Corporation (CMC) in the mid-1970s. However, the restrictions on imports of hardware, the banning of software imports and poor enforcement of the Copyright Act constrained the growth of the industry. Private software firms initially operated as data entry operators in the domestic market by developing their own software at the low end.

The government of India started to generate favorable conditions for exports of software in the early 1980s when it started to provide finance, infrastructure, legal, and marketing assistance. The policy was made more liberal in 1984 in allowing 100 percent foreign subsidiaries, and imports of hardware and software (Heeks, 1996). One of the most successful software firms, Infosys, was set up by a small group of technocrats headed by N. R. Murthy. After the initial struggles waged to overcome institutional constraints, Infosys grew into a major player by adopting a model that reduced its dependence on local infrastructure and institutions. As it grew through exports, it invested in its own electricity generation, water treatment, satellite links, and transport services for its employees in order to meet the standards of global markets.

One of the important landmarks of the industry was the entry of Texas Instruments (TI) in 1985 by its setting-up of an R&D unit in Bangalore. At that time, most TNCs were reluctant to enter India, as it was perceived as an economy of high transaction costs and red tape. The establishment of the subsidiary was made possible by the initiatives taken by the then Indian Prime Minister, Rajiv Gandhi, and one of the senior vice presidents of TI, who happened be an Indian expatriate (Mohan Rao). At that time, the government did not permit private firms to own and install their own satellite communication facilities. TI's managers brought in the most current communications equipment (a 64 Kbps data link) and gave it to the government (the Department of Telecommunications). TI, in turn, then established a link with the Department of Telecommunications for the company's own operations.[9] The communication facilities made it possible for the R&D teams in Bangalore to be in direct and instant contact with the parent operations in the US. The excess capacity on the satellite link initially allowed local firms to get the link and facilitated their movement from onsite projects to offshore development (Patibandla and Petersen, 2002).

The sequence of the exit of IBM and the entry of TI had important implications for the evolution of the industry. As mentioned before, IBM's departure in 1977 helped local firms such as TCS to grow. By the time of TI's arrival, some local firms had achieved a critical level of maturity and competence. A few large local firms in Bangalore moved up on the quality ladder of offshore development from onsite development by linking up to the satellite communication infrastructure brought in by TI. Furthermore, TI's success spurred other major TNCs to set up their operations in India. The 1990s world market boom coincided with the entry of several TNCs in India to overcome the skill shortage in the US and western Europe (Desai, 2005). The subsequent recession in the 2000s caused an expansion of the existing TNCs and witnessed the entry of new TNCs into the country for the purpose of realizing cost-competitiveness.

The economic reforms of 1991, accompanied by a devaluation of the rupee, gave a boost to software exports. The world market boom of the 1990s and Y2K business gave tremendous opportunities for Indian firms to grow rapidly through exports. The high degree of export orientation of the industry relaxed the domestic market size constraint and allowed the entry of a large number of local firms and TNCs. The increase in the number of firms and their rapid expansion in the 1990s and the early 2000 resulted in a rapid growth in demand for labor with both general and specialized skills.

Consequently, wage rates for skilled software professionals increased at an annual rate of 30 percent from the mid-1990s. During this period, there was intense competition among TNCs and large Indian firms for skilled people with a few years of experience in project development and management. This provided incentives for people to acquire both general and specialized skills. The increase in demand for education led private firms to enter the education market. There are about 2,300 recognized private training institutes in the country. The large private firms NIIT and APTECH account for 60 percent of private training. Apart from this, there have been initiatives from the center and state governments in collaboration with private sector firms to set up educational institutions. The Indian Institutes of Information Technology, set up in Bangalore and Hyderabad with the coordinated efforts of state governments, Microsoft, IBM, and Satyam Computers, illustrate this collaboration.

### Evolution of institutions

First, I discuss the evolution of institutional conditions within the industry, and later how the growth of this industry facilitated the expansion of markets and the evolution of institutions in other spheres. Copyright enforcement is a critical institution for the development of industries such as software, book publishing, and movies, etc. Intellectual property rights emerge and are enforced in an economy when domestic agents or industries become major wealth generators and develop strong interest in

enforcing them. Until the early 1990s, there was rampant piracy of software in India. At around the same time, India's software industry had
become a major wealth generator and a source of employment to a large
number of young professionals. The software industry association
NASSCOM lobbied the Indian government and succeeded in having the
Copyright Act amended in 1994 to make it on a par with the best in the
world. However, enforcement by the government was weak. The industry
association took an active role in enforcing the act by educating and training the police force.[10]

To recall, one of Douglas North's propositions for institutional change
involves a change in the attitudes of economic agents, especially those that
have strong political constituency. India's software industry demonstrated the
benefits of openness to international trade and multinational investment.
Industry growth through openness to foreign trade and investment contributed not only to foreign exchange earnings, but also to employment generation for skilled labor, who were mostly from the middle class. This, in
turn, changed the attitudes of both the government and the middle class positively towards openness to international trade and multinational investment

### Application of IT and institutional change: a few examples

The application of IT in general has implications for private and public
sector organizations and a consequent decline in transaction costs. As
mentioned before, the implementation of IT in the railways and the
banking sector reduced transaction costs to consumers significantly. A few
state governments in India, such as the Andhra Pradesh state government
under the chief minister Chandra Babu Naidu, adopted e-governance to
improve government services to the public. It resulted in improvements in
some spheres and reduced informational imperfections to the public.
Institutional economics shows that public governance, in terms of the
accountability of government agents and reduction in corruption,
improves under decentralized governance with transparency. The application of information technology to governance can nevertheless result in
contradictory outcomes. On one side, it can reduce informational imperfections at the micro level, and on other it can lead to centralization by
making possible a greater availability of information at the center, which
can increase the powers of a single individual at the top of government
(Patibandla *et al.*, 2000).

### e-choupals[11] and rural market expansion

As has already been mentioned, close to 65 percent of India's population
is engaged in the agriculture sector and lives in rural areas. It is observed
that a lack of infrastructure destroys close to 35 percent of agricultural
output. Apart from this, farmers do not realize the right prices owing to

informational imperfections caused by middlemen, and the lack of futures commodity markets. Small farmers are trapped into poverty cycles because of high interest rates, the transaction costs of rural credit markets, the high risk of production due to environmental uncertainty, and underdeveloped output markets (Patibandla and Sastry, 2004). The case of e-choupals demonstrates how the application of information technology to the rural commodity market reduced informational imperfections and helped small farmers realize competitive product and input prices.

The idea of e-choupals was initiated and executed by one of India's leading private companies, ITC (Indian Tobacco Corporation), in 2000 to expand its trade in agricultural commodities. The e-choupal concept is basically an e-commerce technique of procuring agricultural output from small farmers in villages by making information about prices of output, input and productivity-enhancing methods available through a Web-based portal. The computer is placed in the house of the sanchalak, who is basically an educated middle farmer who is trained to make the information available to other farmers. For these services the sanchalak is paid a small commission of 0.5 percent of each tonne of soya bean originating from the e-choupal. The farmers gather at the choupals and check the prices, and sell their output at the collection centers. The process of measuring and checking the quality is streamlined so that transaction costs are minimized for the farmers. The e-choupals have eliminated middlemen, as farmers can have direct access to prices and sell directly at the ITC collection centers. Interestingly, the company entrusted middlemen with the role of aggregating the output from different collection centers and supplying it to the main ITC center for a commission.

The e-choupal service was later extended to other crops such as wheat, coffee, shrimps, etc., covering a larger number of villages. By 2004, the e-choupal services reached more than two million farmers in about 24,000 villages. The company intends to scale it up to ten million farmers covering 100,000 villages by 2010. The websites are created in relevant local languages. The information services are expanded for farmers; from the services, they can learn about best farm practices, the prevailing prices both in India and the world markets, and risk management, as well as the weather forecast in order to plan their seeding and harvesting. Apart from this, farmers can order inputs, seeds, fertilizers, and other services. The e-choupal is basically a supply chain innovation through the use of information technology, which has reduced informational imperfections and transaction costs to small farmers, and helped them to realize fair prices and improve productivity, thereby expanding the market.

## The pharmaceutical industry

The pharmaceutical industry is a knowledge-intensive industry in which intellectual property rights (IPRs) play a critical role. I examine how IPR institutional arrangements shaped the industry, which, in turn, affected the evolution of IPRs. At the global level, the pharmaceutical industry can be divided into two kinds of firms: innovative firms and producers of generic drugs. The innovating firms are located mostly in developed economies. The research-oriented pharmaceutical companies are among the most multinationally oriented in the world. Protection of IPRs (patents) is a crucial requirement for firms to invest in R&D owing to the associated high costs and uncertainty of investment.[12] The effective patent period for a successful drug ranges from fourteen to twenty years, for which an innovative firm will have monopoly status. In countries with comprehensive patent protection, generic drugs come into production when the patent expires. When a drug becomes generic, its price declines steeply because of competition among a large number of firms. In countries where patent protection is non-existent or weak, all drugs are generic. Firms in these countries undertake the reverse engineering of new pharmaceutical drugs produced in developed countries and sell them at low prices to local users.

To assess the market size for pharmaceutical products in developing economies, one has to make a distinction between two types of diseases: those that are primarily present in poor countries, such as malaria, and those that are found in all parts of the globe. Protection of intellectual property rights for drugs restricts the market size in developing economies, as most people in these countries cannot afford the prices that the global pharmaceutical companies charge (Kremer, 2002). In the more advanced developing countries, such as India and Brazil, local firms are able to supply pharmaceutical products at low prices under generic production.[13]

Patent protection of pharmaceutical products in India was based on Great Britain's laws until 1970. Consequently, the prices of essential drugs were among the highest in the world and the market was dominated by TNCs until 1970 (Huang and Hogan, 2002). The Patent Act was modified in 1970 such that it recognized only process patents and not product patents. Apart from this, the government also enacted price controls on certain pharmaceutical products. These measures were implemented to make certain essential drugs affordable to low-income groups.

The Patent Act of 1970 allowed firms in India to reverse-engineer new drugs produced in developed economies and sell them in India at low prices. Through this practice, the Indian pharmaceutical industry grew very rapidly, averaging a 35 percent annual growth rate during the period of 1982 to 2002. In the year 2003, the industry was valued at about $5 billion. There were about 24,000 firms in the industry in 1997, including several small and a few large Indian and multinational firms. Multinational firms cater to about 38 percent of total industry sales and have been active in formulations (branded products), as compared to Indian firms, which concentrate more on bulk drugs and generic pharmaceutical products. Indian companies manufactured drugs in virtually every therapeutic category and marketed them under their own brand names. The major Indian companies, such as Cipla and Reddy's Laboratories, grew rapidly over the years by adopting the reverse-engineering of drugs from developed economies. Because of the generic nature of the market, drug prices are among the lowest in the world. Furthermore, some of the Indian firms have become major exporters of generic drugs in the world market (Smith, 2000). Regionally, the industry is concentrated in the south in the city of Hyderabad, and in the west in the cities of Ahmedabad and Pune.

In 1994, the Indian government signed the WTO (World Trade Organization) agreement which mandated a higher level of protection of trade-related intellectual property rights (TRIPS). As a result, India has to implement a patent regime protecting drug products by January 2005. During this transition period, India has to provide five years of exclusive marketing rights to any entity that files a patent application in any WTO member country after January 2005. Furthermore, the government implemented a reduction of the price controls in 2002. Recently, several large Indian firms which reached large sales volumes and technological maturity started to refocus their strategies of investing in R&D and formed joint collaborations with multinational corporations for R&D efforts in discovering molecules (Smith, 2000). The recent scientific discoveries on the human genome have had a significant effect on boosting the nascent biotechnology industry in India. Synergies among the pharmaceutical, information technology, and biotechnology fields confer comparative advantages for undertaking R&D in India. In the other words, the modification of the patent regime, the endowment of a large pool of scientific manpower and of complementary industries, and the vast biodiversity in India provide incentives for firms which have reached a critical level maturity to undertake R&D.

For example, an Indian company, Reddy's Laboratories, which became a major player through reverse-engineering practices, invested in R&D in collaboration with the Danish pharmaceutical company Novo Nordisk and the Swedish company Novartis. This led to the discovery of three molecules that have been licensed for diabetes drugs. Recently, this company lobbied the Indian government to adopt product patents (Huang and Hogan, 2002). Another Indian large firm, Ranbaxy, has entered into a licensing agreement with the German multinational Schwarz Pharma AG, under which the TNC will launch Ranbaxy's chemical discovery NCE for treating benign prostatic hyperplasia. Under the licensing agreement, Ranbaxy would receive $50 million in licensing fees and a percentage of royalties. In 2004, there are two groups of firms: one group that favours the adoption of the product patents, and the other that resists the adoption of the product patents. The interesting aspect is that the Reddy's Labs company, which grew rapidly by the adoption of reverse-engineering, favours the adoption of product patents by 2002.

## A comparative analysis of the software and pharmaceutical industries

The analysis of India's software and pharmaceutical industries provides qualitative evidence to support the proposition that the enactment and enforcement of IPRs are viable only when local firms become major wealth generators and develop a strong economic interest in the protection of IPRs. On the other hand, one can argue that a knowledge-intensive industry would not develop in a developing economy in the absence of the protection of intellectual property rights. The Indian software industry took an indirect route of becoming a wealth generator through exports first, and subsequently the Copyright Act was enacted and enforced to generate the local market. In the case of the pharmaceutical industry, the story is simpler. Indian firms became major wealth generators because of the weak patent regime, which not only allowed local firms to undertake reverse-engineering practices but also shielded them from competition and entry barriers from the globally established TNCs. This helped local firms become major wealth generators over time. The imposition of IPRs through the WTO agreement in 2005 is now viable, as several large Indian firms have reached a critical level of technological maturity and have been developing an economic interest in the protection of product patents. In essence, institutional change in developing economies is possible only when local firms and agents become major wealth generators and develop a strong economic interest in the change (Patibandla, 2005b).

## The textile and garments industry

Historically, the textile industry was important for India's industrialization. Prior to the arrival of the British in the country, India was known for the production of the finest handmade textiles. Under British rule, the handloom industry declined as the British promoted British mill-made textiles and discriminated against the native handlooms. One important aspect of India's industrialization is that, as discussed in the previous chapter, local industrialists emerged from the trading communities of Parsis, Marwaris, and Gujaratis and entered the mechanized textile industry in the early nineteenth century. The Indian textile industry continues to be the largest industry in the country, accounting for 20 percent of total industrial output and with an employment of twenty million people and nearly 30 percent of total exports. Modern textile processing facilities coexist with hand-printing and traditional processing.

At the time of independence, India's textile industry was observed to be internationally competitive (Jalan, 1996). However, the import substitution policies, which imposed several restrictions on the mill sector and promoted the small-scale sector, caused the industry to lose its competitive edge. Jalan observes that

India has enjoyed a comparative advantage in this industry [textiles] for long. Yet, within a few years, India whittled away its traditional advantage by severely restricting output of cloth (through licensing restrictions), increasing costs (through widespread interventions in the labor and cotton markets), and preventing induction of new technologies and new fibres. In 1973–74, India's share in world markets for textiles and clothing exports was the same as that of China (4.5 percent). Korea's share was 7.7 percent and that of Pakistan only 1.7 percent. By 1985–86, China's share increased to as much as 14.6 percent and that of Korea to 13.6 percent. Other developing countries, like Pakistan, Thailand and Hong Kong, also increased their shares substantially. India was the only country among major developing country exporters whose share actually fell from 4.5 percent to 3.8 percent during this period.

The industrial policies which gave incentives in terms of excise duty concessions and the reservation of several segments of garments production for small firms caused the entry of a large number of small-scale firms, competing with low cost and prices. This led to the rapid growth of the power-loom[14] sector with a large number of small firms, which marginalized both the large-scale mill sector and also the handloom sector (Patibandla and Amarnath, 1994). Subsequently, in the typical market failure of large-group competition, the structure led to small firms being unable to invest in technology upgrades, which, in turn, trapped India's exports of textiles in the low-quality and low-value segment. On the other hand, in the case of the garments cluster in Tirupur in the south of India, the export market dynamics and cooperative behavior between large and small firms through subcontracting helped small firms undertake technological upgrading and move up on the value chain (Cawthorne, 1995).

The garment industry has been one of India's largest-exporting industries. Most of the production takes place in the unorganized sector and employment generation in this industry takes place via backward linkages with the textile industry, both with the power-loom and the mill sector. However, the export competitiveness of the industry was damaged by inefficient input industries such as low-quality cloth, threads, and buttons and also the high transaction costs associated with ports and roads, which increased lead times. Additionally, most of the exports had been under the Multi-Fiber Arrangement (MFA), which restricted garment imports by quotas in certain markets (the USA and western Europe).

### The effect of the reforms

In 1985, the textile policy removed industrial licensing as well as expansion and restructuring barriers for mills and power-looms. The trade policy reforms of 1991, apart from the devaluation of the rupee, substan-

tially reduced tariffs on the import of equipment and generic intermedi-
ates, which, in turn, reduced the costs of acquiring new capacities and
technology and imports of yarn. The reduction in the tariffs had a significant effect on domestic prices. It forced the largest producer of synthetic
yarn, the Reliance Industries Corporation, to reduce prices, which, in
turn, resulted in a steep decline in prices of man-made fabrics. This, in
turn, expanded the markets for man-made textiles by making them access-
ible to lower-income groups. Domestic consumption and demand for
man-made fibers increased at a rapid rate during the 1990s at an annual
growth rate of 8.5 percent. As the real incomes of the lower-income
groups go up, they shift their consumption to man-made fibers, which
have longer life and manageability. In other words, the effect of the
reforms on this industry increased the real incomes of low-income groups
and expanded the market for man-made fabrics in the domestic market.

The policy reforms provided an opportunity for the revival of the large-
scale mill sector through investment in technology. The investment rate in
terms of gross capital formation as a percentage of value-added had grown
from 51 percent in 1986–7 to 106 percent by 1991–2 in the mill sector.
The expensive technological modernization of the mills augmented their
export orientation (Roy, 1996). In other words, although the mill sector
could not compete with the power-loom sector in the domestic market,
owing to the price-elasticity of domestic demand, the reforms, both
internal and external, allowed them to restructure and increase their
export competitiveness.

The total exports of this sector grew at an annual average rate of 12
percent in the 1990s. Garments emerged as a major exporting sector
during this period, with a 30 percent annual growth. In order to undertake exports, a few large mills restructured by adopting highly integrated
production, from the production of yarn and textiles to branded garments. For example, Reliance is considered the lowest-cost producer of
synthetic yarn, and the Arvind Mills Company the largest producer of
denim in the world. The interesting aspect of the trend of the market
expansion is that before the reforms, the domestic demand for ready-
made garments was very low. In the 1990s, the large exporters of garments
first branched into exports, catering to the high-quality segment of
exports of blended-cloth-based garments and then generated the
domestic markets for ready-made branded garments. Since the mid-1990s,
the domestic consumption of blended cloth (by the relatively higher-
income group, urban consumers) began growing at a rapid pace, integrating the demand preferences of domestic and export markets (Roy, 1996;
Ghemawat and Patibandla, 1999). The production of the high-value
segment of branded garments is concentrated with the large-scale mills
that virtually created this market in the 1990s. One way these firms were
able to break into high-value branded garments in the international
markets was by getting into collaborations with well-known international

branded companies.[15] A few recent studies show that there has been a significant improvement in the productivity of the textile industry in response to the reforms (Kambhampati, 2003).

One of the structural outcomes of the reforms, especially with regard to the garments sector, was a gradual regional shift of the industry from the north and the western part of India to the south. Typically an exporter in the north operates through subcontractors who employ labor on a piece-rate basis. The average size of a unit varies from twenty to fifty machines. Exporters avoid setting up larger factories and the employment of workers on a salaried basis so as not to suffer from union problems. As a result, an exporter operates through a network of twenty to thirty fabricators. Large orders have to be split among the fabricators, which results in quality control problems and delays. Apart from this, a piece-rate worker is less interested in improving quality. In Bombay, the increasing cost of real estate (owing to the Rent Control Act) is one of the major reasons for the shift.

The relative advantages of locating in the south are: a more literate workforce; a disciplined and docile workforce with a large number of women workers; workers are not migrant and, since they are more settled in one place, skill upgrading through training is possible; the south has access to Madras (Chennai) port, which is close to Sri Lanka where a lot of offshore manufacturing takes place to take advantage of quota availability; and cities like Salem and Coimbatore provide access to fabrics. The south also has a well-developed base for accessories like zippers and linings.

The removal of MFA by 2005 provides not only great opportunities to increase exports but is also expected to increase competition from other low-labor-cost countries such as China. It is thought likely to cause a decline in prices in the absence of quota premiums, and in rent and floor prices, increase competition, provide a better quality match, quicken response time and result in higher levels of service. In order to prepare the ground for this, the government of India set up the Textiles Techno-logy Fund to finance the technological upgrading of the industry. Several segments of garments production were de-reserved from small-scale pro-duction, and there is some progress in improving the infrastructure of ports to reduce lead times of exports.

I briefly summarize the main effects of the reforms on this industry. One is that the reduction in tariffs and restrictions on imports of yarn forced domestic monopoly producers to reduce the prices of raw mater-ials, which, in turn, generated a market for man-made fibers from the low-income groups. Second, the large-mill sector, which lost out in the pre-reforms period, was able to restructure itself through integrated pro-duction and realize high cost-efficiency. The trade policy reforms helped them to undertake exports to overcome their disadvantage at home, and then generate domestic markets for ready-made and branded garments. In the post-reform era, the firms that were able to invest in technology and quality were able to prosper, while those that could not slowly faded away. Furthermore, export activity requires quality control and low lead times; for this, part of the garment industry moved to the south. As already mentioned, this industry has a large domestic market-base and is also highly export-oriented. The removal of MFA could further increase the exports of the industry. Garment production is highly labor-intensive. An increase in exports will further increase employment in the sector, which, in turn, can further the strategic interests of the sector for open trade and investment policies.

## Income growth and distribution

The differential growth rates of different industries and sectors could change income distribution, which, in turn, results in the formation of interest groups whose interests may or may not conform to the reform process. I will briefly point out the income distributional outcomes of the growth process. For the decade 1990–2000, India's annual average GDP growth was 6.2 percent and GDP per capita was 4.4 percent. For the decade 1980–90, it was 5.9 percent and 3.8 percent, and it was 3.7 percent and 1.5 percent for the period 1950 to 1980. There is a significant increase in per capita income in the post-reform era. The studies of Sundaram and Tendulkar (2003), Deaton and Dreze (2002) and Bhalla (2003) show that, since 1993, poverty levels in India declined but income distribution has worsened and there is a wide disparity in the decline in poverty across different states. This is consistent with the proposition that the reforms benefit those with initial endowments of durable assets and skills more than those who lack these initial endowments. However, the decline in poverty is an indication of the expansion of the markets, which takes place through both increase in employment and decline in prices. A study by the National Council for Applied Economics Research (NCAER, 2002) shows that the percentage of low-income groups with income less than Rs 5,000 declined from 58.8 percent in 1989–90 to 39.7 percent in 1998–9. For the same period, the lower middle class with incomes of Rs 35,001–70,000 increased from 26.9 to 34.5 percent, the middle class with incomes of Rs 70,001–105,000 increased from 10.1 to 13.9 percent, the upper middle class with incomes of Rs 105,001–110,000 increased from 2.7 to 6.2 percent, and the high-income groups with incomes above Rs 140,000 increased from 1.4 to 5.7 percent. As shown earlier, the use of durable consumer goods such as refrigerators, two-wheelers, and household appliances grew rapidly in the post-reforms period. However, the increase in income and consumption grew higher in the urban areas than the rural areas with the widening rural and urban divide. Furthermore, the increase in incomes is highly skewed across regions, with the regions with an initially favorable market and institutions growing faster than the others. In a nutshell, the middle class, both the lower- and upper-middle groups, mostly from the urban areas, is the one that drew major benefits in employment and consumption gains in the post-reform era.

## Regional distribution of growth

One of the propositions is that the regional distribution of growth in the post-reform era depends on the initial conditions in different regions. As the previous chapter showed, both in British India and under the import substitution regime of independent India, despite government efforts at generating regional equality in growth, industrial development was concentrated in the western and southern part of India, while it declined in the eastern part of West Bengal. These disparities in regional growth only increased in the post-reform period. The Gini coefficient of inequality among states was 0.15 in 1980–1, which increased to 0.17 in 1990–1. This increased rapidly to 0.23 by 1991–8 of the post-reform era. The annual growth rates in per capita GDP for the interior (landlocked) northern states such as Bihar, Uttar Pradesh and Rajastan declined. An even more striking aspect of regional disparities was that regions within the states also showed wide disparity in development levels. Banerjee (2004) observes, "According to the 1991 census, less than 7 percent of villages in the Vishakhapatnam district in Andhra Pradesh (AP) had middle schools and just over 46 percent had some educational facility, as opposed to 55 percent and 100 percent in Guntur." The market reforms obviously benefit those who had a favorable initial market and institutional and asset endowments, further improving the growth and evolution of markets and institutions in the well-developed regions. How do a few faster-growing regions benefit others in spreading markets and institutions? It could take place in two ways: migration of labor into the growing regions, and the demonstration effect on people and governments of low-growth regions.

Clark and Wolcott (2001) show that during the Britain's industrial revolution in 1750–1860, there was not much productivity growth in the southern half of the country, where two-thirds of the population lived. Most of the growth in productivity occurred in the north in the textile industry. However, through the twin forces of labor migration and international trade, Britain's success in this one sector was translated into widespread economic growth. Can this be applied to India in the 1990s and 2000s, a time in which most of the growth is concentrated in the south and the west, while the landlocked northern and the eastern parts of India remain backward? India differs from Britain on one major ground: while Britain is a small, homogenous country, India is a large and highly diverse country with multiple languages and cultures.

In 2001, India's population was a little more than one billion. About 65 percent lived in rural areas. From 1951 to 2001, the proportion of the population living in urban areas increased from 17.3 percent to 32.8

percent (Srivastava and Sasikumar, 2003). India, as is well known, has sixteen major languages and different dialects across the country. This regional difference in languages and culture, coupled with illiteracy, functions as a mobility barrier for the migration of labor. It was observed that despite regional disparities in development levels, population mobility in India was low (Kundu and Gupta, 1996). However, the notable outcome of the reforms is that there is a modest increase in migration levels in the post-reforms period. The National Sample Survey (NSS) for 1992–3 and 1999–2000 shows an increase in migration rates from 24.7 percent to 26.6 percent. The pattern of migration depends on the literacy and skills of people. Illiteracy, being a source of high transaction costs, imposes mobility barriers for migration into different regions. For an illiterate migrant, lifetime migration or migration a long way from home has large uncertainties owing to poor knowledge of the job market and high search costs. However, the increasing regional disparities in development levels result in labor-demand and supply imbalances in different regions. This led to the emergence of middlemen and contractors who recruit workers to supply them to employers in different regions, thereby reducing transaction costs to the illiterate workers (Srivastava and Sasikumar, 2003). In other words, as new labor-market institutions emerge, reducing the transaction costs of labor mobility, migration levels should increase.

As far as the social costs are concerned, it requires an understanding of whether a group of people belonging to a specific region migrates together, or whether migration of one member leads others to follow (chain migration). The mobility of skilled labor among different regions is observed to be quite high. High skills mean low mobility barriers, low search costs, and high employment opportunities, leading skilled workers to take advantage of wage arbitrage. Apart from this, for skilled people, social mobility or status is high, irrespective of regional residence – both social and economic externalities can be high for the educated. For example, the software cluster in Bangalore employs skilled people from all over the country, but few locals. Another example is the state of Kerala, which has the highest literacy rate in India, but low levels of industrial development. This state has a very high emigration of males, both to overseas and within India.

As far as permeation of market institutions from the developed regions to regions with low development is concerned, I do not have evidence, except for press reports that indicate some degree of competition among a few state governments in the west and the south to attract both domestic and foreign capital with tax incentives and allotment of land, etc. This competition is among the relatively more developed states rather than among the poor states. The study by Fisman and Khanna (2004) attempts to show that the large-group affiliated firms, because of their ability to internalize labor and capital markets and generate their own infrastructure, may locate in the backward regions to make use of tax incentives and low labor costs. But their evidence is tenuous and is based on only a couple of case studies. More than labor costs, the availability of the right kind of skills locally and low labor disputes may be dominant factors in location decisions. Ghemawat and Patibandla (1999) show that several garment producers, both small and large, moved from the north to Tamil Nadu in the south owing to the availability of literate labor, and the low incidence of labor disputes.

Rao and Singh (2002) show that there is competition from the state government for obtaining transfers from the center for consumption. In India's federal system, the center has more political and economic powers than the states. The interesting aspect is that some of the states in the south and the west, which had lower political representation and received much lower transfers from the center since independence, are more developed than the northern states, such as Uttar Pradesh and Bihar, which have higher political representation in the center. One conjecture is that centralization has encouraged states that had greater power and more representation at the center to depend on, or draw their major consumption expenditure from, the center, rather than concentrate on developmental efforts. If the political economy factors of these large northern states makes the ruling parties look at development as a threat to their powers in a typical prisoner's dilemma interactions, the political parties in government have an incentive to block the demonstration effect from the growing states. A low level of development can be the result of a two-way relation between the scarcity of material wealth and the resultant institutions and rules that perpetuate the low level of development. A simple example can be found when one stands in the queue to buy movie tickets for a newly released movie in some major cities in India.[16] When the police are not around, getting the ticket is a matter of muscle power. Moreover, there is a black market that operates in collusion with the ticket sellers of the theaters, specific outside agents, and the police. Once the black market institutions become entrenched, they develop a strong incentive to create or perpetuate the scarcity. The political economy in the states dominated by feudal institutions is similar to the black market.

One of the ways people can escape from the low-development trap is through an increase in mobility across different regions, similar to the effect of the railroads in the British times. Investments in infrastructure could enhance people's mobility and increase both direct and indirect interactions of people from different regions. This, in turn, could cause both migration and a demonstration effect. I offer an example of the effect of central government investments (but not state governments), similar to the interference of an exogenous agent who breaks a prisoner's dilemma trap. In the year 2001, the central government initiated the building of large national highways across the country, with private participation. The project, called the 'Golden Quadrilateral', envisaged the construction of 5,952 km of new roads connecting the whole of the country.

The highway was planned to connect Delhi from the north to Kolkata in the east, along the 1,469 km of national highway 2. Kolkata to Chennai in the south would be linked along national highways 5, 6 and 60, covering a distance of 1,745 km. From Chennai to Mumbai in the west, national highways 4, 7 and 46 would form the next part of the grid, making a further distance of 1,302 km. From Mumbai, the quadrilateral would link Delhi through national highway 8. By 2004, out of the total of 5,846 km, 3,038 km had already been completed. The literature on economic geography shows that villages and towns in the proximity of national highways demonstrate higher growth and development than the unconnected ones (Fernald, 2003). Infrastructure development should contribute to some degree of economic development of poorly developed regions in the long run. Apart from this, as mentioned before, the Indian economy's international trade has shown a trend of increase. An increase in regional and international integration may result in the spread of growth benefits across regions. However, as has been said, commodity trade between states is still subject to taxes and high transaction costs, blocking development of national markets. In the latter half of the year 2004, the central government announced that twenty-six states in India had agreed to implement VAT (value-added tax), which was expected to reduce barriers to trade across regions.

# 5  Competitive dynamics

To recall, I draw from North's (1993) propositions of institutional change:

1  The continuous interaction between institutions and organizations in the economic setting of scarcity and hence competition is the key to institutional change.
2  Competition forces organizations to continually invest in skills and knowledge to survive. The kinds of skills and knowledge individuals and their organizations acquire will shape evolving perceptions about opportunities and hence choices that will incrementally alter institutions.

The underlying assumption is that there are critical initial institutional and market endowments, on the basis of which reforms increase competition by reducing policy-based entry and expansion barriers. One of the main propositions is that competitive dynamics leads to the convergence of best practices of firms, which triggers a process of market and institutional evolution.

As discussed in Chapter 3, reforms in India have been gradual and piecemeal. In the mid-1980s, the industrial licensing policies and expansion barriers applicable to large firms were removed and a gradual liberalization of the entry of multinationals was initiated. Although there has been a progressive evolution of the capital markets in the post-reform era, they still remain imperfect in the sense that the market still involves high transaction costs for absolutely new entrants to raise capital and compete with large incumbents.[1] Consequently, most of the new entrants are actually incumbent industrial houses who have branched out into different areas of new opportunities, and TNCs. There are only a few areas, such as the software industry, in which there are some great success stories attributable to new entrants, like Infosys.

Competitive dynamics between local incumbents and new-entrant TNCs have interesting implications for the evolution of markets and institutions as TNCs enter developing economies with technologies and organizational and marketing practices generated in developed

economies. The competitive dynamics will have implications on comparative economic organization of convergence of best practices, which
improve micro level efficiency. This, in turn, affects the evolution of
markets and institutional environment.

As discussed in Chapter 2, the new institutional economics is based on
the notion that the institutional environment determines micro-level governance choices. Although TNCs adapt their governance in the host
economy in relation to the prevailing institutional environment, there are
certain elements of their governance that could be quite foreign and
independent of the local institutional environment. These, in turn, have a
feedback effect on the evolution of institutions. For example, when Suzuki
entered the Indian car industry in the early 1980s, it adopted Japanese
management and vendor development practices, which had significant
effects on the industry in general.

## Convergence of best practices

Convergence refers to the diffusion of superior practices among firms
within an industry and across industries under comparative economic
logic.[2] The convergence of best practices among firms takes place through
competitive dynamics, joint ventures, and the process of spillovers of best
practices (Patibandla and Sanyal, 2005b). The effect of convergence is
more significant when we take the case of new-entrant TNCs and local
firms. The qualitative behavior of incumbents and new-entrant TNCs in
response to competition from each other is an attempt to overcome their
relative disadvantages. The other mechanism is deliberate copying of each
other's superior practices through conscious effort and through a
spillover process. This happens when TNCs enter the Indian market with
far-superior technology, organization and products, which has implications for micro level governance changes and the consequent evolution of
the institutional environment.

Intense competition between incumbents and new-entrant TNCs
induces firms to copy the efficiency-enhancing resources of rivals. For
example, the Japanese automobile companies acquired their unique managerial and production floor practices in relation to the market environment in Japan, which provided them with a competitive advantage in the
global market. Competition between Japanese companies and their American counterparts led to the imitation of some of the organizational practices of the Japanese companies by the American firms over a period of
time (Adler, 1999). However, differences in several elements of firm-level
practices between the Japanese and the American firms persist, owing to
the importance of firm-specific elements.[3]

To understand the convergence of best practices among competing
rivals and its implications for markets and institutions, one has to trace the
possible asymmetries among the incumbents and new entrants and

observe how these asymmetries trigger the process of convergence. The following conceptual framework is derived in the context of India's institutional conditions, the policy reforms and the qualitative information regarding events in the post-reforms era.

For the purpose of simplification, let us take it that the new entrants are TNCs. In entering developing economies, TNCs possess relative advantages in two dimensions: in intangible assets, and in capital markets. The intangible-assets theory of TNCs shows that, for a firm to conduct foreign production, they must possess some kind of firm-specific ownership advantages, such as superior technology (patent), brand name and marketing, which provide it with an advantage over local firms in the host country (Hymer, 1960; Caves, 1996). The decision to invest in a foreign country is essentially a decision to control some firm-specific proprietary asset rather than transact it via the market. Whether a firm will exploit that advantage through licensing or FDI depends on the type of advantage and the degree of market imperfections in the host market. The higher the degree of market imperfections, the greater will be the need to control the asset through direct investment. Generally, TNCs' advantage in intangible assets, such as global brand names and technology, tends to be more dominant in developing economies than in developed economies, because local firms in developing economies are underdeveloped. However, since property rights concerning intangible assets are underdeveloped, they are partially public goods and others can use assets developed by one firm at a small cost. If local firms, through deliberate effort or spillover, obtain the superior practices of TNCs, it improves industrial efficiency in the host countries (Caves, 1996; Dunning, 1981). This, apart from the competitive dynamics, has important implications for the issue of convergence under comparative economic organization logic.

The capital arbitrage hypothesis of TNCs is also relevant to developing economies, because highly underdeveloped capital markets cause real interest rates in these countries to be higher than in developed economies (Aliber, 1970). For example, in 2004, real interest rates in India ranged between 6 and 7 percent, while they were between 2 and 3 percent in developed economies (and zero in Japan). The ability of TNCs to tap global and internal (to a firm) capital markets gives them an advantage over local firms in developing economies. This disadvantage faced by local firms and their consequent efforts to overcome it have implications for institutional change in the capital markets.

In order to organize the process of the competitive dynamics between new-entrant TNCs and incumbent local firms, I use a simple analytical framework of Cournot-Nash oligopoly rivalry.[4] The competitive dynamics of oligopoly is partially consistent with the approach of comparative economic organization logic, which is illustrated below. Competitors have to adopt the superior practice of a firm with a relative advantage in order to safeguard their market share.[5] The benchmarking possibilities operate at two levels: in the Schumpeterian world of creative destruction, if one firm innovates and other firms imitate; and the entry of new firms into the market propagates superior practices. The arrival of new firms not only increases the number of firms but also introduces diversity in technology and organizational practices among firms. This, in turn, augments the possibilities for benchmarking and increases the opportunities for imitation by relatively inefficient firms.

I take two major sources of asymmetric advantage of firms: first mover and cost advantages. If a firm is able to move into the market first it derives advantages on both the demand and supply side. On the demand side, it can occupy a major part of the market through investments in fixed and sunk costs, which also helps it block and create disadvantages for new entrants (Dixit, 1980). Second, if there are significant learning economies in production, it could internalize them, which can give it a cost advantage with respect to new entrants. The time dimension in the qualitative behavior of firms is germane in the present context because I deal with two time periods: pre-reform and post-reform.

On the supply side, cost of production is a function of technology and organization. Firms derive technological advantage over rivals through innovation of new processes and products. In the context of emerging economies, the issue is the introduction of new technologies by TNCs and the ability of local firms to adopt and imitate technologies from developed economies.

As discussed in Chapter 2, organizational aspects for efficiency considerations involve several issues such as diversification behavior (vertical integration and horizontal diversification into unrelated activities), internal organization issues of hierarchy, teamwork and incentives, and agency relations of corporate governance. When policy changes take place, firms have to alter their organizational practices in order to improve efficiency. For example, policy reforms reduce transaction costs in general. A firm which is able to adapt to this by reducing its diversification and take advantage of economies of specialization in the market will realize higher production efficiency than one that does not adapt to the change. I sketch the qualitative behavior of firms in the post-reform period in general terms in the following. The micro level details of technological and organizational behavior of firms are discussed in detail in the following two chapters.

## Competitive dynamics between local incumbents and TNCs

According to the intangible asset theory, TNCs possess significant advantages in terms of superior technology and products, financial resources, and advanced marketing and management skills while entering developing economies. However, the intangible assets are developed by TNCs primarily in relation to the institutional environment of the home market.

TNCs have to take into account the prevailing institutional environment in the host country, such as the transaction costs of doing business and the degree of protection of property rights in deciding the governance choices in realizing their advantage with regard to intangible assets, which may impose additional (adjustment) costs. In the case of incumbents, their accumulated experience in dealing with the local output and input markets, well-established dealer networks and distribution, mechanisms of contract formulation and enforcement could provide an advantage over new-entrant TNCs in the short run.

In entering new markets, TNCs can overcome their lack of country-specific institutional knowledge by forming a joint venture with a local firm. This involves hazards for both TNCs and local firms. A TNC faces the risk of appropriation of its intangible assets by the local partner. A well-established local firm fears losing ownership control to a TNC. Therefore, a well-established local firm may prefer to buy technology through licensing rather than giving ownership rights to a TNC. In such a case, a joint venture may take place between a TNC and a local partner who is not already established in a specific industry.[6] If joint ventures are of this kind, the argument that established local firms in a specific industry have a firm-specific relative advantage over a new-entrant TNC in respect of distribution and institutional knowledge is still valid (Patibandla, 2002a). The finer issues relating to joint ventures are examined later.

By incumbents, I mean the large Indian firms that operated through the pre-reforms period into the post-reforms era. The incumbents who operated in the institutional environment of the pre-reforms period have to adapt to the changes in the institutional environment and compete with new-entrant TNCs. As the policy reforms are partial shifts in the institutional environment, incumbents derive certain relative advantages and disadvantages with respect to new entrants in the short and medium run of the post-reforms period, which determines their qualitative behavior. In response to competition from TNCs, incumbents have to get rid of some of the assets acquired specific to the institutional environment of the pre-reforms era and acquire new assets to enhance technological and organizational efficiency.

Under the institutional conditions of the pre-reforms era, Indian oligopoly firms were able to pre-empt entry by cornering industrial licenses and blocked competition from imports by investing significant human and physical resources in cultivating politicians and bureaucrats. This investment ceased to be useful for entry prevention in the post-reforms period and a major part of this specific asset became redundant. These types of specific human assets acquired by Indian firms may not be easily redeployed into a more productive mode. Most Indian firms have been family-run businesses with a highly centralized organizational structure. In the pre-reforms period, economy in the design of organizations was not a major concern for Indian firms, as they had access to a highly protected and non-contested home market.

Lebenstein's (1966) theory of X-inefficiency shows that a lack of competition causes the cultivation of less efficient operation modes within the firm. Indian firms appeared to have a fondness for creating too many hierarchies; one explanation could be drawn from cultural factors. In a typical large Indian firm, hierarchy levels ranged between fifteen and twenty categories and within five or six broad categories; there were three or four subcategories (Patibandla, 1998). It is well established in the literature on economic organization that the higher the centralization and larger the number of hierarchies, the more imperfect will be information transfer and the higher is the susceptibility to information overload at the top, leading to organizational inefficiency. On the technology front, most Indian firms were observed to have made minimal investment in R&D assets in the pre-reforms period (Lall, 1987). Generally, older-vintage technologies were imported and minimal efforts were made in adapting them and building technological dynamism. Consequently, most Indian firms were far below international technology frontiers.

In response to competition from new-entrant TNCs in the post-reforms period, local firms in India appear to replace technological assets more easily than organizational assets. Local firms adopted more efficient technologies through imports, international purchase of technology, and increased expenditure on R&D. But organizational change among Indian firms is subject to a high degree of path-dependency and inertia (Patibandla, 2002a). This inertia and other institutional factors, such as India's labor laws and trade unions, constrain firms while firing or replacing employees, and make organizational change a difficult process. Second, as most Indian firms are family-run businesses, owner-managers themselves are reluctant to change the prevailing organizational practices and bring in decentralization (*Business Today*, 1999). A few local firms were able to adopt more efficient organizational practices while starting new plants in the post-reforms period but the employees in older plants resist the change.

Assuming that the adjustment costs of technology are taken into account, new-entrant TNCs have a cost advantage over local firms owing to their superior technology and organization. However, low cost alone, though necessary, is not sufficient for a new-entrant TNC to penetrate the Indian market when institutional elements are considered. At the beginning of entry into the Indian market, new entrants have negligible knowledge of dealing with market institutions. This implies that it takes time for a new entrant to penetrate the market, irrespective of its superior technology and organization.[7] This experience in dealing with local institutional conditions is an advantage that local firms have over new-entrant TNCs.

These (exogenously given) relative advantages (or disadvantages) of incumbents and new entrants determine their behavioral response in the post-reforms period. Local firms and new entrants have to acquire different types of assets to compete with each other. Local firms increase their investment in R&D assets to enhance technological efficiency. As TNCs bring in advanced technologies that are developed and market-tested in the international markets, they do not have to invest in R&D in their Indian subsidiaries. However, since the relative technological and organizational advantage of TNCs can be neutralized by their lack of well-established distribution networks and knowledge of Indian institutions in gaining market share, they invest more in promotional assets and in acquiring networks and local institutional knowledge.[8]

While new-entrant TNCs invest in promotional assets to build distribution networks and gain knowledge of local institutions, domestic firms increase investment in promotional assets (distribution and advertising) to safeguard their market shares in the face of new competition. To recapitulate, stickiness in some of the assets retards the efforts of local firms in augmenting their production efficiency. Given this relative disadvantage, domestic firms could concentrate on their relative strengths. For example, they make efforts at strengthening their distribution channels.[9] These are some of the possible short- and medium-term competitive behavioral responses of local firms and TNCs.[10] In the long run, relatively inefficient firms will be eliminated and there should be convergence in the efficiency levels of competing firms. And even TNCs might have to invest in R&D in local markets to able to compete with local firms and adapt their technologies and products to local market conditions.

To test some of the above arguments empirically, I have undertaken an econometric exercise on the basis of firm-level panel data for a set of industries covering the post-reform era. The data and the methodology are discussed in Appendix 2. One of the most significant results of these exercises is that market share of firms is positively associated with relative production efficiency (*TE*) of firms in all the industries with statistical significance. As I have discussed in Chapter 3, several studies had shown that firm size and market share had no relationship with relative production efficiency in the pre-reforms era. The results in the present case imply that markets have become competitive, with more-efficient firms gaining at the cost of the inefficient in the post-reform era. This also implies prices approaching long-run marginal costs, which means an increase in consumer welfare. The other result of the exercises is that TNCs are able to increase their market share by increasing selling costs more than local firms. This results supports the arguments that TNCs have to incur distribution and market expenditure in gaining local market share and institutional knowledge more than incumbent local firms.[11]

## Competition among TNCs

The above discussion concentrated on competition between TNCs and local incumbents by simplifying their relative advantages. However, the relative advantages of TNCs in intangible assets could be very diverse, differentiating TNCs within an industry. For example, the unique intangible assets of the Japanese TNCs are their managerial and vendor development practices, which were quite distinct from the American and European ones. A TNC's ability to adapt its unique advantages to local markets and institutions and its ability to generate new markets to take full advantage of its unique position determine its relative success. Competition among TNCs could result in convergence in some of their practices with important implications for the evolution of markets and institutions in India. This point is enlarged upon in the following paragraphs, using India's automobile industry as a sample case.

Prior to the mid-1980s, two firms dominated India's automobile sector, producing substandard models with a captive market. The Japanese firm Suzuki entered the Indian industry in 1982 with a joint collaboration with the Indian public sector for production of small cars with a 50:50 equity stake under the brand name of Maruti-Suzuki (MS). The Indian government patronized and protected the venture from new entry until the early 1990s. Within a short period, MS became the largest producer of cars in India, with a market share of 65 percent in 1995, and realized the highest level of cost-efficiency in producing small cars in the world (with one of its low-end cars selling for about $5,000 in 2004). Its success can be attributed to two reasons: adapting to highly price-sensitive local consumers, and transforming the local production organization to utilize its firm-specific unique intangible assets of internal organization and vendor development. It derived its cost advantage by indigenizing close to 70 percent of the production of components, meticulously developing local vendor firms through technology transfer, long-term commitment to contracts, and encouraging spatial concentration of vendors around its plant in the state of Haryana in north India (D'Costa, 1995; Okada, 2004; Tewari, 2005). This, in turn, caused the development of intermediate product markets by transforming supplier relations in the Indian automobile industry in a significant way. This case is a good example to support the proposition that TNCs can induce micro-level changes partially independent of the institutional environment, which, in turn, can influence the evolution of the institutional environment.

In the early 1990s, the government of India liberalized the policy of free entry into the small car segment and allowed fully owned foreign subsidiaries into the automobile sector. This led to the entry of sixteen new TNCs into the industry. However, the government imposed tariff rates of 35 percent on imports of components. The TNCs that were able to adapt to the local market conditions in a rapid manner succeeded in penetrating the Indian market, while the others who failed on this front struggled to get a foothold. Two striking examples are Hyundai and Mitsubishi. Hyundai undertook development of local vendors through technology transfer and thereby reduced its dependence on imports of components.

This, in turn, allowed Hyundai to penetrate the Indian market rapidly both by catering to the expanding market and also by cutting into Maruti-Suzuki's market share in the small-car segment. On the other hand, Mitsubishi introduced a luxury car with high dependence on imports, which led to its relative failure in the Indian market. Ford Motors adopted a mid-path of introducing larger cars, but not the very expensive luxury ones, and undertook the local development of vendors in a slow fashion with a long-term commitment to the local market and also for utilizing its base in India for exports (Tewari, 2005).

Hyundai's strategy involved competing with MS by adopting practices favored by MS, namely, catering to local price-sensitive consumers with cost-efficiency of production. On the other hand, Ford's strategy focused on generating markets for intermediate-range cars with the expectation of long-term changes in income levels of the Indian middle class, who would then move from small cars to the mid-sized cars as their incomes went up. This behavior has resulted in the development of local intermediate product markets both in terms of their emergence and also in terms of improvements in the institutional conditions of contractual relations. In the late 1990s, there was further development of the intermediate input markets with the entry of new TNCs, in all about sixteen of them. Intense competition among TNCs for local markets leads to copying of best practices among them, which, in turn, engenders development of local intermediate input, labor, product markets, and exports of both components and finished products.

## A methodology of observing convergence

I have undertaken a simple statistical exercise in examining the proposition of convergence, which is presented in Table 9. The conceptual methodology is given in Appendix 3. I have taken the case of two firms in the two-wheeler industry as samples – one, Bajaj Auto, a local firm, and one, Hero Honda, a TNC. The reason is that these companies have been competing intensely for a long period ever since 1985, when Honda entered the industry in response to the reforms. Detailed firm-level time-series data for these firms is collected from the CMIE for the period of 1989–2003. The time period is segregated into three segments, each one consisting of five time observations. I measured a set of variables for the two firms. I have taken the means of differences (squared) for each of the time periods and for all the variables between the two firms. If there is a convergence, the values of the means of the variables should decline over the three periods. As shown in Table 9, there had been a significant decline in the differences in relative efficiency of production ($TE$) and corresponding market shares. In the case of the response variables of distribution, advertising and R&D to sales variables, there is an increase in the differences from period 1 to period 2, but there is no noticeable

*Table 9* Convergence: motorcycle industry – Bajaj Auto and Hero Honda

|       | *1989–93*        | *1994–8*         | *1999–2003*      |
|-------|------------------|------------------|------------------|
| TE    | 48.93 (6.22)     | 40.19 (6.72)     | 17.71 (19.46)    |
| MS    | 17.68 (4.25)     | 14.18 (3.6)      | 7.35 (5.92)      |
| DIS   | 0.0016 (0.0008)  | 0.003 (0.001)    | 0.002 (0.001)    |
| ADS   | 0.0067 (0.0063)  | 0.005 (0.005)    | 0.0059 (0.0004)  |
| RDS   | 0.0002 (0.0002)  | 0.0005 (0.0005)  | 0.0004 (0.0001)  |
| PLS   | 1.48 (1.71)      | 2.83 (1.73)      | 2.09 (0.64)      |
| VI    | 7.43 (1.51)      | 8.02 (2.75)      | 4.09 (3.46)      |
| EXS   | 0.046 (0.046)    | 0.013 (0.012)    | 0.024 (0.019)    |
| IMS   | 0.998 (1.72)     | 0.579 (0.423)    | 0.91 (0.71)      |
| AMS   | 0.009 (0.012)    | 0.019 (0.012)    | 0.014 (0.003)    |

Notes
TE    technical efficiency of production
MS    market shares of firms
DIS   distribution expenditure to sales
ADS   direct advertising expenditure to sales
RDS   R&D expenditure to sales
PLS   plant and machinery to sales
VI    vertical integration, value-added/sales
EXS   exports to sales
IMS   imports to sales
AMS   administrative expenditure to sales
Figures in parentheses are standard deviations.

decline from period 2 to period 3. Similar is the case with respect to plant and machinery to sales, administrative expenditure and the organizational choice of vertical integration. The overall statistics show that there had been a noticeable degree of convergence of the basic characteristics of the competing local firm and TNC.

There is evidence for the convergence of the product differentiation strategies of the rival firms in the two-wheeler industry. Prior to the reforms, scooters manufactured by the Indian firm, Bajaj Auto, were predominant in the market. In the post-reforms period, the Japanese firms Honda and Suzuki, in collaboration with local partners, introduced motorcycles using Japanese technology. As mentioned before, Hero Honda grew rapidly, taking market share away from Bajaj. In the middle of the 1990s, consumer preferences shifted away from scooters to motorcycles, giving an advantage to Hero Honda with four-stroke motorcycles. Bajaj and TVS-Suzuki then invested in R&D and developed four-stroke engines, imitating Hero Honda. The TVS Victor and Bajaj Pulsar motorcycle models were able to gain market share at the expense of Honda's Splendor. Honda, on the other hand, was able to break Bajaj and TVS's stranglehold over the economy segment (Patibandla, 2002c). Honda's CD Dawn took the market share from Bajaj's Boxer. By the year 2004, the model sold by all three firms looked quite similar in characteristics and features.

## Joint ventures between TNCs and local firms

One of the mechanisms of diffusion of superior technology and organizational practices of TNCs to local agents is through joint ventures. TNCs form joint ventures with local partners in a developing economy for two reasons: policy stipulations, and economic factors. A joint venture between two parties takes place when there is higher output (value) through joint production than from going alone. In a similar way to the arguments of the theory of the firm, if two firms possess complementary assets, there could be a joint venture or internalization depending on the transaction costs and asymmetric incentives for the investment in the relation-specific assets in the post-contractual stage. As discussed in Chapter 2, Aoki's formalization of the T-form (temporary) of organization is similar to a joint venture in that, when firms face uncertainty in the institutional environment, they may form joint ventures in spite of the contractual hazards of appropriation of each other's proprietary assets. In the present context, one can treat the TNC's assets as the intangible assets and a local firm's assets as country-specific institutional knowledge, and well-established distribution networks.

Diffusion of the best practices of TNCs can take place in joint ventures if the local partner has direct access to them. The issue that follows is that the type of technology and practices a TNC brings into the joint collaboration determines the magnitude of technological spillovers and diffusion. This is a matter of the governance choices of TNCs, which are a function of the local institutional environment. If a TNC finds poor protection of intellectual property and easy appropriation of its intangible assets by local partners and rivals, it may not bring in the best of its technology, but an older vintage. Furthermore, the potential market growth for income-elastic differentiated goods also determines the nature of the technology transferred to local market.

To give an example, the Japanese TNC Honda, which entered the Indian two-wheeler industry in the mid-1980s through a joint venture, retained its R&D activities in Japan. This put the venture in India at a disadvantage with respect to Indian rivals. Later on, Honda branched out as a fully owned subsidiary in India to cater to the rapidly growing Indian market. On the other hand, the Korean automobile TNC Hyundai, which entered the Indian car market in the mid-1990s as a fully owned subsidiary, started to introduce its latest car models into the Indian market and utilizes its production base in India for exports to international markets.

The kind of technology and products brought in by TNCs determines the magnitude of changes in local organizations and institutions. If technologies and organizations brought in by new-entrant TNCs are far superior to those of local incumbents, they have strong implications for the comparative economics of benchmarking and inducement of rapid changes in local practices. On the other hand, older or outdated technologies of TNCs will have weak effects on inducing changes in local organization. The type of technology and products brought into a joint venture by a TNC are determined by how well property rights are defined and protected in the venture, and the ex ante calculations of the partners about the future state of environment.

The partners have to negotiate the equity structure and management control, which, in turn, determines property rights, namely, the control and the residual rights of the respective assets of the partners. A TNC that has equal or greater control rights may have an incentive to bring in the latest technology. As the technology provider has an interest in protecting its property rights in order to prevent a defecting partner from appropriating them, it would be interested in setting elaborate conditions about what is to be transferred, how it would be utilized, and the conditions for the sharing of the returns. As contracts in high-tech industries are highly incomplete, and costs of contract enforcement in developing economies high, a TNC may hold back on transferring technology. In other words, firms forming joint ventures face a fundamental conflict between the desire to learn from the ventures and the need to protect themselves from the opportunistic behavior of partners. One way to deal with it is, to put it in Williamson's transaction cost logic (1983), that firms invest in 'credible commitments' at the ex ante stage. Each one undertakes investments at the ex ante stage so that the break-up of the venture abruptly by any one partner is costly, a similar tactic to taking hostages.

The T-form (temporary) nature of the arrangement is motivated by the fact that TNCs have an interest in acquiring local institutional knowledge through the local partner and a local agent has an interest in acquiring the knowledge of the intangible assets of TNCs. Once the individual objectives are served, joint ventures may not last. (This is, however, not the central issue here, but that of the convergence of best practices through joint ventures.) It is at this stage that ex-ante calculations and the adoption of appropriate strategies by partners matter in determining the magnitude of technology diffusion to the local agent. To illustrate this argument, in the mid-1980s when Indian policy opened up to TNCs with foreign equity stipulations of 40 percent, several Indian agents formed joint ventures with TNCs. However, the equity stipulations have been gradually relaxed in several industries over the years. As TNCs acquired local knowledge, several of them broke the joint ventures to set up their own fully owned ventures. The local agents who had expected this outcome at the ex ante stage of the venture had built up their technological capabilities to be able to compete with the independent operations of TNCs. In such a scenario, local agents are able to converge towards the superior practices of TNCs. The others who did not foresee this at the initial stages lamented at the time of break-ups. These possible outcomes are illustrated with a few case studies.

## Case studies of joint ventures

In the year 2000, there were about 1,300 joint ventures between TNCs and local firms. The well-known names are Maruti-Suzuki in the car industry, Hero-Honda and TVS-Suzuki in the two-wheeler industry, and Modi-Xerox in the electronics industry. A qualitative analysis of a few of the case studies shows that in some cases the joint ventures led to the development of local partners at the time of their break-up.[12]

### *Maruti-Suzuki*

As briefly discussed earlier, the joint collaboration between Suzuki and the government public sector is probably the most successful collaboration in India. Suzuki benefited immensely from the collaboration because the government of India patronized the firm by giving it a monopoly status in the production of small cars for about ten years. On the other hand, Suzuki made technology transfer both to the Indian subsidiary and also to local vendor firms to indigenize the production of the components to the extent of 70 percent. However, it kept production of crucial components such as gearboxes at the home unit under the logic of quality control, which led to a dispute in the mid-1990s between the partners. Nevertheless, the collaboration still continues successfully, although the Indian government undertook privatization by issuing equity to the Indian public in 2003 and diluting its stake to 26 percent.

Although Suzuki benefited from the collaboration with the Indian government, there was one disadvantage of the institutional arrangement. At the time of the setting-up of the plant, the economic efficiency criteria suggested locating the plant closer to the coast; but political interference caused it to be sited in the central part of northern India. The firm generated a highly dynamic cluster of component producers, spatially close to its plant. As mentioned before, policy liberalization in the early 1990s led to the entry of several new players. The new entrants could decide on the location of plants purely on the basis of economic efficiency criteria. Once the new entrants establish themselves, Maruti Udyog will be at a disadvantage in competing with the later entrants regarding the locational asset specificity. A simple reason is that undertaking exports and imports from the coast is less costly than from the land-locked areas.

The interesting feature of Maruti's operations is that it played an active role in developing small local supplier firms by forming equity joint ventures with several of them. It facilitated joint ventures between local suppliers and its suppliers in Japan to enable technology transfer and the upgrading of local vendor firms. Apart from this, MS diffused its organizational practices to the supplier firms in India. It encouraged and helped them to adopt lean production practices and its own organizational practices of teamwork and employee suggestion schemes. Several of these organizational practices diffused to local component producers and assemblers such as TELCO (Okada, 2004).

## TVS-Suzuki

The TVS-Suzuki joint venture was formed in 1982 between the TVS Motor Company of India and Suzuki of Japan for producing two-wheelers. TVS was originally a leading manufacturer of automobile components. Under the joint venture, Suzuki was expected to provide technology. Over the years, the venture became quite successful, with the firm gaining market share in motorcycles, scooters, and especially mopeds. In 2001, the joint venture broke up, with the local partner buying out Suzuki's stake. Suzuki's technological contribution in the venture was mainly in two-stroke motorcycles. The local firm invested significant amounts in R&D, not only to learn Suzuki's technology but also to develop new models independently for the Indian market. Its most successful products in the moped segment were developed indigenously without any technology transfer from Suzuki. In the early 2000s, the company launched a four-stroke motorcycle, which was also developed indigenously. In 2003, the company was awarded the coveted Deming Prize for Total Quality Management and has become a world-class producer of two-wheelers. This case shows that the local partner developed technological and marketing capabilities by the time of break-up in 2001, and is in a position to compete effectively with the TNC that pulled out of the venture.

## Hero-Honda

The Hero-Honda joint venture was started in 1984 between the Indian firm Hero and the Japanese Honda to produce four-stroke motorcycles, with equal equity stakes. The agreement was that Honda would supply the technology and the designs from its home operations to the Indian subsidiary. The venture has been highly successful. Within a few years, it has become a major player in the Indian market, taking away a major chunk of the market share from the leading Indian firm Bajaj, and became the largest producer of two-wheelers in the world by early 2000.

However, the underlying characteristics of the venture show that there is significant asymmetry between the partners, with Honda having total control over technology. The local partner did not, or was not allowed by the TNC partner to, invest in R&D and was left with total dependence on Honda for design and technology support. As the competitors, Bajaj and TVS, gained ground in the motorcycle market by developing indigenous products for the needs of the local market, Hero-Honda's dependence on Honda in Japan placed it in a position of disadvantage in its ability to respond quickly to local market conditions. In the early 2000s, Honda has set up a fully owned subsidiary in India with the agreement that it would not produce motorcycles until 2004. As the local partner did not develop its own technological capabilities, it will be in an unfavorable position to be able to compete with the defected TNC and other competitors. This is a case of a TNC making sure that the local partner would not become a serious competitor in the future. It also demonstrates the myopic outlook of the local partner at the ex ante stage, and is an example of too great an initial market success of the venture leading to complacency on the part of the local agent.

## Joint ventures in the financial services

The following analysis of case studies of joint ventures in the financial markets illustrates how joint ventures between a local bank and TNCs has generated and expanded new markets.

### *State Bank of India (SBI) and GE in the credit cards market*

In early 1998, two joint ventures were formed between a large Indian bank, the State Bank of India (SBI), and a globally established TNC, GE Capital, to market, issue, and service credit cards under the name 'SBI Cards'. One was SBI Cards & Payment Services, which markets and distributes SBI Cards in India. The other was GE Capital Business Processes Management Services, which handles the technology and processing needs of SBI Cards in India. This venture leverages the brand equity, customer relationship, and wide network of SBI with GE Capital's technology, processes, risk management, retail marketing, and service capabilities to offer credit card products. In this joint venture, the brand name that has been used belongs to the Indian bank, while the TNC provides technical support.

At present, SBI is the largest commercial bank in India, with a country-wide network of 9,019 branches and employing about 214,845 people. It commands one-fifth of deposits and loans of all scheduled commercial banks in the country. GE Capital is the financial services arm of the General Electric conglomerate. GE Capital Services is a global diversified financial services company with twenty-eight distinct businesses. GE Capital Services India was established in October 1993 as a wholly owned subsidiary of GE Capital Services. It has two types of operations in India, one catering to Indian financial markets, and the other encompassing back-end technical support units for its global operations. The motivation behind the latter operation is to take advantage of low-cost skilled and semi-skilled workforce, proficient in English, for its global operations. GE Capital's Indian market focus includes consumer finance, commercial equipment finance (including truck financing), and commercial finance.

When the SBI–GE venture was launched in 1998, there were an estimated 2.5 million cards in circulation in India, with foreign banks such as

Citibank accounting for 40 percent, and Standard Chartered, HSBC, and ANZ claiming a chunk of the rest. These banks have concentrated their card business on high-income groups in a few large metropolitan areas. With its countrywide banking network of approximately 14,000 branches, SBI targeted middle-income groups, most of whom were already its customers. The company underpriced its credit card annual fee at Rs 500, compared to the industry average of Rs 750. Then, it leveraged its back-end operations with GE Capital to ensure that applications were processed within two weeks, beating the industry norm of five weeks. The back-end technical processing support of GE Capital facilitates fast and efficient bill processing, which reduces the incidence of customer default. Within sixteen months of the launch, SBI Cards achieved a customer base of 0.25 million in twenty-five cities. In 2000, 0.9 million cards had been issued, covering about forty-one large and small cities across the country.

### SBI and Cardiff joint venture in the insurance market

SBI established the joint venture with Cardiff in mid-2001. Cardiff owns a 26 percent equity stake, while SBI holds the rest. Cardiff will play a silent role in the partnership, although it will take a key part in devising products for the joint venture that are specifically targeted at bank customers. The joint venture in India is marketed under SBI's brand name, SBI-Life Insurance, but not under the brand name of Cardiff. Through this joint venture, SBI intended to provide a number of products to suit different segments of the population in the Indian market, given its large network of branches and banking customer base in the country.

The important point from the illustration of these joint ventures is that they have generated and expanded financial markets, especially for middle-income groups. In both cases, the local bank's brand name is utilized instead of that of the TNC. A major reason is that SBI has a strong brand image and a nationwide network, and also the public may trust the local bank more than a foreign bank with safeguarding their deposits. The main aspect of this case is the generation of markets, which benefits the consumers; a second issue is the spillover of the practices of TNCs to the local bank. The latter aspect involves the ability of SBI to learn the back-end service technology of GE and to internalize the intangible assets of the insurance product services of Cardiff. It is difficult at this point to speculate whether these joint ventures are likely to continue in the long term, because they could become natural collaborations of firms specializing in different branches instead of temporary arrangements for appropriating each other's technology or intangibles. However, it is more likely that SBI, with its strong national brand and network, is in a better position to learn the back-end service technology of GE over time and break the joint venture.

As mentioned before, joint ventures are basically temporary types (or T-forms) of arrangements and most of them break up once the objectives of one of the partners are served. In the case of new-entrant TNCs and local agents, the joint ventures are motivated by the fact that TNCs use local agents to get access to local institutional knowledge and distribution, and local agents get access to the TNCs' technology. Both partners should therefore take these calculations into account at the ex ante stage of the ventures and adopt strategies in conformity with their objectives. When local firms build their technological capabilities through the venture, there will be a degree of convergence in terms of local firms moving up on the technology ladder. This will put them in a position to compete with the erstwhile TNC partners, should the joint venture break up.

## Intermediate-input markets

The following discussion deals with the issue of the convergence of practices of new-entrant TNCs and local firms in dealing with intermediate input suppliers. In several Indian industries, subcontracting activity between large final-goods producers and small- and medium-scale intermediate inputs producers has been prevalent since the mid-1970s. As discussed in Chapter 3, small-firm component producers operate in the unorganized labor markets with the flexibility to hire and fire workers, which helps them to keep labor costs low. Large final-goods producers operate in the organized labor markets and face policy constraints in replacing inefficient workers with the more efficient. Apart from this, several component industries were reserved for small-scale firms (for example, bicycle parts). In order to overcome the institutional constraints in the labor market, several large firms started increasingly to resort to subcontracting production of labor-intensive intermediate inputs to small- and medium-scale firms. The contractual relations between the large and small firms were highly asymmetrical, with large assemblers being in positions of greater bargaining power (Nagaraj, 1984; Patibandla, 1988, 1994). Consequently, large assemblers used to extract maximum rents and pass on the costs of uncertainty to small component producers.

The issue that follows is whether both assemblers and suppliers realize higher productivity if the relation is based on cooperation rather than being an asymmetrical relationship! If such is the case, policy changes or exogenous effects that induce collective efficiency can bring about improvements in the institutional environment. If policy reforms cause the entry of new players into final-goods production, monopsony power of the buyers in intermediate input markets goes down, thereby increasing the bargaining position of the suppliers. Furthermore, the new entry of final-goods producers increases product market competition, which drives firms to search for productivity-enhancing practices, both internal and external to a firm.

There can be instances where exogenous effects such as the foreign practices of new-entrant TNCs may engender forces that facilitate collective efficiency and thereby improve the overall productivity of both buyers and suppliers. This is illustrated by the case of the Japanese TNC Maruti-Suzuki, which induced improvements in supplier relations in the automobile industry in the early and mid-1980s. Later on, further improvements started to take place with the entry of new players from the mid-1990s. Buyer and supplier relations based on cooperative arrangements can reduce the constraints of capital market imperfections and market transaction costs to the small supplier firms and aid technology transfer from the buyers to the suppliers.

As is well known, Japanese automakers revolutionized the organization of production by adopting lean production practices which consist of four elements: transformation of design, restructuring of assembler–supplier relations, reorganization of production along the lines of just-in-time (JIT) delivery, and total quality management (Gulyani, 2001). Maruti-Suzuki brought in these practices into Indian industry. It was able to develop a local supplier base rapidly because small local firms that could function as suppliers already existed, but their technological capability was below its requirements (Okada, 2004). It brought about a significant transfer of technology and continuous technical assistance to its key suppliers. It arranged joint ventures between local suppliers and Suzuki's suppliers in Japan. It also helped them with capital by holding equity stakes in about a dozen such joint venture suppliers. Maruti encouraged and pushed the suppliers to improve quality, price, and delivery and forced some of them to adopt JIT. Consequently, several of the component producers achieved performance levels (quality and productivity) of world standards, and have become internationally competitive and undertake exports.

At present, Maruti has about 400 suppliers in India. Of them, 248 are located in proximity to Maruti's plant. In order to implement its lean production practices under the inefficient infrastructure conditions in India, Maruti encouraged many of its suppliers to locate close to its plant in Gurgaon in north India. The disadvantage for the supplier firms was that they had to invest in location-specific assets, which locks them into Maruti's buying and imposes the risk of opportunism by the buyer. The costs of this risk could be significant, especially in the case of Maruti, because, as mentioned earlier, the company is located in a land-locked area with locational disadvantages. However, over a period of time, Maruti and its suppliers in the vicinity have generated agglomeration economies, which prompted other TNCs, such as Honda and Daewoo, to locate nearby so as to tap into the suppliers of Maruti. Moreover, as Maruti's suppliers became technologically advanced, many of them diversified to produce components to other assemblers in India, and to export markets.[13]

The diffusion of Maruti's organizational practices to other local supplier and assembler firms was given a stimulus with the 1991 reforms, which led to the entry of new TNCs. The increased competitive conditions in the product and input markets forced companies to search for productivity- and quality-enhancing practices in Indian industry. For example, the Tata group's TELCO, which is a major player in both the production of components and final goods, was a vertically integrated firm with 'arm's length' relations with suppliers. TELCO started to change its supplier relations in 1996 by creating a special unit, called the Supplier Quality Improvement Group, to provide technical assistance to suppliers and improve product quality for its indigenous development of a small car (Okada, 2004).

An even more striking example is the Indian firm Mahindra and Mahindra (M&M), which was a leading producer of commercial vehicles and tractors. M&M achieved high cost-efficiency within a short period by adopting Maruti's practices of outsourcing. In 1994, the company undertook a major restructuring and increasingly adopted outsourcing of its components and sub-assemblies to local suppliers. It embarked on the indigenous development of the Scorpio van by purchasing the Italian design. The company developed a network of 110 local suppliers and pushed the outsourcing policy to high levels, outsourcing a major part of its component requirements. Consequently, it was able to launch the van at a competitive price and with a great degree of market success (Sutton, 2004).

The cases of Hyundai and Ford are interesting. They located their plants in the coastal region of south India in Chennai city in Tamil Nadu state. Their location has sowed the seeds for the development of a vibrant cluster of component producers. The location of the plants close to the port of Chennai facilitates their long-term objective of using India as a base for exports. Second, the state of Tamil Nadu has a well-developed base of engineering industries, which is a significant source for developing supplier firms.

Hyundai adopted outsourcing practices similar to Maruti and was able to indigenize the production of components to the extent of 70 percent by developing supplier firms in and around Chennai. There are around seventy suppliers in the vicinity, out of which sixteen are Korean component suppliers of Hyundai who set up their plants jointly with local partners. Hyundai facilitated technology transfer to the suppliers to enhance quality and cost-efficiency in order to compete with Maruti in the small-car market. Within a short period, it has been able to achieve a high degree of local market success and undertake exports from the Indian plant to the home market and markets in other developing and developed economies. TNCs such as Ford entered the Indian industry by encouraging some of their home (international) supplier firms, such as Visteon, to locate their plants in India. GM and Daimler Chrysler also brought in a few of their supplier firms from overseas. Unlike Hyundai, Ford undertook the development of local supplier firms in a slow manner to maintain

*Table 10* Auto-component production and exports: India

| Year | Value of output (US$ million) | Value of exports (US$ million) | Exports/output % |
|------|-------------------------------|--------------------------------|------------------|
| 1997 | 2,406 | 299 | 12.4 |
| 1998 | 2,599 | 314 | 12.0 |
| 1999 | 3,271 | 366 | 11.1 |
| 2000 | 3,571 | 541 | 15.1 |
| 2001 | 4,203 | 555 | 13.2 |

Source: Sutton, 2004.

quality standards for supplying the local market and for exporting from India.

The entry of TNCs into the component industry is allowed under the policy stipulation that they export 50 percent of their output. These policy stipulations and the achievement of international quality standards have made the TNC supplier firms become major exporters of components. As shown in Table 10, since the late 1990s India's exports of auto components started to grow in a rapid fashion. Out of the top ten component exporters, all were TNC joint ventures, while three form part of a single domestic group, the TVS Group (Sutton, 2004).

The evolution of the outsourcing practices of both TNCs and local assembler firms led to the emergence of a three-tier system of supplier firms. The first tier includes the large TNC joint ventures and local firms supplying to the assemblers. The second tier comprises the small- and medium-scale firms supplying to the first-tier firms, and at the bottom are the small firms supplying to the second-tier firms. The diffusion of best practices permeated quickly to the first-tier firms, but not to the ones at the bottom. In order to realize high quality standards and cost-efficiency, the first-tier firms increased the capital and skill intensity of production, thereby gradually eliminating bottom-tier suppliers.

Sutton (2004) observes,

> Underlying the rapid advance of first-tier producers towards world-class levels of quality has been a rapid absorption and diffusion of those working practices which originated in Japan in the 1960s and '70s and became standard in the US and Europe during the 1990s. These include a strong emphasis on cooperation and team-work, the steady improvement of quality through diagnosis of sources of defects by groups of operatives, and the immediate implementation of strategies to pre-empt recurrences ('quality circles'), the organization of a tightly coordinated inflow of raw materials and parts and the outflow of finished products, thus minimizing inventory costs and so on.

Sutton, in comparing the auto-component industries of China and India, finds that the productivity of Indian firms is significantly higher, with all of the top three firms being Indian.

This provides evidence for one of the propositions of this chapter with regard to the diffusion of best practices, some of which are exogenous to the local institutional environment, which triggers institutional change. One of the elements of the institutional change is the improvement in the bargaining position of supplier firms. Tewari (2005), based on her field study of supplier firms, observes that first-tier suppliers have become discriminating towards getting into a supply relation with assemblers by taking account of volumes, the size and nature of investment, and the price range of assemblers. It is interesting to note that it is the larger firms within the component industry, who could adopt capital-intensive technologies in a labor-abundant country, who have been able to improve their bargaining position with respect to assemblers. Furthermore, adapting to the inefficient local infrastructure conditions required the TNCs to develop supplier firms' agglomeration into clusters. Cluster activity can result in collective efficiency and reduce the transaction costs of contract formulation and enforcement through repeated interactions.

## Competition in the labor markets and the convergence of practices

In this part, I examine the development of labor markets in response to the entry of TNCs. The main proposition to be examined is whether wage rates and the organizational practices with respect to workers in TNCs and local firms tend to converge. It is qualitatively observed that TNCs pay higher wages for a given skilled worker than local firms in developing economies (Patibandla and Petersen, 2004). In the microeconomics textbook case, firms are taken to be price-takers in the labor market, and by this logic it is irrational for any firm to pay higher wage than others. One explanation from development economics literature is the efficiency wage hypothesis – higher wages elicit higher productivity and reduce the costs of attrition. In the present context, one of the ways to resolve this is by taking into account differences in technology and organization between TNCs and local firms. If TNCs have superior technology and organization to local firms, they realize higher productivity for any skill levels. By paying higher wages, they attract skilled workers from local firms. The rational response for local firms would be to strive to realize similar productivity levels to TNCs in order to pay similar wages. This requires adopting similar technology and organizational practices to those of TNCs. If such is the case, the organizational practices of human resource management should converge between local firms and TNCs, which, in turn, will have implications for the evolution of the institutional environment. This outcome is likely in those labor markets in which the endowment of skilled labor is relatively scarce and there is intense competition among firms for good skills. It is unlikely to take place in Indian labor markets for unskilled and semi-skilled labor owing to the abundant availability of labor (Patibandla and Petersen, 2002, 2004).

As discussed in chapter 3, labor markets in India are segmented into the organized and the unorganized sectors, with different institutional environment conditions. The unorganized labor markets have flexibility in hiring and firing workers with little or no benefits or social security, unlike the organized markets. One aspect of the evolution of labor markets that needs to be studied is whether the fragmentation of labor markets is reduced in terms of increasing flexibility and the adoption of employee benefits, and whether the qualitative behavior of firms in the labor market changes in conjunction with changes in the institutional environment conditions.

## The labor market in the automobile industry

As discussed earlier, the entry of Japanese TNCs into the automobile industry resulted in some degree of convergence in subcontracting and organizational practices. Product and labor market competition and the convergence of some of the practices of TNCs and local firms in the intermediate inputs markets have implications for the labor market.

An increase in the number of producers increases the demand for skilled and semi-skilled labor. An increase in product market competition results in firms adopting productivity-enhancing technological and organizational practices, which, in turn, can have contrary effects on the demand for labor. If efforts to improve productivity result in firms adopting capital-intensive technologies, as illustrated before in the case of auto component industry, it results in a decline in the demand for labor or necessitates the replacement of semi-skilled labor by skilled labor.

Okada (2004) from her extensive fieldwork shows that in the late 1990s in the automobile industry, the quality of jobs improved at both the assembler and supplier levels with respect to an increase in wage rates, increased worker participation in production processes, and increased skill-training opportunities. However, employment did not keep pace with the growth in output, as even component producers increasingly adopted capital-intensive technologies.

As discussed earlier, Maruti-Suzuki started the process of change in organizational and supplier-relation practices in the Indian industry. The first dimension of this change was the payment of higher wages than local firms to skilled and semi-skilled workers on efficiency wage grounds of developing employee loyalty and a low turnover of skilled workers. As a part of its lean production organization, it adopted quality controls, employee training, employee participation, and teamwork. As a result, for the period of 1985–6 to 1995–6, employment grew at the annual average of 5.8 percent, while value-added per worker grew at 27.4 percent. Faced with this growth of worker-productivity of the TNC, local firms had to adopt similar practices to be able to compete. Maruti's organizational practices, such as internal training, teamwork, employee suggestions and rewards, and technology transfer to workers of supplier firms, diffused to a notable degree to local firms such as TELCO, and Mahindra and Mahindra. However, although wages paid by local firms increased in the 1990s, especially to skilled workers and managers, Maruti's wage rate still remains higher than the industry norm (Okada, 2004).

Okada's study shows that the assembler firms initially employ casual labor in order to achieve a degree of flexibility but they are increasingly being replaced or removed as firms improve productivity by adopting capital- and skill-intensive technologies. Similarly, in the component industry, the third-tier small firms, which operate in the unorganized markets with labor-intensive technologies, are being gradually eliminated over the years. In the case of the first-tier and second-tier firms, there has been an increasing adoption of capital-intensive technology and the employment of educated workers (graduates and engineers). The evolution of labor markets has been tilting more in favor of skilled workers, while the role of semi-skilled and unskilled labor is declining in the industries, with the increasing adoption of global standards of productivity and quality. Direct employment of unskilled labor has declined in specific industries. On the other hand, if the expansion of the capital-intensive and service industries leads to their increasing linkages with the semi- and unskilled service industries, it could result in an increase in the employment of unskilled workers. There is some qualitative evidence for this in the software and business process outsourcing (BPO) industries in India. Their expansion has resulted in an enhanced demand for support services.

### The labor market in the software industry

India's software industry presents a very interesting case for understanding labor market dynamics in a context of globalization through exports and the increasing presence of TNCs. India has developed quite a few large, internationally competitive software firms. As discussed in Chapter 4, India's comparative advantage in low-cost, English-speaking manpower has led, since the mid-1980s, to the large-scale entry of TNCs catering to their home and global markets. Competition among TNCs and local firms for local product markets has been very marginal. However, the competition between them in the labor market, especially for high-end skills, has been intense, generating positive dynamics in that market. The previous propositions with regard to wage and organizational behavior of firms are tested for this industry with the following qualitative analysis, a part of which is based on my fieldwork for my paper with Petersen in World Development (Patibandla and Petersen, 2002, 2004).

In the early and mid-1980s, there were a few Indian firms and TNCs undertaking low-end programming, coding, and data-feeding activities. The large pool of skilled labor and high levels of market concentration engendered a high degree of monopsony power to firms. Consequently, both TNCs and local firms underutilized skilled labor, using it for mundane tasks catering to overseas markets. In other words, firms could afford to use skilled labor far below its potential productivity owing to imperfect product and factor markets in the Indian economy. However, the market structure started to change in the late 1980s. As mentioned earlier, the entry and successful operation of TI in India gave an impetus to the entry and expansion of a large number of TNCs, mainly utilizing low-cost skilled labor to support their home market operations.

The rapid increase in the number of firms (both TNCs and local firms) increased the demand for skilled labor and resulted in an annual increase in the wage rate of 30 percent throughout the nineties. The increase in wage rate results in two types of response at the firm level. One is the utilization of labor in accordance with its potential productivity. The other is the differentiation of skilled labor in accordance with differences in skill levels, whereby tasks are assigned in line with the potential productivity of differently skilled workers. My field study in the early 2000s in the cities of Bangalore and Hyderabad demonstrated that as market structure became more competitive in the labor market, firms assigned tasks in accordance with skill levels and paid higher wages for better skills. The first aspect implies change in organizational practices. In the context of increasing wage rate, it is more imperative for local firms to upgrade technology and organization than it is for TNCs. In the late 1990s, Indian firms, especially the larger ones, made systematic efforts to upgrade their organizational capabilities by imitating practices introduced by TNCs, to improve productivity and retain skilled manpower. In other words, increased competition in the labor market for skilled labor drives firms to adopt the best practices of benchmarking so as to attract and retain high-skilled labor.

## Capital markets and convergence

While discussing the competitive dynamics between TNCs and local firms, I mentioned that one of the sources of firm-level relative advantage could be the cost of capital. TNCs' ability to tap global financial markets provides them with a relative advantage over local firms in a developing economy. Local incumbents have to adopt strategies to overcome this relative disadvantage. Leading from this is the question about whether their strategies result in the convergence of costs of capital in the long run. India's capital markets are subject to a gamut of complex institutional arrangements. Here, I confine the discussion to the organized capital markets. The changes in capital markets and costs of capital are governed by both the policy changes at micro and macro level and changes in the qualitative behavior of firms. The main focus, here, is on the latter aspect.

The theory of financial markets shows that different firms may end up paying different prices for capital in both the bond and equity markets owing to risk and liquidity premiums, even if they operate in a similar institutional environment. A firm which is perceived to undertake high-risk investments pays a higher capital price. Furthermore, a firm that operates in a less liquid market pays a higher capital price than a firm that operates in more liquid capital markets. The liquidity of markets is determined by the development level of financial markets in terms of the transaction costs incurred by investors and borrowers. A TNC which operates in highly liquid developed-country markets such as the US has access to capital at a lower price than firms in India. Within the Indian capital markets, larger and more-established players have better access to capital than newer or smaller firms (Patibandla, 1998).

As discussed in Chapters 3 and 4, the large Indian corporate houses had privileged access to capital through their capture of the government financial institutions. Once a promoter secured an industrial license, they received full funding from the financial institutions without having to stake a single rupee of their own. The risk of failure and the personal cost of capital were both low because product markets were non-competitive, resulting in monopoly profits. On the other hand, the prevailing bankruptcy laws constrained financial institutions from making claims on the assets of loss-making companies. Although, loans were given at concessional interest rates, the interest costs of capital were higher than the world market because of the closed capital markets in the pre-reforms period. But in the post-reforms period of the 1990s, the importance of public financial institutions started to decline because of the drainage of government funds for subsidizing the non-performing loans of the institutions. This, in turn, put pressure on the large firms to tap alternative capital markets owing to increased competition in the product markets.

An important element of the development of local capital markets is equity joint ventures between local firms and TNCs. As discussed in Chapter 1, in the case of China, the Chinese private firms established equity joint ventures with TNCs to overcome capital availability constraints and high costs of capital (Huang, 2002). In the case of the Indian corporate sector, most joint ventures, as discussed earlier, were formed to tap the intangible assets, and the equity arrangements were more a question of defining efficient control rights between the local and foreign partners. Several large incumbents (such as Bajaj, TELCO, and Mahindra and Mahindra) who did not want to give up their control rights set up technology license arrangements but not equity joint ventures. When firms formed equity joint ventures, the tendency was for TNCs and local firms to put in equal or unequal stakes, covering a portion of the capital structure, and the rest was raised both from government financial institutions and through a limited equity issue to the public. Several of the joint ventures broke up over the years, with TNCs setting up their fully owned subsidiaries. This means that the local partner firms have to compete with the defected TNCs, and one of the asymmetric relative advantages of TNCs is the cost of capital.

The issue here is the qualitative behavior of local firms in overcoming the capital cost disadvantage with respect to the competing TNCs, and its implications for the evolution of capital markets. One strategy for Indian firms could be to improve their functioning in Indian capital markets. Since capital costs include transaction costs incurred by both the lenders and borrowers, apart from the opportunity costs of capital, a reduction in the transaction costs of capital markets would also help improve the liquidity of the market. One of the ways of reducing the transaction costs of investors is to improve disclosures by companies. This gives positive signals to investors regarding good corporate governance and low agency costs. Although it involves costs to companies in terms of adopting good accounting standards, the long-run benefits can outweigh the costs.

There was an increasing presence of foreign institutional investors in Indian capital markets. FIIs have a two-way effect on the improvements of capital costs to firms. One is that firms can attract investment from FIIs by being efficient and adopting good disclosures. A second is that, once FIIs invest in specific firms, they monitor them and ensure that the firms improve their performance. In other words, for firms to raise capital in the more competitive markets, they have to invest in better corporate governance, which improves their efficiency. Another important dimension of the qualitative behavior of firms is that quite a few Indian firms branched out into tapping the capital markets of the developed economies, such as Global Depository Receipts (GDR) and American Depository Receipts (ADRs) to get access to low-cost capital. Registering in these markets requires the high costs of adopting global accounting standards. Therefore, the larger among the Indian firms, which are able to invest in the additional costs, are the ones that have succeeded in these markets.

By 2004, the government and the Reserve Bank of India implemented a series of policy changes in reforming the Indian banking sector and reducing the transaction costs of deposits and loans. Apart from this, they also implemented policies such as a reduction in the reserve requirements of banks to reduce real interest rates. Consequently, real interest rates in India declined significantly, despite large government budget deficits (Rajan and Shah, 2003). One reason for this outcome is the lobbying of the organized industrial sector for rationalization of the costs of capital. Furthermore, the Indian middle class has become an important political constituency. The consumer boom and the housing market needs of the middle class also prompted the government to implement measures to reduce interest rates on loans. Apart from the government banks, several multinational financial institutions, such as HSBC and GE, have entered the Indian capital markets for consumer and corporate financing. Thanks to all these measures, capital costs are being pushed to international levels.

## Feedback effects on the evolution of markets and institutions

The analysis, so far, traced out the competitive dynamics between TNCs and local firms in the product, intermediate input, labor, and capital markets and qualitatively tested the proposition of convergence of best practices. In the following, I bring forth explicitly different elements of the evolution of markets and institutions as outcomes of competitive dynamics.

The analysis has focused on TNCs for two main reasons. One is that most new entrants in the post-reform era are TNCs and local established players branching out into different areas, mostly through joint ventures with TNCs. There have been very few demonstrated cases of entrepreneurial dynamism exhibited by absolutely new entrants succeeding in a significant way in the Indian industry except for a few cases, such as Infosys in the software industry, Bharat Biotech and Biocon in the biotech industry, and Air Deccan in the low-cost airlines. Part of the reason for the lack of entrepreneurial dynamism is that the institutional environment in India is still not conducive for new entrants to succeed. The capital markets are still underdeveloped and markets still impose high transaction costs. There is, however, a small and increasing presence of venture capital in a few high-technology areas such as software and biotechnology, which, in the long run, may generate entrepreneurial activity.[14]

The second reason for the focus on TNCs, as mentioned earlier, is that if TNCs bring in technologies and organization far superior to those prevailing in India, it has important effects on the evolution of markets and institutions, especially if they diffuse to local firms. Although TNCs adapt their governance to the local institutional environment, some of their practices could be independent of the prevailing institutional environment. These practices will have significant implications for the evolution of institutions. The example that was given earlier was the supplier relation model adopted by Maruti-Suzuki that transformed the Indian automobile industry.

As defined in Chapter 2, the evolution of markets is seen as product and input prices approaching their long-run marginal costs (opportunity costs) and the emergence of new markets. I trace out these outcomes of the competitive dynamics in the following paragraphs.

The econometric results show a statistically significant positive association between the market share of firms and production efficiency, as reported earlier, which implies prices approaching long-run marginal costs. A decline in prices increases the real incomes of consumers, which, in turn, enlarges their consumption basket and also creates surplus savings for investment. The relationship between advertising and markets can be seen as the emergence of markets for information. The theory of information economics shows that one of the ways of avoiding the problem of adverse selection of low-quality products flooding the market owing to informational asymmetry is through signaling by sellers. Spence (1976) shows that product warranties can be a means of signaling of quality of products and advertising is one of the means of providing information about quality and warranties. In other words, the transaction costs associated with assessing the product attributes decrease as a consequence of competitive rivalry. In conjunction, advertising, building distribution networks, and product warranties together can eliminate inefficient markets. To give an example, prior to the entry and expansion of Maruti-Suzuki in the automobile industry, the supply of low-quality spurious parts was rampant all over the country. Maruti, by developing a nationwide service network, eliminated most of the spurious component market in India by obliging their customers to deal only with authorized service vendors. Other producers adopted this practice, which has almost eliminated the market for bogus parts.

Another offshoot of competitive dynamics is the emergence of the market for consumer finance. Competitive dynamics enlarges the product basket and real incomes of consumers. The resultant consumer boom has led to the emergence of several local and multinational financial institutions and banks catering to the financing of consumer durables and housing markets. Furthermore, the cases of the joint ventures between SBI and GE, and SBI and Cardiff, show that the joint ventures between well-established local banks and TNCs in the financial services sector generated and expanded markets for financial services, especially for middle-income groups who were left out of the market previously for services such as credit cards. The incidence of high agency costs associated with moral hazard and adverse selection through informational imperfections is more dominant in the financial markets than in the other markets. This, in turn, can block the emergence and expansion of financial markets such as insurance. SBI, with its large network of branches and experience with local customers, in conjunction with the back-end technical processing of GE Capital, is able to reduce adverse selection costs and expand the credit card and insurance markets.

In the case of intermediate input markets, as illustrated by the auto component industry, the bargaining position of supplier firms in the formulation and enforcement of long – term contracts improved significantly in the post-reform period. In other words, the transaction costs of contracts of supplier firms declined significantly in comparison to the pre-reforms era. However, as the supplier firms have become more capital- and skill-intensive, the role of small third-tier suppliers has diminished.

The improvements in supplier relations (institutional change) have led to an increase in the quality of output and productivity of the supplier firms, which, in turn, has contributed to export competitiveness and market expansion.

The qualitative evidence in the labor markets demonstrates that the wage rate of skilled labor increased significantly, especially in the internationally oriented industries, such as software and automobiles. On the other hand, the capital price has gone down. This result is similar to the predictions of the general equilibrium trade theory of comparative advantage. The wage increase can be traced to two main factors: an increase in the number of firms, which reduces the monopsony power of few buyers in the input markets, and thereby improves the bargaining position of labor; and improvements in labor productivity. In the case of the automobile industry, the process of increase in productivity was initiated by Maruti, which adopted efficiency wage practice and the development of supplier firms through long-term contracts and technology transfer. The supplier firms, especially the first- and second-tier firms, improved their productivity and have become increasingly export-oriented. Export competitiveness required the adoption of world-standard technology and organizational practices, which means that Indian firms have narrowed the technology gap with the advanced economies.

Similar outcomes took place in the case of the software industry with one major difference: while the auto component industry became internationally competitive thanks to a strong base in local demand, the software industry did not have a local market base. This meant that while product and labor market competitive conditions operated in the case of the auto component industry, in the case of the software industry it is competition in the labor markets that has been the underlying driving force. The increase in the number of TNCs and local firms put upward pressure on wages, which, in turn, induced local firms to improve technology and organization to augment workers' productivity. Irrespective of the large increase in the volume of exports (output), the wage rate of lower-end skilled labor remains lower in India than in the advanced trading economies (for example, the US), because of the abundant supply of semi-skilled labor in India. Higher-end skilled labor is paid a relatively higher wage rate owing to its relative scarcity.

In the case of capital markets, a series of policy changes and firm-level qualitative behavior led to improvements in the institutional arrangements (which, in turn, improved the liquidity of markets), and a decline in capital price. In order to raise capital, both domestically and internationally, Indian corporations had to invest in improvements in disclosure and corporate governance, which, in turn, augmented the efficiency of firms (by reducing agency costs) and resulted in an increase in the participation of investors in equity markets.

The interesting aspect of the above discussion is how competitive dynamics alters the interests of different groups and thereby contributes to institutional change. Competition among local firms and TNCs benefits consumers at the cost of monopoly incumbents. In the long run, the incumbents who have been able to survive and compete with TNCs are better off compared to the pre-reforms period, as their increased productivity expands markets and opportunities in both local and export markets. Another outcome is that the decline in interest rates benefits the corporations, but at the cost of households with savings. The improvements in the protection of investors' interests in the capital markets are implemented to protect large institutional investors and the large number of middle-class investors. It has mutual benefits for both investors and borrowers by reducing transaction costs, bringing about improvements in corporate governance, and thereby increasing the liquidity of the market. In other words, the institutional change that has improved the property rights of investors in the equity markets benefits both the investors and the corporations.

However, the government of India so far (2005) has not adopted a systematic competition policy. The objective of competition policy is to restrain the anti-competitive conduct of firms – any behavior that is detrimental to consumers in terms of increasing prices above long-run marginal costs, and misinformation and behavior that blocks the entry of efficient firms and eliminates rivals through predatory pricing. In the case of the institutional reforms in the capital markets, these are crisis-driven. So far, the competitive dynamics in the market benefited consumers by increasing the number of differentiated goods and causing a significant decline in prices. From the producers' side, although local firms lobbied for a level playing field with regard to the entry of TNCs, they did not make strong demands on the government to adopt a competition policy. Part of the reason could be the fear of the control Raj of the previous regime, and second, that competition policy also forces large local incumbents to subject themselves to scrutiny and legal action.

Douglas North, in his proposition of institutional change, observed that competitive dynamics changes perceptions and opportunity sets of agents and thereby contributes to institutional change. As mentioned briefly in the beginning of the last chapter, one of the important structural outcomes of competitive dynamics is the change in the attitudes and perceptions of different economic agents. One of these perceptions in the present context refers to TNC operations in India. In the pre-reforms period, there was a general inimical attitude towards TNCs, among both the policy circles and the public. One reason was India's history of British colonial rule. There was a partial liberalization towards the entry of TNCs initiated in the mid-1980s. However, there was still opposition in policy circles and incumbent industrialists in the name of economic nationalism. As TNC operations started to show positive outcomes in both the product and labor markets, apprehensions about TNCs declined and the policy has been made more liberal, thereby contributing to improvements in the property rights of TNCs. They are allowed to set up fully owned subsidiaries in several industries and also in those areas where they had joint ventures with local partners.

# 6   Technological change

Technological change at the micro level, as characterized in the previous chapter, is driven by competitive dynamics. Apart from this, policy reforms change the incentives for investing in technological progress at the macro level of a national innovative system. The objective of this chapter is to trace how the policy reforms have contributed to technological changes at the firm, industry and economy level and its implications for the evolution of markets and institutions. In the first part, I discuss different elements of technology conceptually in order to understand how they change in response to the reforms. For a developing economy, most of the technological change involves catching up with developed economies by imports and the purchase of technologies. I discuss the effect of the policy reforms on incentives for the adoption of technologies from developed economies and the process of adaptation of the technologies to the local markets and factor endowments. I provide empirical evidence, both qualitative and quantitative, of the adoption of new technologies in the Indian industry. The characterization of the process of technological adaptation has important implications for understanding the emergence of appropriate markets and institutional conditions. Following this, I discuss the evolution of the national innovative system (NIS), which refers to the institutional environment for technological activity and encompasses issues such as the public stock of knowledge, externalities, human capital accumulation, industrial clusters and incentives and the abilities of individual agents to tap the public stock of knowledge. This, in turn, should throw light on how technological institutions evolve in response to the behavior of firms.

To recapitulate, the policy reforms are treated as parameter and qualitative shifts in the institutional environment. They have implications for technology through changes in the market and institutional dimensions. The market conditions that are important for technology are competition (as opposed to monopoly or collusion), the extent of the market (division of labor), labor market conditions, and the development level of financial markets. Market opportunities refer not only to the expansion of markets but also to the decline in informational asymmetries and transaction costs of product and input markets. Institutional factors that play an important role in the generation (innovation), adoption, and utilization of technology are incentives determined by property rights (both physical and intellectual), linkages between different economic actors, which are determined by the costs of contract formation and execution, and the organization of labor and financial markets.

Technology is basically an engineering relationship between a set of inputs and (observed) output. The inputs are generally taken as skilled and unskilled labor, R&D, and plant and machinery (capital). When functional forms of the production function are derived, the inputs are substitutable, which depends on the relative prices of labor and capital. This is treated as a smooth technical relation in mainstream economics under the black-box view of the firm. However, the process is also an organizational one. Technological factors are governed by organizational issues such as incentives due to workers and managers, organization of centralization and decentralization and agency relations between owners (principals) and controllers (agents) of capital, which, in turn, determine the utilization of technology, the extent of learning by doing on the job and possible innovations.[1]

Organizational economics, as discussed in Chapter 2, assumes away technology so as to simplify the analysis of factors that determine governance choices and organizational efficiency. In reality, technology and organization are interlinked in determining the overall performance of firms. Changes in policy may present several complementarities and trade-offs to firms in determining overall efficiency. For example, the importation and adoption of modern technologies in the post-reform period require changes in organizational practices. Piecemeal adaptation of some technology and some organizational practices may not result in the desired potential productivity. Similarly, in terms of trade-offs, new technological opportunities may generate economies of scale and scope to firms, which should increase vertical and horizontal integration. On the other hand, a decline in transaction costs provides incentives to reduce integration. Firms that are able to assess these possibilities and adapt to them in the changed institutional environment will have a relative advantage over the late movers. In this chapter, I concentrate on technological issues, while the following chapter deals with the organizational issues.

What are the different elements of technology and how do they change in response to the reforms? Solow's neoclassical growth theory takes economic growth as a function of labor, capital accumulation, and technology as the residual, and exogenously given. In his Nobel lecture, Solow (1988) himself commented on the neoclassical approach,

> The idea is to imagine that the economy is populated by a single immortal consumer, or a number of identical immortal consumers. Such a consumer, or his dynasty, is supposed to solve an infinite-time

utility maximization problem ... For this consumer, every firm is just a transparent instrumentality, an intermediary, or a device for carrying out an inter-temporal optimization exercise, subject only to techno-logical constraints and initial endowments.

The new growth theory treats technological change as an endogenous process; that is to say, the incentives for innovation arise from institutional factors such as protection of intellectual property rights and market struc-ture dynamics. The new growth theory gives a lot of weight to human capital. Thus, a country with a larger endowment of highly skilled workers generates technological innovations. Unlike physical capital, human capital accumulation leads to increasing returns to scale in cumulative production. In Romer's (1990) model, spillovers of knowledge are the main source of increasing returns to investment in human capital and research and development. This takes place owing to two main character-istics of innovations: non-rivalry and non-excludability conditions. Non-rivalry implies that the use of a new technology or a blueprint (or a new idea) does not preclude others from its use. There can be a simultaneous use by a large number of agents. It implies that, once in place, the social marginal cost of production of an additional unit for another consumer is zero. The larger the number of users, the larger is its aggregate value. International trade and investment increase the number of users. The non-excludability condition implies that a new technology cannot be fully appropriated by an innovator owing to spillovers and possible imitation by other agents in the economy.[2] This, in turn, determines the public stock of knowledge.

Lucas (1988) focuses on human capital accumulation, although phys-ical capital plays an essential but subsidiary role. Human capital accumula-tion takes place in schools, in research organizations, and in the course of producing goods and engaging in trade. In the Lucas model: $Yj=A(H)$ $F(Kj, Hj)$, where $Y$ is output, $A$ represents technology as the scale variable, $Kj$ is the stock of physical capital, $Hj$ is the stock of human capital. Techno-logical change is a function of human capital. From this, one can see a two-way causation between workers' productivity and technological change. The level of human capital stock in terms of both number and level of skills determines the productivity. Human capital invested in research and development leads to new ideas and blueprints, which, in turn, further increase productivity. New ideas and technologies, and learn-ing-by-doing economies associated with new technologies further enhance human capital accumulation (skill levels). Romer (1990) shows that an economy with a larger stock of human capital will experience faster eco-nomic growth.

However, for analytical tractability, the new growth theory treats a firm similar to the original neoclassical approach – as a black box, instead of as an organization. Internal organizational conditions play an important role in determining the incentives of workers and managers in realizing learning by doing, and investing in productivity-enhancing internal practices. Furthermore, the non-rivalrous characteristics of new technology involve tacit and codified elements. Non-tacit elements of technology can be codified, digitalized or turned into blueprints and transferred across agents with little costs. Tacit elements of technology involve closer interaction between inventors, innovators,[3] skilled personnel, and managers for its adoption and adaptation, which involve adjustment costs, especially if it is transferred across different economies with different factor endowments and market conditions.

As argued before, the initial technological endowments at the time of the reforms determine how the reforms cause further development of technology through changes in competitive dynamics, market opportunities, and institutional conditions. As discussed in Chapter 3, the previous policies of import substitution generated a critical level of technological endowment in terms of a large industrial base, skilled labor endowments, and public and private research institutions. The Indian government pursued the policy of developing indigenous technologies by building an extensive network of science and technology institutions under the public sector, providing tax incentives to private firms to undertake R&D, and offering financial and technical support to private-sector firms (Katrak, 2002). The previous policies also led to a significant presence of mature private-sector firms in several industries, although they operated with technologies that were below international frontiers. The issue under consideration is how do reforms provide incentives to firms to adopt new technologies and how does the adoption of these new technologies develop markets and engender institutional evolution?

## Market reforms and the adoption of new technologies

The policy reforms, which are qualitative and parameter shifts in the institutional elements, can be treated as enabling an economy in which firms had been using some technology at $t < T$ to move to $t = T$, which implies that firms in a developing economy context have greater access to new or superior technology. The adoption of new technologies involves adjustment or adaptation costs. The question is, will firms adopt newer technologies that offer higher levels of productivity and output? If yes, why and under what conditions?

Under the previous policy regime, the large oligopoly firms in India colluded and derived long-run monopoly power. Collusive oligopolies have no incentive to adopt superior technologies. When we talk of collusion versus competition, it refers to oligopoly of strategic interaction between a few large players. The mainstream economics literature talks about market failure of innovation when markets are competitive because a large number of small firms lack surplus rents and the non-appropriability condition of perfectly competitive markets is a disincentive to investing in innovation. One of the possible institutional mechanisms of small firms investing in new practices is through cooperative arrangements with competitors (unlike collusive oligopoly), and upstream producers, which will be elaborated on later, with a few case studies.

The above observation requires a conceptual distinction between two notions of competition. One is the perfectly competitive market with firms selling homogenous items, under which none can influence prices acting alone. It is impossible for any mutually beneficial contract to take place between two firms in a competitive market of this kind. Owing to the presence of transaction costs, collective arrangements can be initiated only by higher-level bodies than the firms (governments or external agents) or by a substantial majority of firms initiating the move. Hence, collusions are not seen in these markets. The second is the potential competition, where even though existing (large) firms have market power and can influence prices, they face competition from potential entrants (under perfect capital markets). This kind of competition provides incentives for innovation; in fact, Schumpeter's praise of capitalism was based on competition such as this. Collusion can take place only among firms of this kind; when it does, it reduces incentives for innovation (technology adoption).

I take the reforms as qualitative shifts that break collusion among large oligopolies by eliminating barriers to new entry. In competitive oligopoly, strategic interactions result in technological rivalry. In the previous chapter, it is argued that policy reforms have resulted in the entry of new players, which has augmented competitive conditions. In order to induce technological change, the new entrants must possess technology that is superior to that of the incumbents. As defined in Chapter 5, the new entrants are TNCs from developed economies. The kind of technology that they bring into the local markets depends on the existing institutional factors like property rights, market conditions (such as the extent of competition from local player, size of the market and its potential for growth), and input endowment conditions (such as skilled labor and support industries producing intermediate goods).

The Indian economy presents a large, growing market, which had an annual average growth rate of 6 percent throughout the 1990s and the early 2000s. There are well-established and mature local firms in several Indian industries. Over the years, Indian policies have improved the property rights of TNCs by allowing them to set up fully owned subsidiaries in several areas, which implies a decline in policy-based entry costs to TNCs. To give the example of the automobile sector, the growth in incomes and the improved property rights of TNCs have resulted in the introduction of the latest technology and new car models into the market, with the entry of the fully owned subsidiary of the South Korean TNC Hyundai, and also other TNCs, like Ford and GM in the early 2000s. The higher the technology levels brought in by the new entrants, the greater is the need for incumbent local firms to adopt newer and higher-end technologies. In a developing-economy context, the first step is to utilize the internationally available non-proprietary technologies and purchase proprietary technologies. R&D is then to be undertaken for their efficient utilization and for incremental innovations.

The development of product markets is essential for firms to find adoption of new technology profitable. When adoption of a new technology improves productivity and increases output, the underdeveloped product markets can make producers worse off by making product prices fall below long-run average costs. Development of the product market implies not only market size but also transaction costs of exchange. High transaction costs of search, and assessment of product attributes, storage and distribution can impose high costs on producers and consumers, and dissipate profits.

The importance of market size for technological adoption follows from the famous statement of Adam Smith, "division of labor is limited by the extent of the market." For the adoption of new technologies, the domestic markets should be large and growing, and present low transaction costs of market exchange. Complementing domestic market size, international trade is one of the means of extending market size. Openness to international trade is one of the important incentives for the adoption of new technologies. This happens through two mechanisms: extending the market size, and providing access to internationally traded differentiated intermediate goods, which reduce the adjustment costs of new technologies. The division of labor through trade also means structural changes in the economy, as discussed in Chapter 4. Some sectors which have initial comparative advantage grow rapidly through trade, and some may decline. If the growing sectors are technology-intensive, international markets make the industries adopt newer technologies. If these sectors have linkages with other sectors, overall productivity gains can be realized.

Large domestic market size is not a necessary condition for export-oriented industries such as India's software industry. India's software and BPO industries have introduced a significant amount of product, process, logistical, and organizational innovation, but the domestic market for these industries has been minimal. Porter's (1990) framework of competitive advantage of nations, inspired by the Japanese success story, argues that even to grow through export markets, a large domestic market is a precondition. By producing for a large domestic market, an industry realizes its scale and learning-by-doing economies, and it can utilize them to compete overseas and grow further. However, this is just a generalization from historical experience of export industries in the last hundred years. There is no compelling theoretical reason for this to be true. If an industry, product, or practice is new to the world, then firms of any country can grow and develop with reliance on overseas markets, and can then innovate and excel. Another extension of this is that access to global markets can help firms to avoid entry barriers and high transaction costs of the domestic market (Patibandla, 1995; Ghemawat and Patibandla, 1999). This has always been theoretically possible. Now, with globalisation, this theoretical possibility has become a reality.

The resource endowments of a developing country are different from those of a developed one. As discussed in Chapters 3 and 4, India's duality is characterized by the fact that there is an endowment of skilled labor comparable to developed economies in certain pockets, and in others there is a large amount of unskilled labor. Similarly, there are well-developed research institutions, technical universities, and engineering capabilities in several pockets. Under these conditions, some industries find that adoption of new technologies and investment in adjustment costs are productivity-enhancing and profitable, while others may not find it so. According to a study by consulting company McKinsey & Co., the abundance of low-cost unskilled labor in India makes automation in industries such as garment manufacturing unattractive (Patibandla and Sinha, 2005).

John Hicks observed that the industrial revolution in Britain became feasible because of the development of financial markets. Before liberalization, the Indian public had few investment options. India had traditionally enjoyed one of the highest savings rates in the world. However, as discussed in Chapter 3, the institutional arrangements of the public financial institutions and big business houses resulted in the misutilization of capital. From the latter half of the 1960s, the government sold financial assets only in the organized sector. The public, therefore, had to invest their savings either in land or gold, or they had to buy government securities. There were, of course, large informal markets, but ordinary savers shied away from them owing to high risks and the fact that specialized lenders dominated these markets.[4] The public sector financial institutions made public savings available to large businesses at low rates and with little monitoring; as a result, businessmen were able to use those funds for personal objectives with impunity.

Liberalization brought in financial reforms. The contribution of financial sector reform has been to make these lending institutions cost-conscious and thus more efficient. The entry of foreign institutional investors brought greater discipline into the markets. There was an increase in the cost of capital of firms in terms of improving corporate governance to attract capital (Patibandla, 2005a). The reforms also forced collusive firms into non-cooperation. In the post-reforms era, the government of India brought in a series of additional measures in the financial sector, which improved liquidity and also contributed to greater regulation and market discipline.[5] Thus, perhaps the major contribution of liberalization was that it not only brought Indian firms access to new technology, but that it changed the nature of competition among them, both in the product and input markets.

Intellectual property rights have implications for technology adoption at two levels: whether the adoption of new technology takes place at all in a specific industry, and ownership modes. When the value of assets protected by patents and trademarks cannot be fully realized by owners, the incentive to invest in these technological and marketing-based assets is reduced. Under a weak property rights regime, higher ownership modes are more efficient because of reduced cost of unwanted dissemination. The policy reforms on the IPR front have led to changes in the legal definition and transaction costs of enforcement. As discussed in Chapter 4, the Indian government reformed the Copyright Act in 1994 upon the initiative of the industry association (NASSCOM). As government enforcement was weak, the association itself played an active role in enforcing it. However, enforcement of the Act is still weak in many aspects, for example the widespread piracy of both locally and foreign-made movies and music in India. As the Indian market started to become lucrative, a few Hollywood studios opened their offices in India and invested in the enforcement with some success.[6]

Similarly, Maruti-Suzuki in the automobile industry eliminated the spurious-component market by investing in the distribution system all over the country. These examples tell us that if there are legal rights on paper and the market is profitable, firms have incentives to invest in costs of enforcement for the adoption of technologies that are subject to appropriability. This is one of the aspects of the adjustment costs of adoption of new technologies, which is discussed in the following section.

## The adaptation or adjustment costs of new technologies

The notion of adjustment costs refers to adapting a new technology to India's input and product market conditions. In a developing economy context, it refers to adapting an imported technology to local conditions. This involves costs such as mastering codified and tacit elements of technology and the adaptation of these to local factor endowments, the market demand of modifying product characteristics, training local skilled labor and developing supplier firms. The adoption of new technologies and undertaking adjustment costs are determined by trade-offs between combinations of different factors. These factors include the extent of market size, competition, initial endowment of skills, and technological capabilities. A large, growing market reduces the costs of the trade-offs. For example, in the case of India's software industry, firms employ personnel with generic engineering and mathematical skills and invest in training on their technology platforms. The industry's high degree of export-orientation overcomes the domestic market size constraint.

Similarly, in the case of the automobile industry, the fast-growing local market gave incentives to TNCs to invest in the development of the intermediate-product industry. This involves technology transfer, costs of contract formulation, and enforcement among the assemblers and intermediate-input producers. As discussed in the previous chapter, the Japanese TNC Maruti-Suzuki invested substantial resources in the development of vendor firms, which drove local firms to undertake similar investments to be able to compete with Suzuki.

The other dimension of adjustment costs involves the modification of product characteristics to fit in with local conditions, such as consumer tastes, infrastructure, and weather conditions. For example, the TNCs like Hyundai and Ford had to modify some features of their latest-vintage cars to local infrastructure and weather conditions. Likewise, the Indian firm Titan Industries developed a high-torque stepper motor for quartz analog watches that could operate in environments with high levels of dust (Bowonder and Richardson, 2000; Krishnan and Prabhu, 1999).[7] In other words, if the country has a critical level of skill endowments, rapidly growing and competitive markets, and protection of intellectual property rights, it offers high incentives for firms to adopt newer and more sophisticated technologies and invest in the consequent adjustment costs.

Technologies from developed economies tend to be capital-intensive. Adapting to factor endowments in India involves finding the right skills and providing training on the job. Since skilled labor is less expensive than in developed economies, those firms that are able to invest in adapting the technology to skilled-labor-intensive techniques derive allocative efficiency in production. If technical efficiency of operating at the frontier of a given technology is combined with the allocative efficiency of utilizing relative factor endowments (inexpensive skilled labor) inline with their relative prices, firms in India can realize higher cost-efficiency than firms in a developed economy, owing to the low cost of skilled labor.

A good example, as discussed in the previous chapter, is the auto component industry in India. Market dynamics have made the first-tier firms in this industry adopt capital-intensive technologies and at the same time they have been able to derive cost advantages thanks to low-cost skilled labor, which has made them internationally competitive in exports. Another interesting case is the software industry in India. A few software firms invested in their own infrastructure and internal labor markets by training skilled workers in order to reduce their dependence on the inefficient infrastructure and institutions in India, and became 'islands of competitiveness'. This is an additional expenditure Indian firms have to incur, as they have to operate in a generally inefficient economy with inefficiencies reflected in higher physical capital intensity in comparison with similar activities of firms in advanced economies. However, this disadvantage is neutralized by the advantage in low-cost skilled manpower for export competitiveness. This forces firms to achieve the highest possible allocative efficiency in order to neutralize the additional costs of self-infrastructure building.[8]

## The adoption of new technologies in the post-reforms era

Fulfillment of the above conditions for the adoption of new technologies depends on the initial endowments such as skilled labor, income levels (market size), industrial development, and how the policy reforms change competitive conditions and market opportunities. Market opportunities are not only in terms of an increase in domestic demand but also the realization of comparative advantage in exports. The realization of comparative advantage on the basis of initial endowments implies that a dormant comparative advantage for different industries did exist, but the previous policies such as the overvalued exchange rate and high transaction costs masked it. Once the policy reform had rectified the policy distortions, industries could realize the comparative advantage based on the initial conditions, which means that they did not have to change technology to exploit the market opportunities. The examples could be India's software, garments, diamond-cutting, and leather industries, whose exports increased at a rapid rate immediately after the reforms of 1991, without much initial technological change. Technological change by definition is a long-run phenomenon.

However, the case of the auto component industry shows that the first-tier firms adopted capital-intensive technologies. This is because the first response of the firms was towards the domestic market to cater to the assembler firms, which had been facing intense competition in the domestic market. The linkages between the assemblers and the first-tier firms of the component industries caused the first-tier component firms to adopt world-class quality standards. The process of upgrading took almost ten years from the inception of the reforms in 1991. In the early 2000s, the industry became highly export-competitive. The export activity of these firms had been an offshoot of domestic market dynamics. As they had combined capital-intensive technologies with low-cost advantage of skilled labor, they derived a comparative advantage in exports.

The software industry is mainly driven by exports but also presents a picture of duality. On one side there are firms that merely take advantage of low-cost skilled labor for export of services without having to adopt markedly advanced technologies, and on the other side there are several TNCs that have set up R&D operations in India for high-end technology development for their home and global operations. In other words, the incentives to adopt modern technologies vary across industries and across firms within industries. In the following paragraphs, I present qualitative and quantitative evidence for the adoption of new technologies, both at the industry and firm level, by Indian industries in general.

One of the indicators of technology adoption is the rapid increase in the number and variety of differentiated consumer durable and non-durable goods available in India in the post-reforms era. The differentiation is on vertical and horizontal lines to cater to both rich and middle- and lower-middle-class groups. In 2004, one could find the latest electronics products, such as televisions and household items, computers, motorcycles, and automobiles. The real prices of these goods declined significantly over the years.[9] Furthermore, consumer services, such as after-sales services, and warranties of product quality provided by companies, improved significantly. This signals technology adoption of high-quality products and the generation of markets for information to consumers.

Most of the new technology flows and adoption of technology are through local firms purchasing technologies from developed economies and multinational firms, and imports of capital goods. From the panel data obtained from seventy-eight Indian industries, as discussed in Chapter 4, the annual average growth rate of the royalties and technical fees expenditure (normalized by sales) for eleven years between 1989 and 1999, showed a 67 percent growth, which implies increased technological purchases by Indian industries. The industries that showed higher than average growth with regard to the technology purchases consist of both capital goods and consumer goods industries such as cosmetics, bicycles, photographic material, textile machinery, and steel. The annual average growth rate for this period for imports of capital and intermediate goods to sales was 9.5 percent. The industries that showed higher than average growth rate were air-conditioners and refrigerators, bicycles, textiles, cosmetics, drugs and pharmaceuticals, and auto component industries.

As discussed in the previous chapter, there has been a significant increase in the presence of TNCs with modern technologies and differentiated goods in several industries. TNCs enter India for two reasons: first, to serve local markets for which they have to compete with local firms, and second, to undertake exports by taking advantage of India's comparative advantage in low-cost skilled and semi-skilled labor. In the latter case, the level of technology they bring in depends on the endowment of skill levels and supportive institutions such as universities and public stock of knowledge. Given the range of skill levels in India, TNC operations vary between high- and low-end technology operations while catering to export markets. To give a few examples of high-end technology, General Electric set up the biggest R&D lab outside the US to utilize the large existing pool of Indian scientific manpower, equipped with advanced degrees in science and engineering, to support its global operations. Other examples in the software industry include companies like Texas Instruments, Microsoft, Adobe, and Oracle. At the same time, there are several TNCs that undertake low-end service activities like coding and programming and BPO operations.

When TNCs enter India primarily to serve local markets, the level of technology they adopt, as mentioned earlier, depends on the degree of local competition, market size, and property rights. Their R&D operations could be an extension of their local market focus. For example, Samsung and LG Electronics, which have become successful in selling consumer electronic goods, set up R&D centers in India. Similarly, in the automobile industry, the South Korean TNC Hyundai, which became a successful producer of small cars, set up its R&D center and uses the production base to export cars from India. Following from this, if TNCs realize that in general the costs of undertaking R&D are low owing to low-cost scientific manpower, these R&D operations can be extended from the mere adaptation of products to local markets to undertaking or complementing innovative R&D for the home market base.

One of the indicators of increased technological activity in the post-reforms era is the technical collaboration between local firms and foreign firms. Table 11 shows the number of technical and financial collaboration approvals in India from 1991 to 2001. The technical collaborations are the largest in the capital goods industries, followed by basic goods and consumer non-durable goods. On the other hand, financial collaborations are the largest in the service industry followed by capital goods.

Investment in R&D expenditure is one of the indicators of technological adoption. In the pre-reforms era, most of the R&D in India (close to 90 percent of the total expenditure) was undertaken by the government both for defense research and for the generation of the public stock

*Table 11* Industry-wise breakdown of foreign collaboration approvals in India (August 1991 to March 2002)

| Industry | Number of approvals | |
|---|---|---|
| | Technical | Financial |
| Basic goods | 1,517 | 1,942 |
| Power | 21 | 246 |
| Oil refinery | 111 | 144 |
| Capital goods | 3,237 | 3,301 |
| Electrical equipment | 893 | 768 |
| Electronics | 158 | 327 |
| Transportation | 562 | 610 |
| Intermediate goods | 251 | 560 |
| Consumer non-durable goods | 1,387 | 2,976 |
| Pharmaceuticals | 236 | 247 |
| Textiles | 151 | 576 |
| Food products | 134 | 613 |
| Consumer durable goods | 37 | 122 |
| Passenger cars | 6 | 65 |
| Services | 571 | 5,601 |
| Computer software | 86 | 2,267 |
| Telecommunications | 126 | 675 |
| Financial services | 8 | 406 |
| Total | 7,000 | 14,502 |

Source: *Economic and Political Weekly*, 31 August 2002.

of knowledge. In the case of the latter, the government of India set up the Center for Scientific and Industrial Research (CSIR) as an autonomous society. The CSIR has thirty-eight national laboratories all over the country for coordinating both pure and industrial applied research, and it also undertakes collaborations with scientific bodies in various countries. The R&D activity by private firms in the pre-reforms era was very marginal, barring a few pockets where private firms imported technology and undertook adaptive R&D. In the post-reforms era, public expenditure on R&D declined, while a few large Indian firms stepped up their R&D investment. The total spending on R&D by the top ten firms in India was about $150 million in 1999 (Forbes, 2002). Table 12 shows the growth in R&D expenditure by large Indian firms.

The outcome of increased technological activity by large Indian firms is that some of them have become world-class players. To give a few examples, the Reliance Industries group set up the largest grassroots refinery in the world in the west of India and has also become the lowest-cost producer of polyester yarn in the world. Tata Steel has become the lowest-cost producer of hot-rolled steel in the world. Moser-Baer is the third-largest manufacturer of optical media in the world and the lowest-cost producer of CD-writers. Sundaram Fasteners, a firm in the auto component industry, was awarded the coveted Deming Prize for Total Quality in 2002 and has been regularly winning the Supplier of the Year award from General Motors. TELCO, the Tata group firm, developed an indigenous small car successfully and is now exporting it. Larsen and

*Table 12* R&D expenditure by the large Indian companies

| Firm | 1998–9 | 1992–3 | Growth multiple |
|---|---|---|---|
| Reliance Industries | 751 | 24 | 31 |
| Mahindra & Mahindra | 414 | 33 | 12 |
| Ranbaxy | 523 | 84 | 6 |
| Eicher Ltd | 222 | 40 | 5 |
| Wockhardt Ltd | 156 | 33 | 5 |
| Indian Oil Corporation | 772 | 185 | 4 |
| Crompton Greaves | 217 | 54 | 4 |
| Hindustan Lever | 373 | 113 | 3 |
| TELCO | 1,000 | 308 | 3 |
| Ashok Leyland | 217 | 94 | 2 |
| Bajaj Auto | 315 | 144 | 2 |
| Indian Telephone Industries | 338 | 212 | 2 |
| Bharat Heavy Electricals | 527 | 430 | 1 |
| Steel Authority of India | 483 | 395 | 1 |
| Oil and Natural Gas Corporation | 250 | 221 | 1 |
| Bharat Electronics | 661 | 705 | – |
| DRL | 212 | 31 | 7 |

Source: Forbes (2002).

Toubro indigenously designed and developed the world's largest fluidized catalytic converter. In the pharmaceutical industry, several large firms refocused their strategies of investing in innovative R&D as a reaction to the WTO agreement on product patents. For example, Reddy's Laboratories is the first Indian company in the industry to obtain a US patent for a new molecular product that can be used for treating insulin-resistant diabetes. Several of these firms are attempting to translate their technological success in the domestic market to global markets by increasing exports, undertaking green-field ventures, and acquiring overseas companies in developed economy markets.

As discussed in Chapter 4, India's software industry has come to be known globally for competitive software services. The industry is mostly focused on markets in the developed economies such as the US and western Europe. The opportunities in these international markets range from providing low-end programming and coding to complex consultancy services. Consequently, one sees software firms with varying levels of technological sophistication. The software industry benchmark for measuring software performance is the Capability Maturity Model (CMM 2001) developed by the Software Engineering Institute at the Carnegie Mellon University. The model classifies the technology level of firms and software from 1 to 5, with 5 being the best. By early 2000, twenty-seven Indian companies achieved a CMM level-5 certification. The incentives for the adoption of technology are mainly driven by the global market focus of the industry.

However, there are several large firms that failed on the technology front in the changed market and institutional conditions of the post-reforms era. Forbes (2002) lists the winners and losers in this period. If we take two large firms facing similar market and institutional environments, and one is successful and the other is a failure, it should to be attributed to managerial failures in assessing the right kind of technology purchases and adapting them to local markets and/or high agency costs of managerial decisions. However, if we take size differences into account, the prevailing institutions may operate differently for different-sized groups of firms. For example, if capital markets remain imperfect, a small firm with a good project proposal may still find raising capital and the adoption of technology more costly than a large firm. I illustrate this by considering technology adoption in the agriculture sector.

The Green Revolution in agriculture is one of the successful policies of the past policy regime. The government policies of the introduction of new seeds and fertilizers, and product market support to farmers helped India achieve self-sufficiency in food production in a very short period of time. The Green Revolution was mostly concentrated in the northern states of Punjab and Haryana. In the early part of the 2000s, press reports revealed that several middle-level farmers (owning three to five acres of land approximately) committed suicide owing to debt burden in the southern states of India, Andhra Pradesh and Karnataka. One of the underlying reasons for these suicides could be the adoption of technology under the conditions of underdeveloped product and capital markets.

In rural areas of states, the capital and product markets are interlocked such that small and middle farmers borrow capital and sell the output to middlemen. The interest rates of informal markets are far higher than formal markets owing to the adverse selection outcomes of the rural markets, poorly defined land rights and the high risk due to environmental uncertainty. Furthermore, commodity and futures markets are not developed, which results in small farmers realizing low prices or even distress sales at the time of harvest. The farmers cannot avail themselves of credit from the formal government banks owing to high transaction costs and collateral requirements. The poor and very small farmers do not invest in productivity-enhancing practices because of high interest rates. However, it is the middle farmers who generally take the risk of investing in technology. When the adoption of technology results in higher output but product prices fall proportionately more, or even necessitate distress sales at harvest time through the middlemen, the debt burden becomes very high. This is one of the underlying reasons for the incidence of suicides among middle farmers (Patibandla and Sastry, 2004). In other words, technology adoption becomes viable only under a critical level of development of product and capital markets.

Competition among a large number of small players can also hamper the adoption of new technologies. Apart from the market failure arguments of large-group competition and innovation, competition of a destructive kind worsens the condition of small firms. Destructive price competition between large numbers of small (power-loom) firms in the textile industry of the Bhivandi cluster made the firms decline technologically. On the other hand, cooperative behavior among small firms in avoiding a destructive type of aggressive price cutting and generating cooperative relations among downstream and upstream firms in the garments cluster of Tirupur helped even small firms adopt superior practices and achieve international competitiveness in exports (Cawthorne, 1995). In other words, cooperative behavior among small players can overcome prisoners' dilemma-type competition and reduce transaction and informational costs of the product and input markets, which could facilitate adoption of superior practices for higher productivity.

Empirical evidence and explanation of productivity gains in India's industrial sector is presented in Appendix 4. The econometric results for both the industry and firm-level panel data indicate significant productivity gains in the post-reform era. The micro level processes of realization technological change and productivity increases are discussed in the following section on the basis of qualitative information and case studies.

## The micro-level process of technology adoption and adaptation

Forbes and Wield (2002), in their book titled *From Followers to Leaders*, analyze how countries such as Japan in the 1960s and 1970s purchased and imitated technologies from the West and improvised on them to become internationally competitive in the spheres of electronics and automobiles. They list three main factors for building technological capability in the context of technology followers:

- Technological competence: the ability to master the particular technologies relevant to the needs of the enterprise.
- Entrepreneurial competence: the ability to generate and implement strategies for research and development coherently linked to the enterprise strategy, taking account of long-term trends in the evolution of technology, markets and competition.
- Learning ability: the ability to adapt organizationally and culturally in order to accommodate technological change.

In the present context, technological competence involves initial endowments at the firm, industry and country level in terms of technical skills, industrial endowments, and managerial talent. Given the initial endowment, the subsequent step is adoption of modern technologies, which requires purchase and transfer of technology from developed economies. As mentioned before, the major element of technology transfer is, apart from the purchase of blueprints and machinery, mastering tacit elements of technology for its transfer to local production needs. The transfer of technology and adaptation to local conditions requires investments in R&D, skills and organizational change, which mean the adjustments costs at the initial stages are high. Additionally, tacit characteristics of technology make technology transfer partial. The process could lead to either of two outcomes. The utilization of technology may be below the frontier of the original technology of the seller, or the transferee may realize higher productivity than the original technology through improvisations and learning by doing, as the Japanese did in the case of electronics and automobiles. Once the technological capabilities are realized, the adjustment costs of the adaptation of newer technologies could decline over time. I discuss a few case studies to identify the processes of technology transfer and building of technological capabilities in post-reforms India.

At the onset of the economic reforms, the Tata Steel Company in India was an inefficient producer of steel compared to international levels, because of outdated processes, excess workforce and an inward-looking mindset. In the late 1980s, the firm initiated a process of restructuring. It bought and transferred technology from overseas and modernized the plant. The modernization and improvements in operational efficiency took ten years of concerted effort. The organizational change that was implemented resulted in a flatter structure of three levels, as against the eleven levels prior to the change. Consequently, the raw material consumption efficiency improved from 4.81 tonnes per tonne of saleable steel in 1990–1 to 3.71 in 2000–1; labor productivity improved from seventy-nine tonnes of saleable steel per man-year in 1995 to 189 in 2001 (Krishnan, 2003). By 2005, the company is considered the world's best steel maker. Out of twenty-two major steel makers in the world, which include South Korea's Posco, US Steel, and Bao Steel of China, the company is ranked number one by World Steel Dynamics.[10]

The TELCO firm, a part of the Tata group, developed a small car successfully in India. The firm diversified into the production of automobiles from the production of commercial vehicles by utilizing its technical expertise gained in truck manufacturing. It sent a group of its engineers and top managers to different countries in the world to understand the tacit elements of technology, and bought technological services from firms in developed countries.[11] It sourced the body and styling from Italy, engine design from France and instrumentation from Japan. An unused Nissan plant bought in Australia was dismantled into about 800 containers and reassembled in Pune at a cost of $22 million. The firm implemented mechanization (with robots). It brought about organizational coordination between the R&D department and plant engineers. The product was improvised through concerted efforts as a part of learning by doing and overcoming failures and technical snags, and improving the product. In terms of organizational change, it strengthened interdepartmental horizontal cooperation and feedback mechanisms. It established an Ancillary Development Department and the Supplier Quality Improvement Program to develop vendor firms and assist them with technology transfer and training (Okada, 2004). By early 2000, it had become successful in competing with TNCs such as Hyundai and Maruti-Suzuki, and today it undertakes exports to Europe under the brand name of Rover.

The Indian two-wheeler and automobile industries have become vibrant sectors marked by technology, product, and market development in the post-reforms era as a consequence of competition between local firms and new-entrant TNCs. The following example illustrates how the leading local firm Bajaj Auto transformed itself through technological efforts in response to competition from the entry of TNCs such as Honda and Suzuki. Until the mid-1980s, only a few local players, with Bajaj Auto as the leader, dominated the two-wheeler industry. As a result of the reforms, TNCs such as Honda and Suzuki entered the Indian market with contemporary models of motorcycles and mopeds and grew rapidly, posing a serious threat to Bajaj's market position. In response, Bajaj, like the other firms mentioned above, sourced technology and licenses from countries such as Austria, Italy, and Japan. It enhanced in-house investment in R&D. It undertook organizational restructuring for the adaptation of the technology and for achieving operational efficiency. The new organizational approach is shifting from a top-down approach, typical of a family-run, highly centralized organization, to a bottom-up approach. On the shop floor, workmen and section managers were grouped into cells and the members were guided by the self-management approach. All the cells were interlinked for a smooth information flow and coordination system. Close to 5,000 workers were given voluntary retirement. Manpower productivity in terms of the number of vehicles produced per man-year improved by 88 percent between 1988 and 1998 (Bhudiraja *et al.*, 2003). The company developed selective vendor firms for the supply of specific components with long-term contracts and facilitated joint ventures with overseas firms for technology development. In the late 1990s, when consumer preferences shifted away from scooters to motorcycles, the company was able to adjust by indigenously developing motorcycle models. By the early 2000s, Bajaj, which had almost lost out to the TNC Hero-Honda, was able to derive a relative advantage over the TNC owing to its focus on cost-efficiency and its responsiveness to market trends. On the other hand, Hero-Honda depended on the home R&D base in Japan for technology, which hampered quick response to market trends. Bajaj is able to respond swiftly to market trends and is able to introduce an entire range of two-wheeler models. In the process, it is able to launch innovative product developments such as two-wheeler model hybrids between motorcycles and scooters to cater to the consumer preferences in India.

In the case of TNCs, technology choices should take account of consumer preferences and price-elasticity of demand. For example, the US cosmetic firm Revlon entered the Indian market with a substandard product. This allowed the Indian firm Lakme to trounce Revlon (Forbes and Wield, 2002). Apart from being able to compete with Revlon's technology, the Indian firm also had the relative advantage of local institutional and market knowledge. Another case is Mitsubishi, which introduced a luxury car with high dependence on imports. This pushed up its costs of production and it could not get a foothold in the Indian market. On the other hand, Hyundai brought in latest technology for producing both small and middle-size cars, adapted the technology to local conditions, and systematically developed local vendor firms, which helped it to derive cost-competitiveness. This, in turn, helped the TNC quickly to gain a market share at the cost of the established Maruti-Suzuki and enabled it to undertake exports from India in a significant manner.

In the case of the export motive of TNCs, their strategy would be to utilize low-cost skilled labor for global operations. However, the low cost of skilled labor alone is not enough for a TNC to be successful in utilizing the comparative advantage in a developing-economy context. Infrastructure and local technology institutions should support it. If the cost advantage of skilled labor is dominant, a TNC may invest in its own internal institutions and infrastructure. As discussed in Chapter 4, when Texas

Instruments entered the Indian software industry in 1985, it had to bring its own modern telecommunications facilities. Additionally, TNCs may have to generate internal labor markets by training skilled labor on their technology platforms, both in the Indian subsidiary and also in the home-based technology operations.[12]

From the discussion of the case studies of the Indian firms, the different elements of the process of technological build-up can be seen as the following steps: having a critical level of initial technological capabilities of skilled labor and managerial talent (historically given); conceptualizing the technology needs in relation to the changed market and institutional environment; identifying the sources and sending technicians and managers to the source, not only for the purchase of blueprints and services but also to learn the tacit elements of the technology; adapting to local conditions and realizing the learning-by-doing economies; and undertaking organizational change, such as coordination and developing effective technological linkages with supplier firms. As we can see, these processes imply institutional change within the firms and changes external to the firms. To state it explicitly, the internal institutional change involves the generation of internal labor markets through the training of skilled labor and adopting incentive-compatible practices through organizational change. The external institutional change includes the building of linkages with technology suppliers from developed economies and intermediate supplier firms within India.

Is it possible to generalize these processes to the follower firms and industries in developing economies? After reviewing the literature on technology from Schumpeter to Rosenberg and several other scholars, and the analysis of several hundred case studies in the US, Bhide (2000) observes that "noteworthy developments of new products or processes result from a large number of steps undertaken by many individuals and companies over several decades."

If technological change is an incremental process, the question that follows is, if Indian firms are able to compete with the technologies of TNCs of developed economies in the domestic market, is the next step innovative activity? There is some evidence that the process of local firms responding to fierce competition in the local market is an incremental process. This is substantiated by product improvisations in the two-wheeler industry, such as hybrids of scooters and motorcycles that combine the best features of the two products to cater to the changing preferences of Indian consumers.

One of the success stories of the post-reforms era is the software industry. This industry, which started out with low-end programming, coding, and data feeding for exports in the early 1980s, has become one that undertakes several complex services for export. The procedure of replacing older technological assets and training workers in the manufacturing industries is somewhat different in the case of the software industry. Here, the physical capital intensity is low, while human capital intensity is high. The developments in information and telecommunications technologies make the global diffusion of new technologies rapid and inexpensive. Furthermore, in this industry, the production activity itself embodies technological learning, while in manufacturing this is not often the case. A software engineer thus learns and upgrades as she/he does her/his work, while in manufacturing companies there may be little learning from production alone. Therefore, technological capacity-building in the software context is interpreted as drawing on the basic skills of workers acquired in the universities and the ability of firms to train and retrain workers on new technologies, rather than replacing physical capital. The learning costs and time periods involved are thus much more significant in upgrading complex manufacturing activities than in moving up the software technology ladder.

The issue that follows is to understand how Indian firms were able to move up the learning and quality ladder. Indian firms grew by undertaking low-end programming and coding for the booming world market of the 1980s, mostly doing onsite projects. The next step was to shift to offshore development by building their internal infrastructure and by training skilled workers in order to reduce their dependence on the inefficient Indian infrastructure conditions. Firms recruited people with generic skills in mathematics and engineering, and imparted training in-house on software development. Their basic R&D activity involved the tracking and absorbing of the latest developments in the software field by setting up their units in the US (especially in Silicon Valley), and training their skilled workers on these platforms to deliver services based on new tools (Patibandla and Petersen, 2002).

The industry's major focus had been exports rather than the domestic market. By the early 2000s, in addition to a large number of TNCs undertaking a wide range of activities for the support of their home market operations and for global markets, there were also a few billion-dollar Indian companies, such as Infosys, TCS, and Wipro. Is there any technological innovation possible after achieving billion-dollar company status among Indian firms? One innovation that Indian firms generated and mastered is the global software delivery model. This is the process of understanding and designing the needs of clients abroad, developing software operations in India and delivering and implementing this software at the clients' sites. TNCs such as TI pioneered the offshore development model through modern telecommunications, which Indian companies later imitated.[13]

Otherwise, one can say that there is no significant innovation among Indian companies. The immediate question is, why? There are several possible underlying reasons. An excessive focus on large global markets and little local market focus (domestic demand base) deprive the firms of the intense competitive pressures exerted by local markets. In other words, a plausible conjecture is that a local market with limited demand may pose stronger competition than the world market with a larger opportunity set for diversifying through wage arbitrage. Since the later part of the 1990s, there has been increasing international outsourcing of a wide range of services by companies in the US and western Europe to Indian firms. Consequently, Indian firms find opportunities to increase revenues through diversification into a wide range of services rather than focusing on a few activities. Furthermore, the input of skilled labor is not a binding constraint. In India, there are a large number of graduates with basic engineering skills whom companies can employ and who can be trained quickly in three to six months on different services for their diversification. Lastly, the local technological institutional environment is not adequate for innovations. India lacks a national innovative system that provides effective linkages between different advanced technological institutions.

## The evolution of the national innovative system (NIS)

NIS is a set of institutional conditions at the national level for the generation of technological innovations in terms of the existence of private and public firms, universities, research institutions, funding and undertaking of research by government agencies, intellectual property regimes, and the linkages between these different elements of the institutional environment. The technological capabilities of these organizations and the interactive processes amongst them determine the technological activity at both the firm and national level (Freeman, 1997; Nelson; 1987). Intarakumnerd *et al.* (2002) observe,

> NIS is the interactive system of existing institutions, private and public firms (either large or small), universities and government agencies, aiming at the production of science and technology (S&T) within national borders. Interaction among these units may be technical, commercial, legal, social and financial as much as the goal of the interaction may be development, protection, financing or regulation of new S&T.

In the case of developing economies it is not innovation but imitation of technologies, which is the pertinent issue. The germane issue is how do the prevailing institutions in a developing economy facilitate effective imitation and narrowing of the technology gap with more developed economies.

The evolution of NIS in an emerging-economy context refers to the evolution of the institutional environment that engenders effective imitation of technologies from developed economies and the process leading to institutional development generating innovative capabilities. Given the initial conditions and endowments, the policy reforms result in technological rivalry among firms, which drives them to seek relative advantage both by internal restructuring and by tapping external (to a firm) sources of advantages. This, in turn, triggers the process of evolution of the technological institutional environment at the national level. Also, policy reforms may result in different growth rates of different industries in an economy. Rapid growth of science and knowledge industries in response to the reforms may generate incentives for both the private and public agents to generate conditions for the evolution of NIS for augmenting national and international competitiveness. International competitiveness is germane if the knowledge-intensive industries are highly export-oriented, as in the case of India's software and pharmaceutical industries. This, in turn, can trigger a two-way causation between the increased technological activity of firms and the evolution of NIS in an emerging-economy context.

It is necessary to identify the different elements of NIS in order to understand their emergence and evolution. These are the human capital endowments, which are generated by primary and secondary education, universities; on the job training and learning by doing; the public stock of knowledge, that includes all the research done in universities and research institutions, both the publicly and privately funded; technological externalities caused by the public and private investments in research and a degree of technological activity of firms and industries; the linkages between different actors; and development of financial institutions for risk-taking and investment in innovation.

After the industrial revolution in Britain in the latter half of the eighteenth century, the other west European countries imitated technologies from Britain and developed their NIS for generating innovative activities. In the case of countries such as Germany, the government played an active role in undertaking massive investments in building the infrastructure for generation of the NIS (Rosenberg, 1972). The role of government in generating innovative capabilities in western Europe can also be seen as an offshoot of the war efforts during the First and Second World Wars. These required government to invest in defense-related technologies such as improvement of the performance of jet aircraft and the conversion of basic research in physics into nuclear energy research, which were later commercialized. In the case of the US, the main role of the government in the initial stages of nation-building in the nineteenth century consisted of building a large number of universities. One sociological explanation for this was that the working-class immigrants from Europe wanted to climb the social ladder through education. Government investments in the establishment of universities and universal primary and secondary education led to the generation of a large homogenous middle-class market in the US, which gave it a great advantage later on in becoming the technology leader of the world in the twentieth century (Rosenberg, 1972).

It is common knowledge that Russia, under communism, built highly advanced space technology, while the US was a follower. Under communism, the state was the sole driver of technological activity and innovations, which resulted in its own kind of NIS, in which private incentives were irrelevant. In order to catch up with Russia, the US government took an active role in developing space technology in the 1960s. In America, defense research investments by the government both during the Cold War era and afterwards have become a major source of technological inventions and public stock of knowledge upon which private agents can draw for the commercialization of products.[14]

The difference between the communist and capitalist NIS was that, in the latter case, the government initiated the technological activity by involving private firms. The private agents had the incentive to commercialize the inventions ensuing from government investment in technological advancements. This was one way of drawing on the public stock of knowledge. Therefore, the additional element of the institutional framework of a capitalist innovative system is the combination of private and public technological activities. The role of the government was not, therefore, merely confined to defining a legal system of property rights, and the regulation and facilitation of efficient contract execution, but also the generation of the public stock of knowledge on the basis of which private agents were given incentives for inventions and innovations, and commercialization.

For example, the National Science Foundation in the US funds research in pure sciences in a significant way. The question is, why did or why does government investment in technology have such an important role in the free market economies? The neoclassical economics talks of market failures that occur when private agents do not invest in inventions, either because the returns on research cannot be appropriated by the investors, or projects have a long gestation period, or they do not result in immediate commercial gains, or it requires simultaneous investments in different complementary assets. The essential point here is the role of the government in generating the public stock of knowledge of a country's NIS.

One germane question is the incentive of governments in shaping an NIS by using the taxpayer's money. Subsidizing higher education is politically unpopular in the US, while it is accepted in India. In democracies, governments have to justify their spending and involvement in NIS to the public. In Europe, the incentives came from rivalry among the nation-states, and old European intercultural rivalries. In America, since the Second World War, the main motivating factor for heavy government investment of the taxpayers' money in the NIS was the paranoia of the Cold War, exhibited by both the government and the public. However, after the end of the Cold War, in recent years, nation-states are rapidly losing their economic power to TNCs consequent to globalization. This implies that each nation may complain about the others benefiting more from their investments in public knowledge and technology.[15]

In the case of India, which today is termed an emerging economic power, the middle class is getting international recognition and globalization has also created job opportunities for this section. This is a result of government's heavy investments in higher education in the past and present. Consequently, there would be support for government investment for the generation of the public stock of knowledge. The popular press in the West gives space to the fact that many service and high-tech jobs are moving to countries such as India. There are a few studies which attempt to determine who benefits more from the outsourcing of jobs to India. On one side is the argument that the West is losing jobs to India, while the other side points to the cost savings and surplus generation for TNCs, and considers whether TNCs save more for each dollar they pay to a skilled worker in India (Dossani and Kenny, 2004). If TNCs' savings are a lot more than the wages paid to skilled labor, government investment in subsidizing higher education in India can be termed politically non-viable, provided the real tax-paying public realize it.

India's technology policy prior to the reforms was shaped by the import substitution and self-reliance objectives. In order to achieve these objectives, government subsidized higher education heavily and set up several institutions of higher learning, government research institutions, and public sector firms. By the end of the 1990s, there were 229 universities of national importance, 7,199 undergraduate and postgraduate colleges for general education, 162 medical colleges, and 325 pharmacy colleges, in addition to numerous engineering colleges, including the IITs. Apart from this, there are several institutes that are of international repute. These include the Jawaharlal Nehru University, Madurai Kamraj University, the National Center for Biological Sciences, and the Indian Institute of Science that grant world-class doctorate degrees. The government of India set up several research institutions, such as the Center for Scientific and Industrial Research (CSIR), the Department of Science and Technology, the Department of Defense Research, the Indian Space Research Organization, the Indian Council of Medical Research (ICMR), and the Indian Agricultural Research Institution, which generated about 1,000 R&D institutions and laboratories across the nation.

As Forbes and Wield (2002) observe, by 1980 the Indian government invested 0.6 percent of GDP in R&D, which was more than any other newly industrializing country at the time. This was about the same level as South Korea and Taiwan, two countries whose technological progress has been much more rapid. The concern, is why did India realize lower productivity than South Korea and can we generalize it across all industries or are there islands of success? The second issue is whether India's prior investments have enabled new industries to emerge and traditional industries to restructure themselves effectively in the post-reform era.

I briefly discuss the comparative analysis of the computer industry of South Korea and India. Evans' (1995) comparative study of South Korea, India, and Brazil showed that the information technology industry in these countries was born because of policy intervention and support. In the 1960s, no private entrepreneur could even see the potential of this industry in a developing economy. The initiatives taken by these governments in public sector funding (in India's case, the setting-up of the Bharat Electronics Company) and in supporting private investments led to the birth of the industry in these countries. While the South Korean government nurtured the industry by investing an adequate amount of capital in a targeted and systematic way and building effective linkages between government agencies and private producers, efforts by the Indian and Brazilian governments fell short of making the industry competitive. Consequently, the South Korean semiconductor industry became internationally competitive, while the Indian and Brazilian industry could not grow.

One of the reasons for the lower technological progress in India was the lack of linkages between the public sector investment in R&D and the commercialization efforts of the Indian corporate sector. Under the protectionist regime, Indian corporations had low incentives to undertake technological upgrading as they had captive markets. They made minimal technological efforts, which meant that they did not have incentives to tap the public stock of knowledge. On the other hand, in the case of the pharmaceutical industry, the government made considerable efforts to promote indigenous capabilities for developing mass drugs for the population during the import substitution regime. The government provided tax incentives and relaxation of import licensing to R&D units, and set up various R&D units like the Technical Consultancy Organization (1973), the Risk Capital Foundation (1975), and the Technology Development Fund. The government also developed linkages between the R&D institutions and private sector firms. For example, the National Research and Development Corporation was made to transfer the R&D results of the research institutes to industrial entrepreneurs (Aggarwal, 2004). These efforts made India's pharmaceutical industry one of the most vibrant science-based industries in the post-reforms era.

One more exception was the development of tractor technology in India. The Swaraj tractor was the culmination of governmental efforts. First, the Planning Commission took on the role of conceptualization, and later the Central Mechanical Engineering Research Institute undertook the development and transfer of the technology to private firms (Roy, 2004). The objective was to assist in agricultural development through the Green Revolution. As I have discussed in Chapter 4, one of the government's great success stories (in terms of social objectives) of active intervention in the pre-reform era was the Green Revolution in agriculture. The active role of the Indian Agricultural Research Institution in spreading the use of new seeds and fertilizers was supported by complementary policies of price support, product procurement, and infrastructure development in terms of grain storage facilities. The policies and implementation were comprehensive in terms of developing complementary institutional conditions instead of piecemeal R&D efforts.

The Indian government also embarked on the space research program by setting up the ISRO (Indian Space Research Organization) to meet defense and social objectives. The social purposes comprise weather forecasting for farmers and the spread of literacy to the masses. Nevertheless, these objectives notwithstanding, the importance of the faults of islands of technological activity can also be illustrated by the following example. In 2004, the ISRO launched a satellite for spreading education to the rural masses through communications technology. However, this was not effective in fulfilling its objective, because most villages did not have adequate electricity-supply infrastructure.

As Chandrashekar and Basvarajappa (2001) observe, space technology has direct links with the agriculture sector through remote-sensing satellites, with the IT sector via communications services satellites, and to the weather, ocean and environment sector through both meteorological and remote-sensing satellites. However, the benefits are not fully realized because of the absence of investment in complementary assets. The country is marked by a lack of focus in rural communications, ineffective organization and management of disasters, distorted and inefficient markets for agricultural products, and the inability of government departments dealing with resources management to integrate new technologies into their operations.

The case with respect to universities, engineering institutes, and the corporate sector is very similar. The Indian corporate sector did not build any linkages with the universities and technical institutes for sponsoring research or for commercialization of research, except in a few cases where the large businesses houses such as Tatas and Birlas set up scientific institutions like the Indian Institute of Science, Tata Energy Research Institute, and Birla Institute of Technology. Nevertheless the Indian corporate sector did benefit from subsidized higher education.

## NIS in the post-reform era

One point of interest is how industrial growth and technological progress in the post-reforms era benefit from government investments in technology. A striking example is the emergence of India's software industry. Although in popular parlance it is wryly observed that the software industry developed because it was not targeted for government intervention, Patibandla *et al.* (2000) argued that India's software industry was a by-product of the import substitution policies. The government's policies of subsidized higher education in engineering and basic sciences became a source of comparative advantage in skill endowments from which the industry drew for its export success. Second, private firms, both local and TNCs, were able to poach skilled labor and scientists from the public sector institutions. In the 1990s, most senior managers or project managers in Indian firms and TNCs were ex-employees of the public sector institutions. The other science-based industry that has been able to emerge and grow rapidly on the groundwork of past efforts is the nascent biotechnology industry. The industry is able to draw from the capabilities built in biological sciences, including scientific manpower and public R&D institutions, and also from the pharmaceutical and software industries (bio-informatics) for its emergence and growth in the post-reform era. Similarly, the engineering capabilities acquired under the import substitution regime also became useful for manufacturing industries such as the auto components industry to achieve international competitiveness in the post-reform era.

Given the initial endowments of the NIS at the time of the reforms, there are two notable effects of the reforms that have influenced its evolution: the policy reforms that have altered the incentives of public R&D institutes to commercialize basic research, and the incentives of the private sector firms to tap the public sector institutes. An additional dimension could be the government's efforts at building upon the past capabilities under the changed institutional environment. To give an example of the last observation, the pharmaceutical industry is a success story of the past policies, having become one of the leading players in the world market in the manufacture of generic drugs. The government of India took further initiatives in 1994 for promoting collaborative research between the public institutes and private sector firms for developing new drugs. Aggarwal (2004) observes that the government program supports joint research projects normally on the basis of 50:50 sharing of financial requirements between industry and institutions. This has resulted in twenty-eight alliances, three product patents and nine process patents.

Let us go back to the first issue of altering the incentives of the public R&D institutions – allowing the scientists of the public sector institutions to share in the profits of the commercialization of R&D. Under the previous policy regime, most of the public scientific institutions were controlled by the Indian Civil Service, which imposed various restrictions on salaries and commercialization. In several cases, career bureaucrats belonging to the Indian Administrative Service (IAS) headed public sector firms and technology institutions, instead of scientists, resulting in a mismatch between management and scientific efforts.

## Linkages

Krishnan (2003) shows how the incentives in several of public research institutions are altered in the post-reforms era for more active linkage building and commercialization of technologies. In the post-reforms era, the CSIR laboratories filed 310 Indian patent applications in 1998–9, as against 120 in 1987–8, and were awarded 133 Indian patents in 1998–9, against seventy-six in 1987–8. Apart from this, the external fund flows reached Rs 2,040 million in 1998–9, with 18.1 percent of it coming from private industry and 7.3 percent from foreign sources. This was possible because of the institutional reforms that government implemented in these laboratories. These included allowing the laboratories to retain net earnings from externally sponsored projects, with the freedom to use the funds for internal incentives of scientific manpower.

Krishnan gives the example of the National Chemical Laboratory (NCL), in which the top management implemented organizational changes such as the creation of separate business planning and scientific information divisions, medals for obtaining US patents, and awards for technology development and support functions. As a result, it transformed itself into a global R&D platform in terms of licensing technologies and undertaking contract research for TNCs. The Indian Institute of Science in Bangalore formed the Society for Innovation and Development and started to collaborate with industry in developing and commercializing technology. It has about eighty projects with private industry. Several TNCs, such as IBM and Texas Instruments, sponsor research undertaken by the IIS. It also provides incubation to start-up technology firms, where scientists hand-hold a start-up until it becomes successful. In government higher education technical institutions such as the IITs, incentives for undertaking consultancy research for industry were adopted, with outstanding results leading to increasing linkages with private sector firms for the commercialization of technology. For example, the revenue from sponsored research at the IIT in Kanpur increased tenfold and the consultancy income went up about sixteen times between 1993–4 and 2002–3.

How do incentives for linkages among the private sector change in response to the reforms? The backward and forward linkages among private firms take the form of different types of institutional arrangements depending on the objectives of the agents and external institutional environment. They could be short-term or long-term contractual arrangements, joint ventures, and technology licenses. The governance choices of short- and long-term contracts and integrated operations are determined by the technological capabilities of firms and their ability to find complementary assets and skills among each other, transaction costs of contracts, and protection of intellectual property rights in the knowledge industries. The larger the linkages, both short- and long-term, the higher should be the technological diffusion and generation of public stock of knowledge or spillovers. As against this, highly integrated operations of firms do not contribute much to technological diffusion.

Linkages could be at the higher or lower end of technologies. The former cause a higher degree of technological spillovers than the latter.

This is determined by the technological capabilities of firms and their ability to find complementarity at the higher end of technology. For example, TNCs with modern technologies have an incentive to build linkages with local firms if the local firms have achieved a critical level of technological maturity. Linkages at the higher end of technological activities require the ability of firms to formulate and execute complex contracts in the context of frequent technological changes, which makes transaction costs of incomplete contracts high.

The telecommunications sector is a good example. By 2005, the telecommunications sector in India has become one of the most vibrant and rapidly growing sectors, with both local firms and TNCs playing an important role. The sector was opened to private operators in the early 1990s as a part of the reforms process. The natural monopoly properties of the sector make government intervention necessary in terms of giving licenses to the private operators. For this, private firms have to get into contracts with government to obtain license fees, establish prices, and agree on services. Second, the sector has been subject to rapid technological changes, with frequent decline in average costs and increase in bundling of services. In this context, the contracts between government and the private operators are subject to complex calculations. In the late 1990s, the sector was opened to TNCs, with equity restrictions. This saw the entry of a few TNCs through joint collaborations with local firms. Therefore, the contractual agreements are between the government and the private operators, and the local firms and TNCs, encompassing issues relating to licensing fees, revenue sharing, bundling of different services, equity agreements and control rights. This caused several miscalculations on both sides, especially in the context of rapid technological changes, which resulted in losses, the break-up of joint ventures and the exit of firms, until 2004, when the policy was settled to a 'revenue sharing model' and debundling of certain services.

I have extensively discussed in the previous chapter how the changed institutional arrangements of subcontractor relations in the auto industry transformed it into an internationally competitive one. The linkages between the assemblers and auto component firms resulted in technology transfer and made the first-tier component firms internationally competitive. Although the linkages of subcontractor activity were prevalent to some extent in the pre-reforms era, the Japanese TNC Suzuki brought an institutional change in cooperative relations with component firms for technology transfer and organizational change. When the intermediate products are firm-specific or product-model specific, the firm's assembler and component firms need to develop long-term contracts by undertaking asset-specific investments. Thus, Maruti-Suzuki encouraged several supplier firms to locate their units close to its main factory to facilitate long-term linkages with them. Similarly, TNCs such as Hyundai and Ford brought in their own supplier firms from the their home countries on the basis of long-term relations.

Nortel in the telecoms-software industry provides a good example of linkages with local firms on a short-term contract basis, which resulted in technology diffusion to local firms. Nortel has operations in India for developing telecoms-related software. It entered India in 1989 through a joint R&D collaboration with large Indian firms such as Tata Consultancy Services (TCS), Infosys, Wipro, and Silicon Automation Systems to make use of mutual complementary assets in technology, human capital, and infrastructure. The partnership became possible because Nortel could formulate non-disclosure contracts with each of its partners. Nortel created infrastructure, provided state-of-the-art telecoms hardware and a large capacity for communications in each partner's location. It also invested heavily in training the employees of the Indian firms. As the partnership became successful, Nortel transferred complex technologies to these firms. The partnership benefited Nortel significantly by reducing the costs of developing telecoms-related software. The Indian partners gained in terms of the transfer of the latest technology and Nortel's international management practices and markets. Owing to the transfer of technology, one of the Indian firms has been able to develop a new product and market it globally (Basant *et al.*, 1998; Patibandla and Petersen, 2002). In this case, part of the learning of the local partners consisted of Nortel's technology, but not the whole. In order to restrict the local firms' learning, Nortel formed joint ventures with four Indian firms, with each one assigned a part of the development (independent subprojects) with Nortel alone responsible for the integration (Lema and Hesbjerg, 2003). As Nortel gained experience with Indian market institutions through the partnerships, it set up its own subsidiary in Bangalore in 2000, after which the contracts with local partners were terminated.

The case of Hewlett-Packard in India presents a policy of pursuing linkages with local firms on a consistent and regular basis. On the basis of my fieldwork in 2000 (Patibandla and Petersen, 2002), the HP linkages model consists of three types: outside specialists – consultants are brought in regularly in order to work on short-duration special projects; out-tasked specialists – employees of an Indian firm are given a site at HP and work on a project; and outsourced specialists – the project moves out to an Indian firm. One of the three different outsourcing models is adopted depending on the project needs. HP outsources some projects to a group of small companies who are selected after rigorous screening and bidding, and are made to sign non-disclosure contracts. The firms are provided with HP technology and some training is given to the employees. HP deliberately selects small firms because entrepreneurs of small firms are highly motivated by their linkage with HP, which is a strong source for growth and helps in establishing their reputation for high-quality work.[16] Some of the problems that HP faces in relation to outsourcing are delivery time, cost overruns, and the attrition issue of employees on a given project. In order to mitigate these problems, HP sometimes employs more than one firm on a similar task. However, the higher-end technological activity of HP in India is retained with the subsidiary.

In the case of industries such as software, the main input is skilled labor. To overcome the shortages of skilled labor and identify the right kind of skills, software firms built linkages with educational institutions for the generation of a skilled workforce. In the case of TNCs such as Microsoft, the additional interest is the promotion of firm-specific technology platforms with lock-in characteristics. To give a few examples, the TI subsidiary has developed linkages with the universities and research labs in and around Bangalore through funding the establishment of research labs in about twenty universities and through collaborations with university professors in designing and upgrading the curriculum of engineering education. Since the curriculum is outdated in several universities, this last task is stated to be an important element of TI's linkage with educational institutions. Similarly, Motorola built linkages with fifteen engineering colleges in Bangalore, after screening 100 colleges in and around the city. Motorola provides the institutions with technology, tools, and training. Furthermore, faculty members are brought in for sabbaticals at Motorola's center. The company has also invested in the courses of the Indian Institute of Information Technology (IIITs) of Bangalore and Hyderabad. The TNC and a few large, local software firms, in collaboration with the state and central governments, initiated the setting-up of the Indian Institutes of Information Technology in major cities in India. Infosys, a leading Indian software firm, set up software engineering educational centers in and around Bangalore. Apart from this, it built linkages with the Indian Institute of Management, Bangalore for the setting-up of management education specifically for the software industry in 2005.

The strategy of building extensive linkages by Microsoft in India presents the case of the firm promoting its technological platforms. In this way, Microsoft employs a fairly active and aggressive approach in getting collaborative arrangements with almost all the leading Indian firms. Microsoft's sales operations, barring the R&D center in Hyderabad, actively invest in education to spread Microsoft's technology. This is very unlike Texas Instruments, which does not have local market focus. Microsoft provides certified technical courses at Microsoft Authorized Technical Education Centers (ATEC) and end-user training courses on Microsoft products via Authorized Training Centers (ATC). Furthermore, the company organizes seminars and hands-on, lab-based and video courses which emphasize skill transfer by providing the necessary technology, and help to build, implement, and support real-world business solutions that take full advantage of Microsoft technology. Microsoft is also involved in the course development of the Indian Institute of Information Technology in Hyderabad. The operations of Microsoft's R&D center in that city are carried out without any outsourcing or collaborations with the local firms.

**Industrial clusters**

Industrial cluster dynamics are considered an important dimension of the NIS of a country because cluster activity generates technological externalities by reducing the transaction costs of linkages among various actors. The external economies of cluster activity imply that for given inputs, the output of an individual firm is larger in direct relation to the aggregate output of other firms producing a similar good in a cluster or a region. Apart from this, clusters make the benchmarking of best practices and their imitation and diffusion easier than under diffused location of firms, by facilitating closer interaction and promoting the demonstration effect among firms. The larger the number of firms in a cluster, the higher are these possibilities. In the case of the famous Silicon Valley cluster, Saxenian (1994) showed how a decentralized system of dense social networks linking a large number of large and small firms, research institutions, and universities generates conditions for entrepreneurship. The cluster demonstrates both intense rivalry and cooperative networks of communication and collaborative projects among a large number of actors, with a high degree of benchmarking, learning, and diffusion of best practices and ideas.

In the present discussion, there are two pertinent issues relating to clusters. The first is, how do the reforms contribute to the generation and expansion of industrial clusters? And second, how does cluster activity engender institutional change within and outside a cluster? Initial conditions or historical incidents and geographical advantages lead to a concentration of industrial activity, which generates self-perpetuating agglomeration economies. On the institutional front, the issue is, how does cluster development promote collective action for bringing about institutional change, in other words the formation of 'social capital' through repeated interactions, which reduce the transaction costs of market exchange?

The effect of the reforms on the cluster dynamics is that the elimination of industrial licenses, liberalization of entry of TNCs, removal of restrictions on the regional location of firms, and reduction in political interference can allow firms to make their location decisions purely on efficiency considerations, which, in turn, may lead to the formation of new clusters and augmentation of the dynamics of prevailing clusters. If the industries that form into clusters have comparative advantage in exports, policy reforms such as trade liberalization further enhance the cluster dynamics by expanding output through trade. The software industry cluster in Bangalore and the garments cluster in Tirupur took roots much before the reforms – the software cluster in the early 1980s and the Tirupur garments cluster as early as 1935.

The policy reforms on the international front in 1991, especially the devaluation of the rupee, gave a significant boost to exports by the clusters and consequently led to their rapid growth. The export orientation of clusters accentuates external economies because the learning of international practices through trade diffuses more effectively in a cluster than in a geographically diffused industry. In contrast to the above example of Tirupur in garments, the textile cluster of Bhiwandi (in Maharastra) presents a cluster on the decline in the post-reforms period. This cluster prospered prior to the reforms through inward orientation and under stagnant technological conditions. In the 1990s, it had started to decline under the changing textile production scenario induced by the reforms owing to inadequate investment in technology by the small-scale power-loom firms. Bhiwandi had about 400,000 small-scale power-loom firms in production, amounting to about Rs 4,000 million turnover per day in 1999. The inability of the firms to upgrade technology and generate surplus through collective action led to cut-throat competition in the form of price cutting, and even unethical practices among the firms within the cluster, which contributed to its decline.

On the other hand, in the case of traditional, labor-intensive and low-technology export industries such as diamond cutting, the agglomeration economies of technological learning may not be as dominant as in high-tech industries because these industries are not characterized by frequent technological change. One of the reasons for the dominance of the Bombay-Surat cluster of this industry in the western part of India is the practice of informal trading contractual practices among an ethnic class of Gujarati traders. In this industry, the key resource was monopolized access to rough diamonds by ethnic traders from the international cartel De Beers. Trading of diamonds and large sums of working capital among the traders takes place through informal contracts. Diamonds were cut and polished mostly by semi-skilled labor, which did not belong to any particular location. The cheap labor can be trained in any part of the country, whereas relocation away from the existing Bombay-Surat cluster may reduce poaching of trained labor by competitors. There was some movement of firms away from Bombay-Surat to the southern cities of Chennai and Bangalore in the late 1990s (Ghemawat and Patibandla, 1999). In other words, a pertinent question, is does the need for the clustering decline if the hold of the industry by traders bound by an ethnic background goes down?

The automobile industry presents an interesting case of cluster formation and dynamics. As mentioned in the previous chapter, Maruti-Suzuki was set up in central north India in the city of Gurgaon. Suzuki, by bringing the Japanese practices of outsourcing and just-in-time production, developed the region into a vibrant auto-component cluster. In order to implement its lean production practices under the Indian conditions of inefficient infrastructure, Maruti encouraged many of its suppliers to locate close to its plant in Gurgaon. At present, it has about 400 suppliers in India, 248 of them located in the proximity of its plant. The Japanese practices led to cooperative relations between the final producer and the suppliers for the transfer of technology and organizational practices. Maruti and its suppliers in the location generated agglomeration economies, which prompted other TNCs such as Honda and Daewoo to locate nearby to tap the suppliers of Maruti, in the post-reform period.

Another automobile cluster that took root and has been growing in the post-reforms era is the one in the coastal region of Tamil Nadu state in the south. This is driven by two major TNCs: the South Korean Hyundai, and the American Ford. The coastal location gives them an advantage for international trade. Furthermore, they were able to tap the well-developed engineering base and skilled manpower available in the state. The initial endowment of engineering capabilities helped the firms to develop local component suppliers through technology transfer under long-term cooperative contracts. The cooperative behavior led the component suppliers to invest in location-specific assets for the needs of the final producers, and the final producers, in turn, undertook technology transfer to the component producers. In other words, both the assemblers and component producers invested in credible commitments for mutual benefits.

A lot is being written on India's software industry and the Bangalore software cluster, both in academic and popular literature. In 2004, India exported close to $10 billion worth of software and services, of which one-third comes from Bangalore alone. In 2004, there are close to 300 leading technology companies which operate low-end call centers and high-tech R&D operations. In 2002, of the fifty-five software companies in the world that had reached CMM level 5 authorization, twenty-two of these were located in Bangalore (Lema and Hesbjerg, 2003). The origins of the Bangalore cluster have some similarities with Silicon Valley in terms of the role of government institutions at the initial stages. During the Second World War, the US government set up a defense research base in the Bay Area. Subsequently, the setting-up of Hewlett-Packard there gave an impetus to the formation of the cluster. Similarly, the government of India set up defense-related research institutions and high-technology public sector firms in Bangalore in the 1950s and 1960s. Many small private-sector firms came into Bangalore as subcontractors to these public sector firms, which sowed the seeds for Bangalore to become a dynamic high-tech cluster later on.

As discussed in Chapter 4, the entry of Texas Instruments in 1985 and its successful operation served as a demonstration effect to several leading world players in the software industry to enter Bangalore. Around that time, the government of India developed the concept of software technology parks (STP), which the government's Department of Electronics implemented in 1991. The STPs not only provided the infrastructure necessary for exports but also procedural assistance such as project approval, import approvals, and bonding and export certification. They provide assistance to new entrants by giving access to incubation infrastructure and high-speed international gateways.

Motorola, Texas Instruments, HP and local firms such as Infosys built varying types of linkages in and around Bangalore. The linkages of firms are mostly with educational and research institutions, rather than amongst each other. Linkages among firms are limited because most firms, especially the Indian firms, are largely focused on software services, which reduces the scope for collaboration among firms. Lema and Hesbjerg (2003), on the basis of their extensive fieldwork in Bangalore, observe that managers of firms associate collaborative relations with a high degree of risk. They are therefore less willing to engage in collaborative relations as they grow, because most large companies in Bangalore are service companies, which is a domain of low entry barriers that is characterized by a high risk of customers being stolen. They also observe that coordination activities tend to take place within ownership-based hierarchies and there is little institutionalized coordination at the inter-firm level. This shows that linkages between input suppliers and assemblers are not static. An input supplier can become an assembler by drawing away the customers of the assemblers when there are low costs of entry. By reducing the transaction costs and informational imperfections of the output, labor and financial markets, cluster activity may result in a decline in entry costs to new entrants.

The major focus of the firms in the Bangalore cluster is on inter-cluster relations and vertical relations, especially with the US customers rather than local firms because the industry has been mostly export-oriented with a low domestic market focus. In such a case, external economies develop through informational and technological externalities of international trade. A high degree of international orientation exposes firms to practices in developed economies, which facilitates the imitation of these practices. If one firm adopts international practices, other firms, even those with a domestic market focus, may be driven to imitate them owing to competition in the skilled labor market. Skilled workers are attracted away by firms with superior employee-incentive practices and technology. Poaching becomes easier in a cluster than in a spatially diffused industry. In my fieldwork in 2000, several TNC executives observed that they were able to attract the best talent because of the adoption of employee incentives, flat organizational structures, and allowing highly skilled workers to work on advanced technologies with a high degree of learning on the job.

The rapid growth of the cluster in the 1990s and the early 2000s led to the emergence of supportive institutions and markets in Bangalore. Figure 3 demonstrates the linkages of a set of complementary industries and services with the IT industry of the Bangalore cluster.[17] Markets for services such as campus management and financial services emerged in Bangalore in response to the growth of the industry. The emergence of support industries and services reduces the transaction costs of the backward linkages of software firms. However, since the mid-1990s, the Bangalore cluster experienced an exponential expansion with an increasing

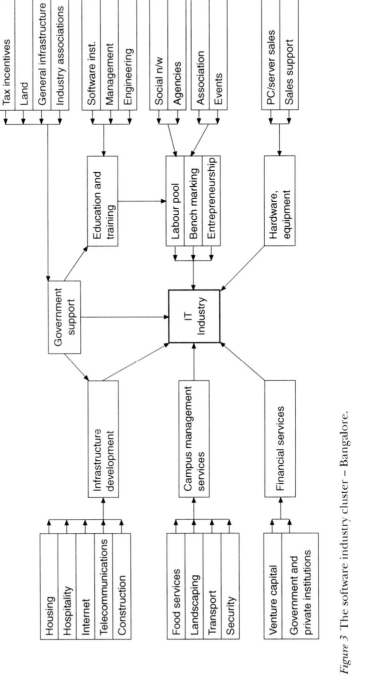

*Figure 3* The software industry cluster – Bangalore.

number of TNCs setting up their outsourcing operations. This, in turn, pulled in a large number of skilled workers to Bangalore and also increased wage rates (Patibandla and Petersen, 2002, 2004). The escalating wage rate of skilled workers and the increasing establishment of new entrants, in turn, resulted in exponential expansion in construction, housing demand, and rental costs, and an increase in the number of automobiles on the roads. Public services such as water and roads could not cope with the growth, which resulted in significant negative externalities to the local public, leading to traffic congestion, pollution, and water scarcity.

I discussed in Chapter 4 how companies such as Infosys became 'islands of international competitiveness' by generating their own infrastructure. However, this has limitations, especially when the industry grows at a rapid pace and is geographically concentrated in a specific region or city. I have also argued earlier that a high degree of export orientation relaxed the domestic market size constraint, which allowed the entry of a large number of both local firms and TNCs. Theoretically, a developing economy is a price-taker in the world market, which means that firms face an infinitely elastic demand. Firms can thus sell as much as they can at a given world price. In such a case, if the production of output, growing at rapid pace, is concentrated in one city within the country, the output expansion should be supported by institutional change that facilitates public goods provision within the region at the same pace.

Institutional change is, however, a slow process. To illustrate this, the government of India monopolizes the building of infrastructure such as roads, airports, and water supply. I have been in Bangalore since July 2003 and I see private housing buildings and offices of world-class standards coming up rapidly all over the city. The private sector has been able to respond quickly to the opportunities, with the emergence of specialized contractors who have acquired the ability, for example, to build, within nine months, world-class campus facilities that can accommodate 5,000 employees. The contractors have also developed innovative organizational forms, such as build, operate, and transfer, in order to reduce the transaction costs of entry to new TNCs, which I discuss in the following chapter. But the construction and improvement of the roads and water supply remains in an abysmal state. Until 1995, the government alone took the responsibility for building roads. Later, it allowed private contractors to participate with local governments. Political interference and the contracts' distorted incentives for corruption make construction activity subject to delays and haphazard progress. Furthermore, to promote the software industry, the government provided several tax breaks to the industry, which means that local government could not generate sufficient revenues in line with the growth of the industry to invest in the infrastructure needs.

**Negative externalities**

Industrial growth in general gives rise to both positive and negative externalities, and clusters magnify both. In the Coasian theorem, as discussed in Chapter 2, collective action in the absence of transaction costs could rectify negative externalities. The presence of transaction costs requires government to interfere and establish appropriate public order institutions. However, both government institutions and the collective action of the people subjected to negative externalities may be ineffective in a developing economy, especially with the rapid growth of markets which are not matched by institutional change at a similar pace. In the following, I illustrate the negative externalities of cluster activity.

In Chapters 3 and 4, I discussed how small firms played a prominent role in exports. Most small firms tend to be in the labor-intensive areas, in which India has a natural comparative advantage. Apart from this, several of these industries are also pollution-intensive, such as the dyes and pigments, leather, and shrimp farming industries. Several of these products were reserved for small-scale firms, for example leather processing up to the semi-finished state. The trade policy reforms, especially the devaluation of the rupee in 1991, enhanced the comparative advantage of labor-intensive goods produced by small firms and there has been a rapid growth of exports by the small-scale sector. In 2003, the small-scale industry comprised 40 percent of industrial production, employed about seventeen million people, and accounted for 35 percent of India's total exports. Exports of small firms will be even higher if one takes into account indirect exports through subcontracting with large exporters. Small-scale firms belonging to a specific industry have a tendency to form geographically concentrated clusters. To give a few examples, there are textile dyeing industries in the states of Gujarat and Rajasthan, the leather industry is in Tamil Nadu, the diamond-cutting industry is located in Surat, and hosiery and garments are found in Ludhiana and in Tirupur.

Industries such as leather tanning are generally located on the river belts, for leather treatment purposes. Several of these clusters resulted in significant pollution of river and groundwater and agricultural lands in the nearby regions. The main reason is that it is too expensive for small firms to adopt pollution-prevention technology individually and regulation in India has been ineffective despite a large number of rules and laws governing environmental protection. For example, in Tamil Nadu state, the leather industry in the Palar Valley and the garment industry cluster in Tirupur have resulted in vast tracts of agricultural land becoming unfit for agricultural use, and a large section of the local population have been deprived of their sources of drinking water. Similarly, the clusters of textile-dyeing units polluted the Pali, Balotra, and Jodhpur rivers in Rajasthan and Gujarat, and rivers such as the Bhavani and Noyal in Tamil Nadu. Harris-White (2003) observes that the state has been indifferent or slow to act against the business class of these clusters because of their collusive powers with the state. The consequence of this is that the costs of the negative externalities fall mostly on those who are least able to bear the costs, namely, the disenfranchised and diffused rural poor, for whom the transaction costs of undertaking countervailing collective action are too high.

I briefly discuss the internal collective efficiency of the Tirupur cluster and its effect on the local environment. About 70 percent of cotton knitwear production and exports are concentrated in Tirupur. An ethnic community called 'Gounders' of Tamil Nadu state, hailing from an agricultural background, initially started the cluster. In the initial stages, the community ties of the Gounders fostered cooperative behavior in raising capital, subcontracting, and undertaking export orders in order to economize on transaction costs. From the late 1980s, as the cluster had become highly export successful, a number of people from all over the country entered the cluster. In the 1990s, after the reforms, the cluster experienced rapid growth, with an annual export growth rate of about 50 percent. By the mid-1990s, half of the producers were Gounders and the rest were outsiders (Banerjee and Munshi, 2002).

Later on, the cluster developed its own norms of cooperative behavior. The firms range in size from five to 500 workers. The large variation in size and capital-intensity of the firms is a result of decentralization and outsourcing among firms through job work and indirect exports. The firms in the cluster developed cooperative norms, such as refraining from price undercutting for securing export contracts. Clustering improved the flow of information about export markets and how to serve them, reduced fears about buyer/supplier hold-up that might prevail with smaller numbers and facilitated organized cooperative efforts in areas such as lobbying the government for infrastructure (Ghemawat and Patibandla, 1999; Cawthorne, 1995). However, as mentioned before, the rapid growth of output through exports resulted in negative externalities, such as the destruction of neighboring agricultural lands, and river and groundwaters.

Annually, the cluster exports about 71,000 tonnes of knitwear and produces about 50,000 tonnes for the domestic market, with about 4,000 small firms involved in various processes, including bleaching and dyeing. About ninety million liters of water are consumed in a single day. This production activity polluted nearby rivers and agricultural land. The local government and environmental boards ignored the problem until a group of farmers, with the help of NGOs, filed a public litigation against the polluting units of Tirupur, which led to direct intervention by the Supreme Court of India. This led the Tamil Nadu Pollution Control Board to take action and close 140 units. The producers of the regions responded by forming eight groups to construct Common Effluent Treatment Plants.

In the case of the leather industry in Tamil Nadu, it was again the interference of two external agents that led firms to adopt pollution free technologies. The first was direct intervention by the Supreme Court of India, and the other was the banning of leather products containing tanning chemicals from India by the German government. The German ban was effective in mobilizing the whole industry to adjust quickly. Since low-end cleaning of leather was reserved for small firms, a large exporter, who depended on the small firms for the leather, mobilized the small firms and helped them to adopt pollution-free technology under a 'forced cooperation' (Tewari and Pillai, 2003). In the case of the Palar Valley leather cluster, the state government enforced and subsidized collective treatment plants for tanning effluents. This aspect of the emergence of private order institutions for collective action is elaborated in Chapter 8. The essential point here is that policy reforms, by changing the relative prices that do not capture the costs of negative externalities, can result in the expansion of output and input markets, causing high social costs. In the absence of appropriate institutions, the costs of negative externalities can be severe and the important issue is who bears the burden. The latter aspect determines how soon the appropriate regulatory institutions come into existence. Most of the polluting industries expanded through trade in the post-reforms environment. With an increase in international trade and expanded output, certain elements of institutional change that rectified the negative externalities also arose from external (international) sources, namely, countries like Germany, Sweden, and Switzerland that banned garments dyed with azo benzidine and other similar amines, forcing local firms to change their production practices.

A counter-example of TNCs causing negative externalities is the case of Coca Cola. In the soft-drinks industry, Pepsi was the first entrant in the 1980s. Under the prevailing government stipulations TNCs were expected to contribute to exports. This obliged Pepsi to develop agricultural markets for tomatoes and potatoes in Punjab and Haryana, which benefited small farmers. However, the entry of Coca Cola into the Indian market in the 1990s led to intense competition between the two. Interestingly, the two giants could not make much profit from the soft-drinks market in India. As a response, they developed markets for bottled water in India in a big way. Thus, Coca Cola in the south Indian state of Andhra Pradesh buys water from the government at the rate of about Rs 0.30 per liter and sells the treated bottled water in the market at Rs 10. Extensive extraction of water by the TNC resulted in a scarcity of drinking water for common people. It is observed that the Coca Cola plant in Plachimada over-exploited groundwater resources, resulting in the drying-up of wells and other natural water resources in the surrounding areas and adversely affecting agriculture and drinking water for the populace. Apart from this, the company was accused of supplying its plant wastes, containing high levels of lead and cadmium, as fertilizers to farmers (Jayaraman, 2002; Srivastava, 2004). This has led the state government of Kerala to close the operations of Coca Cola in its state.

In other words, openness to international trade and investment can generate positive and negative externalities. Minimization of negative externalities depends on both the effectiveness of the government regulatory bodies and private order institutions, and the ability of the victims to organize themselves and undertake countervailing actions.

## Feedback effects

In the following section, I discuss explicitly how increased technological activity in post-reforms India contributes to the evolution of markets and institutions. One of the aspects of the evolution of markets is the emergence of new industries in response to the technological and market dynamics of other industries. I take the case of the biotechnology industry to illustrate this aspect.

The growth of the biotechnology industry in India since the late 1990s can be attributed to complementarities arising out of the capabilities of the pharmaceutical and software industries, given the initial endowments of skilled labor and public sector scientific institutions. In the early 2000s, the popular talk of the press, the business community, and government agents was: "We have done it in IT and next big thing is BT [biotechnology]." This reflects changes in attitudes and perceptions as a consequence of the international success of the software and pharmaceutical industries, which, as Douglas North says, is an important driver of institutional change. I provide qualitative evidence for this observation in the following paragraphs.

Although the government sowed the seeds of the biotechnology industry before the reforms by establishing the public sector research institutions in biological sciences and the Department of Biotechnology in 1986, the industry started to grow only after the late 1990s.[18] Indian biotech firms have taken four distinct routes to development: diversifying from large-scale industrial activities such as chemical manufacturing, creating start-ups focused on the indigenous production of first-generation recombinant proteins, investing profits and expertise from generic pharmaceutical manufacturing to move into discovery, and combining expertise in biology and information technology to create bioinformatics and genome companies.

The leading pharmaceutical firms such as Reddy's Laboratories and Ranbaxy, started bio-pharmaceutical divisions for the development of vaccines and molecules. Apart from this, the leading software companies started bioscience divisions for the development of bioinformatics using software skills for gene mapping. To give an example, the largest Indian software company, TCS, has developed software for the biotechnology and the pharmaceutical industries. This is a software package called 'Bio-Suite' which can be used for analyzing and accelerating drug-discovery processes in partnership with the CSIR. The software has been developed with the objective of bringing forth cost-effective indigenous technology for developing the biotechnology industry. It consists of eight blocks covering all aspects of computational biology, ranging from genomics to structure-based drug design. It comprises more than 200 individual algorithms and is designed to be modular so that new algorithms can be added as scientific advances take place. This bioinformatics software is developed in collaboration with the Indian research institutions, such as the Center for DNA Fingerprinting and Diagnostics, the Center for Biotechnology, and the Indian Institute of Science.

On the part of the government, the Department of Biotechnology of India has developed a nationwide network called the Biotechnology Information System. This network provides grants and discipline-oriented information to public institutions all over the country. The DBT has initiated twenty master's-level courses in general biotechnology, agricultural biotechnology, and medical and marine biotechnology, and diploma courses in molecular and biochemical technology. In the case of the IT industry, it was the government that took the sole initiative in setting up the STPs. The result of the demonstration effect of the success of the software technology parks is the active participation of the private sector in the biotechnology industry for the development of biotechnology parks. The state government of Andhra Pradesh in collaboration with the ICICI bank set up the Genome Valley technology park in Hyderabad with 200 acres of land. The infrastructure not only provides self-contained facilities to local companies and TNCs, but the ICICI bank and the state government also set up a venture capital fund for new start-ups in the park. In 2002, the government launched India's first biotech venture fund with a corpus of $30 million. It was a joint venture between the Andhra Pradesh Investment Development Corporation and Dynam Venture East of the US. Similarly, the Tamil Nadu and Karnataka state governments set up biotechnology parks in collaboration with the ICICI bank and American and German TNCs. Consequently, there has been an increasing presence of TNCs and local firms. Several of them are new start-ups, especially in the southern cities of Bangalore and Hyderabad. Hyderabad city has started to form a bio-pharmaceutical cluster of firms, given the development levels of the pharmaceutical firms and the leading public sector research institutions such as the Indian Institute of Chemical Technology, the Center for Cellular and Molecular Biology, the National Institute of Nutrition, and the Center for DNA Fingerprinting and Diagnostics. Given the presence of well-developed software firms and public research institutions such as the Indian Institute of Science, the bioinformatics cluster started to form in Bangalore. The interesting aspect of these developments is that highly specialized science-based clusters are taking root in a developing economy, indicating evolving capabilities in high-tech industries and the NIS of India.

Unlike the software industry, which has been mostly export-oriented with little domestic market focus, the biotechnology industry has been increasing its outward-orientation with a domestic market base. The industry has a large and growing domestic market for vaccines and agricultural biotechnology. For example, the Shanta Biotech firm in Hyderabad developed India's first indigenous r-DNA-based hepatitis B vaccine. Shanvac-B, the company's first product, is the largest selling hepatitis B vaccine in the country. Every time an Indian company introduces a vaccine in the country, TNCs have to slash their prices owing to the cost-competitiveness of Indian firms. At the same time, the industry has been increasing its international orientation through exports and the increasing presence of TNCs. Several TNCs have built linkages with local firms for contract research outsourcing on a vertical chain of product development and linkages for collaborative research for the development of molecules. Another dimension of the internationalisation of the industries is that several local companies have obtained international patents for the discovery of molecules. The Bharat Biotech Company in Hyderabad obtained a patent for the lysostaphin molecule covering more than 100 countries, including the US. The interesting side of the story is that the company is a new start-up, established only in 1996.

## Labor markets and human capital

The relevant issue in the present context is, how does the increased technological activity in Indian industries contribute to the evolution of labor markets and the associated institutions, increased skills and productivity, demand for labor, and decline in the transaction costs of labor markets? To recapitulate, in Lucas's specification of growth model, growth is a function of the stock of human capital in the economy that is generated by educational institutions and by learning on the job. The latter aspect implies a two-way relationship. The initial endowments of human capital generate technological activity in response to the altered incentives of the reforms. Increased technological activity changes labor markets in two ways: increase in productivity (and wages), and demand for skilled labor, which means that there are incentives for the generation of a pool of skilled labor. This increase in the pool of skilled labor has to be seen in the context of a labor-surplus developing economy. Adoption of newer technologies by firms requires training labor on the job, which means an increase in the productivity of the labor employed. Demand for skilled labor increases when demand for output expands more than the output expansion of increased productivity through on-the-job training of employed workers.

On the basis of a rigorous of study of India's auto component industry in the post-reform era, Sutton (2004) observes, "The theme of India's excess supply of highly qualified individuals with poor employment prospects is an old one." Firms increasingly employ skilled labor to maintain quality standards, the pay-offs of which outweigh the increase in wage costs. One important dimension of the changes in labor practices is that employers are increasingly adopting training on the job to upgrade the skills of employees in a sustained manner, which contributes to a significant increase in productivity. As firms, especially the first-tier ones, adopted modern technologies, the demand for skilled labor increased but direct employment of unskilled and semi-skilled labor declined.

In the case of the IT industry, the major technological change that contributed to an increase in the skill labor pool is the move from on-site projects (onshore) to the offshore model since the late 1980s. Basant and Rani (2004) observe that software companies could only hire engineers from good institutions for onshore projects because the nature of the tasks was complex and diverse. The offshore model allows firms to employ both engineers and non-engineers from both good and less-renowned universities to undertake both complex and less-complex tasks. As a result, more people with different skill-sets can participate in the labor market. The offshore model, made possible by technological changes in telecommunications and information technology, allowed India's software industry to expand in three broadly segregated groups: offshore software development (programming and coding), investment in research and development, and business process operations such as medical transcripts, back-office operations, call centers, data processing, etc. The pattern can be observed in greater detail in terms of the segments, such as integrated circuit design (IC), systems software, application software, and communications software. In the case of IC, both semi-conductor and related software development takes place. These different segments require different levels of labor skills and sophistication. IT-enabled services is the least skill-intensive part. Programming and coding require basic skill, while the other segments require highly specialized skills. For example, in the case of telecoms-related software development, the skill requirements are high because it is necessary to have software skills and also an understanding of telecoms technology. While Indian software firms are mostly focused on services, several TNCs, such as IBM, HP, and Oracle, have operations in India in all three segments.

The rapid growth of the industry in the 1990s through the increasing presence of local firms and TNCs increased the demand for skilled labor at different levels of skills, which caused an average annual increase in the wage rate of about 30 percent. The supply-side response of the labor market is an increase in the supply of skilled labor from the formal institutions, and also through increasing the presence of private software-training institutes and engineering colleges in India. The number of software professionals increased from 7,000 in 1986 to about 0.7 million in 2002. The increase in the wage rate put pressure on firms to augment productivity, not only by internal training and organizational restructuring, but also by differentiating skilled labor and assigning tasks in accordance with skills rather than using high skills for mundane tasks, a practice which was widely prevalent in the 1980s, when the market structure was concentrated. As labor markets deepened, the markets for differentiating skilled labor developed, with the emergence of specialized employment agencies, which also contributed to a decline in the transaction costs of the labor markets.[19]

The wage increase is more at the higher end of the skills market than at the lower end because of India's labor market. Despite the large increase in the volume of output, the wage rate of lower-end skilled labor remains lower in India than in the advanced trading economies because of the abundant supply of semi-skilled labor in India. Labor supply responds quickly to changing demand conditions in this segment. Higher-end skilled labor is paid a relatively higher wage rate owing to its relative scarcity. However, the wage rate is not equalized with the US in this segment because the technology in India is still inferior to that of America (Patibandla and Petersen, 2004).

A major part of the growth of the software and services industry is still at the lower technological paradigm as compared to the advanced economies. This has certain negative implications for the evolution of NIS because the market then acts as a disincentive for the acquisition of highly specialized skills with doctoral degrees. The wage rate of scientists with doctoral degrees is far lower than that of software professionals with a few years of experience, thereby making it unattractive for bright young people to acquire doctoral degrees. This, in turn, results in a shortage of good teachers and of specialized skills for fundamental research, which restrains the innovative capabilities of the economy in general.[20] In my fieldwork, a few executives of leading local and TNC software firms in Bangalore mentioned that there was a shortage of teachers because they were attracted away by companies offering high salaries.

## Venture capital

One of the outcomes of the growth and technological activity of the software industry in the post-reforms era is the emergence of venture capitalist institutions. At the early stages of its evolution in the 1980s, entrepreneurs such as Narayana Murthy of Infosys had to depend on personal finance and some funding from the public financial institutions. As the industry grew and became internationally successful, venture capitalists entered the scene to fund new entrepreneurs. Initially, a few large TNCs, such as Intel and Cisco, funded some start-up companies. Venture capital funding by TNCs can be a significant element of the evolution of the industry, as TNCs are geographically insensitive, whereas a typical venture fund in the US tends to be provincial (Dossani, 1999). A few non-resident Indians who made fortunes in Silicon Valley started venture capital funds in the software industry. In 2000, it was estimated that there was about $200 million worth of venture capital, especially in Bangalore, to fund start-ups in the software industry (Patibandla *et al.*, 2000). By 2003, there were about seventy venture capitalists operating in India, with about $5.5 billion worth of funds. The focus of the venture capitalists diversified into areas other than the software industry, such as health, biotechnology, IT-enabled services, and wireless applications. Some of these areas, such as biotechnology, have a long gestation period. Furthermore, several local financial institutions and banks, such as ICICI and IDBI, have set up venture capital funds to identify potential start-ups both in the science-based and manufacturing industries.

Venture capital institutions are one of the conditions for entrepreneurial and innovative activity. Entrepreneurial activity can be start-ups focusing on the imitation of technologies from the advanced economies, or they may be of the innovative kind. Most of the technological activity in Indian industries has been of the imitative kind, both by large, established players and new entrants. The question is whether there has been any increase in innovative activities as a result of the increased technological efforts of Indian industries in the post-reforms era. The number of US patent filings from India increased from 183 in 1997 to 883 in 2001. These are mostly in the software, pharmaceutical, and biotechnology industries. The patent filings are made by large local firms, such as Reddy's Labs and Ranbaxy in the pharmaceutical industries, public research institutions (CSIR), TNC operations in India, and few small and start-up firms. In 2003, small IT firms filed about thirty-five patents in the US. Start-up firms such as Bharat Biotech and Shanta Biotech in the biotechnology industry were successful in obtaining patents for vaccines. TNCs in India like Cisco in the IT industry took 245 patents in 2002, out of which 145 were filed from India. The HP subsidiary in India encourages its employees to file for patents with reward-sharing agreements, and it secured about sixty patents filed from its India operation. The Indian subsidiary of the US-based $1.2 billion Adobe Systems, Adobe India, has developed Acrobat Reader for handheld devices from concept to the final product at its R&D center in Noida (Patibandla and Petersen, 2002).

As discussed in Chapter 4, the institutions for legal rights and their enforcement of IPRs are viable in a developing economy only when local industry and firms generate a strong economic interest in IPRs The government of India signed the WTO agreement, which means that the implementation of IPRs of WTO rules must begin from January 2005. The central government of India issued the ordinance regarding the implementation of IPRs in January 2005, despite opposition from the left-wing parties who are the coalition partners of the Congress party, which is in power at the center. But this issue is subject to complex interpretations regarding whether it is the result of lobbying from TNCs to suit their interests, or the larger economic interests of the nation.

To illustrate this, the editorial of the *New York Times*, January 18 2005, observes that the ordinance works against the poor, not only in India but in the world, by taking the example of the generic version of the antiretroviral drug treatment for Aids patients developed by Indian pharmaceutical companies, which brought down the price of the drug from $12,000 to $140 a year. The editorial observes,

> Industry lobbyists managed to insert two noxious provisions in the decree that go well beyond the WTO rules. The decree would limit efforts to challenge patents before they take effect. Also, it is uncomfortably vague about whether companies could engage in 'evergreening' – extending their patents by switching from a capsule to tablet, for example, or finding a new use for the product. This practice, a problem in America and elsewhere, extends monopolies and discourages innovation.

In other words, the attitudinal changes made use of by organized vested-interest groups (right-timing of the powers of lobbying) can go overboard and exaggerate the short-run benefits of free markets in a country that is moving from over-control to freer markets.[21]

Another dimension of the evolution of technological institutions is the emergence of markets for the management of IPRs Since 2002, a few specialized service firms have emerged in India to provide consultancy services in the technical and legal aspects of patent research, and patent registering and enforcement.[22] The interesting side of this development is that these markets emerged not only to serve the domestic market, but also as a result of the increasing outsourcing to India, from the US and western Europe, of business service functions such as patent research.

# 7    Organizational change

The new institutional economics, as I have discussed in Chapter 2, had its origins in the analysis of the firm as an organization. The organization of economic activity is as important as technology, and the two are interdependent in determining the utilization of resources and consequent economic growth of an economy. The mainstream neoclassical economics talks of high-powered individual incentives of free choice driven by individual self-interest. Individual incentives face only resource constraints, typical of the world of Robinson Crusoe. Organization, on the other hand, basically implies collective action through individual incentives subject to collective or societal rules. Countries or societies which are able to find a fine balance between individual incentives and the constraints of collective action are the ones that are able to realize higher value out of given resources than others that tilt the balance either by imposing too many controls or where lawlessness reigns. These are basically organizational issues at a broader level.

The new institutional economics talks of resource allocation within an economy driven by both the so-called 'invisible hand' of free markets and the 'visible hand', referring to the internal organizational hierarchy of firms, as well as the constitutional and governmental regulation of economic activity (by fiat, incentives, and a combination of the two) at the economy level. Fiat is an outcome of the delegation by society (collective action) to an individual or to a set of individuals for enforcing the agreed-upon rules of collective action motivated by the aim of economizing on the sum of the transaction costs of each individual acting alone. The delegated are subject to removal depending on performance. If this arrangement is under frictionless competitive markets, there is no problem. However, informational asymmetry and transaction costs determine the degree of effectiveness of the group, which can sway the institutional arrangements towards the exercising of powers by the delegated beyond the social contract for rent-seeking, because all contracts are incomplete and subject to high costs of enforcement. The issue of the evolution of institutions is a matter of finding a fine balance between these two, at both the micro level of firms, and the broader level of an economy or a society.

It is a continuous process because there is nothing called an optimum. This chapter focuses on the organizational changes at the firm and industry levels in the post-reforms era.

Organizational restructuring has been a major facet of corporations in the India of the post-reform era in its attempts to compete with new entrants in product, capital, and labor markets. Competition and market opportunities drove several large Indian firms to adopt new technologies, which required changes in the internal organization and building of external linkages with input suppliers. However, organizational change encompasses several other broader (interrelated) issues such as ownership and control rights, diversification behavior, and corporate governance. In this chapter, I focus on the underlying mechanisms of organizational change at the micro level of firms and industries. In the first part, I discuss how the ownership arrangements of large corporations, especially family business groups, are changing in the post-reforms era. Following that, I discuss issues relating to governance, namely, centralization versus decentralization, and thereafter, diversification behavior and changing corporate governance in India's corporate sector. I discuss the emergence of stand-alone companies in the post-reforms era and their organizational strategies. Lastly, I briefly discuss organizational innovations in the context of the globalization of industries, such as the software and BPO industries in India.

To recapitulate, I characterize the initial conditions on the basis of which the policy reforms cause qualitative and parameter shifts in certain elements of the institutional environment, which induce changes in the organizational arrangements for adaptation to the changed parameters and rules of the game. In Williamson's logic of organization, choice of governance is discrete among markets, hierarchy, and hybrids. In this schema, parameter shifts in the institutional environment change the transaction costs of exchange in the dimensions of uncertainty, frequency, and asset-specificity, which makes economic agents choose the governance depending on the extent of changes in the trade-offs of the transaction costs of markets and the costs of bureaucracy of internal organization. We have to combine the parameter shifts with the qualitative shifts in understanding organizational change.

As I argued in Chapter 2, organizational change is not necessarily discrete. It could be a slow process owing to path dependency and inertia considerations. In this context, the extent of the difference between the discrete and continuous change in response to the reforms depends on the effects of the qualitative shifts. Let us take a simple case, assuming that before the reforms, firms in general adopted governance of $k$, and parameter shifts in the institutional environment make governance $k1$ more economical, after adding the additional costs of moving from $k$ to $k1$. Incumbent firms may continue with governance of $k$ even after the reforms, owing to inertia and collusion among the incumbents. The qualitative shifts cause the entry of a new player (a TNC), who adopts the governance of *k1* in accordance with the new institutional environment. Assuming both incumbents and new entrants have the same technology, the significance of the cost difference between adoption of *k* and *k1* determines the speed of response of incumbents in moving from *k* to *k1*. Larger the cost difference, the greater is the need for incumbents to change their ways in accordance with the changed rules of the game. The need for change emanates from product, labor, and capital markets because the stakeholders are multiple and include consumers, owners of capital, managers, and workers. There have been significant changes on these fronts in the Indian economy as a consequence of increased competition from new-entrant TNCs with superior technological and organizational practices, reforms in the capital markets, and increased demand for skilled and semi-skilled labor and managerial talent.

One of the most important aspects of organizational economics is the ownership (control rights) issue, which determines the organization of hierarchy and incentives of different actors for resource allocation and utilization within a firm. Control rights within an organization arise out of the ownership of inalienable assets. At the basic level, organization arises when an owner employs a worker to augment the value realization from the asset. A worker has the incentive to accept the control rights of the owner because his or her productivity and wage is higher than not having the ability to have access to the asset. There is an increase in organizational complexity when the owner of the asset employs a manager to monitor workers and to decide the wages or surplus sharing. From this starting point, organizational complexity increases when firms grow and develop different layers of agency relationships and incentives of owners, managers, workers, and providers of capital.

One of the important features of modern capitalism is the coexistence of self- or family-owned and professionally run businesses under a wide variety of institutional arrangements among different stakeholders. This is an important issue in the present context because of the importance of family-owned business groups in emerging economies, and how the reforms change the rules of the game for these business groups. The interesting dimension of the Indian family business groups, as I have discussed in Chapter 3, is that business families have been able to exercise a high degree of control rights, not with their own capital, but with the capital raised from public financial institutions. In other words, it is an institutional arrangement of family-run businesses with high agency costs, paid for by the public at large (public savings and taxes).

## Organizational change of family-run business groups

At the beginning of 2005, one of the most discussed news items in India was the tug of war between the two brothers who inherited India's third-largest business, Reliance Industries, from their father, Dhirubhai Ambani.[1] One of the most influential concepts in management literature in the 1990s was that of 'core competence' developed by Prahalad and Hamel (1990), which prompted several large corporations in the US to divest unrelated businesses and adopt focused strategies. In the present context, an ironic twist can be provided by saying that the break-up of the company was due to the differences in 'core competencies' of the brothers. In a more serious vein, the question is whether the rift is merely a 'power struggle' problem within a family business, as compared to the agency problems of professionally run corporations.

A simple ownership arrangement like a self-owned and managed firm in which there is no separation of ownership and control rights should be more efficient than a firm in which there is a separation of the two. This is because in the former case there are no additional costs of moral hazard of agents (managers) and monitoring costs involved. In Britain, the Industrial Revolution was made possible by the family firm (Payne, 1978). Similarly, industrialization in the US in the initial stages was driven by innovative entrepreneurs such as Ford, Carnegie, and Rockefeller, who built large and highly integrated businesses, some of which became publicly held and professionally run later on. The recent examples of rapid industrialization initiated by family business groups are the *zaibatsus* of Japan and *chaebols* of South Korea, which became global players. One similarity of the institutional arrangements of Japanese and South Korean family businesses with that of Indian businesses was the collusion among the government, big business, and banks, coupled with poor corporate governance and transparency practices. However, while the Japanese and South Korean firms became major global players, the Indian firms became monopolies in the protected domestic market. With their growth, the management of Japanese and South Korean firms by family members was passed on to professional managers.

India's diversified family-run businesses came into existence under British rule in the nineteenth century. Beginning with ethnic trading communities in the western, southern and, later, the eastern parts of India, these family firms first forayed into textiles and later diversified into the steel and engineering industries. Under the free market economy of British India, the industrialists drew capital mostly from family and friends and adopted the managing agency system. Nenadic (1993) argues for the legitimacy and relevance of family-based business in British India:

> In a situation of low business ethics and considerable instability, as doubtless prevailed in Britain throughout the eighteenth century and nineteenth centuries, the successful entrepreneur will be the individual who is able to create and sustain a stable business institution with a reputation for moral integrity.

> This is essential since a great deal of entrepreneurial activity in a

market economy will focus on the need to improve trading arrangements through the reduction of transaction costs, and such costs are high in a low morality environment. In the absence of state regulation the only way of achieving reduced transaction costs is to link the reputation of the market institution, that is the firm, to some organization or institution that is non-market defined and innately identified with high levels of morality. . . . The family provided the entrepreneur with one of the best available vehicles for reducing transaction costs through improved 'intermediation' on the basis of family reputation.

The above observation indicates that in the presence of high transaction costs and underdeveloped capital markets, the institution of family and friends became a major source of capital and business development for the Indian entrepreneurs.

Business development has several stakeholders, including capital providers, managers, workers, consumers, and government. The morality of the closely knit family group is similar to the morality of 'Though shalt not steal from thy neighbor'. A small group of family and friends develops a code of conduct and discipline for their collective actions for achieving material prosperity. However, once these groups become effective and powerful they are capable of capturing external institutions like government and indulge in rent-seeking at the cost of the less organized. As I have discussed in Chapter 3, under India's import substitution regime, family business groups were able to capture industrial licenses and public financial institutions and had access to public money for building family business empires. The distribution of wealth in favor of the organized happened in two ways: the channeling of public savings into the capital of the organized groups through public financial institutions;[2] and through the monopoly rents of the product markets in extracting consumer surplus by blocking competition through capture of the government.

To give an example of the diversified family business groups, the Tata group, India's first and the largest, consists of eight-two companies, with a turnover of $8.8 billion and a value of assets of Rs 368 billion in 1998. The group encompasses businesses in sectors as diverse as metals, automobiles, energy, engineering, chemicals, consumer products, finance, information technology and communication, agro industries, and several service industries. Another contrasting example is the TVS group, which was founded in 1911 as a small transportation company. Later on, the company diversified into related areas to create a range of independent subsidiaries for the production of a variety of auto components and the provision of automotive services. The diversification was primarily intended to capture a prominent position in India's growing auto industry. In addition, there were two other driving factors: to remedy the inability to source spare parts for the production of complex automotive systems, and to reduce the distribution bottlenecks of the underdeveloped markets of the time.

By 2005, the group had become a leading player in the two-wheeler indus-try and grown into a highly competitive exporter of auto components in the world market. These two cases present contrasting objectives of diver-sification – one into unrelated areas, and the other in a focused manner in related areas, to overcome market failures in the input and capital markets.

By the late 1990s, there were about seventy family business groups in India, accounting for some 25 percent of total industry revenues, 18 percent of the assets, and 32 percent of the profits after tax (Piramal, 1999). Most of these were diversified business groups. Operating linkages among the businesses were minimal, especially in the more diversified groups, and corporate strategy was usually the responsibility of family managers. In other words, the family's hold on the business meant a highly centralized and hierarchical organizational structure. Obviously, control was passed on from generation to generation of fathers, sons, and daughters. Lack of transparency owing to poor monitoring by the govern-ment institutional lenders helped the business groups move funds across firms within the groups without adequate disclosures. The institutional arrangements of high debt capital and the political capture of public financial institutions, major equity held by the groups, and financial inter-locking among the member firms helped them to block the threat of takeovers.[3]

Williamson (1981) characterizes a business group as a hybrid form of economic organization that combines the primary functions of both firms and markets in terms of a major corporation associated with a set of sub-sidiaries and affiliates. In the case of family groups, the family is at the top of the pyramid in determining the extent of centralization or decentraliza-tion and the degree of autonomy of the subsidiaries. The higher the control of the family, the lower is the role of markets (or prices) in deter-mining the resource allocation among the subsidiaries. The excessive control may arise out of the family's desire to control the businesses or market failures in allocation of capital and labor markets in developing economies (Khanna and Palepu, 2000). In the case of the first aspect, relating to family control, it is a question of the costs of centralization in facing up to competition in the post-reforms era. If the costs are high in relation to decentralized and professionally run new entrants, especially TNCs, the family business organization comes under pressure to change. A further dimension of this issue is the relative costs and benefits of man-agement resting in the hands of family, and of the employment of profes-sional managers. In the case of the market failure aspect, if the reforms lead to the development of capital, labor, and intermediate markets, the need for a high degree of centralization should decline.

In the US, over 65 percent of business is family business. As Piramal (1999) observes, "Bill Gate's Microsoft is as much a family firm as Dhirub-hai Ambani's Reliance, Galvin's Motorola and Ratan Tata's Telco." Then where is the difference and what is the crisis of the Indian family business? One difference lies in the capital structure, and another in the organization of management. With the demise of the license Raj, the importance of the public financial institutions in funding the long-term projects of the family business groups declined in the post-reforms era, forcing the groups to look for alternative means of raising capital, both internally and internationally. Consequently, there has been an increasing pressure on firms to improve transparency and to adopt efficient organizational practices (Patibandla, 2005a). One important element of organizational change is the issue of ownership and management, specifically, whether the top management is drawn from the family and its generations or from the competitive markets. Gurucharan Das (1999) observes, "The Indian business world is still largely feudal, where the owners treat their employees no better than they treat servants. In fact one industrialist, I recall, literally referred to his finance manager as a servant within earshot of his foreign collaborator."

As the environment becomes more competitive with the entry of new firms and TNCs, the markets for managerial talent deepen. The development of these markets depends not only on the increasing demand owing to an increase in the numbers of producers and the supply-side response of institutions, but also on the emergence of markets for information and reputation that reward managers who demonstrate high performance levels and low levels of moral hazard. On the supply side, one of the indicators of the expansion of markets is the increasing number of business schools and the growing presence of companies specializing in head-hunting for managerial talent in India (Patibandla, 2002a). As a measure to increase supply, the government of India also set up two more management schools to join the four other existing IIMs. Furthermore, private management schools imparting management education have started to mushroom all over the country.

Apart from this, if the legal mechanism of corporate governance and organization of investors improves, the market for professional managers develops in terms of weeding out inefficient or unethical professional managers. Since the early 1990s, the salaries of professional managers and management graduates have increased at a rapid pace owing to the increasing presence of multinational firms and consulting companies, and the opening-up of businesses to the world market. Under these institutional changes, the family organization based on feudal codes would lose out, as the best managers would leave for better companies.

The advantage of a professionally run business is that it can draw managerial talent from competitive markets, if they are well developed, while in a family business, management may change hands within the family itself. One of the ways of overcoming this disadvantage for family businesses is the generation of internal professional managerial markets. A first step in this respect is imparting professional management training to the next generation before they become managers. For example, Aditya Birla, who took over the top slot of the Birla group, acquired an MBA from the London Business School, and the two sons of Dhirubhai Ambani of Reliance Industries secured MBAs from the Wharton and Stanford schools.

Several of the family businesses introduced human resource management practices, such as intake-recruitment programs to recruit talented youngsters as well as senior managers. For example, India's largest family group, the Birla group, 'which rarely hired outsiders directly at senior levels, hired a former director from Levers, an ex-deputy chairman from ITC Ltd, and an ex-CEO of Blow Plast Ltd. In 1997 alone, the group hired fifteen MBAs as general management trainees and continued hiring more MBAs over the next two years' (Manikutty, 2000). Several other family groups, such as Reliance Industries, RPG enterprises, the Thapar group, BPL and the Ranbaxy group, started to hire managers for the top positions. This form of organizational arrangement of managerial control can be treated as a hybrid between family control and professional management, where professional managers are allocated the right kinds of powers and incentives while retaining a degree of family control. In such a case, if the control rights and incentives of the professional managers are well aligned with the interests of the business, this organizational arrangement should perform better than purely public-held and professional companies. This is because the organizational arrangement could reduce agency costs by the direct involvement of the owner-managers. At the same time, it could utilize the managerial talent secured from competitive management markets. In other words, this type of hybrid management system arises from competing in the capital markets and in markets for managerial talent. In support of this argument, the study of McConaughy (1994) for the US showed that the performance of large publicly traded firms controlled by their founding families is superior in terms of profitability, growth, stable earnings, and lower dividends as compared to purely professionally run and family-dominated companies.

The next dimension of organizational change of groups is the issue of centralized versus decentralized governance structures. One form of decentralization prevalent in the Indian family groups is that different sons manage different units of the family business. One of the jokes in this connection is that 'every time a son is born, a new family business unit is started'. In the case of the Bajaj group, at the top of the pyramid is the father, Rahul Bajaj, who runs the Rs 25,000 million Bajaj Auto. His son, Neeraj Bajaj, runs the Rs 2,000 million Bajaj Electricals, and a cousin, Neeraj, runs Mukund Iron and Steel.

One feature of family businesses is that family disputes can result in the splitting-up of the companies. This can take place in two ways. The groups can split strategically on business lines and this generates viable and focused businesses. Groups can also split illogically putting family interests first and such fissures are not able to create viable businesses and syner-gies between the divided companies (Das, 1999). However, even after the split, several units do retain links through informal ties in terms of cross-investments and trading (transfer pricing) practices, as long as the capital markets remain inefficient. Some of the leading groups form holding companies as a means of decentralization and professionalization by retaining family control. The families have controlling stakes in the holding companies, such that with much fewer resources they are able to maintain control over the constituent companies and also make takeovers difficult.

In order to generate competent professional managers, the Tata group developed its own cadre of professionals, named Tata Administrative Ser-vices. Similarly, the Birla group transformed its Birla Management Center into a corporate center for deriving synergies from different units of the group (Manikutty, 2000). On the other hand, given the historical weak-ness of the market for corporate control in India, controlling families enjoyed significant discretion in setting corporate strategy in ways that did not necessarily maximize profits. The Tata group may be an example: in the beginning of the 1990s, Ratan Tata appeared to have embarked on a program of reasserting family control by strengthening financial and other interlocks among the group companies instead of undertaking a major downsizing (Ghemawat and Khanna,1998).

The decentralization issue has two dimensions: one, as illustrated above, from the top of the group pyramid to the autonomy of different subsidiaries; the other within the organization or units. Different layers of hierarchy are created within the unit. As I discussed in Chapter 3, in typical family-run business units, the hierarchy levels ranged between fifteen and twenty categories. Within five or six broad categories, there were three or four subcategories. One explanation for this type of organi-zational structure is the feudal ethos of Indian organizations and the absence of competitive markets. This organizational structure became non-viable in the post-reforms era of highly competitive markets. Several firms, in their attempts to adapt to the changed market conditions, under-took painstaking organizational restructuring. Bajaj Auto, in order to compete with TNCs such as Honda and Suzuki, undertook technological upgrading and organizational restructuring. It reversed the top-down approach of the management of a family business to a bottom-up approach. On the shop floor, workmen and section managers were grouped into cells and the members were guided by the self-management approach. All the cells were interlinked for better information flow and for a superior coordination system. Consequent to these changes, man-power productivity in terms of the numbers of vehicles per man-year improved by 88 percent between 1988 and 1998 (Bhudiraja *et al.*, 2003).

Khanna and Palepu (2000) provide empirical evidence to demonstrate the superior performance of group-affiliated subsidiaries as compared to stand-alone firms. According to them, the groups, by generating internal capital and labor markets, overcome the disadvantages of the institutional inefficiencies of a developing economy. One other way to look at it is, 'Father save me.' A father has several sons, of whom some are doing well and others are faring badly. In such a situation, what does he do? He helps the ones who are not doing well, which is basically cross-unit subsidization. However, in economic terms, it is not necessarily an efficient institutional arrangement.

Wipro, the diversified family business firm, has come to be known as a leading software company in India since the 1990s. Originally it was a diversified business group, which had interests in multiple areas of manufacturing. It branched out into the software business from hardware in the early nineties, when the export market for software services was booming. It was able to make large profits in the software business through wage arbitrage. Instead of investing the surplus revenues in the software business, it diverted the surplus to other businesses, which were not doing as well.[4]

Wipro's decision to cross-subsidize different businesses should be evaluated on the basis of the trade-offs of demand-side expectations and the supply-side adoption of core competence. For a family or a conglomerate, the objective function is the long-run aggregate profit summed over all its subsidiaries. The decision to cross-subsidize should depend on parameter values. A family business holds a portfolio of a number of industrial assets. Depending on long-run expectations, gains from one can be invested in others or some of the assets can be divested. The issue is mainly a matter of expectations about the demand side of the market. Core competence, on the other hand, is a supply-side concept. It arises from a firm's technology, organization, and previous learning. Given the features, it helps a firm to improve efficiency by sorting out its core competence and sticking to it. It is necessary to note that the natural unit of core competencies is a firm, not a conglomerate.

The relatively better performance of the group-affiliated firms as compared to stand-alone companies can arise out of Khanna and Palepu's explanation of the advantages of the internal capital and labor markets of the groups, cross-unit subsidization by groups, which a stand-alone company lacks, and lastly the professionalizing of family-owned firms, which can derive the benefits of the best of both worlds of family involvement and the utilization of professional managerial talent.

## Organization of small-scale business

To recapitulate from Chapter 3, the government of India adopted a gamut of policies to correct for the policy bias against small-scale firms under the heavy industrialization strategy of import substitution. Among these were the reservation policies, policies granting excise duty concessions and concessional finance, etc. On the capital markets side, the government set up financial institutions to provide loans at low rates for small firms. However, high transaction costs associated with formal financial institutions helped only the relatively large among the small firms and the organized large firms, which set up smaller firms to avail themselves of formal capital. The small firms depended on family capital or informal capital markets. The bankruptcy laws, which limited the rights of debtors in claiming the assets of defaulting companies, provided perverse incentives for the firms, which took capital from the government institutions. Generally, they declared bankruptcy and diverted the capital into the personal pockets of the promoters. As a consequence there was high incidence of sickness among small firms (Patibandla, 1994).

On the other hand, the reservation and excise duty policies served as disincentives for the efficient small firms to grow. These firms adopted premature diversification into either multiple units in the same area (registered under the names of different family members) or into multiple areas. On the other hand, a few small firms adopted innovative practices to remain registered as small firms, although they realized high sales turnover. To recall, the government had defined a small firm on the basis of its net assets criteria. A small firm which adopted a highly labor- or variable input-intensive technique and a high degree of outsourcing of intermediate goods could realize high sales turnover with low net assets.[5]

The government of India implemented a series of reforms in the 1990s, such as the dereservation of several products and an increase in the net asset limit to Rs 100 million in classifying small firms. Although the series of reforms targeting the capital markets reduced the interest rates of the formal markets, most small firms still operated in the unorganized capital markets owing to the high transaction costs associated with dealing with formal financial institutions.

Have there been any notable organizational changes among small firms in response to the reforms? The qualitative evidence shows a mixed picture. Piecemeal changes in the institutional environment with little change in the transaction costs in several spheres of regulation do not have much effect on the organizational behavior of small firms and, in fact, may even lead to perverse outcomes. On the other hand, increasingly competitive conditions and better export market opportunities have led to cooperative behavior between large assemblers and small component producers. The linkages between the two have helped small firms in some spheres to improve technology and organization.

Bhide's (2004) extensive study of new start-ups and small firms in the city of Bangalore shows that successful small firms show a tendency to diversify into multiple areas rather than grow in one specific area, so as to overcome the institutional constraints of government policies and administrative apparatus. A large number of small firms do not comply with the registration requirements. Only about 26 percent of the 5,000 small firms supposedly operating in the different areas of production and services had valid registration. Of those registered, 90 percent reported employment below twenty personnel.

Although the actual employment including the casual and full-time employees was generally more, firms underreported employment because those with twenty or more employees had to contribute about 10 percent of the wages to a provident fund scheme and to the payment of bonus, since the Bonus Act required the unit to pay a bonus after being in operation for five years. Second, businesses with less than Rs 10 million in revenues were exempt from paying excise taxes, levied at the base rate of 16 percent of sales. Once a firm registers above twenty employees, it is subject to government inspectors' scrutiny on various accounts. As I mentioned in Chapter 4, small firms are more-frequent victims of harassment and bribe extraction by the inspectors. Harassment by the inspectors coupled with the disadvantageous costs of complying with the rules serves as a disincentive for small firms to expand: – "have to pay a bribe to pay your taxes."[6] The choice for a small firm to overcome this is either to grow or remain invisible to officials.

Furthermore, expansion of the business in specific and narrow areas calls for the extension of the market beyond the city and the state. This requires making use of the highly inefficient transport system based on trucks. Moreover, excise inspectors and the police extract bribes from the trucks transporting the goods. This rampant practice adds additional costs. The natural question that follows is, how do the last two observations affect small firms in a different manner as compared to large firms? Bhide observes that the "The system of indirect taxation has a powerful influence on the decision of entrepreneurs to operate many small businesses instead of one large business." In addition, apprehensions about the long-term consequences play a role in discouraging businesses from expanding. Once a business registers with the excise tax authorities or enrolls in the provident fund scheme, it cannot easily withdraw, even if its revenues or employment subsequently fall below the prescribed thresholds. In a similar way to my argument of convergence under competition in Chapter 5, if one firm is able to avoid taxes, the other firms have to follow suit to remain in the competitive race to survive.

On the capital markets side, the sources of capital for small firms are self-finance or family funds, debt capital from formal banks with collateral such as the ownership of real estate, and the moneylenders. The moneylenders are resorted to when there is no collateral on the part of the borrowers. There are two types of institutional arrangements among the moneylenders. The first are the lenders who charge high interest rates and consequently face high default rates because of their unsystematic approach – a typical outcome of the adverse selection problem. The others are professional moneylenders who invest in information on the creditworthiness of borrowers and defaulters. These lenders form an association, mostly based on ethnic ties. They pool the information about good borrowers and probable defaulters and they are thus able to overcome the adverse selection problem, charge lower interest rates, and realize high turnover of funds.

On the labor market side, the efforts of small firms to overcome the government labor regulations provided incentives for the use of contract labor, a practice that has become increasingly widespread. This is because a large number of firms started to use contract labor rather than full-time employees because of the weak protection of contract workers, and because the contract suppliers could avoid governmental registration and controls because they did not operate under fixed premises (Bhide, 2004). Within this field of small firms providing contract labor, the number of licensed contractors showed a drop in the early 2000s, due to a decline in compliance.

The above study shows that as long as the transaction costs associated with government regulations are high, piecemeal reforms do not provide sufficient incentives for small firms to change their organization to more efficient modes. On the other hand, reforms can result in organizational changes for the better as a result of private order arrangements of cooperation among firms as demonstrated below.

The case of the auto-component industry presents the development of the intermediate product markets through effective linkages between large assemblers and small- and medium-scale component suppliers. The Japanese style of subcontracting practices, initiated first by Maruti-Suzuki, developed the intermediate-goods industry, which gradually became internationally competitive through the development of a three-tier system of supplier firms. The first-tier firms or the larger firms were able to adopt capital-intensive technologies due to active linkages with assembler firms and joint collaborations with TNCs. The third-tier firms or small firms carried out low-end work with mostly unorganized labor. Similarly, in the case of the Tirupur garment cluster, the linkages between small and large firms helped small firms to overcome the transaction costs of capital and product markets and become highly successful exporters.

## Changes in the diversification behavior of large business

Conceptually, the diversification behavior of firms can be segregated into three broad groups: vertical and horizontal scopes, and diversification into unrelated businesses. In India's case, the diversified business groups, with a history of family ownership, increased their diversification under the licensing Raj of the import substitution policies. In the Western capitalist economies of the 1960s and 1970s, too, capital markets rewarded diversified businesses. In the 1990s, however, the business strategy mantra changed to core competence of focused operations (Prahlad and Hamel, 1990). The conglomerate and merger wave of the 1960s and 1970s was partly fueled by the belief that internal capital markets were more efficient than external capital markets.[7] Recent literature, however, suggests that internal markets do not work well and companies that are more focused fare better in the market than diversified firms (Bolton and Scharfstein, 1998).

The theory of the firm explains vertical integration and mergers. There is, however, no systematic theory that justifies horizontal mergers and unrelated diversification. Khanna and Palepu (2000) extend the logic of the theory of the firm and the new institutional economics by rationalizing that diversification into unrelated areas in developing economies occurs on the grounds of economizing on the transaction costs of capital and labor markets. According to their argument, in developing economies underdeveloped capital markets limit equity financing of risk capital. Labor markets are deficient in skill availability and managerial talent and are beset with transaction costs. Contract formulation and execution in securing intermediate products are subject to high transaction costs and distribution and infrastructure bottlenecks. Diversification into multiple areas helps the business groups generate internal markets and synergies among the different affiliated subsidiaries. Furthermore, Ghemawat and Khanna (1998) observe that the tax code also plays an important role in encouraging diversification by the groups. Sales-based taxation, rather than value-added taxation of products, offered incentives for vertical integration[8] (as in the original thesis of Coase, 1937).

The Tata Engineering and Locomotive Company (TELCO), a particularly large company within the Tata group which assembles commercial vehicles, is an example. When TELCO set up a large, new plant in Pune in the 1970s, there were hardly any component suppliers in the vicinity, forcing it to undertake backward vertical integration. While there had been some movement in the emergence of input suppliers, TELCO continued to be significantly more integrated than its only (and smaller) domestic competitor, Ashok Leyland, in spite of evidence suggesting that it could, in fact, end up paying twice as much for certain parts that were manufactured in-house as opposed to their purchase from outside. It is only in recent years, when TELCO branched into the production of small cars, that it undertook the development of vendor firms in a systematic way so as to be able to compete with other small-car producers such as Maruti-Suzuki and Hyundai. In other words, competition was responsible for rooting out inefficient governance.

However, Khanna and Palepu's explanation is incomplete, owing to the fact that the relation could be the other way round, in that capital market imperfections could have worked in favor of the large groups in getting privileged access to scarce capital, which, in turn, helped them to build family empires. New entrants, on the other hand, even with more efficient ideas and projects, had difficulty in raising capital. Second, it can be argued that the emergence of collusive oligopolies in most industries through the licensing policies could have resulted in diversification by blocking the emergence of efficient intermediate-product industries and capital markets. In the pre-reforms era of highly protected markets, diversification and vertical integration could have been one of the business strategies of deriving monopoly power instead of overcoming institutional deficiencies. To give an example, vertical integration in the production of synthetic yarn by Reliance Textiles gave it a degree of monopoly power in the 1980s. When the tariffs on the yarn were reduced in the early 1990s, the firm reduced the prices of yarn significantly and with immediate effect. Of course, later the firm used the vertical integration to realize economies of scale in the post-reforms era and increased forward vertical integration by acquiring overseas firms, which led to a drastic decline in the costs and prices of synthetic textiles (Ghemawat and Patibandla, 1999).

As I discussed in Chapter 3, the small-scale sector policies resulted in the emergence of a large number of small firms producing labor-intensive manufacturing and engineering products. However, these industries were unable to develop or mature because of two reasons: government policies and the monopoly powers of the final-goods producers. Most small firms were afraid to invest in capacities and technologies because of a few large buyers who had monopsony power. When subcontracting took place, especially from the mid-1970s, the bargaining power was always in favor of the large buyers, with a major part of the burden of transaction costs falling on small firms. Some of the small firms, in order to reduce their dependence on a few monopsony local buyers, branched out into the export market despite an overvalued exchange rate, because export markets, once they were able to break into them, presented lower transaction costs than local markets (Patibandla, 1994, 1995). When a large number of TNCs entered the four-wheeler and two-wheeler industries, the tables turned the other way round and improved the bargaining power of small- and medium-scale supplier firms as a result of their willingness to invest in technology through cooperation and industry- and firm-specific assets, which, in turn, developed the intermediate-product markets.

## Vertical integration in the post-reforms era

Chandler (1977) shows that large, integrated firms have dominated most sectors in the US since the early part of the twentieth century. Large corporations enjoyed economies of scale and scope and an extensive brand image, and gave formidable competition to new entrants. The firms were vertically integrated because they were set up when the industry was young and very few suppliers of intermediate goods existed. Apart from this, as in Williamson's thesis, the suppliers could not be persuaded to set up units because all they could see for the foreseeable future was a monopolist buyer and investment with a high degree of asset-specificity. In other

words, any supplier of intermediate input would have to produce a specialized product with only one buyer or a very few likely buyers. Consequently, most transactions took place within the firm and very few
between the firms. In the 1980s and 1990s, the organization of large corporations went through drastic changes in the advanced capitalist
economies. Large conglomerates were broken up into separate stand-
alone companies. Several large corporations reduced the degree of vertical integration (Rajan and Zingales, 1998).

At the same time, the 1990s saw a wave of both national and cross-
border merger activity, on both vertical and horizontal lines. National and
cross-border mergers grew about 42 percent per annum, reaching $2.3
trillion in 1999. One quarter of them accounted for cross-border mergers.
In 1999, they accounted for about $720 billion. Big mergers, defined as
those worth over $1 billion, accounted for 68 percent of the total merger
activity. India, too, experienced a high degree of merger activity in the
post-reforms era, in both the domestic market and the international
market, with local firms acquiring firms abroad. Most mergers, in the early
1990s, appeared to be among firms belonging to the same business
groups, operating in similar product lines, probably to face up to the
emerging competition from TNCs. In the second half of the 1990s, the
participation of foreign-controlled firms in mergers increased significantly
(Beena, 2000, and Table 13). In the period between 1990 and 1995, there
were a total of 291 mergers, and for the period between 1995 and 2000
there were 743. During the three years between 2000 and 2003, Indian
firms acquired about 119 business units abroad, out of which sixty-seven
belonged to the software industry, while twelve belonged to the pharmaceutical industry. Most of them were acquired in the US. Almost all the

*Table 13* Sample of acquiring firms involved in the M&As process between 1995
and 2000

| Year | Domestic-owned acquiring firms | | Foreign-owned acquiring firms | | Total acquiring firms | |
|---|---|---|---|---|---|---|
| | Total assets | Number | Total assets | Number | Total assets | Number |
| 1995–6 | 12,770 | 6 | 3,432.16 | 7 | 16,202.69 | 13 |
| 1996–7 | 6,771.82 | 15 | 5,445.1 | 7 | 12,216.92 | 22 |
| 1997–8 | 9,342.03 | 16 | 856.81 | 4 | 10,198.84 | 20 |
| 1998–9 | 127,217 | 13 | 1,225.69 | 4 | 128,442.69 | 17 |
| 1999–2000 | 41,267.39 | 34 | 4,463.42 | 9 | 45,730.81 | 43 |
| Total | 197,362.2 | 84 | 15,423.18 | 31 | 212,798 | 115 |

Source: Beena (2000).

Notes
Assets figures are in tens of millions of rupees.

overseas acquisitions by Indian companies were in related fields. Thus, software companies acquired software firms and pharmaceutical companies acquired pharmaceutical firms. The Indian steel firm Tata Steel acquired Natsteel, Tata Tea acquired Tetley of the UK, and Reliance Telecom acquired Trevira. Most of these mergers were efforts at forward integration in an attempt to get access to customers and brands, and backward integration in an endeavor to access technology and processes.

The above observation illustrates both divesting and merger activity by large corporations happening together. This is not necessarily a contradiction, because when one company divests a part of its business, another one buys it. Unrelated activities could be divested while merger or buying could refer to a company buying into vertically or horizontally related activities. In other words, these phenomena show a tendency to become more in tune with the theory of the firm and its principles of governance.

Stigler (1951) argued that at the initial stages of development of an economy, vertical integration would be high, but as the economy developed through the emergence of institutions supporting the division of labor, vertical integration would decline. The institutional elements are the development of formal legal mechanisms of contract formulation and execution, and development of capital and intermediate-product markets. In recent years, another dimension is the increasing power of human capital, especially in human-capital-intensive industries. To draw from modern property rights literature, Rajan and Zingales (2001) argue that when the capital markets are highly developed, ownership of physical assets by a firm is not endurable, as skilled personnel can raise capital freely. This makes the power of organizational hierarchy low and the attrition of skilled workers high. At the same time, firms as organizations respond to limit the attrition of skilled workers, especially those appropriating their technology. One of the ways in which firms could do this is to build firm-level unique advantage by combining their technology with organizational practices, which generates complementarity between different skilled workers and departments within the firm. This may lead to the adoption of focused strategies. Rajan and Zingales (2001) observe that complementarities between assets and growth opportunities help a firm retain control of its technology. This may explain why the response of many firms to the financial revolution has been a greater emphasis on focus. Focus ensures that the growth opportunities the firm generates are in areas where it has a comparative advantage, so that it has a greater chance of retaining them.

On the other hand, too narrow a focus can also lead to a loss of opportunities. Rajan and Zingales argue that perhaps the best way to capture all the possible growth opportunities in an area is to maintain the widest possible competence in that narrow area. This implies that as the capital market develops, firms may reduce horizontal diversification. However, the outcome is not straightforward in the case of vertical integration. If vertically integrating some of the processes increases complementarities between different skilled workers, the organizational power in holding on to skilled workers increases. This could be especially relevant in high-tech industries in which human skills are important. In other words, firms may reduce horizontal diversification but adopt vertical integration to build the widest-possible competence in a specific area as capital markets develop.[9] The example could be telecommunications-related software development, in which a telecoms company may integrate software development instead of outsourcing it to software companies.

The above logic assumes that diversification occurs because of inefficient institutions. Thus, if the institutional change in the post-reforms era were to cause the development of capital, labor, and intermediate-product markets, then diversification and excess vertical integration should decline in Indian industries. However, the outcome may not be that simple for the Indian industry, because rapid economic growth starting from a low base results in the simultaneous operation of a gamut of forces on technology, institutions, and markets. Some of these elements might be operating in harmony, and others in opposing directions in determining organizational choices for different industries. For example, technological change that increases the division of labor (separability of production processes) combined with a decline in transaction costs in the intermediate-product markets results in a decline in vertical integration. On the other hand, when technological adoption or change is such that the economies of scope and scale become more dominant than economies of specialization (plus transaction costs) of securing inputs from outsiders, vertical integration increases. With increase in technological sophistication, complexity of contracts and associated transaction costs increase, thereby necessitating vertical integration.

On the one hand, as development proceeds, one expects to see increased investment by companies in reputation assets, which can increase the viability of market exchange, and thereby decrease the need for vertical integration. On the other hand, development typically also leads to greater reliance on specialized differentiated inputs, which, other things being equal, tend to be less conducive to market arrangements than less specialized inputs. The process of economies of specialization would be more important in industries involving complex technologies with rapid technological changes than for matured technologies. However, there are contradictory forces with regard to vertical integration in high-tech industries. High-tech firms have to adopt integration to protect proprietary nature of innovations. At the same time, the increasing complexity of technologies drives firms to specialize in narrow areas, which requires collaboration with other firms to innovate new products and technologies.

In commodity industries such as steel, yarn, and textile production, with matured technologies, vertical integration may be adopted for reasons of economies of scale, rather than to protect proprietary technologies. As I discussed in Chapter 4, after the reforms several large textile mills restructured themselves through a high degree of vertical integration, starting from the production of yarn, manufactured textiles, and branded garments, which made them both locally and internationally competitive.

On the other hand, the automobile industry shows the case of an increase in subcontracting through the development of intermediate-product industries. I have discussed in Chapters 5 and 6 how subcontracting activity was initiated by the Japanese TNC Maruti-Suzuki and imitated by local firms, which led to the development of the intermediate product industry. The increasing use of subcontracting between the assemblers and first-tier auto-component firms under relational contracts in the automobile industry meant a decline in the vertical integration of the assemblers. The qualitative evidence shows that the first-tier auto-component firms increasingly adopted capital-intensive modern technologies and increased vertical integration in order to upgrade technology to world standards. Tables 19 and 20 presented in Appendix 5 show the top fifteen industries with the highest decline (descending order) and highest increase in vertical integration respectively.

If we consider Table 14, the auto-component industry increased vertical integration by 1.64 percent, while the passenger car and jeep industry reduced it by 0.16 percent for the period 1990–9. In other words, increasing technological sophistication in the component industry required the supplier firms to increase vertical integration.

However, there could be non-linearity in the subcontracting behavior of the assembler firms, especially in terms of numbers of vendor firms. Initially, some of the assembler firms increased subcontracting to a large number of small players. As the transaction costs of dealing with a large number of component producers and technological sophistication increased, they reduced the numbers to fewer suppliers, with long-term

*Table 14* Annual average growth rate of vertical integration, 1990–9 – a sample of commodity and manufacturing industries

| Industry | GVI | Industry | GVI |
|---|---|---|---|
| Paper and paper products | 0.58 (0.02) | Auto components | 1.64 (0.036) |
| Steel tubes | 0.79 (0.02) | Synthetic fabrics | 1.7 (0.04) |
| Steel wires | 1.25 (0.03) | Footwear | 1.2 (0.04) |
| Aluminum products | 3.4 (0.06) | Glass and glassware | 0.28 (0.03) |
| Cement products | 0.3 (0.02) | Dyes and pigments | 0.87 (0.04) |
| Tiers and tubes | 1.6 (0.06) | Communications equipment | 1.6 (0.05) |

Note
Figures in parentheses are standard deviations.

systematic relational contracts under which the suppliers also increased relation-specific investments. For example, Bajaj, in the two-wheeler industry, started to outsource 60 percent of its component needs in the early 1990s to about 300 firms. Later, however, it reduced the number of supplier firms to about 200, developing long-term relational contracts with the fewer suppliers in order to reduce transaction costs and to deal with the increasing technological complexity of the product. This could be one of the reasons why the annual average growth rate of vertical integration for the two-wheeler industry shows a positive figure of 2.0 percent in Table 20.

The comparative picture of Tables 14, 19 and 20 presents interesting trends. Table 19 shows that industries which showed a decline in vertical integration had high levels of vertical integration in the base year 1990 with the average at 0.44, while it is lower, at 0.32, in Table 20 for industries with positive growth in vertical integration. One possible conjecture is that the industries that had adopted excess vertical integration reduced it after the reforms. The industries that adopted low vertical integration because of the government policies of reservation for small-scale industries and the fragmented domestic market increased their vertical integration after the reforms. Table 14 provides qualitative evidence for this argument. Industries such as dyes and pigments, footwear, glass and glassware, and paper and paper products, which were fragmented before the reforms, show a positive annual average growth in vertical integration.

Interestingly, the software industry, which is skilled-labor-intensive, increased its integration by 5.2 percent. As discussed before, for technology-intensive industries, if the proprietary nature of technological activities increases in the post-reforms era, vertical integration should also increase. Another knowledge-intensive industry, pharmaceuticals, also increased vertical integration by 0.13 percent. However, the case of the software industry is slightly different. The success of the software industry stemmed mainly from the generation of 'islands of competitiveness' in terms of firms generating their own infrastructure to overcome inefficient domestic market conditions. It appears that the software firms increased this, instead of reducing it, in the post-reforms era. In January 2005, the leading software company Infosys announced that it would build its own hotel in Bangalore because it had become extremely difficult to get hotel accommodation for their visiting customers from overseas. The major element of backward integration for a software company is into the labor market. The Infosys company established a major software-training center in the nearby city of Mysore, which graduates close to 1,500 people in a year, and embarked on collaborative agreements with educational institutions for the training of software professionals. Most software companies recruit skilled people in bulk with a diverse background of engineering and general mathematical skills and then undertake both intensive and brief training on software skills. If this activity has increased over the period, it reflects in the increase in vertical integration.[10] Furthermore, several large software companies increased their forward integration by setting up subsidiaries in developed economies to be closer to the customers.

I have undertaken econometric explanation of vertical integration by a set of variables for the industry data. The results are presented in Appendix 5 and discussed in detail. The results show inverted 'U' shape (convex) trend changes in vertical integration over time in Indian industries. As markets and institutions start to develop, vertical integration decreases over time, in a similar way to the pattern experienced in developed economies such as the US.

## Diversification behavior of unrelated business

Competition in the product and capital markets and increased market opportunities in the post-reforms era have implications for the diversification of corporations into unrelated areas. On one side, corporations divest unrelated business areas and focus on those areas in which they have a competitive advantage. On the other hand, increased market opportunities provide incentives to diversify into new and growing fields of opportunity such as the software, telecommunications, and infrastructure areas. For example, Reliance Industries, which had been relatively focused on textiles and petrochemicals, diversified into telecommunications, infrastructure, and computer animation. Several business groups set up software units to take advantage of wage arbitrage in global markets. Groups have not been allowed to own banks, but most have taken advantage of the recent liberalization in the financial sector to launch their own non-bank financial institutions. Some of this diversification probably makes sense for some of the groups that have developed the capability to budget and manage large, complex projects on time (e.g. Reliance Industries). The question is, if the mature capital markets, especially the equity markets dominated by institutional investors, punish diversified businesses, how is the latter behavior possible? One possible explanation is that the business groups still enjoy the reputation advantage in the capital markets, and, second, the groups could utilize internal cash flows to diversify instead of paying dividends.

Is there a relationship between vertical integration and diversification into unrelated areas of business groups in the changed institutional environment of the post-reforms era? From the previous discussion, one can suggest the proposition that a reduction in unrelated diversification results in an increase in vertical integration in the focused area for the realization of economies of scale, both in the physical assets and management of capital. The analysis of the case of Ballapur Industries (BILT) by Ghemawat and Khanna (1998) is a good illustration to provide qualitative evidence for the proposition.

BILT is one of the top five family-controlled business groups operating in the areas of paper, chemicals, glassware, food products, leather, and telecommunications equipment. In response to increasingly competitive conditions in the post-reforms era, it undertook organizational restructuring. Ghemawat and Khanna (1998) observe that BILT, in response to competitive shocks, split their portfolio of businesses into three categories: businesses where it was or could become a market leader on its own (in spite of global competition), businesses where it had a valuable lead, and all other businesses. It focused on the first category and diverted resources into these businesses. In the second category, it formed joint ventures with TNCs, and the third category was divested. The paper industry belonged to the first category. It made use of modern, imported technology, purchased from the Swedish multinational firm Stora. It expanded capacity and adopted a high degree of backward integration into plantations, pulp, chemicals, and captive power generation. This helped the firm realize economies of scale and cost competitiveness. In other words, reduction in diversification behavior was followed by an increase in vertical integration in the focused area of the business. Ghemawat and Khanna observe that, apart from increased competition from TNCs (Sinar Mas of Indonesia), the increasing costs and scarcity of capital in the changed institutional environment were also underlying factors for the organizational restructuring of the group.

Broad patterns of qualitative behavior of the corporations show that divesting and restructuring of the organizational structure has been taking place in two ways: the sale of unrelated businesses and the adoption of core-competence practices, and decentralization by the groups, i.e. giving more autonomy to different units and resorting to external capital markets by the autonomous units. The following are some examples of restructuring.

In some instances, such as the original Goenka and DCM family-owned groups, restructuring has been accomplished by splitting up portfolios of businesses among brothers. Grasim Industries of the Birla group shut down the sea magnesia plant and one of the caustic soda plants and focused on its core businesses, namely cement, fibers, and textiles. In the core businesses, it expanded on a horizontal scale by acquiring two plants from other firms in cement. The main business of the Raymond Company of the Singhania group is worsted textiles. The company nevertheless diversified into steel and cement, which adversely affected its performance. It therefore sold off its steel plant to the German EBG Gesselschaft, and also disposed of its cement plant. Greaves, the engineering firm of the Thapar group, has been a leader in gearbox technology for over forty years, with a market share of 50 percent. It divested its power transmission units by selling them to BTR European Holdings of the Netherlands. The semiconductor unit of Greaves, too, was divested in favor of Teamasia Greaves Semiconductors, which is a joint venture company with Teamasia.

The Essar group increased its diversification at the onset of the reforms and ended by divesting before the end of the decade. In the early 1990s, it diversified into steel, power, oil and gas, and telecommunications. In the late 90s, it started to sell off its units in power and minerals. DCM Ltd, which has been a major player in the textile industry, sold off its real estate business and the foundry division in order to focus on branded textiles. At the same time, it diversified into the software industry. Godrej Soaps Ltd divested household insecticides, Godrej properties and investments, and the distribution of photo processing equipment. The Tata group, which, as mentioned before, did not show any inclination towards the adoption of core competence, started to divest certain activities. For example, it exited from the paints industry by divesting its 28.5 percent equity stake in Goodlass Nerolac in favor of Kansai of Japan.

On the decentralization front, Mahindra and Mahindra, whose core business is automobiles and tractors, had been grouping unrelated activities into separate independent companies. Larsen and Toubro, the large professionally managed conglomerate, split its construction, engineering, and cement businesses into three major companies with focused lines of business. Several of the company's smaller, non-focused businesses such as shoes and glass bottles were sold off. Hindustan Lever, the largest company in India, implemented extensive organizational restructuring in terms of decentralizing its main business lines into several smaller units. It is expected to result in anywhere between forty to fifty new units to be managed by independent business managers, as against a few centralized units. This is similar to the adoption of Chandler-Williamson's decentralized M-form (multi-divisional) organization to manage the large organization. The size of organizations within the focus areas has been increasing both in the home market and also through forward integration into overseas markets through acquisitions.

The qualitative information obtained from press reports shows that, after adopting focused strategies, several firms followed market diversification strategies to translate their cost advantage into the international markets. This has taken place in two ways: through an increase in export-orientation, and by acquiring overseas firms in related areas as a forward integration strategy. Several business group units, after undertaking organizational and technological restructuring, branched out overseas by acquiring firms abroad. Reliance Industries acquired Trevira, a polyester company in Germany, to become the world's largest producer of polyester. The Tata group, which is worth Rs 650,000 million in 2005, has a presence in forty countries. Its software unit, TCS, has subsidiaries in all the major developed countries. The group acquired Daewoo, the Korean firm making trucks, a steel plant in Singapore, a telecoms company in the US, and a tea company in Britain. Most of the acquisitions were aimed at forward vertical integration into overseas markets. The organizational change in diversified business groups is decentralization of different units and an increase in the vertical integration of each of the units.

However, some of the overseas acquisitions were not smooth and were beset with problems. A case to illustrate this was the acquisition of the UK's Tetley group by Tata Tea. Tata Tea has fifty-four tea estates and employs 59,000 personnel in India. The acquisition was undertaken to generate a vertically integrated global value chain from the tea gardens to the end-packaged product under Tetley's brand equity. Press reports show that in the bidding for the Tetley group, Tata Tea paid $100 million dollars more than the market price and, as in the classic case of the winner's curse, the value of the company fell after the acquisition. The group was supposed to have subsidized the acquisition by revenues generated by the software business of TCS.

Another example is the acquisition of the South Korean Daewoo by the Tata group unit TELCO, for production of commercial vehicles. The acquisition ran into problems because of differences in the geographical dispersion, culture, and internal organizational structures of the firms. The deal provided a pool of talented professionals from Daewoo who were more productive than their counterparts in India. The salaries and incentive structures of Daewoo were higher than those of the Indian firm, which caused several post-merger problems in labor negotiations. In other words, as in the typical prediction of modern property rights literature, the incentives of the workers and managers of the acquired firm altered in the post-merger phase, subjecting the management to complications.

On the other hand, the overseas acquisitions by India's software companies have been success stories. As discussed before, India's software industry is the most globalized. This means that managers and the skilled manpower of the companies are quite familiar with the organizational practices of firms of developed countries. Joint ventures and strategic alliances with TNCs helped companies in India to learn the organizational and technological practices of TNCs, which, in turn, helped them to manage the acquired firms in the US and western Europe efficiently (Patibandla and Petersen, 2002; UNCTAD: World Investment Report, 2002).

The changes in organizational practices as illustrated above are determined by changes in factors external to the organization caused by the reforms, and a set of internal changes in managerial practices, size of organizations, and diversity of operations. The new management practices and culture forced some of the changes in organizational practices. We can argue that the changes have come more directly from management and organization dynamics, and indirectly from the reforms.

## Stand-alone companies

The previous discussion concentrated on business groups. How do stand-alone companies come into existence and differ? The development of capital and product markets should facilitate the emergence and success of stand-alone companies. Companies such as Infosys and Satyam Computers in the software industry, and Bharat Biotech, Shanta Biotech, and Biocon in the biotechnology industry, are representative of the success stories of stand-alone companies that came into existence in the 1980s and 1990s. It is important to note that these success stories are in the new areas of market opportunities rather than in the traditional areas where domestic business groups and vested interests were entrenched. The case of Infosys illustrates this. The success of the company came through exports; it had no domestic market focus and, consequently, it did not pose any threat to the entrenched business groups or large incumbents in the domestic market. Second, in the software industry, the capital requirements for entry are not as high because it is a skilled-labor-intensive industry. As I discussed in Chapter 4, four technocrats with personal finance and some debt capital from the state-level public financial institutions started Infosys. Later, internal revenues and foreign financial institutions in India financed its rapid expansion. These institutions were the ones that had discovered it in the equity market in the first place, leading to its listing on the Nasdaq. Globalization made the success of Infosys feasible.

I illustrate the example of the emergence of a stand-alone company in the domestic airlines business. The Indian airlines business is dominated by three major players: the government-run Indian Airlines, and two private airlines, Jet Airways and Sahara. In 2003, Captain Gopinath, a retired army captain, launched a low-cost airline, Air Deccan. The airline began selling air tickets at rates that were 30 to 40 percent cheaper than the established airways. Prior to starting the airlines, Mr Gopinath started his business career with a helicopter business in 1995, financed mainly through personal funds, since formal banks and financial institutions refused financing. The success of the helicopter business was attributed to the minimization of the costs of operation at all stages and to the employment of pilots who had retired from the army. The venture generated markets that served remote and small towns, provided medical emergency evacuation facilities, and promoted helicopter-tourism, which were non-existent prior to its entry. Within one year of the start of its operation, the business turned profitable. Mr Gopinath, like Mr Narayana Murthy, was a pioneer, since there were no incumbents or other business groups prior to his entry into the field. Following the success of the helicopter business, Mr Gopinath branched out into the low-cost airline sector in 2003. Interestingly, capital for the airline was provided by self-finance, a local company (Brindavan Beverages), a non-resident Indian firm, a Japanese investor, and a few other promoters. Later, the local bank ICICI Venture and the US-based Capital International funded its expansion. Furthermore, in 2005 it signed a $1.4 billion contract with Airbus for purchase through financing of thirty Airbuses and thirty ATRs (turboprop regional aircraft), out of which fifteen were on lease. Today, Air Deccan has 100 flights a day and a turnover of Rs 5,000 million. The interesting aspect of the firm's progress is that the major part of capital at both the initial and expansion stages came from overseas agents.

Air Deccan's success can be traced to the adoption of an innovative organizational structure in reducing costs at every stage of operation. It implemented e-commerce-based selling of tickets and thereby eliminated the costs of travel agents. While low-cost airlines in the US and Europe use the proprietary software of a particular company for Internet-based reservations, Air Deccan created an in-house reservation system by giving the mandate to an Indian software company to create an Internet-based system for the Indian context, which took into account the fact that a large number of people in India do not have Internet access and credit cards. It set up a central computerized reservation system (CRS) on the Internet, linked to a virtual private network (VPN) which was leased to a call center. The call center uses local languages for different regions and is open twenty-four hours and seven days a week, with one mobile number for each state and one common telephone number for the whole country. The number operates as a local number for ticket purchasers and not as a toll-free number, which is thus affordable to the customers. A customer without an Internet connection and credit card can make the reservation and pay for the ticket within twenty-four hours at any of its 2,500 collection points and its collaborator agents in small towns.[11] It has turned out to be the largest e-commerce site in the country, doing business worth $350,000 a day. Figure 4 shows the organizational structure of the company.[12]

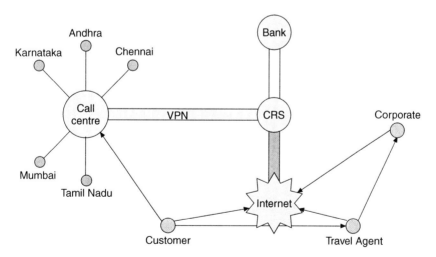

*Figure 4* Air Deccan Organization (source: The Air Deccan Office in Bangalore, Patibandla (2005c)).

Notes
Karnataka, Andhra, and Tamil Tadu are the names of states in the south of India.

As Gopinath observed during my interview, the organization they adopted is "very local, very global, and it is very robust and scaleable" (Patibandla, 2005c). However, the major constraints the airline faces are the infrastructure bottlenecks, since the government has the monopoly of the airport infrastructure. Gopinath actually had to beg the airport authorities for hangar facilities for his aircraft. This again shows the mismatch between private entrepreneurial talent, market growth, and institutional change owing to government controls over infrastructure. Government agents resist giving up control, since the major pay-offs come from infrastructure building contracts. Air Deccan's case shows that for a stand-alone entrepreneur to succeed in the context of India's institutions, he or she has to adopt organizational innovations to overcome the institutional constraints and to face competition from the business group units.

There are several pertinent questions concerning stand-alone companies, such as, why have stand-alone companies started to appear only in the 1980s and 1990s and why were they virtually absent till then? Why are such companies more prevalent in some sectors and not in others? In the present Indian context, is it becoming a better mode of doing business than other modes?

As I discussed in chapter 3, the import substitution policies generated a certain level of industrial and human capital endowments in the country by the middle of the 1980s. In the case of the new software industry, a few technocrat entrepreneurs who could perceive global market opportunities and harness the underutilized domestic endowments of human capital succeeded in launching and developing successful enterprises. This was also the case with the new and fast-growing biotechnology industry. The new market opportunities, especially the export markets, do not pose an immediate threat to incumbent large houses. However, the strategy of Air Deccan is different. The entrepreneur perceived a business opportunity in low-cost airlines, which incumbents did not bother about. The growth of the Indian economy in terms of the increase in incomes provided positive signals to overseas investors to fund the project. Air Deccan challenged the incumbents by charging prices 30 to 40 percent lower than existing fares. It will be interesting to see how well the airline succeeds in the long run as incumbents respond to the threat and diversified business groups enter this line. To recapitulate, most of the capital for these companies came from foreign sources. Most stand-alone companies are in new and rising businesses. Going global helped to overcome the constraints of inefficient institutions at home. Once they are able to find a foothold, they may turn out to be better than the incumbents because they are professionally managed, have no organizational dead weight to handle and derive the advantage of flexibility to change in accordance with changes in the external environment.

## Corporate governance

The major driving force for the restructuring of corporations was the increasingly competitive conditions in both the product and capital markets. Second, the decline of the public financial institutions owing to non-performing assets reduced the institutional advantage enjoyed by large incumbent businesses in the capital markets. The textbook economics shows that increase in demand results in a rise in prices and a consequent supply response. The demand and supply response of capital markets in modern capitalist economies is governed by the agency arrangements of the separation of owners (the principals) and controllers (managers or agents) of capital at different layers of an economy, right from banks, pension funds, insurance companies, and stock markets up to government receipt of taxes. Corporate governance is basically an issue of arriving at institutions that minimize the conflict of interest among the owners and controllers of capital. At the corporate level there are two tiers of agency relationships: at the top, between corporate headquarters and investors, and, below that, between corporate headquarters and division managers (Bolton and Scharfstein, 1998). Here, I discuss how the market and institutional conditions of corporate governance changed on these fronts in the post-reforms era.

At a general level, external finance is undertaken from two sources: debt and equity finance. In the case of debt finance, there is a legal obligation on the part of the borrower to pay back the money with the agreed-upon returns, which requires the institutional mechanisms of contract formulation and execution and bankruptcy laws. In the case of equity finance, there is no legal obligation on the part of the managers (the agents) to pay back the investment. For equity markets to take place and develop, investors should have the confidence that managers utilize their capital efficiently and obtain adequate returns. This depends on both the legal framework of a country and on how the investors are organized in monitoring the agents and exercising their control rights.

As I discussed in Chapters 3 and 4, the demand for equity finance was low in the pre-reforms era because the large business houses had privileged access to long-term finance from the DFIs and the liquidity of the markets was limited owing to the monopolization of the Bombay Stock Exchange by a few stockbrokers. Except in the case of one large business house (Reliance Industries), most business houses never had any interest in developing the equity market as they were able to exercise strong control rights with access to debt capital from the DFIs. The agency relationship between industrialists and the DFI lenders was governed by political economy factors, namely, collusion of the government agents controlling the DFIs and the large business houses. Thus, once a business house secured an industrial license, it was automatically given long-term loans by the institutions. In several instances, some of the business houses could pre-empt the licenses and the finance to block entry or competition. As the DFIs used the taxpayers' money, the moral-hazard costs were high, since the taxpayers' ability to discipline the agents was low because of informational imperfections and the monopolistic nature of the mobilization of households' taxes and savings by the government. Once a business group got loans from the DFI, the representatives of the DFI were passive partners, functioning as dummies on the board of governors, and had the least incentive to monitor the agents. A part of the debt would be diverted as the equity of the promoters to derive strong control rights. This, in turn, resulted in a peculiar agency problem. As Verma (1997) observed, the main problem in Indian corporate governance was not a conflict between management and owners but between dominant shareholders and the minority shareholders; and the minority shareholders (the promoters) were the managers. In other words, there was an ambiguous distinction between the principals and the agents in the corporations. To put it in the right perspective, the dominant agency relationship was between the taxpayers and government agents, and the government agents and corporate managers, with the final burden of the moral-hazard costs of the government agents and minority shareholding managers falling on the taxpayers and small shareholders.

One of the immediate outcomes of the reforms of 1991 was a series of stock market scandals. Until 1992, the Controller of Capital Issues of the government (CCI) controlled the prices of issued shares. As a part of the reforms, the control of the CCI on share prices was eliminated in the absence of a regulatory body and an effective legal framework of corporate governance. The outcome of the diminution of the role of the CCI was the stock market scandals. This serves as a simple example of the costs of piecemeal reforms. The first scandal was that of 1992, engineered by a stockbroker called Harshad Mehta of the Bombay Stock Exchange. The second was the case where TNCs started consolidating their ownership by issuing preferential equity allotments to their controlling groups at steep discounts. The third scandal was that of disappearing companies in 1993–4 (Goswami, 2001).

In the first case, Mehta had access to large sums of funds through illegal deals with a few public sector and private banks and used these funds to manipulate stock prices. In the true spirit of 'animal spirits', several small investors imitated Mehta's investment pattern. Once the stock prices zoomed, Mehta would sell and make huge profits. The discovery of the practices employed by Mehta was made by a journalist, Sucheta Dalal, not by the government, and led to the bursting of the bubble. This resulted in the wiping-out of billions of rupees of small investors' savings. The stock market scandals were caused by multiple players in the capital markets, apart from the brokers of the Bombay Stock Exchange. Several promoters in the Indian stock markets engineered incomplete or wrong information using strategies such as inflating project costs, fixing high premiums, and raising money for projects which existed only on paper. This took place with the active collusion of merchant bankers, underwriters, advertisers, financial weeklies, and other sundry marketers under the very nose of the regulatory bodies (Bhole, 1995). Furthermore, the financial institutions owned the credit rating agency, Credit Rating and Information Services of India Ltd (CRISIL). Ultimately, the small investor was at the receiving end.

The government's response to the stock market scandals took the shape of crisis-driven institutional reforms and was on two fronts: the setting-up of the regulatory body, the SEBI, and of the National Stock Exchange (NSE) to eliminate the monopoly power of the Bombay Stock Exchange. Interestingly, while the NSE was given full autonomy by the government, the SEBI was not. The initial resistance was from the stockbrokers, who were reluctant to reveal information to a statutory body and to register their operations. Most corporate bodies expressed a preference for executive powers to rest with the government rather thatn an autonomous regulatory body, obviously to make use of the pecuniary economies of their investments in cultivating the politicians. The SEBI's powers remained subordinate to the government and it was denied executive powers. The government retained the powers to override the SEBI's decisions (Mukherjee Reed, 2002). Obviously, the incumbent business houses and government agents would not easily relinquish their institutional advantages in rent-seeking.

However, these qualitative shifts in the policies have resulted in gradual improvements in corporate governance over the years, in a country in which most corporations were clueless about what corporate governance was all about. The SEBI steadily acquired regulatory teeth and started to impose codes to improve transparency, introduced controls on insider trading, and forced firms to adopt accounting standards. The NSE established screen-based trading all over the country, thereby reducing the monopoly power of the Bombay Stock Exchange and its brokers.

In 1993, the government of India announced the opening of the country's stock markets to direct participation by foreign financial institutions (FIIs), such as pension funds, mutual funds, investment trusts, and asset management companies. They are permitted to invest in all the securities traded on the primary and secondary markets. These instruments include shares, debentures, warrants, and schemes floated by domestic mutual funds. This has led to an increasing role of FIIs in India's equity markets. The FIIs started to play an important role in monitoring and improving the corporate governance practices of the corporations. Their entry into India had implications at two levels. First, foreign financial institutions, as privately owned and managed entities, have higher incentives to monitor corporate managers to ensure returns on their investment than the public financial institutions. Second, these institutions possess more-efficient tools for monitoring managers than do local private financial institutions in developing economies. It is observed that FIIs have steadily raised their demands for better corporate governance, more transparency, and greater disclosure. Forbes (2002) observes that FIIs account for fewer than 10 percent of the total market capitalization, but for a disproportionate share of daily trading. Their buying preferences have led to the imposition of a penalty on the stock valuations of those firms that have group cross-holding or inadequate disclosure, or are closely held.

My paper in the *Journal of Economic Behavior and Organization* (2005a) examined how the capital structure of India's corporations in terms of the different shareholdings of the FIIs and DFIs, and the public sharehold- ings, determined the performance of India's corporate sector. Instead of reproducing the results, I briefly discuss the basic findings.[13] The empiri- cal analysis was based on firm-level panel data for twelve industries relat- ing to the post-reforms era (1989–2000). The performance of firms was taken as net profits to sales. The results show that the share of foreign equity explains the profitability of firms positively and is statistically significant. However, the relationship is non-monotonic – the profitability of firms increases at a decreasing rate as the percentage of foreign equity increases. The non-monotonic association can be interpreted in terms of the benefits and costs of large institutional investors. On the positive side, large institutional investors are in a better position to invest in informa- tion and to monitor agents than a large number of small investors (Shleifer and Vishny 1997). On the negative side, an increase in the share of large outside investors beyond a certain point could result in collusion among the managers and the large investors to redistribute gains from dis- persed small investors. Apart from this, the costs of risks associated with instability in macroeconomic variables such as interest and exchange rates are high in the case of foreign equity. Small changes in these variables may cause foreign capital to move in or out frequently, imposing costs of uncertainty on the performance of firms.

The empirical results of the paper indicate that the higher the share of the DFIs in the capital structure, the lower is the performance of firms, which implies that firms that depend on DFIs perform poorly in the post- reforms era. The incumbents could no longer take privileged access to capital from the DFIs for granted as the institutional reforms of the latter made them more conscious of the quality of lending. Here, the difference could be the organizational dead weight of the DFIs and incumbent large business houses, which slows down their adoption of more efficient modes. The results also show that firms in general made higher profits in the latter part of the 1990s than in the earlier part of the 1990s, a possible result of the restructuring of firms that had been taking place. However, the corporations that depended more on debt finance (from DFIs) per- formed poorly through out the 1990s and, in fact, their performance was even worse in the latter part of the 1990s.[14]

The overall results of the paper suggest that under the changing product and capital market conditions, newer and more professionally run companies perform better than traditional corporations that depend mostly on raising debt-finance from public financial institutions. The newer and younger units belong mostly to the industries that had market opportunities for growth, such as the software, auto-component, and biotechnology industries. Goswami (2001) observes,

> The dominant characteristic of today's top 50 companies is the preponderance of first generation enterprises or professionally run businesses. In 1991, 22 out of the top 50 companies were controlled by family groups that held their sway during the license-control regime. By February 2000, the roles were reversed: 35 were professionally managed, of which 14 were first generation businesses; only 4 out of the 50 were run by older business families.

It is necessary to note that there are other factors at play apart from the sources of finance. As I discussed earlier, new and young enterprises are in the rising industries and are better managed, with no organizational dead weight to deal with. Under these conditions, even if both new and old enterprises were getting their funds from the same type of source, the younger enterprises would do still better.

There are two driving forces for improving corporate governance in firms. One is the role of regulatory institutions, and the other is increasing the competition and globalization of the markets. Globalization here refers to the increasing role of FIIs in the equity markets, the increasing competition from TNCs in the product markets, and the need to tap cheaper capital globally, such as through ADRs and GDRs, and the international stock markets. However, adopting high standards of corporate governance involves costs. Corporations have the choice merely to comply with the minimum requirements of the regulatory bodies, or to adopt the global standards of governance. I discuss below the case of Infosys in the software industry, the first company to adopt the world-standard US GAAP (Generally Accepted Accounting Principles) of corporate governance.

## Infosys and corporate governance

India's software industry is the most globalized in India in terms of its export-orientation, the presence of TNCs, and Indian companies going multinational. Infosys is one of the most successful stories of a global player in all respects, namely, export-orientation, the setting-up of its subsidiaries overseas, listing on the Nasdaq, and the adoption of global standards of corporate governance. A more remarkable side of the story is that it is the first Indian company to adopt employee stock options by lobbying the government to change the rules. It is the first company listed on the

Nasdaq, and the first to adopt GAAP. What are the underlying motivating factors for a company that came into existence as a stand-alone company in a sea of rent-seeking companies to adopt these ground-breaking practices? Was it the exogenous altruism of the founding members to share wealth with all the stakeholders, or was it a conscious visionary business strategy?

As far as investment in the costs of adopting world-standard corporate governance is concerned, the capital needs of software companies are not high, as it is a skilled-labor-intensive, rather than a sunk-cost or fixed-capital-intensive, industry. This makes it all the more intriguing why Infosys invested in the high costs of adoption of GAAP. Looking at possible underlying reasons, Khanna and Palepu (2004) concluded that Infosys adopted the stock options for two reasons. First, because of its leader, Narayana Murthy, who believed in wealth generation by sharing it with the stakeholders, and, second, the company wanted to signal in the global product markets, not the capital markets, that it was a world-standard company in all respects. This, in turn, contributed to its reputation and international growth.

What have been the demonstration and externality effects of Infosys and the software industry's practices on the rest of the corporations? Prior to the reforms period the Indian corporations did not have much understanding of either corporate governance or the idea of independent directors. Infosys demonstrated the possible benefits of adopting good governance in a globalizing developing economy to other corporations. The Confederation of Indian Industry (CII) set up a committee on corporate governance headed by Narayana Murthy to spread good governance across corporations in India. Furthermore, the practices adopted by Infosys became a benchmark for the regulatory body, the SEBI, to learn about international standards of corporate governance and to change and impose regulatory rules on the other corporations. Murthy played an important role in helping to design the SEBI's guidelines on corporate governance. The SEBI gradually implemented regulations in two broad areas: the stipulation that boards should be composed of independent directors, and improvements in the disclosure standards of accounting practices. These covered areas such as the consolidation of accounts, disclosure of accounting results by business and geographical segments, deferred tax accounting, and related-party disclosures, mainly to enforce the rights of minority shareholders (Khanna and Palepu, 2004).

In other words, the market forces of globalization have been instrumental in driving firms in the software industry to adopt high standards of corporate governance. The benchmarks set by firms such as Infosys in this industry helped the SEBI to become a catalyst in spreading good governance to other sectors. By 2001, over 140 listed companies, accounting for almost 80 percent of the market capitalization, had to follow a mandatory code laid down by the SEBI, which was in line with some of the best international standards. By 2003, every listed company had to adopt the SEBI code (Goswami, 2001).

## Internal governance

Internal agency relations refers to the organizational aspects of the board of directors, and the chairperson of the board, the composition and size of the board, the independence of the board with respect to the CEO or managers, interlocking of directorships, and division managers and employees. The Anglo-American corporate governance model gives crucial importance to shareholders as the legal owners of companies and residual risk bearers. In this institutional arrangement, it is imperative to provide shareholders with accurate information, on the basis of which they can exercise their control rights in hiring and firing the board and the managers. The information requirements need an independent external auditing agency to assess the information and turn it into performance indicators. The policy-makers in India have adopted the Anglo-American model as the benchmark for bringing forth institutional reforms on the corporate governance front.

The objective of having these different bodies is to establish countervailing powers in reducing moral hazard behavior among any one of them. In several instances an ambiguous distinction existed between owners and managers because managers or promoters often also happened to be minority shareholders. Boards and their chairmen or women were mostly family members and friends, and dummy members of the DFIs. One of the most dominant features of the board membership was the interlocking of directorships across several business units, a mechanism of collusive family business to retain control over a major part of the organized business. For example, in the early 1970s, seven leading industrial families held 303 directorships or partnerships. Of these, two families, the Goenkas and the Bangurs, alone held 136 directorships. De (2003) shows a substantial extent of director interlocks in eighty-nine Indian business groups that were influential in financial and information exchange in the early 1990s.[15] In most of the family business groups, the auditors were either from the family business or were associated with the business over generations. There was, therefore, a shroud of secrecy enveloping the overall auditing process; the whole thing was a family affair. Capital, however, came from mostly the taxpayers. How have these institutional arrangements changed in the post-reforms era?[16]

Apart from the committee headed by Narayana Murthy, the SEBI, the CII and the government of India set up two other committees, the Birla Committee and the Naresh Chandra Committee, to suggest measures to spread corporate governance practices on par with global best practices. On several accounts, while referring to the internal structures, the recommendations are quite similar in terms of increasing the independence of directors, restricting interlocking across companies and improving disclosures.[17] A vast majority of companies ignored the recommendations. The SEBI, based on some of the recommendations of the Birla Committee, mandated changes in the board structure and independence of directors and audit committees. Despite these measures, the promoter CEOs of most corporations retained their control of boards by managing to install their own cronies. Given the institutional arrangements of most Indian corporations, business houses are reluctant to relinquish their control. Ideally, corporate boards should have the powers to evaluate the performance of the directors and remove them in the case of poor performance. However, this never took place and board compositions remained unchanged, since managers and board members generally developed crony comfort relationships.

A few companies in India adopted the Anglo-American model in good spirit to raise capital in the US and western Europe. Nevertheless, the imitation of the model at present is only piecemeal. Shareholders still do not possess sufficient rights to discipline managers and board members, one of the reasons being that most business groups resist relinquishing their control of the business. Moreover, the legislative mechanism is not fully in conformity with the model. Thus, the regulatory body is denied full autonomy, and the courts are plagued by the high transaction costs of enforcing contracts.

One of the indicators of shareholder rights is the takeover code. Takeover threats are considered to be one of the mechanisms of disciplining incumbent managers and directors (Shleifer and Vishny, 1997). Capturing the public financial institutions helped the business houses in India reduce the threat of takeovers. In most cases, the agents of the DFIs sided with the promoters to block the takeovers. In 1997, the SEBI established the takeover code, according to which, if an acquirer's shareholding exceeded 10 percent, he or she had to make an open offer for an extra 20 percent of the shares. The public offer would carry a minimum price, which was the average of the last six months. The existing management was allowed to consolidate its holdings through the secondary market. Goswami observes that the regulation had two positive effects: first, it created a transparent market for takeovers, and second, the legislature in favor of open offers ensured that the minority shareholder would have the right to obtain the market-driven price in any takeover.

Most of the above discussion has revolved around the agency costs of managers. Generally, in the initial stages of the evolution of businesses, an owner/manager resorts to self-finance and debt capital, and at a later stage to equity finance. Once a firm grows into a critically large size, managers prefer equity finance to debt finance in order to exercise greater control, provided that equity financers are dispersed and are not large institutional investors similar to big banks. Once the separation of ownership and management of capital is total and clearly defined, the agency problem becomes highly germane and the issue of shareholders' rights important. However, apart from the entrepreneurs and owners of capital, workers and managers create the wealth of a business. Excessive control rights of shareholders, especially the large ones, can have negative implications on the performance of firms. If a large investor has strong control rights over the firm, managers and employees may not have incentives to acquire the firm specific capital, thereby reducing potential efficiency gains.

As shown in the case of corporations in India, when control rights are concentrated in the hands of a few investors, information can be distorted and cash flows can be distributed in their favour at the cost of dispersed small investors and employees. This can reduce efficiency by reducing employee incentives to acquire firm-specific human capital (Crémer, 1995). If the costs of risk-taking can be passed on to other investors, large investors can force managers of a firm to take undue risks (Shleifer and Vishny, 1997). In several instances, the productivity of managers and workers may depend on unobservable inputs. Excessive monitoring may induce managers and workers to shift their efforts to observable inputs away from the unobservable, in a similar way to the argument of the pressures of showing annual and biannual profits to shareholders (Patibandla and Chandra, 1998). In such cases, corporations may not realize their potential productivity and long-term wealth-generation gains. Williamson (2002) has a similar argument with respect to debt finance. Debt finance is generally undertaken by large banks that effectively monitor managers of firms to ensure returns on their loans and to be able to appropriate the assets of firms in the case of insolvency. In such cases, firms that rely more on debt capital are restrained from investing in assets with a high degree of non-redeployability by the banks. If the assets with a higher degree of non-redeployability are more productive than redeployable assets, firms that depend more on debt capital perform worse than others.

The Anglo-American model of corporate governance should understand and incorporate issues concerning not only the protection of the shareholders' and capital providers' interests but also the adoption of organizational conditions of incentives for workers and managers. The case of Infosys shows the adoption of governance mechanisms that protect shareholders and at the same time provide appropriate incentives for managers and workers to acquire firm-specific capital.[18] In the case of the Japanese automobile company Maruti-Suzuki and its component suppliers, there is evidence to show that they invested in efficiency wages to elicit the maximum productivity gains from managers and employees. I do not have information about other industries and firms regarding the issue of changes in shareholder rights, and managerial and employee incentives. That is a subject for further research.

## Changes in the debt finance institutions

The DFIs had been the major source of long-term debt finance for the industrial houses. Most of the banks were nationalized during the pre-reforms era. The positive outcome of the nationalization was the mobilization of savings from far-flung areas of the country. Most of the savings mobilized by the government were used to finance government budget deficits and a major component of that was used to subsidize the public sector firms and the public financial institutions. By the early 2000s, the DFIs ended up with large amounts of non-performing assets. For example, one of the institutions, the UTI, was bailed out by the government in 1998 with a sum of Rs 33,000 million of taxpayers' money. Some estimates show that the government of India has earmarked over Rs 200,000 million of taxpayers' money in 2002 to bail out just three of the public financial institutions: UTI, IFCI, and IDBI (Dalal 2002). Some of these institutions have started to adopt institutional reforms. For example, the ICICI, originally a government-owned development bank, shifted into merchant banking and the funding of high-technology activities, assisting their listing on the public stock exchange since 1994. In the early 2000s, IDBI started to shift to merchant banking. On the banking sector side, as I discussed in Chapter 4, the government of India implemented a series of reforms such as the deregulation of interest rates and compulsory lending and relaxation of the reserve requirement. Although, most banks were still under government ownership, there was a partial privatization of banks by allowing them to issue a part of their capital structure to the public equity. However, banking failure remains highly protected by the government.

The major constraint for the development of the debt financial institutions had been the property rights of lenders diluted by the bankruptcy laws. In India, the government defined bankruptcy as erosion of net worth but not debt default. The government body the Board of Financial and Industrial Reconstruction (BIFR) was responsible for the reorganization of bankrupt companies and its procedures were notorious for the long delays and high transaction costs. The creditors were not allowed to make any claims on the assets of bankrupt companies until the BIFR cleared them. The legal process was a cumbersome procedure. With all this put together, it was almost impossible for creditors to make claims on the assets of a company that declared bankruptcy. The press reports in 2003 showed several companies, public figures, and politicians defaulting on loan repayments to banks and institutions and hiding under the rules. In 2003, the Indian parliament passed the rule that the creditors could make claims on the assets of the defaulters without the BIFR and the courts, by directly sending legal notices and treating these as public notices. Although loopholes do exist, with the defaulters resorting to delays, it has nevertheless helped the debt financial institutions to harass the defaulters and put pressure on them. This has so far made a marginal positive difference in increasing the property rights of creditors.

## Market structure dynamics

Chapters 4, 5, 6 and the current chapter have shown the broad structural changes, competitive dynamics and firm-level technological and organizational changes in response to the reforms. In the final analysis, these outcomes should result in an increase in the welfare of large sections of the society. In purely positive terms, this should translate to a fall in the prices of goods and services, and an increase in incomes. Economists look at this in terms of the market structure of industries under the logic that competitive markets result in the Pareto efficiency of prices approaching long-run marginal costs. I briefly discuss the changes in the market structure of industries. A detailed analysis can be found in Patibandla and Sinha (2005).

Technological and organizational improvements in general should result in an increase in output and a fall in prices. In Schumpeterian characterization, large firms are in a better position to invest in innovations than competitive markets. If one firm is able to innovate a new technology and realize high-cost efficiency, it ends up dominating the market. If the market is contested by potential entrants, the firm will price output at long-run average cost, which benefits consumers. If one oligopoly firm adopts a superior technology and organizational practices, others are forced to adopt these practices or otherwise lose out in the market. If all firms implement these procedures, the productivity and output of industries increase, resulting in a decline in prices. When prices, especially of intermediate and capital goods, decline through general improvements in productivity, the entry costs of new entrants decline over time.[19] Even by taking the standard arguments of sunk and fixed costs as entry barriers, general improvements in productivity can result in a decline in the prices of investments. Apart from this, if new markets are able to convert fixed and sunk costs of exiting companies into economic value, the contestability conditions improve by reducing exit costs.[20]

Figure 5 shows the behavior of prices in the post-reforms era. The real prices of capital goods show a significant decline, there is a decline in the growth of inflation, real interest rates show a gradual decline and there is a steady and slow increase in FDI in flows. I have shown in the previous chapter that there has been a significant increase in productivity in general in Indian industries, which should be reflected in a decline in real prices at different levels.

## Globalization and organizational innovation

Organizational change that has been taking place in industries such as software and BPO in India could be attributed partly to the endogenous

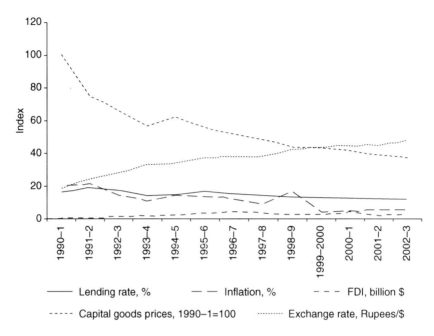

*Figure 5* Some economic indicators in post-reform India.

process of market reforms and partly to exogenous factors, such as technological and institutional change at the global level. The software and BPO industries in India had been able to take advantage of the global market changes owing to the endowment of initial conditions and the right-timing of the reforms since the mid-1980s. This was around the time when worldwide technological changes in telecommunications and the software industry took place, and the market boom of the industries presented great opportunities to India, because of the initial endowments.

To recapitulate, the rapid growth of the software industry was through exports, mostly to the US. Once software companies adopted the offshore model, they had to cater to the standards of customers in a developed economy by conducting their production operations in India, where they were hampered by pervasive infrastructure bottlenecks and institutional inefficiency. To overcome these problems, some of the companies, such as Infosys, adopted the organizational structure of 'islands of competitiveness' by investing in the self-generation of infrastructure. Once Indian companies imitated the offshore model of software development by TNCs such as TI, they mastered the global software delivery model, which became a worldwide benchmark for worldwide software development and delivery.

The logic of the theory of the firm is the most amenable for application to the underlying economic costs and benefits of the global outsourcing of services. In 2005, India is considered the preferred destination for TNCs to undertake the development of software and BPO services for their global operations. There has been a significant increase in the presence and expansion of operations of TNCs in these sectors since the late 1980s. The governance choices facing TNCs are outsourcing, joint ventures, and the setting-up of fully owned subsidiaries. Outsourcing to a local firm could involve long- or short-term contracts, with two subsets of governance, one being purely arm's length contracts, and the other being captive supplier contracts. I discuss the implications of these different governance choices in the Indian context.

## Outsourcing governance

For a global firm, the first issue involves the transaction (search) costs of identifying a country where it can derive maximum cost and quality benefits, considered against the trade-offs of the transaction costs of doing business in a foreign country. India has developed a good reputation on this front. The second issue is investing in the transaction costs of identifying the right kind of partners in India and verifying the credibility of a provider of the particular service. The third stage is getting into a comprehensive contract. Contracts have to incorporate specifications about the service, delivery parameters, payment terms, security and confidentiality of the data, the availability of the data on demand, the response time in case of unexpected problems, refund criteria in the case of failures, the conditions of termination of the contracts, and the proprietary nature of the data provided by the outsourcer. Apart from this, there could be costs of training the outsourced firm, which are asset-specific investments, in that, if the contract breaks down, these investments are useless. The more complex the service becomes, the more complex is the contract.

One of the organizational arrangements of outsourcing that took place was that of the captive supplier, in which a TNC embarks on a contract with a local firm which provides its infrastructure and skilled manpower on a fixed-commission basis, enabling the TNC to make use of it for software development.[21] However, it had incentive incompatibility because a TNC paid a mark-up commission based on local wage rates and made huge profits through wage arbitrage. Unless the collaboration is based on equity and profit-sharing, it has inherent instability and breaks down. The only way that a local firm would expose itself to this would be that it had no access to overseas customers. Once a local firm is able to vertically integrate into overseas markets, these organizational arrangements break down.

Additionally, there is the quasi-hierarchal governance choice, in which the outsourcer enters into a contract for the delivery of a specific service and retains the right to monitor job work while the provider firm in India controls its employees through prices and monitoring as the incentive mechanism for the output. Williamson's notion of hybrid governance is that partners in a contract invest in credible commitments (hostages) to incorporate safeguards. Once they invest in credible commitments, partner firms are autonomous with a certain degree of cooperation. In the case of the above-mentioned quasi-hierarchy, the autonomy of the Indian firm is rather ambiguous because the outsourcing firms retain some degree of hierarchy in monitoring the job.

In the case of Williamson's logic of governance, the partners at the ex ante stage make calculations regarding the transaction costs of asset-specificity, uncertainty, and frequency, and make the governance choice. However, in the context of rapid changes in technology and market development, contracts are highly incomplete and ex ante calculations may not be in line with changes in the future. I illustrate this by taking the case of the joint venture between the State Bank of India and GE Capital, which I discussed in Chapter 5 to show how the joint venture led to the generation of markets for credit cards from the middle-income groups. Here, the focus is on the governance of the partnership.

The SBI was the largest commercial bank in India, with a large customer base all over the country. GE Capital Services India was established in October 1993 as a wholly owned subsidiary of GE Capital Services, with two types of operations in the country: one that catered to the Indian financial markets, and another that encompassed the back-end technical support units for its global operations. The company's motive was to utilize the wage arbitrage of skilled personnel in India. In early 1998, two joint ventures between SBI and GE Capital were formed to market, issue, and service credit cards under the name 'SBI Cards'. SBI had the customer base and identified the potential customers for the credit card service within the pool. GE undertook the back-end processing of the customer profile before the credit cards were sold. The ensuing stage was the processing of information on the usage and payment patterns of the customer base to minimize the defaults.

According to Williamson's theory of governance, parties invest in relation-specific assets once they enter into a contract. In the present context, both the partners had pre-existing investments and capabilities, which demonstrated complementarities for generating markets and realized value through the joint venture. The partners, especially GE, did not have to undertake any major relation-specific investments for the venture; it was able to leverage its existing back-end processing infrastructure in India. On the basis of the existing infrastructure, it added employees to cater to the technical processing aspect of the venture. These employees could be redeployed to other uses or fired without much cost or difficulty if the collaboration broke down. Similarly, SBI had the pre-existing asset of a large customer base. SBI invested in marketing and building the brand name of the credit card, mostly among its large number of depositors. As I discussed in chapter 5, the venture led to the rapid development of credit cards and other financial services, especially to middle-income groups. However, the underlying dynamics of the governance threw up several complexities.

The value-addition in the joint venture through the complementarities of the assets of the partners can be observed by invoking the concept of 'revenue distance' (Aron and Singh, 2002). Revenue distance is the distance between the final sale of the service and the first step of value creation, similar to the 'value chain' concept that reveals the sources of value creation along vertical lines. The point at which the customer buys a credit card is the one where the revenue distance is zero. There are multiple processes and steps behind providing a specific financial service or product. The first is determining the customer profile so as to separate out potential defaulters, which requires the processing of information about a large number of customers. The information is generally collected from credit rating agencies, but in this situation, since SBI has a large base of banking customers, it already possesses the information. The greater the number of steps involved in collecting and processing the information, the greater is the revenue distance. After the credit service is sold to a customer, the next crucial step is the task of processing the usage and payment patterns of the customers and getting timely payments with minimum defaults.

As the financial services become more sophisticated and complex in response to intense competition, firms are compelled to create new sources of value and strengthen the means of monetizing the value (Aron and Singh, 2002). The lock-in and switching costs for SBI with GE may increase. This means that GE's firm-specific advantage may become more sticky and difficult to replicate by SBI in the future. In other words, GE's service, which began as low-end technical support at the beginning, may develop strong intangible-asset properties as market complexity and back-end processing sophistication increase. The degree of lock-in depends on the kinds of services that are outsourced to GE. If complex financial services such as real-time updating of customer balances, operating expenses control, and yield computations are outsourced to GE, SBI will become highly dependent on GE's services.

When the complexity of the services increases and the revenue distance decreases, it is better for the final service provider, in this case SBI, to set up its own captive processing unit instead of outsourcing. This is where the issue arises of how sticky or firm-specific GE's advantage is in dynamic terms. This assumes a crucial influence on SBI's ability to develop capabilities to replicate the back-end service assets of GE. As the complexity of the financial services provided by SBI increases, the costs of hold-up increase, which may eventually compel SBI to set up its own back-end operations. If SBI is able to realize this on an ex ante basis, it can be expected eventually to make efforts at appropriating the back-end technology of GE Capital. GE will have two possible future decisions to address: if its back-end technology can be copied by SBI over time without much difficulty, it would be reluctant to invest in relation-specific assets in dynamic terms; and/or it will make systematic efforts to make its back-end technology advantage sticky and non-tradable. One of the essential points of this case is that the global integration of the Indian economy renders firms, both local and TNCs, able to find increasing opportunities of mutual complementarities and generate or expand markets.

## Joint ventures

As far as my knowledge goes, joint ventures between TNCs and local firms are few and mostly technical in nature, rather than equity ventures in the service industry. One of the examples I discussed in the previous chapter was the technical joint venture between the TNC Nortel and the Indian firms Wipro, Infosys, and TCS in developing telecom-related software. To recapitulate, in order to protect the proprietary nature of its technology, Nortel formed comprehensive non-disclosure contracts with all the partners, utilized their premises and skilled people, and kept the Indian partners at a distance by allotting separate components of the development to each of them. It was a successful venture in the sense that some technology was transferred to local partners. As the complexity and proprietary nature of technology increase, most TNCs set up fully owned subsidiaries instead of forming joint ventures or outsourcing models of governance.

## Fully owned subsidiaries of TNCs

Most of the TNC operations in the software industry in India are fully owned subsidiaries (Patibandla and Petersen, 2002). Theory tells us that when transaction costs are high and property rights are weak, the governance choice is an integrated operation. Several early-entrant TNCs, such as TI, incurred high transaction costs in setting up their fully owned subsidiaries. Later, a large number of TNCs entered Indian industry. Setting up a fully owned subsidiary involves assessing the trade-offs of wage cost advantage of skilled labor in India versus the transaction costs of replicating and operating a plant there.[22] In recent years, a large number of overseas firms from the US and western Europe have set up BPO units in a wide variety of services. Although the government rules concerning clearance of FDI projects in software and BPO industries are a lot simpler than in other industries, they still involve high transaction costs, which include getting government approvals, commercial property and land acquisitions, and the costs involved in verifying legal ownership by checking the land records, implementing the labor laws, obtaining local-level clearances, and environmental clearances, etc.

In response to the entry of large numbers of TNCs in an economy beset with high transaction costs, new market modes of governance started to emerge in the 2000s. One of them is the build, operate and transfer (BOT) mode of governance undertaken by local firms to minimize the transaction costs for TNCs to set up their BPO operations.[23] BOT governance is generally prevalent in infrastructure industries, which necessitate high sunk and fixed costs in setting up.[24] It is now happening in the BPO and software industry in India, although it is very unlike infrastructure industries because it is skilled-labor-intensive, with low fixed and sunk costs.

A TNC which has the intention of setting up its subsidiary in India enters into a contract with an Indian company to facilitate a BOT. The Indian company obtains all the necessary clearances, acquires the commercial land, and builds the infrastructure, recruits the necessary personnel and, in collaboration with the TNC, even undertakes the requirements for knowledge transfer. When the subsidiary is fully operational, it is transferred to the TNC. The initial contract incorporates the payment and transfer issues. The whole process minimizes the transactions costs incurred by the TNC in setting up and making its subsidiary operational.

One of the outcomes of the growing software development and BPO operations is the emergence of specialized training institutions. With the increasing complexity and variety of services outsourced to India, both large and small firms in India lack complete expertise in all the fields. Some large firms are able to invest in internal training in different service segments but there are limits as the variety of services increases. In recent years, specialized institutions have emerged to train young graduates in medical transcriptions, call center jobs, and voice modulation for computer animation services. There are even training centers where prospective employees are trained to imitate American and British English-language accents for call center jobs.

In essence, there has been significant organizational restructuring by corporations driven by increasing competitive conditions in product, capital, and labor markets. Organizational change is both internal and external to firms. Internal changes are a reduction in excess diversification, followed, in some industries, by an increase in vertical integration. Internal changes also encompass organizational restructuring in terms of a reduction in excess hierarchies and the adoption of employee incentive practices, especially in family-run businesses in their attempts to become more professional in the competitive markets. In industries such as automobiles, assembler firms have developed vendor firms systematically which has not only led to the development of intermediate-product markets, but has also prompted the auto-component industry to become internationally competitive. Policy reforms and an increase in competition in capital markets have driven firms to improve on corporate governance practices, which, in turn, resulted in the emergence of markets for information. For the first time after independence, stand-alone companies, especially those started by entrepreneurs from the middle class, have emerged, particularly in skill-intensive and highly globalized industries. Globalization has also contributed to organizational innovations by firms in order to achieve international competitiveness operating in the Indian economy still weighed down by high transaction costs.

# 8 The evolution of public and private order institutions

This chapter discusses the evolution of the formal and informal institutions of collective action in response to changes in the economic dynamics in the post-reforms era. The public order institutions refer to the formal institutions of the constitution, the government, and the judiciary, while the private order institutions refer to the collective action of private agents. Improvements in property rights through changes in the laws and the administrative apparatus of government bodies are an example of public order institutional change. Industry and consumer associations that work for improvements in the formal laws and institutional arrangements for overcoming the constraints or failures of government bodies through repeated interactions with government agents and with each other are private order institutions. These can be defined as collective action in consultation. Even if a number of private agents were to act in a similar fashion, but independently of each other, it cannot be termed a private institution. Neither is a one-off collective action an institution. Repetitive collective action by private agents alone can be called a private institution.

The conceptual link between economic reforms and the evolution of public and private order institutions is that economic reforms as parameter and qualitative shifts are basically changes in the public order institutions in scope and objectives which trigger a growth process through structural and micro level changes, as shown in the previous chapters. This, in turn, leads to the emergence or shifting of economic interests of private agents, which can trigger private order actions for changing both formal and informal institutional arrangements. The interaction between the formal and private order institutions determines the efficiency of economic activity and further improvement (or deterioration) of the prevailing institutional environment. It is important to note that some changes in the public and private order institutions are independent of the reforms, while others are triggered by the reforms. I discuss both these aspects in this chapter.

In the first part, I broadly delineate the different types of institutions and their role in the functioning of capitalism, and in the second part, I discuss the evolution of these institutions in India's post-reforms era.

To recapitulate, Coase's theorem shows that collective action can rectify the costs of negative externalities in the absence of transaction costs. In the presence of transaction costs, government as a public order institution has to establish and enforce property rights. It is possible, especially in countries like India, that the government or legal bodies impose high transaction costs, which can be higher than the sum of the transaction costs of individuals acting alone before government came into play. This may lead to varied outcomes. For example, individuals who are unable to incur the transaction costs may accept the costs of negative externalities, some may resort to private order institutions (such as mafia) to enforce their property rights,[1] and some may form collective action groups to deal with government by incurring the transaction costs of formation of the group and dealing with government agents. These outcomes, if they are widely prevalent, can trap a country or a society into economic stagnation and retard potential growth benefits.

How is it that the governments and legal institutions of some countries are able to generate institutional environments marked by low transaction costs and efficient economic activity, while others get trapped with inefficient institutional environments? Why is it that politicians of countries with inefficient institutions and stagnant economic growth do not imitate the efficient institutions of other countries, so that larger sections can be better off? Examining the history of different nations provides some answers to these questions (North, 1990, Olson, 1982).

In the case of the US, the first European immigrants modified some of the political and economic institutions of the European Anglo-Saxon model into a presidential system in which government's powers were restricted by setting up countervailing institutions. They also adopted a high degree of decentralization of governance. However, American government institutions such as the postal services, and big businesses such as the railroad companies, were quite corrupt during the nineteenth century (Glaeser and Shleifer 2003). How did the corruption decline? Douglas North observes that the US was historically lucky for two reasons: first, it was a young country without strong entrenched interest groups, and second, some great visionary leaders, who helped in shaping the institutions, emerged at the right time, before the vested-interest groups entrenched themselves in perpetuating the inefficient institutions. In India's case, at the time of independence, a major part of the constitution of India was copied from the British. The constitution also incorporated several social objectives for government. As I discussed in Chapter 3, the parliamentary system assigned a lot of powers to the government, which adopted a high degree of centralization of powers, despite being a democracy. This political arrangement, where the government adopted a developmental role with all-round intervention in economic activity, conferred vast powers to government agents.

India, despite having inherited several features of the British legal system (including a large number of lawyers) and capitalist institutions, is observed to have performed poorly as compared to China, which began its economic take-off in the 1980s when it had only a rudimentary legal system (Posner, 1998). The interesting aspect is that in the post-reforms era of the late 1990s and the early 2000s, when the government reduced controls on economic activity, India's economic growth accelerated remarkably on the basis of the initial endowments. Some scholars (Huang and Khanna, 2003) observe that India may do better than China in the long run, owing to superior capitalistic and democratic institutions at the micro level. However, the major constraints for India's economic growth are inefficient governance and the fact that close to 30 percent of its population is still illiterate, below the poverty line, and outside the market mechanism. One of the important aspects of the evolution of public and private order institutions is the issue of improving governance and the emergence of private order institutions in reducing poverty and illiteracy.

## Public order institutions of capitalism

I briefly discuss the role of public order institutions in advanced capitalist countries. I broadly delineate them into two: support institutions and regulatory institutions.

## Support institutions

Support institutions include the legal framework, social security, primary education, macro policy management, and provision of public goods.

Generally, support institutions are of two kinds. One group defines the environment for the functioning of the economy, like the legal framework, and the fiscal and monetary institutions. The other group is redistributive, and consists of social security of all kinds, e.g. unemployment benefits, old age, maternity and sickness benefits, credit and disaster insurance by governments, and so on.

Regulatory institutions are efficiency-improving in intention. However, regulatory institutions are often so framed that they become redistributive. This happens because of the political process of legislating new regulatory institutions. This point can be illustrated in the Indian context. The licensing and MRTP policies and the DFIs in the pre-reforms era were established to channel investments and control monopolies. In practice, they were captured by powerful groups of incumbent industrial houses and government agents in order to distribute wealth in their favor, at the cost of consumers and taxpayers. The reforms, by overhauling these institutions, benefited consumers. The prominence of DFIs started to decline in the post-reforms era as a result of a series of financial market reforms. The establishment of regulatory institutions such as the SEBI improved the functioning of the capital markets.

The link between distribution and regulation can be seen by looking at the reforms as a one-shot distributional change and the subsequent emergence of regulation. Thus, privatization can result in initial one-time pay-offs to collusive government and private agents, and later bring in the establishment of regulation. To give a specific example, in the case of the telecommunications reforms, which I discuss in detail later, there were several scandals reported in the press relating to large money transfers and pay-offs to concerned ministers in issuing the licenses. However, later on, the regulatory bodies came into existence and started playing an important role in the functioning of the markets.

By equating the origins of capitalism with the emergence of private property rights, the establishment and enforcement of property rights required public order institutional support. In Marxian dialectic materialism, under primitive communism there was no difference between the public and private order institutions: everybody shared and took care of each other. In Marx's characterization, the first institution of ownership was slavery, and later the feudalism of land ownership. The issue, is how did the property rights of land emerge and how were they enforced by the state? In medieval Europe, kings and queens were synonymous with the states that maintained armies and power over the citizens. In several instances, the kings not only invaded other countries to plunder wealth but also predated upon their own citizens. The predatory powers not only related to tax collection, but also consisted of making property rights tenuous in order to retain powers of discretion. However, excess predation led to a decline in the generation of wealth (due to poor investment in productive durable assets by citizens) and a fall in revenue collections by the rulers. This forced the rulers to establish credible commitments of property rights of landowners and the business class and compelled them to provide protection and enforcement in order to maintain a steady stream of revenue (North and Weinghast, 1989; Pirenne, 1937).

Once a king established the military and the administrative apparatus, invading smaller kingdoms and amalgamating them led to economies of scale in utilizing the administrative apparatus, similar to the behavior of the East India Company in India in the eighteenth and nineteenth centuries. Using this analogy, the question that follows is, does a country have a boundary similar to the boundaries of the firm, determined by the transaction costs of markets and internal costs of bureaucracy? When some countries grew large, they had to adopt decentralization by delegating powers to the local landed gentry or government representatives. A similar institution in India was the Zamindari system of land revenue collection under the Moguls and in British India. Credible commitments by governments required the decentralization of power from kings to the judiciary, and later to the legislature, when the democratic institutions came into play after the French Revolution.

After the Industrial Revolution in England, the scope of property rights had to be extended to trade and industrial activity by adopting company laws, such as the limited liability company, and the bankruptcy laws. Over the course of time, as economic activity became more complex, modern capitalism developed complex legal systems of property rights, contracts, and their enforcement mechanisms.

It is necessary to note that, theoretically, it is true that kings or queens could assure themselves of higher revenue and more wealth by developing a number of public institutions. However, in reality, efficient institutional arrangements emerge and become sustainable only when it suits the interests of larger sections and groups. In the case of the French Revolution, populist French institutions were created after the overthrow and execution of Louis XVI. If we take another example from history, the Mongols were militarily far superior to all central Asian and south Asian states. They periodically used to attack these states, loot and burn them, and disappear. If instead, they had occupied some of these countries and developed tax-collecting institutions, they would have generated larger and more stable sources of revenue and wealth. The people of these states would have benefited from security and stable income, which never happened. The basics of the underlying theory are that transaction-cost-reducing institutions emerge and become sustainable when they help many players and it is in the interests of these players to establish the institutions. Whether they succeed or even think of doing so depends on politics, the level of awareness, the power of the status quo, and the ability of the players to act together. If they always succeeded, then governments would have no role to play. In fact, when the players cannot, or have not been able to, succeed, the theory suggests that a well-meaning government should step in and create the appropriate institutions.

One of the biggest lessons the Western capitalist societies learned from the Great Depression of the 1930s, when millions starved, was to establish a social security system in terms of food stamps, unemployment insurance, and minimum-wage regulations. Some countries developed a larger and others a lower base of social security; for example, the Scandinavian countries, such as Denmark, Sweden, and Norway, have a strong welfare economy of food and shelter security, free medical coverage, and primary and higher education, while the US adopted a lower degree of social security in the name of not depressing individual incentives. Another lesson from the Great Depression was that governments and the central banks of the state had to undertake macro policy management to avoid inflation and unemployment, but that issue is beyond the scope of this book.

The provision of free and compulsory primary and secondary education is based on the objective of providing 'equality of opportunity' to citizens. As I discussed in Chapter 6, most of the European immigrants to the US were from the working class escaping from the social hierarchy of Europe. One of the ways they desired to climb the social ladder was through education, which prompted them to invest heavily in primary and secondary education and also in universities. In the US, the provision of primary and secondary education was made mandatory by the constitution and the responsibility was placed on the local municipalities, which were supported by local tax revenues. Consequently, in America, the richer municipalities were able to provide high-quality education, while poorer localities had to be content with a lower quality of primary and secondary education. The upshot of this is that the equality of opportunity becomes unequal.

The provision of public goods by governments in Western capitalist economies presents a mixed picture. Public goods are defined as those that, when used by one agent, do not exclude their use by others. The theoretical rationale for the government's providing public goods is the market failure argument, according to which private agents have low incentives to invest, owing to inappropriability. Environmental regulation is basically a public good provided by the government. According to Coase's theorem, government establishes property rights in order to overcome the transaction costs of private actions. Some governments take a larger role in the provision of public goods, for example investment in R&D and higher education to generate public stock of knowledge. In industries with natural monopoly properties, such as water, power supply, and railroads, government plays both a direct and an indirect role. When these services exhibit natural monopoly properties, they are provided by two possible institutional arrangements. One is that the government provides them with its ownership. The other is that it provides them by entering into contracts with private suppliers.

## Regulatory institutions

I briefly discuss the issues of why a state regulates, and what is an efficient way of regulation. Under Coasian bargaining, government regulation is not necessary in the absence of transaction costs, as private parties can bargain mutually beneficial outcomes of negative externalities. I point out two fundamental reasons for a regulatory state: transaction costs, and the failure of collective action in bargaining. Olson (1965) in his logic of collective action shows that small groups are more effective in organizing themselves for collective bargaining than large groups. This is because large groups are prone to a high incidence of free-riding by members, while small-group members can undertake effective reciprocal monitoring. A simple example is oligopoly. Producers can collude and charge higher prices, while the larger group of consumers fails to organize neutralizing collective action.[2]

Douglas North observes that the anti-trust policies in the US emerged because of the destructive competitive behavior of producers that made everybody worse off, and they needed a neutral government to define and enforce rules of competition. However, Glaeser and Shleifer (2003) observe that regulation in the hands of courts led to its subversion by powerful economic groups (large firms) in the nineteenth century.[3] They observe that, in the US,

> The pervasive distortion of justice through legal and illegal forms of influence decided many cases and had a broad influence on the nine-teenth-century economy. Courts often failed to address the grievances of the parties damaged in the new economy, such as workers suffering from accidents, producers suffering from abusive tactics by the rail-roads, or consumers poisoned by bad food, and ruled in favor of large corporations. . ... The mechanism of subversion ranged from superior legal talent to political pressure to outright bribery.

In the early part of the twentieth century, increasing public awareness and populist leaders led the federal government to set up the autonomous body the Federal Trade Commission, which functions as a monitor and initiator of litigation. The role of the courts changed into that of settling litigation between government and the producers. The fact that the government initiated litigation meant that it was in a stronger position to counter a powerful company than single individuals who were not in a position to undertake the costs involved.

The issue that follows would be the degree of neutrality of the govern-ment regulatory institutions. An increase in the number of players in the system (the government, the courts, and public organizations) through decentralization may make it difficult for one player to be able to subvert the process effectively. A case in point is the anti-trust case against Microsoft in the US, which was initiated by a Congressman from the state in which Microsoft's rival, Netscape, was located. This illustrates the polit-ical factors of a federal or decentralized democracy in shaping the coun-tervailing powers. In the present context, improvements in the regulatory mechanism depend on whether the reforms increase the number of players with countervailing powers and cause a decline in informational imperfections. The different bodies of the autonomous public agencies and the courts, producer and consumer associations, and the independ-ent press all play an important role in regulation.

Improvements in enforcement imply that laws are enforced free from regulatory capture and corruption. Second, the costs of enforcement and compliance decline for both the government and private parties. Becker's (1968) idea of crime-and-punishment-type regulation is the imposition of high penalties on violators of the law with minimum probability of detec-tion to minimize the costs of monitoring by governments. However, this provides strong incentives for subversion and bribes because of the high pay-offs involved. On the other hand, an increase in the degree of moni-toring in terms of a high degree of detection with low penalties can result in high costs to both the government and the regulated. The compliance costs to the regulated increase if the government imposes high costs of disclosures and frequent inspections by government agents. This is especially the case if government agents have incentives for predation. For example, as I have discussed in Chapter 4, agents belonging to tax authorities (income and excise duties) and regulatory bodies such as the environment regulatory bodies in India make frequent visits to small and medium-scale enterprises to extract bribes, imposing high transaction costs on firms. Even when the laws are changed for the better, the practices prevailing from the pre-reforms period can allow government agents to impose high transaction costs and extract bribes from the public, especially from the illiterate and uninformed.

Some of the regulatory bodies in free markets are those concerning food and medicines, competition policy, public goods and natural monopolies, regulation of labor and capital markets, and regulation of environment. As one can see, most of the regulatory bodies target the production side, except in the case of the environment, where both production and consumption can result in negative externalities and degradation of the environment. Examples of such degradation include a private owner of land over utilizing groundwater, or misuse of public goods, such as parks. Regulation, in most cases, is a matter of interaction between government bodies and producers. The underlying logic is that producers, especially of the oligopoly kind, are more powerful than dispersed consumers and they can exhibit implicit and explicit collusive behavior to redistribute wealth or make monopoly profits at the cost of consumers. In the case of large-group competition, a large number of small firms can generate negative externalities through intense competition as I illustrated in the case of the leather and garment industry in Chapter 6. Even in the case of large-group competition, producers appear to form effective industry associations and undertake collective action more successfully than consumers. At the same time, the better-organized are in a more favorable position to undertake regulatory capture, which leads us to the issue of enforcement of the regulatory environment.

Probably the most important issue concerning regulation in India is its enforcement. Formal institutions require the definition of the rules, the setting-up of the administrative and legal procedures, and actual enforcement of the rules. Organizations and the definitions of the rules can be copied from advanced capitalist economies, but enforcement of the defined rules requires the evolution of the embedded conditions. The drafters of India's constitution made it idealistic in the writing. A simple example is the environmental protection. India has a large number of laws protecting the environment, but low levels of enforcement. Although the design and transplantation of organizations is easy, enforcement is more complex. Even when the organizations are replicated, prevailing government agents may resist giving up their discretionary powers of predation. For example, the corporate governance model in India is an imitation of the Anglo-US model. But the SEBI, the regulatory body in the capital markets, is not given full autonomy by the government, so that the ministries can retain their powers. Another example pertains to the tax laws in India, which were framed in such a way that several large corporations did not pay corporate taxes for a long time, profiting from gaps in the laws. In other words, the vaguely defined laws and rules work in favor of the large agents who can incur the transaction costs of finding the gaps. Second, it also gives discretionary powers to government agents to extract bribes by interpreting the rules in accordance with the context.

The administrative discretion on the part of governments and its agents arises owing to informational imperfections and a weak legal system. This can also arise out of the absence of regulatory predictability and procedural transparency. This administrative discretion not only places those who have already invested at great risk, but also causes those who are contemplating investment to think again (Williamson, 1998). This results in predation by governments and by their agents. The distinction is that governments can appropriate property rights by changing policies for political reasons. If the rules are unclear and non-transparent and judicial enforcement costs are high, government agents can predate on private agents for extracting bribes. The credibility and effectiveness of a regulatory framework, and hence, its ability to facilitate private investment vary with a country's political and social institutions (Levy and Spiller, 1996).[4] Under totalitarian systems with no independent legislature and judiciary, predation by government agents is easier than in a democracy. However, the risk of appropriation through changes in the rules and taxes can also arise in a democracy. In a democracy, if there is room for discretion owing to non-transparency of the rules and there is a high transaction cost to the legal process, or if elections, which change power among political parties, determine the status of the property rights, political risk escalates to the same level as under a dictatorship. This issue is especially important in the case of investments in large infrastructure projects which require private agents to invest in high fixed and sunk costs. As I briefly discussed in Chapter 1, the nature of the functioning of democracy in India in comparison to China's totalitarian system is one of the reasons why India performs worse than China in infrastructure investments. I will discuss this issue with reference to the Indian context later by taking a few case studies.

## Private order institutions

This section deals with the different types of private order institutions that emerge and operate in free market economies. As I have discussed in Chapter 2, informal rules and norms, both social and political, are basically private arrangements of collective action that evolve over a period of time. Some norms are a result of learning and cooperation taking place through repeated interactions, which help in avoidance of prisoner's dilemma outcomes. Some norms could be such that they perpetuate prisoner's dilemma interactions, resulting in societies being trapped in low levels of development.

According to Coase's theorem, private order institutions emerge to either overcome the high costs of formal legal systems or to compensate for their absence, both of which reflect a failure of the state to provide effective (low transaction costs) public order institutions. This can result in both efficient and inefficient private order arrangements. In the US, a large number of contract and property disputes are resolved by private negotiation, rather than going to courts, to avoid the costs of legal proceedings. This is an example of efficient private order arrangements. Similarly, I show later how some private arrangements in India have turned out to be efficient substitutes for public institutions. Inefficient private ordering can take the forms of arbitration accompanied by retaliation, mergers (excessive integration), bilateral monopolies, strong-arm tactics such as illegal markets, and costly methods of contractual safeguards with group alliances. These arrangements are expensive substitutes for the formal institutions. They cause economic inefficiency and block the emergence of efficient markets. Apart from this, these work in favor of strong incumbent firms or groups and against new entrants. As Posner (1998) observes, the cumulative costs of doing without law in a modern economy may be enormous.

Private order institutions can emerge mainly for the distributional politics of zero-sum interactions. As mentioned before, Olson's (1965) logic of collective action shows that small groups are more effective in organizing themselves into cooperative arrangements than large groups. Organized groups can effectively capture the policies and governmental institutions and redistribute wealth in their favor. He shows how great empires declined historically when the distributional politics became dominant. This type of private ordering institution could result in the economic decline of nations, especially when these are prevalent under conditions of stagnant economic growth of redistributing a given pie. Dead-weight losses of transfers from one group to the other, especially when they take place cumulatively, result in a decline in the size of the pie.

Coase's theorem holds that collective action may fail owing to the presence of transaction costs. On the other hand, under certain circumstances, the presence of transaction costs could result in collective action that generates higher surplus value than individuals acting alone. This type of private ordering results in efficiency. For example, the collective action of the formation of cooperatives in some agricultural markets in India helped small farmers overcome the high transaction costs of input and output markets and realize higher surplus than they would have realized had each farmer acted alone (Patibandla and Sastry, 2004). Other examples of collective action are mutual funds and financial institutions, and micro-finance institutions in capital markets.

As growth and structural changes in the economy take place in response to the reforms, private ordering institutions come into existence, with agents forming associations to deal with government to change the rules of the game. Existing associations may also change their focus or objectives in dealing with the government for changing the institutional environment of the post-reforms era. For example, the software industry association, NASSCOM, has become quite effective as the industry has become a major wealth and employment generator. Similarly, some of the industry associations which were primarily motivated for distributional gains of controls in the pre-reforms era changed their focus and became more reform-friendly. Thus, the initial lobbying against the entry of TNCs by certain industry associations has changed over time to the extent of becoming TNC-friendly.

## The evolution of the public and private order institutions

Commenting on the emergence of Common Law in England and Civil Law in France in the twelfth and thirteenth centuries, Djankov *et al.* (2003) observe, "England adopted Common Law because decentralized adjudication could be successfully enforced. France adopted Civil Law, sacrificing the benefits of local knowledge, because only more centralized dispute resolution was enforceable." Thus France, facing a higher degree of law and order problems that required centralization, adopted the Civil Law. The Common Law tradition of England was transplanted into India during the British rule and it continued with some modifications after independence. India also inherited some amount of civic capital in the form of bureaucracy, judges, and lawyers from British rule, which expanded after independence. In India, local conditions such as the vastness and diversity of the country posed problems of different kinds across regions which could not be resolved by centralization or decentralization alone. As a result, when the Common Law was introduced into the country, it became a hybrid version that combined centralization and decentralization.

The constitution of India is the supreme law, which guarantees the basic rights of individuals and rationalizes the powers and functions of the various bodies at the center and state levels. Any law enacted by the government, both at the center and state level, that infringes on these rights, when challenged, is liable to be quashed by the courts. The interesting aspect of the constitution is that it acts as a political as well as a financial document. Based on the principles of the constitution, the legislative powers are distributed between the center and the states, with each assigned rights to enact laws based on the delineation. Commercial laws mainly come from the center – the Companies Act, the Consumer

Protection Act, the MRTP Act, the Foreign Exchange Regulation Act, the Copyright Act, the Merchandise Act, the Patent Act, the Income Tax Act, etc. As the government took on the developmental role after independence, it ceded enormous powers both in the legislation of acts and in the administrative apparatus. The government enacted a plethora of rules, laws and by-laws through diverse legislation. Since independence, the central and state governments have brought in about 30,000 laws. The consequence of this is an inordinate number of cases pending with the courts. Jha (1998) observes, "The complexity of procedures, multiplicity of laws and the very structure and organization of courts increase the total period occupied by the trial of suits and criminal proceedings and by the appeals, revisions or reviews arising out of them." Today, in 2005, there are about twenty-five million cases pending with the courts, with 25,000 of them with the Supreme Court. In order to protect consumer interests through speedy decisions from the courts, the government of India set up, in the mid-1980s, consumer courts alongside the mainstream courts to dispose of cases within nine months. However, ten years after they came into operation, the courts ended with a large backlog which resulted in a minimum of two years for a case to get a hearing.

How has the legal system changed for the better in the post-reforms era? The reforms in general were feasible as a consequence of changes in the Companies Act, the MRTP Act and the FERA Act, which can be treated as exogenous changes. As illustrated in the previous chapters, the level and complexity of economic activity increased in the post-reforms era, as also evidenced by an increasing number of both local and foreign firms in industries, joint collaborations, and alliances among firms, which required them to formulate complex contracts. There were about 1,300 joint ventures between TNCs and local firms in 2000. Obviously, some of the ventures were affected by contractual disputes, which forced the parties to resort to judicial intervention. The Supreme Court and High Courts of India passed legal settlements for several cases which serve as legal precedents that provide signals to private agents while making choices between the private and public order settlements of contractual disputes. Moreover, several rulings of the courts supported the reforms process, which serve as signals of the credible commitment of the state to the reforms.

Several of the judicial decisions are in line with the basic tenets of the constitution, whose commercial laws have their origins in British Common Law. The following are a few examples. In the mid-1990s, the Maruti-Suzuki joint venture between the Japanese TNC and the Indian government fell into a dispute over the appointment of the chief executive officer. The TNC claimed that the Indian government had appointed the chief executive officer without its prior approval. The dispute went to the judicial recourse, with the ruling of the court going in favor of the TNC. Similarly, when a TNC with an existing joint venture partnership with a local firm wanted to set up its own subsidiary in a specific field, the local partner took this to the court. The Supreme Court refused to intervene, pointing out that doing business with a subsidiary was not equal to doing business with a joint venture. Twenty-five public interest litigations were filed against the Dabhol (Enron) power project investment. The TNC was able to clear all of them in the courts. These rulings set some standards of legal safeguards of contracts in the post-reforms era. However, in several cases, the procedures involved high transaction costs and long waiting periods for the parties, resulting in potential foreign investors backing out. Since effective and autonomous regulatory agencies similar to the FTC (Federal Trade Commission) in the US are still non-existent or not fully autonomous in India, the burden of understanding and interpreting the economic and legal implications of contracts falls on the Supreme Court and the High Courts. This situation is similar to the earlier stages of the Sherman Act passed in 1890 in the US.

On several counts, property rights in India remain tenuous and subject to high transaction costs of enforcement. While the legal land records in some parts of India, such as Tamil Nadu in the south, can be traced back to a few hundred years, in several parts, especially the northern states of Uttar Pradesh and Bihar, land records do not exist. This makes property rights tenuous and perpetuates the feudal system of domination by large players who can afford to employ private armies. On the other hand, in the state of Tamil Nadu, with better legal records and enforcement of ownership of property, there has been rapid economic development in both the rural and urban areas.

The interesting aspects of the evolution of institutions in the post-reforms era is that in those urban areas where property rights are deter-mined by the institutional constraints of rent control, private agents invested in safeguards in response to an increase in demand. To give an example, as I discussed in Chapters 1 and 3, the city of Bombay could not develop its real estate despite claiming one of the highest real estate prices in the world, owing to the Rent Control Act. In the 1990s, when the demand increased for both commercial and private needs, the outer city of Bombay began to be developed, with developers taking into account the added costs of contractual safeguards relating to the Rent Control Act.

Let us look at the market and institutional response to the increased growth rate and demand in the post-reforms era. One of the outcomes of the rapid increase in demand for real estate is the emergence of large players in the market. In 2005, real estate has been opened up to foreign direct investment. One possible outcome of this is that the large and pro-fessional players could invest in the transaction costs of verifying legal records and dealing with government agencies, and provide better prop-erty rights to small buyers. In other words, a large player can afford to invest in added safeguards by realizing the economies of scale of the trans-action costs of dealing with government agencies. This, however, is possible only when there are critical minimum initial conditions of legal records; otherwise there will be no difference between a mafia and an organized private corporation.

My preliminary research on the land markets in and around Bangalore city reveals the interesting phenomenon of changes in property rights in response to market growth. As I mentioned earlier, Bangalore city has been experiencing exponential growth and the city's expansion has been due to the amalgamation of farmlands around the city. Small farmers own most of the farmlands, which are called Pada lands. The government rule stipulates that farmers have to pay an annual tax on the land. If a farmer fails to pay the land tax for twelve to fourteen years, his or her ownership rights become tenuous. Most farmers are unaware of the rule and, even if they were aware of it, they are afraid to deal with government offices and agents, given the high transaction costs and harassment they have to bear. Large land developers take advantage of this and procure land from farmers at low rates. Subsequently, they incur the transaction costs of dealing with government agents, improve upon the property rights of the land and sell it to the urban middle class at high prices with well-defined property rights.

One more example of the endogenous process of the emergence of property rights is the modification and enforcement of the Copyright Act through lobbying by the software industry association, NASSCOM. The association became politically powerful because the software industry developed into a major wealth and employment generator for the country. Similarly, the institutional reforms in the capital markets and market reforms have opened them to international institutional investors, which has resulted in improvements of the property rights of shareholders over time.

One of the outcomes of the increased economic growth rate in the post-reforms era has been an intensification of judicial activism in defining and enforcing certain elements of property rights. The reforms, for example, led to a rapid increase in the number of automobiles on the roads of big cities, without a corresponding increase in infrastructure. As a consequence, most cities in India ended up with high levels of air pollution. Delhi, the capital of the country, was one of the major victims. As the politicians with different political constituencies could not implement pollution-preventing measures, the courts intervened by banning old vehicles, insisting on the use of cleaner gas and closing polluting small-scale industries on the outskirts of Delhi. Similarly, elsewhere, in a few cases of industries causing pollution, such as the leather tanning industry, the courts compelled firms to adopt cleaner technologies. However, judicial activism has its costs of subverting the legislature and executive bodies and is subject to lack of enforcement. A simple example is the ban on loudspeakers in public places imposed by the Supreme Court of India, which is rarely enforced.

Social security, a public order support institution, is non-existent for the urban and rural unorganized labor. The effect of the reforms is that the problem of lack of social security is actually worsening. This is because the structural changes in the organization of employment have resulted in both large, medium, and small-scale firms increasingly adopting the practice of contractual labor, instead of employing workers on a regular basis. The underlying logic is to avoid labor market institutional constraints and to reduce the costs of social security payments. This is taking place not only for semi- and unskilled-labor-intensive activities, but also in service areas, such as the BPO sector.

The public distribution system (PDS) of fair-price shops was started as one of the basic institutions of food security for the poor. However, the structural adjustment and stabilization policies of 1991, which significantly cut subsidies and reduced allotment to the PDS, weakened the system. The PDS became more or less defunct in the 1990s, except in a few states such as West Bengal. The election results of 2004 are interpreted as a reaction of the rural poor who have been denied the benefits of increased aggregate economic growth. In 2004, the newly elected government at the center announced a Common Minimum Program, which included increasing investment in employment for food programs, and primary education for the poor, especially in the rural areas. The major issue now is the institutional implementation of these programs so as to reach the intended target groups.

Constitutionally, the provision of the services has been in the hands of the state governments with varying levels of initiatives and investments across different state governments, depending on political economy factors. For example, the state of Tamil Nadu in the south has been mostly ruled by regional parties catering to the aspirations of the people of the state. In the 1980s, the state government effectively implemented midday-meal schemes for primary school children, which increased school enrolments. Within twenty years of its implementation, the state improved on all social indicators. There was a decline in the illiteracy rate, a fall in infant mortality, and an increase in life expectancy. Combined with high literacy and low labor dispute rates, the state became a major attraction for investment both in the manufacturing and high-tech industries by the late 1990s (Ghemawat and Patibandla, 1999). Similarly, in the case of the state of West Bengal, the Communist Party rule since 1977 led to implementation of land reforms and decentralization of certain powers to village-level governance, which generated significant improvements in the public goods services reaching the larger sections of population[5] (Bardhan and Mookherjee, 2004).

On the social security front, one of the interesting phenomena in the 1990s is the emergence of privately run old-age homes, especially in small towns in many parts of the country. Insurance markets for health security provided by the commercial banks and specialized agencies have appeared in the post-reforms era.[6] However, the emergence of private order institutions for the provision of social security solutions in response to the failures of the state, is an extremely remote possibility, especially in a developing economy.

In early 2002, the Supreme Court of India gave instructions to the governments to implement the midday-meal scheme for primary school children all over the country. The fundamental problem of government primary schools has been an institutional failure in the delivery of education to children. As the legal responsibility rests with the state government, different state governments have reacted differently. For example, the governments of the large northern states of Uttar Pradesh and Bihar have not shown much interest.[7] In general, in the major part of the country, the primary education provided by the government has been ineffective because most government schools have poor infrastructure, poor teacher attendance, and poor education delivery. One of the institutional outcomes of this is the emergence of private primary and secondary education schools. The process has been started by both commercial and self-help groups as private order institutions, to overcome the failures of the government.

The Indian government spends about 1.7 percent of the gross domestic product on primary education. In spite of this, about forty million children are out of school. An even more serious problem is the institutional failure of existing government schools to deliver education because of the factors mentioned above. The country average indicates that about 25 percent of teachers in government schools are absent on a working day. Teacher absence in India is high relative to that in other low- and middle-income countries. Within India there is significant variation in average absence levels across states, with the poor states having highest average, ranging from 37.8 percent in Bihar to 41.9 percent in Jharkand, 14.6 percent in Maharashtra, 17 percent in Gujarat and 17.6 percent in Madhya Pradesh (Kremer *et al.*, 2004).

Given the poor state of the government schools, the urban and rural middle class send their children to English-medium private schools. The interesting and notable phenomenon in the 1990s, in the post-reforms era, is the increasing presence of private schools catering to low- and poor-income groups (Waldman, 2003). In the past, the opportunity cost of sending children to school was high for the poor because children could be sent to work and earn daily wages. Why is it that the poor now spend a major part of their earnings to send children to private schools? The reason is that in the 1990s there have been increasing job opportunities for the skilled and educated people as compared to the previous decade, and the poor perceive English-language skills as a means of upward mobility. Qualitative information shows that in certain regions of Andhra Pradesh state, the demonstration effect of the families of lower and upper middle class to the poor is one of the motivating factors. If such is the case, why not send their children to the inexpensive government schools? The perception of a poor farmer with respect to the non-accountability of government schools and the relative performance of private schools can be seen from this observation in a village called Naini: "In the private schools, people can put pressure on the teachers to be sure they work. In the government school, even if the teacher doesn't teach half the time, we can't say anything" (Kazmin, 2000). In a larger context, with imperfect information about their rights, the poor perceive that government agents are not accountable to the public, which means high transaction costs to the poor in availing themselves of public goods.

To exemplify the increasing role of the private schools for the poor, in the district capital of Hajipur, in the poorest state, Bihar, there are seventeen private schools. In Andhra Pradesh, there are about 5,000 private primary and secondary schools, charging monthly school fees of about Rs 80. About 40 percent of them are legally unrecognized by the government because it stipulates that they deposit Rs 50,000, a sum that most of the schools cannot afford. As Tooley (2000) observes, private schools have proved to be ingenious – students from unrecognized schools sit for their exams at another friendly recognized school as private candidates. One of the organizational principles of the private schools for the poor, according to Tooley, is that "amongst some of the most disadvantaged people on this planet, the poor help subsidize the poorest, bound together in their shared status as refugees from a failing state system."

## Regulatory institutions in the post-reforms era

One element of regulation is making sure that markets remain competitive and contested, so that prices reflect the true opportunity costs of the resources. The other is reducing any form of negative externalities. In the first case, two aspects are germane: regulation of natural monopolies, especially in the provision of public goods, and formulating and implementing a competition policy.

The objective of the competition policy is to restrain the anti-competitive behavior of private and public agents (government companies as sellers and government departments as buyers), with two main groups involved: producers and consumers. A producer has an incentive to gain, at the cost of consumers and of other producers. The issue is, what are the market conditions required for everyone to have a fair outcome from competition? For the sake of simplicity, economists define a fair outcome as the product prices reflecting long-run marginal costs and input prices reflecting long-run marginal productivity, in the absence of externalities. The government takes the role of ensuring that large firms undertake long-run marginal cost pricing and that the market remains contested by eliminating any form of entry and exit barriers. In the US, the Sherman Act initiated the institution of anti-trust legislation, and later, the autonomous body the FTC was set up, which functions as a monitor of anti-competitive behavior and initiator of legal actions. The Sherman Act defined fair competition in very general terms. As the market became complex through both technological and institutional changes over time, the legal and economics professions became major players in defining what constituted anti-competitive behavior. A large body of literature on industrial organization in economics can be attributed to the public policy issue of competition policy.

As a measure of reducing government controls in India, the MRTP Act was modified. At present (2005), the MRTP Commission enforces a rudimentary competition policy. So far, even fifteen years after the reforms, the government of India has not drafted and implemented a systematic competition policy.[8] For the institution of competition policy to come into existence as an endogenous process in the post-reforms era, powerful interest groups should develop a stake in it. In the Indian context, consumers and potential new entrants into industries are the probable beneficiaries, but not powerful incumbents, unless, of course, they get into destructive competitive mode and need a neutral body to resolve their disputes. Consumers are large and dispersed groups for whom an effective organization is not feasible, and potential entrants are not as powerful as incumbents. So far, the players in the new and politically powerful industries such as software have not developed an interest in local market competition, as most of them are export-market-focused. Furthermore, for those who matter politically, the positive benefits of competition to consumers are high enough compared to the pre-reforms era to worry about competition policy.

However, the dichotomy of the middle class, which has benefited from the increased competition, is rather funny. I illustrate this with my own example. I bought a new Ford car in 2004 in Bangalore. I was truly impressed by the service provided by the distributor before and after the purchase, especially as I had experienced the sellers' market before the reforms.[9] However, every time I drive the car on the roads of Bangalore I get into a state of high anxiety and nervousness. The point is that the provision of roads infrastructure in Bangalore is the responsibility of local governments. The condition of the roads and traffic congestion have increasingly become worse with the market-driven (literally) exponential growth of vehicles in the post-reforms era. The subject of the condition of the roads is another part of the regulatory issue, which I discuss below.

Market reforms in the absence of appropriate regulatory institutions results in a mismatch between market growth and institutional change, resulting in negative externalities. As I discussed in Chapter 6, the devaluation of the exchange rate in 1991 resulted in the rapid growth of labor- and pollution-intensive industries such as leather, dyes, and garments, destroying drinking water and agricultural lands. Similarly, the privatization of public monopolies on one hand results in positive gains of supply responding to demand, but on the other hand, it could result in negative consequences if it is not followed by appropriate regulation. I illustrate this with the example of the privatization of the city bus service in Delhi in the early 1990s.

Prior to this, Delhi's local transport service was monopolized by the local government's bus service, called Delhi Transport Corporation (DTC). In the early 1990s, the local government opened up the service to private bus operators. Before the privatization, any commuter in Delhi could vouch for the fact that taking the DTC service required tremendous patience in terms of waiting time, and also gymnastic abilities for getting in and out of crowded buses. After the privatization, the supply of bus services increased significantly, which, in turn, augmented consumer welfare by reducing the waiting times and the need for gymnastic capabilities. However, the other side of the story is that intense competition between private operators led to a dramatic increase in road accidents because of buses' speeding and overtaking each other. With this outcome, consumer welfare calculations should take into account the increased probability of a commuter getting physically harmed in an accident, as against the benefits in terms of improved service after the privatization. This outcome took place because of the lack of effective regulation of the behavior of private operators. In the absence of effective public regulatory institutions, the private agents themselves may resort to their own method of enforcement (law of the jungle). The competition between private bus operators was intense. Each one tried to cut into the market share of the other, not only by efficient operation (including speeding and overtaking) but also by cheating. As cheating was not restrained by a neutral public institution, each operator monitored the other's behavior and attempted to restrain cheating by whatever means was available. One of the examples of this outcome, from my personal experience of traveling on one of the bus services, was the spectacle of a bus conductor beating up the conductor of another bus, accusing him of violating the time schedule and undercutting the bus fare.

The infrastructure and provision of public goods are generally characterized by natural monopolies, which require government's direct and indirect role in regulating them. As a part of the reforms process, the government of India allowed the entry of private firms to operate public utilities services such as electricity, telecommunications, and road building. Investment and operation in these industries by private firms are subject to a gamut of contractual hazards owing to government regulation at different levels, which include the issuing of licenses, regulation of pricing, and service provisions. In the case of electricity projects, the state governments play an important role in regulation, with diverse regulatory and political economy factors at play across states. The regulatory decisions governing issues such as zoning, land use, and the environment vary from one state to the other.[10] Project approval in India is made at the central level, while implementation is left to state governments. I illustrate the point concerning costs of contractual hazards in these industries by taking the case of a TNC investment in a power sector project.

In 1993, a subsidiary of the Enron Corporation, the Dabhol Power Company (DPC), entered the Indian market in the state of Maharashtra for the generation of 695 MW of electricity with a proposed investment of $2.8 billion. The contract was formulated and signed by three parties: the Central Electricity Authority (CEA), the Maharashtra State Electricity Board (MSEB), and the DPC. The electricity was to be purchased by MSEB at a negotiated price. The contract was formulated in the absence of competitive bidding and under non-transparent procedures, which caused a series of controversies, cancellations, and renegotiations.

In 1995, elections changed the parties in power in Maharashtra. The new government re-examined the terms and conditions of the contract. After a detailed examination by a special cabinet committee, the government of Maharashtra concluded that the contract was not in the public interest and cancelled it. In order to pursue the cancellation legally, the government of Maharashtra filed a suit in the Bombay High Court and presented several government documents to substantiate the various allegations. Interestingly, within three months the government backtracked on its decision without providing any reasons, and renegotiated the contract without any changes. In August 1996, DPC and MSEB entered into an agreement that DPC would supply about 2,000 MW of electricity in the form of available capacity and gas for a period of twenty years. Numerous safeguards were incorporated into the contract for protecting the investment and ensuring future payments by MSEB to DPC for the purchase of electricity. These safeguards included the Power Purchase Agreement, the guarantee by the state of Maharashtra, the State Support Agreement, the counter-guarantee by the Union of India, and the tripartite agreement between the governments of Maharashtra and of India, and the Reserve Bank of India. The Power Purchase Agreement specified that MSEB had to buy all the power produced by DPC, whether there was demand for it or not, and even if cheaper power were available from other sources. The state government offered a lien on all its assets, past, present, and future, in this respect. The Republic of India counter-guaranteed the payments due to DPC. In the case that the government of Maharashtra defaulted in its guarantee, the Indian government would be liable for some of the payments due and would deduct these payments directly from the constitutionally sanctioned share of revenues due to the state of Maharashtra. Arbitration in the event of a dispute over the counter-guarantee would be under English law in England, in exclusion to Indian law.

In 2000, the MSEB, as a result of its bankruptcy, refused to pay DPC a deficit of Rs 790 million for November and Rs 1,520 million for December, stating that DPC had been charging a higher price than its unit costs. Consequently, DPC decided to invoke the central government's counter-guarantee on 6 February 2001. On 12 February the Minister for Power of the central government announced that it would pay all the money owed to DPC by the Maharashtra State Electricity Board.[11]

The above case shows that the investors' rights were protected by contract through a costly and difficult process, but with high transaction costs resulting from inefficient institutions. A portion of the transaction costs arose because of missing institutions at the time of contract formulation, such as a competitive and transparent bidding process. These transaction costs could be higher in a democratic polity than in a totalitarian system because of the political power of various interests groups, and litigation by private parties. Apart from this, because of the uncertainty owing to the incomplete nature of contracts, the costs of safeguards are higher. As a result, there is an incentive for a TNC to recover the investment in a shorter period by inflating the project costs. These costs result in higher product prices to consumers, which, in turn, could be highly politicized.[12] In the case of DPC in India, there are no costs associated with the regulation, as the state government agency is both the purchaser and distributor of electricity. However, owing to the high costs of the electricity sold by DPC to the state government, the State Electricity Board went bankrupt and could not pay its dues to DPC (Patibandla, 2005b).

As far as society is concerned, it is not minimizing the transaction cost of the bidding process, but minimizing the cost of the final service that is important. Even if the cost of tendering is somewhat higher, it ensures that, among rival bids, the best will be chosen, which is a better social outcome. This is the reason why tendering and bidding procedures are used, though they are costly processes. Moreover, there is no reason to assume that the transaction cost will be any lower in a dictatorship. The dictator takes a large bribe – as much as can be squeezed out. Additionally, to increase the potential bribe earning, the contract may be given on terms that are unduly favorable to the producer while harming consumer interest. Implicit in the discussion is the assumption that the dictator is benevolent. Even if a democracy is corrupt, the deal may be no worse for consumers than in a corrupt dictatorship. The reason is that given its cost, a producer (bidder) has a maximum amount that he is willing to bribe to provide the service at any given price. No one, either a dictator or politicians and bureaucrats in a democracy, can get more than that. A dictator will squeeze out the full amount. My argument is that the transactions costs of clearances of large projects could be lower in a dictatorship, as in the case of China, owing to the centralization of power, while in a democracy clearances could be subject to delays owing to the interplay of different interest groups. On the other hand, in a democracy, because of the procedure, the vigilance of the media and opposition, and the likelihood that at least some players could be honest, the involved players may not be able to squeeze out the full amount. This allows the supplier to offer a lower price or higher quality in a competitive bidding process. The

Dabhol fiasco showed the inadequacy of the relevant institutions in India. The effective evolution of these institutions depends on how autonomous and depoliticised the regulatory and legal bodies become over time.

The reforms in the telecommunications sector are considered more successful as compared to other infrastructure industries. The rate of growth of GDP from telecoms increased from 6.3 percent per annum between 1980–1 and 1991–2, to 18 percent per annum between 1992–3 and 2002–3 (Virmani, 2004). However, the reforms and regulatory process have been subject to ad hoc interventions from government, dissipating potential investment, especially from TNCs. Since independence, the telecoms sector was monopolized by the government's Department of Telecommunications (DOT) both as a policy-maker and as a service provider. The reforms allowing private operators into the industry were initiated in 1994. The Telecom Regulatory Authority of India (TRAI) was set up in 1997 as a supposedly independent regulatory authority (IRA). However, its autonomy was eroded by frequent interventions from government, the ministry, and DOT. When the private sector firms bid for licenses, the DOT changed the rules of bidding after the bids were received. At around the same time, the TRAI came out with its first telecoms tariff order in an effort to rebalance tariffs, which placed it in confrontation with the DOT. The government took the side of the DOT and diluted the powers of the TRAI as a regulatory body (Rao and Gupta, 2004). The government set up a new body for arbitrating disputes, the Telecom Disputes and Settlement Appellate Tribunal (TDSAT). Rao and Gupta observe that the telecommunications sector recovered after the introduction of revenue sharing between government and the private firms. Consequently, mobile services have overtaken the fixed-line services. However, the sector has continued to witness running battles between the TRAI, the DOT, and private operators. In most cases, the TRAI comes out second-best.

Virmani (2004) observes that the reforms succeeded despite regulatory uncertainty and policy changes because they were not dependent on large FDI entry into the sector.

> Foreign direct investors from developed countries have a greater intolerance for such uncertainty. The local firms have faced such uncertainty before and learnt how to deal with it. Lack of knowledge of the Telecom sector (among the large pool of entrepreneurs) could have proved fatal if the government had stuck to a purely legal stand. The government's flexible response to the setback and determination to make telecom reforms a success, allowed domestic entrepreneurs time to accumulate knowledge and skills.

This is contrary to Levy and Spiller's argument, discussed earlier, regarding the merits of regulatory rigidity (commitment) as against flexibility to protect against opportunism by governments in developing economies in promoting investments. Here, the regulatory uncertainty and high transaction costs worked in favor of local firms, who could deal with the local institutional environment better than TNCs. Apart from this, the commitment of the government is to make the reforms a success rather than a pure regulatory commitment.

In the case of road construction, the commitment from the central government (with the direct involvement of the prime minister) in building the national highway of the 'Golden Quadrilateral' allowed its successful completion on time in several parts of the country, despite the involvement of local governmental bodies in different regions. However, road construction at the local level of different regions is subject to long delays and corruption in contract formation and execution, making investments by large professional players difficult as a result of large payoffs to government agents.[13]

The rapid growth of the city of Bangalore has not been matched by supportive infrastructure development, resulting in high costs to private agents, both households and companies. Can there be private order institutions to rectify this? As far as the general public is concerned, there has not been any concerted collective action, with the government remaining mostly indifferent. In the early 2000s, the software industry association and the state government formed a consortium, pooling resources for improving the infrastructure. In 2004, state elections changed the political party in power and the consortium went into limbo, as the political dynamics dictated that the government should not have an image as a promoter of the software industry, benefiting the upper middle class but not the rural poor. Around this time, the popular press reported that many large software firms announced plans to move out of Bangalore as their collective bargaining with the state government for improving infrastructure conditions had become ineffective. The press reports in January 2005 show that the government pacified the industry and formulated plans to improve the infrastructure.

## Corruption

Corruption is an important issue of governance and difficult both to define conceptually and to quantify empirically. At a broad level, corruption can be defined as 'misuse of public office for private gain'. Heston and Kumar (2005) make it more encompassing in terms of 'misuse of office' to include corruption in private sector firms. Literature usually classifies corruption by the domain of occurrence or the type of event, e.g. income tax evasion, under-invoicing, kickbacks taken by politicians and so on. This enables researchers to sort out the optimisation exercise of the corrupt agent in a particular kind of offending decision, and helps in understanding the type of corruption (Patibandla and Sanyal, 2005a). All illegal rents can be traced to three primitive sources: scarcity, information, and position. Excessive government intervention in the past generated corruption on all three accounts. The issue at hand is whether corruption has declined in response to the reforms and emergence of institutions in mitigating corruption.

A few international agencies, including Transparency International, the IMF, and the World Bank, publish reports every year which rank countries on the criteria of transparency. These reports generally put the Scandinavian countries at the top and India nearly at the bottom.[14] As I discussed in Chapter 2, Williamson employs the behavioral assumption of 'opportunism' to make the logic of incomplete contracts complete. The basic logic is that in the presence of incomplete contracts and opportunism, agents of a transaction should make calculations and incorporate safeguards at the ex ante stage to reduce the costs of opportunism at the ex post stage. Extending this logic to the larger societal and national level, societies that are able to build institutions that safeguard against the opportunism of private and public agents are the ones that are able to promote productive investments and realize higher material value for any given resource endowments, compared to those with inefficient institutions. Since the initiation of the reforms, there have been major corruption scandals in India. In the early 2000s in the US, there were significant issues concerning corporate governance surrounding Enron, Worldcom, etc. The difference between the two countries is that most of the people who siphoned off funds in India are not punished, while in the US most of them are behind bars and there is an immediate institutional response in order to avoid similar occurrences in the future.

Historically, the US went through cycles of large-scale corruption. Glaeser and Goldin (2004) show that corruption in America rose sharply to peaks in 1818, 1837, and 1857, to a maximum in 1873, with most peaks representing financial crises. From the peaks, corruption declined until 1891, and still further to 1907–11. It then increased again until 1929, and again in 1952. Corruption basically started to decline from the early twentieth century to the 1970s in the United States.

The institutional change that reduced corruption historically can be seen in two ways: big and slow changes. Big changes are initiated in democratic countries when events such as financial crises take place. Why do crises induce big changes? Crises make everyone – or substantial sections of society – worse off as a result of corruption, forcing governments to implement big changes. Slow changes are a matter of changing equations between groups with differential interests in prevailing environments of status quo and of change. In India, the reforms of 1991 were the result of a balance of payments crisis. The stock market scandals of the early 1990s led the government to implement institutional reforms by setting up the regulatory body the SEBI, and the National Stock Exchange. Similarly, the East Asian financial crisis of 1997 prompted the South Korean government to bring forth major institutional reforms in corporate governance, which allowed South Korea to recover quickly from the crisis.

In India, one of the great legacies from the British colonial rule is the civil service (the Indian Civil Service, or ICS), which was a prestigious institution in Britain and British India. This institutional arrangement was effective for colonial exploitation. The British generated both useful institutions for capitalism and inefficient ones. An example of the latter is the civil service to collect land revenues on the basis of the Zamindari system, in which the property rights of farmers were kept tenuous. The civil service apparatus continued after independence under the name of the Indian Administrative Service. Analogously to my comment on the hybrid version of the Common Law in India, Heston and Kumar (2005) observe,

> The established ICS bureaucracy provided India with continuity of administration that would often after 1950, come in conflict with the programs and political debates of elected political leaders. The result has been a decline in the commitment and professionalism of the civil service, while at the same time there is more responsiveness to demand of the public reflected by politicians. While subject to more interference, the bureaucracy has at the same time managed to retain many trappings of colonial administration, in terms of discretion in decisions, internal investigations of complaints, and lack of transparency.[15]

As discussed in Chapter 3, the developmental role of the government after independence led to pervasive government intervention in the economy, which increased the powers of civil servants and the politicians in power. Sanyal (1984) and Bardhan (1984) showed how it resulted in the emergence of powerful interest groups with distributional objectives. On similar lines, there was the literature on rent-seeking, which showed that economic growth was stunted because of pervasive rent-seeking under large-scale government intervention in the economy (Krueger, 1974). The rent-seeking literature can be applied to the South Korea of the 1980s and 1990s, but the country nevertheless experienced rapid economic growth. Theoretically, rent-seeking as a phenomenon has ambiguous implications for economic growth. This is because distribution in favor of the powerful groups should actually result in high savings and investments (capital accumulation), since the money should come back into the economy, unless it leaks out of the country or lies idle as cash or investment in gold. The new institutional economics has a better explanation, which is that the strong predatory powers of government and its agents cause private agents to refrain from investing in productive durable assets and compel them to hide their wealth, which can be a source of inefficiency.

This leads to the issue of corruption that generates growth, and corruption that results in a decline in economic growth. A leading industrialist of

Indian origin in the UK was supposed to have to made the observation that the difference between corruption in South Korea and in India is that "once you pay a bribe in South Korea, you get the things done, while in India, even after giving the bribe, there is no certainty that the things will be done." The multiple layers of bureaucracy in India result in high transaction costs for corruption, because even a peon in a government office can hold up a file. This leads us to two issues. If it is true, why should an economic agent bribe somebody and take the risk in India? If agents are risk-averse, there should be lower corruption in India than in South Korea. Second, what are efficiency and inefficiency generating corruption? The problem with the issue of corruption is that it has to be seen in ex post rationalization terms because there is no systematic theory of the political economy of corruption. The application of a good economic theory is successful in some countries and a failure in others because of political economy factors, which can be understood only after they have taken place.

Bardhan (1997) shows that the negative impact of corruption on efficient resource allocation, investment (particularly foreign investment), and economic growth suggests that these costs are appreciable. Efficiency and growth costs are not limited to direct costs. Indirect cost channels include the reduced information-transmitting efficiency of markets, since corruption is necessarily secretive; business uncertainty, since corrupt favours are not always delivered; and further uncertainty, since corrupt courts cannot be relied upon to uphold property rights and enforce contracts. Continuing corruption eventually reduces respect for the rule of law, which is an important determinant of economic growth (Das-Gupta, 2004).

On the basis of the rent-seeking literature, one can hypothesize that economic reforms that reduce government intervention should result in a decline in rent-seeking and higher economic growth. The policy reforms in India, as we know, have resulted in an increase in economic growth. Have they reduced rent-seeking or corruption? There has been no systematic study to determine whether corruption has declined. My field research on the land market indicates that the stakes of corruption have increased in several spheres. In the early part of 2005, I visited the government land registration offices in and around Bangalore city as a part of my ongoing research. The rapid growth of the city resulted in a swift increase in demand for land in and around Bangalore. On every working day, there are a large number of land transactions and registrations in the offices. I was informed by one of the large land developers that the average price/bribe for each registration was Rs 5,000. The rates were higher if one wanted faster registration of the land. Those who refuse to pay the bribe have to stand in queues for eight to ten hours for several days, until they give up and pay the bribe. One could witness, in practice, the theory of price discrimination, taught in intermediate microeconomics. Agents with high opportunity costs of their time paid higher bribes (Sanyal, 2004).

In the case of illegal rent from scarcity, market reforms are expected to be effective in reducing or even eliminating it. As controls and regulations are removed, product markets tend to find clearing prices at which all who can and want, buy it, leaving no space for illegal rents. At the same time, competition and contestability disable rent-seeking based on the threat of unavailability. Apart from reducing scarcity rent directly, competition also helps establish missing markets behind corruption. The reforms on several accounts, such as getting telephone and cooking gas connections, and the purchase of consumer durables such as two-wheelers, have eliminated illegal rents from scarcity.

Services produced by the government can be classified as those that are related to governance and those that are not. The latter can be produced and sold by the private sector as well. The government has opened up some of them to competition, while others are subject to incomplete but steady deregulation. As the government gradually allows competition in these services, scarcity-related corruption in these sectors is expected to fall. Typically, this is the kind of corruption that increases the cost of living most directly: bribes paid for electricity, water and telephone connection and repairs, railway reservations, admission to hospitals, buying cooking gas, coal and kerosene, and the list continues. These bribes, widespread until fairly recently, are receding and hopefully will disappear if reforms continue.

There are, however, cases where well-developed, not underdeveloped, markets extract rent from scarcity. Can market reform help in these cases? In most cases, it can. Generally, a well-developed illegal market is the reflection of a related legal market which is underdeveloped or regulated. It is the latter that generates the scarcity, while the rent is extracted in the former. For example, transmitting foreign currency through well-developed illegal markets is the result of non-market valuation of currency and/or restrictions on the legal market. The illegal market for gold in India sprang up in response to the Gold Control Act of 1962 and the institutions set up to enforce it. Reform of the legal markets can bring the corresponding illegal markets to an end (Patibandla and Sanyal, 2005a).

In the case of corruption with regard to 'position', the reforms can give opportunities for one-shot rents of privatization. Basu and Lie (1996) argue that reforms may result in a one-time rise in corruption, which may speed the reform process. This, in turn, permanently reduces corruption and the powers of bureaucrats if the reforms give financial stakes to bureaucrats especially those in the middle level who resist reforms. This is similar to the privatization of public sector firms. Politicians can perceive the public sector as a long-term interest of political patronage or a one-shot rental gain through privatization. A ruling party that perceives its tenure as long-term will resist privatization, a situation experienced by the

Congress party in India, which was responsible for the pervasive presence of the public sector prior to the reforms. A ruling party which perceives its tenure as short can promote privatization to obtain large one-shot rents and, in addition, to deny the use of the public sector as a means of political patronage for the next elected (competing) party. In order to gain one-shot rents, there is an incentive for ruling politicians to keep the privatization process non-transparent and sell the assets at heavy discounts through collusion with private buyers (Patibandla, 2002b).[16]

In the way that federal democracy functions in India, a panoply of political and economic calculations combined with the politicians' own perceptions (whether smart or stupid) determine the direction and the manner of the reform process. Some politicians undertake some reforms at the margin and at the same time impose several other conditions to retain rent-seeking powers. An interesting example is the case of a central government minister of India who, in general, supported reforms and privatization at the center but blocked privatization of a large fertilizer plant located in his constituency (Gupta, 2003). In this manner, the minister could make one shot pay-offs from privatazation at the central level and retain the public sector firm in his constituency for political patronage.[17] This exemplifies how the calculations become even more complex when one takes into account the centralization and decentralization of political power and its implications for the reform process and consequent institutional evolution.[18]

The fact that reforms may lead to the possibility of new rent arises from the fact that deregulation, quite ironically, does not do away with monitoring. Just as regulation requires monitoring, so does deregulation. Is it possible that the regulators of the new environment will extract rent for 'selectively regulating', thus re-establishing the familiar nexus of big business and the regulator?[19] The probability of that appears small. The chance of capture of an institution monitoring deregulation is much smaller than one monitoring regulation. The reason is that with fewer entry barriers, the number of players in each industry increases significantly, and industry associations become broad-based. With a large number of members, each with a vested interest in the business environment, associations are expected to keep an effective watch over the official monitoring institutions.[20] In an industry with a broad-based association, the ability of individual members to obtain illegal deals from regulators is small, since it hurts the interests of the majority (Patibandla and Sanyal, 2005a).

As far as petty corruption is concerned, it is pervasive, right from policemen and inspectors of several regulatory bodies taking payments from small businesses on the roadside to small and medium-scale firms. On several fronts, reforms have had no effect on them because many of the regulatory bodies, such as labor and environmental regulation, are relevant even more in the post-reforms era. In certain areas of services such as the provision of drivers' licenses and passports, information technology is adopted in a few states to speed up the processes and reduce corruption. However, it has a marginal positive effect, as I witnessed in securing a driving license in the state of Andhra Pradesh in the south.

One can see petty corruption as a steady state where, in equilibrium the marginal cost of bribes equals the price of the bribes. For somebody to pay a bribe, the trade-off is between standing in a queue for seven to eight hours versus paying the bribe and reducing the waiting time (Sanyal, 2004). This depends on the opportunity costs of the seven or eight hours used in completing the transaction. For the charger of the bribe, the trade-offs are the probability of getting caught and punished versus the income through the bribes. One of the approaches for reducing this type of corruption is to increase salaries, offer incentives for compliance, and have a carrot-and-stick policy where the inspector detecting tax evasion may be given a reward (Das-Gupta and Mookherjee, 1998).

However, giving a reward for spotting evasion does not help. The officer will not report the offence, and demands a bribe from the offending party that is slightly more than the amount of the reward he could get by reporting the offence. To stop this, the government has to give as a reward the whole amount of the avoidance discovered by the officer. That will leave no incentive by the offender to bribe, and hence offend. But that would mean that the government gets nothing from the arrangement. Even this is not long-run equilibrium. Suppose the government says that it just wants to clean its system, and gives officers 100 percent of what they catch. What would happen? The offenders will then stop offending, and officers will not get anything at all, neither bribe nor reward! So they will be better off signaling to offenders that they are willing to take a smaller bribe than 100 percent of the avoidance, and the system will go back to square one (Sanyal, 2000).

One of the effects of the reforms could be that there could be compliance on the part of firms, irrespective of inspections, owing to market forces. For example, as I discussed in Chapter 6, the ban imposed by Germany on leather goods exported from India forced firms to adopt clean technologies through inter-firm cooperation. When income tax levels were reduced in India, there was an incentive for the rich to comply in order to avoid the harassment of income tax officials entering homes and searching the premises for black money. But in several other areas, the stakes of corruption went up after the reforms, which mere salary enhancement for government officials may not be able to match. For example, the increase in demand for land in Bangalore increased the number of land registrations every day, which substantially raised the income from bribes to government agents. One way this type of corruption can go down over time is to increase the transparency of the rules and enhance the public's awareness of their rights, combined with the decentralization of the organizational apparatus of the regulators such that their repeated interaction with the public increases.

*Table 15* Institutions for effective tax administration

| Objective | Operational implementation |
| --- | --- |
| Clarity of goals | • Mission and vision statements<br>• Citizen's charter<br>• Medium range modernization plan |
| Measuring goal achievement or performance | Systems of performance indicators reflecting effectiveness, efficiency, and citizen's service quality, that enable achievement of the administration's mission and modernization plan to be quantitatively assessed. |
| Enabling performance | • Operational autonomy for tax departments<br>• Functional organization |
| Communicating performance | • Annual reports to government on the administration's effectiveness and efficiency in delivering performance<br>• Performance reports for individuals, functional units, and field offices, based on performance indicators |
| Rewarding and motivating performance | • Administration budgets linked to performance<br>• Positive and negative individual and unit performance incentives |

Source: Das-Gupta (2005).

Tax evasion and bribes extracted by inspectors as a result of corruption through the 'information' problem. Because a tax-paying unit owns private information about its own income or transactions, it can get an illegal rent by evading taxes. An auditor extracting rent from a tax offender, like an insider trader, uses the information gathered in his professional capacity for personal rent. Das-Gupta (2005) shows the institutional conditions for effective tax administration. Table 15 from Das-Gupta demonstrates a framework for evaluating tax administration. It puts the emphasis on clarity of goals in line with the social role of tax administration, evaluation of the extent of goal achievement, and aligning incentives with goal achievement.

The conditions listed in Table 15 are basically getting the organizational conditions right in terms of the definition of the rules and the setting-up of the administrative apparatus. However, enforcement depends on the evolution of embedded conditions over time. At least the first step is getting the organizational conditions right. Interactions between the organizations and multiple stakeholders determine the evolution of the institutions over time.

## Surplus-generating private order institutions

In this section, I briefly discuss the emergence of private order institutions, especially as a response to the failure of the state in providing basic social security to the poor. One of the silent institutional revolutions that is taking place, especially in the south of India, is the increasing emergence of self-help groups in the 1990s and 2000s in reducing poverty levels.[21] These have nothing to do with the reforms, except that because of a decline in interest rates and the fact that formal financial institutions such as the public and private sector banks are flush with funds in the post-reforms era, they have started taking part in the development of these self-help groups, which are becoming economically viable institutions. There were about 700,000 self-help groups in 2004 in India. Close to 90 percent of the membership of the groups is made up of women in the rural areas. These groups have a record of 95 percent repayment of the loans on time with interest. In 2003, 11.6 million poor families were assisted through bank credit, with an average loan for a group amounting to Rs 28,560. The interesting aspect is that the formal banks have started to finance these groups. The State Bank of India and the Andhra Bank (in the south) have catered to the maximum number, together disbursing Rs 20,490 million. The amount of net credit given to women by banks reached the target of 5 percent of the total credit (Cuts, 2004).

Coase's theorem holds that the presence of transaction costs inhibits collective action. On the other hand, the presence of transaction costs in the markets may result in collective action generating a surplus, as compared to the situation where individuals act alone, which is illustrated here with a few case studies. The institutional origins of self-help groups in the financial markets can be traced to the concept of the Grameen Bank in Bangladesh (Yunus, 1998). Rural women in Bangladesh were trapped into poverty because highly underdeveloped financial markets made them dependent on local middlemen for short-term finance. Under the institutional arrangement of the interlocking of labor and capital markets, the poor borrowed money from the local middlemen and sold their output to them at very low prices, leaving them with a pittance for their sustenance. The inability of the poor to get access to finance and sell their output at the correct prices trapped them into the poverty cycle. The cooperative institutional arrangement of the Grameen Bank (micro-finance) was initiated by Mohammed Yunus, and made a significant impact by breaking the interlocking of capital and labor markets and thereby alleviating poverty. It is important to notice that an outsider (exogenous) intervention, with almost altruistic motives, was responsible for the emergence of micro-finance institutions. Once it was initiated and organized, the members ran the cooperative without outside intervention. At present, the Grameen Bank has more than two million members in 34,000 villages, organized into subgroups of five members. These are joined together into forty member centers (Pretty and Ward, 2001).

Self-help groups are similar to private order cooperative institutions, which, by pooling the efforts of a group of individuals, generate surplus value. In India, the case of Amul, the rural milk cooperative, presents a good example. At present, Amul is a large enterprise, having efficient horizontal and vertical organizational structures with complex linkages, competing effectively in the national market. The cooperative was started in 1946 to help marginal farmers who could supply one to two liters of milk per day. Prior to this, Polson functioned as the middleman and its advantage was to collect milk from the farmers and supply it to Bombay in bulk. Being the sole purchaser of the milk, Polson, acting as the middleman, could charge high rents. In order to overcome the costs imposed by Polson, farmers were organized into a cooperative by Tribhuvandas Patel and later led by Verghese Kurien, who brought in extraordinary vision and leadership. They invested in the initial transaction costs of organizing the farmers together. Later, as most members were small farmers with strong liquidity constraints, they made sure that they incurred low transaction costs by paying immediate cash for the supply of milk on a daily basis. Subsequently, the organization was expanded horizontally by linking up several villages for milk procurement. They also undertook substantial investment in the infrastructure for storing and processing of the milk and for its transportation. As the cooperative became very successful, it expanded vertically into processing milk to produce consumer products like milk powder and chocolates, etc. (Chandra and Tirupati, 2003).[22]

The above cases show a picture of successful cooperative institutional arrangements. There are also several cases of failures of cooperative institutions. One of the striking examples in contemporary India is the failure of the Urban Cooperative Banks, which destroyed small investors' savings worth billions of rupees. The non-performing assets of cooperative banks across the country amounted to Rs 56 billion in 2000. About 118 urban cooperative banks are under liquidation and another 261 are supposedly in trouble (Reserve Bank of India figures). What are the possible reasons for their disastrous failures?

The first major flaw of these institutions is the motivation and flawed incentives in organizing them. Generally, each bank is formed by a small group of people and attracts depositors by luring them with very high returns or interest rates on their deposits. The capital is loaned to people at high interest rates and under lenient conditions. In a typical 'adverse selection' of information economics, these banks attract low-quality borrowers who have no intention of paying back the loans. The second factor is the organization of the banks with high agency costs. In most cases, capital is loaned to the directors and their relatives. In quite a few cases, local politicians control the banks. One of the worst features of the organization of the banks is that the borrowers are the members, while the depositors have no say in the running of the banks (Patibandla and Sastry, 2004). In essence, the main reasons for their failures are flawed incentives and organization.

I illustrate how cooperative behavior generates surplus on the basis of the case of Amul with a few identities. A cooperative takes place if the surplus for the agents is higher under a cooperative arrangement than when dealing with the middlemen in the market. As discussed in the case of the Amul cooperative, the middlemen's relevance was that small farmers acting alone could not undertake the transportation costs of milk to the consumers in a far-away city. The middlemen did the job by incurring the transaction costs of the collection of milk and transportation, for which he or she charged a mark-up. By this logic, we can express the surplus equation of a farmer:

$$S = P - c - (TC + TP + M)/N$$

Where $c$ is the average cost of production, $P$ is the price realized in the larger city market, $N$ is the number of farmers (and it is assumed that each farmer supplies a unit of milk), $TC$ and $TP$ are the total transaction and transport costs, and $M$ is the total mark-up of the middleman. If the mark-up is competitive, one can argue that the middleman's job has economic efficiency. If the mark-up is based on monopsony behavior, then the cooperative arrangement becomes superior. Even if the mark-up is a competitive price, the cooperative can still achieve a welfare-enhancing outcome. This is because $M$ becomes the income of the cooperative, which can be shared by the members. Apart from this, farmers might be able to save more on transaction costs when organized under the cooperative than when they are dealing with a middleman. Williamson's (2002) theory of contracts shows that in the presence of uncertainty, private agents have to incorporate contractual safeguards, which are reflected in higher costs in transactions. The middleman in the market may pass on these costs to farmers, especially when he or she has higher bargaining power. When farmers form a cooperative with high mutual stakes, these transaction costs go down. The costs go down further in a cumulative way when the organization becomes vertically integrated from milk production to the production of milk-based consumer goods. This is exactly where the creative organization of Amul contributed to the generation of surplus, which is utilized for developing local infrastructure and for investment in the productivity of farmers.

Let us take $q$ as the output and $l$ as the credit (loan). Let there be $n$ farmers $I = 1, 2, \ldots, n$. Assume identical functions, so that acting non-cooperatively, farmers' transaction costs are $\Sigma T(q_i, l_i) = T$ and, acting cooperatively, they are $T_v(\Sigma q_i, \Sigma l_i)$. And if $T > T_v$ then $(T - T_v)$ is the transaction cost saved through collective effort. The surplus generated by a cooperative can be expressed as $[M + (T - T_v) + K] - e$, where $K$ is the surplus realized through the externality effects of cooperative action, and $e$ refers to the internal organizational costs, which can be simplified as the extent of free-riding within the organization. One of the ways $K$ can be realized is that a part of the surplus is invested in enhancing the collective productivity of members. If each member acts alone, these investments will not take place, either because they are too costly for individual agents or because of market failures due to externalities. In agriculture and cattle grazing, just pooling the plots of land together generates a positive $K$. One more source of externality is the cost saved by spreading the risk in the input and output markets through collective action.

Imperfect information, adverse selection, and moral hazard under agency relations do not vanish once a cooperative is formed. These operate within the organization and their incidence increases as the number of members increases. We can argue that as long as the surplus equation is positive, a cooperative has economic rationale. However, this condition alone is not enough. A cooperative has to adopt incentive-compatible practices in sharing the surplus and in the assignment and distribution of control rights for its durability. One of the essential points I would like to bring out from the above discussion is that, even if the middleman's behavior has market efficiency, cooperatives that eliminate middlemen in the market can generate higher surplus to members by providing them with an additional economic role (jobs). This will be especially true of cooperatives made up of people with low income. One more point is that it is generally an outsider with larger or altruistic goals who starts the process of collective action and incurs the transaction costs of organizing the cooperative but, later, members with long-term stakes manage them. In other words, if small farmers have to act on their own to form a cooperative, it might not take place, owing to the transaction costs of getting together.

Banerjee, Mookherjee, Munshi, and Ray (2001) developed and tested a model of sugar cooperatives in Maharashtra. They show that the wealthier farmers enjoy disproportionate power, which they use to depress the cane price paid to poorer farmers and expropriate the surplus. One single price is charged for the output of all members, which means that the price applies to both small and large farmers. The difference between the price of the processed sugar and the output price is the surplus of the cooperative. The strong control rights of the large farmers in the cooperative give them access to the surplus, which they can use to serve their own interests.

The above outcome is likely to take place if a cooperative consists of a large number of small farmers and a few large farmers, where the share of output of the small farmers in the total is greater than that of the large farmers. This makes the loss caused to the large farmers by depressing the price of output lower than the surplus realized from the difference between the price of processed sugar and price of sugar cane. Although there are a small number of large farmers and their output contribution is smaller than the total of the small farmers, the large farmers end up with the control rights in the cooperative because of their outside influence, contacts with politicians and bureaucrats, and their ability to meet market transaction costs. The outcome of the sugar cooperatives is interpreted as an inverse relationship between efficiency and heterogeneity (Hart and Moore, 1998). In other words, a cooperative may be more effective if members are a homogenous group than if it were heterogeneous, so that the more powerful members cannot misuse control rights, as in the case of the sugar cooperatives.

# 9 Conclusion

At the beginning of the millennium, the collapse of communism in eastern Europe, the rapid economic growth of politically communist China through the introduction of free market forces, and the movement of several developing economies away from active state intervention have shown that capitalism is more durable and better at delivering the wealth of nations than socialism, in comparative economic terms. However, the experience of Russia's sudden move to capitalism after years of pursuing the socialist economic system, and the decline of some of the African nations have shown that there is more to the capitalist system than is taught in the mainstream textbooks of economics, i.e. the need to understand the economic institutions of capitalism. A rudimentary understanding of the functioning of free market economies in the advanced Western nations demonstrates that capitalism is functional on the basis of underlying economic, political, and social institutions that evolved over time. A simple sketch of the economic institutions of capitalism is basically arriving at a fine balance between high-powered individual incentives of free choice, and the social, political, and economic constraints of the public and private order institutions of collective action. The nations that tilt the balance between free individual choices (lawlessness) and excessive controls of collective action are the ones that tend to fail. In other words, the effectiveness and appropriateness of institutions of collective action through public and private order institutions appear to have worked better in advanced capitalist economies than in communist nations in which collective action and ownership of resources degenerated into Communist Party dictatorship.[1] Apart from this, capitalism no longer takes the conventional form of a single owner, or a small group of owners, of capital making profits at the cost of the workers. In modern corporations, even small savers, for example workers with savings, can invest and have ownership rights. The more dispersed the ownership is, the less the meaning of the conventional idea of capitalism. This gives rise to the issue of institutions that minimize informational asymmetries and conflicts of interests between, and among, the owners and managers.

The outcome of the economic reforms towards greater free market forces and global integration in India is a success story in general terms. The economic reforms in India are concerned with the reduction of excessive state intervention in the economy within the broad framework of capitalism and democracy. India's economy experienced higher aggregate economic growth rate in the post-reform era in comparison with the Fabian socialist years. However, the pattern of economic growth shows that most of the growth benefits have accrued to the urban middle class and the rich, while close to 300 million people remain below the poverty line. Apart from this, the growth is principally concentrated in the western and southern part of India, while a major part of northern India remains feudal and stagnant. The international and intranational differences in growth in response to the economic reforms can be attributed to the initial endowments of not only technology and capital, but also capitalist institutions at the onset of the reforms.

In this book, economic reforms are treated as exogenous parameter and qualitative shifts in certain elements of the institutional environment on the basis of the initial institutional endowments of capitalism. Consequent changes in absolute and relative prices and the transaction costs of exchange in different spheres have implications for the structural factors of the differential growth of industries, regions, and income groups, and the micro-level governance of competitive dynamics and the associated technological and organizational changes. These changes trigger an endogenous process of evolution of markets and institutions. The direction of structural and micro-level dynamics depends on the initial endowments of markets and institutions.

Theoretical modeling of institutional change is a difficult task as it involves a complex gamut of economic, political, and social factors. Williamson's work in the field of the new institutional economics has provided theoretical rigor because it concentrated on micro-level governance mechanisms by treating the institutional environment as given, and considering institutional change as parameter shifts. I have adopted a broad theoretical framework, but not a model, in order to have a certain degree of freedom to discuss a gamut of interesting factors that govern the institutional change in the context of an emerging economy in which changes are subject to a complex set of factors. The inferences and empirical evidence are based on both quantitative and qualitative analysis of data and case studies. Some of the arguments concerning institutional change, for example changes in attitudes and perceptions of opportunity sets, are difficult to quantify and should be taken in qualitative terms. Furthermore, as far as my knowledge goes, this book is one of the first attempts at research on this complex topic. Therefore, it provides both a broad sketch and micro-level details of institutional change on certain aspects. On several fronts, such as issues relating to labor and capital markets, and public order institutional functioning, future research can concentrate on rigorous micro-level details and quantification. In the following, a summary of the basic inferences is provided.

The post-reform era presents the emergence of new dynamic industries, the restructuring of the old industries, and the emergence of indigenously born global players in several spheres of industrial activity. These positive outcomes are attributable to both changes in structural factors and micro-level competitive dynamics and governance in response to the reforms. The qualitative shifts change the rules of the game, both competition and cooperation, between different actors in the product and input markets of labor and capital, and lead to micro-level technological and organizational change. The parameter and qualitative changes also release resources by reducing transaction costs in both dealing with government and the market exchange mechanism for productive investments, especially if the policy reforms also improve property rights. All this put together, the end result is a decline in real prices, which increases real incomes and reduces the costs of entry to new players, both consumers and producers, leading to further growth of markets and institutional change.

One of the most important structural outcomes of the reforms is a change in the perceptions and attitudes of the middle class towards industry, business, and investment and their international outlook. The reforms resulted in the rapid growth of the internationally oriented industries such as software and services, pharmaceuticals, and auto components. These industries also represented increasing job opportunities for skilled labor coming out of the upper and lower middle class. Furthermore, for the first time after independence, a few highly dynamic entrepreneurs have started to come out of the middle class.[2] They have demonstrated that people with skills and entrepreneurial talent, not necessarily from the business families with political connections and privileged access to capital, can make it big in business and achieve international recognition. Most of these entrepreneurs are in the new and knowledge intensive industries with a global mindset.

The growth of export-oriented, skill-intensive industries, and those such as telecommunications,[3] refrigerators, and passenger cars, represents a two-way effect on economic growth in general. The growth of skill-intensive industries increases the incomes and employment of the middle class, with a consequent increase in demand for goods and services. A decline in the prices of industries such as telecommunications, refrigerators, and textiles increases the real incomes of the lower middle class, thereby increasing their consumption basket and savings. The growth of these industries also resulted in the emergence of several markets and institutions, such as the markets for information (warranties, signaling), consumer finance, and insurance. An increase in consumer incomes increases demand for investment avenues such as real estate, especially for housing. Secure property rights are required for the markets to expand. The increase in demand resulted in the emergence of large developers in the real estate industry who could invest in the transaction costs of dealing with government and sellers of land and improve upon property rights for the expansion of the market, especially in rapidly growing urban areas such as the city of Bangalore. A similar outcome of improvement in property (control) rights took place in the equity markets, which I will discuss later.

In the case of the software and services industry, which is probably the most significant in shaping the opportunity sets and perceptions of the middle class in the post-reform era, the initial conditions, endogenous and (lucky) exogenous factors, played an important role in its growth. The previous import substitution policies, which heavily subsidized higher education, resulted in a large pool of skilled labor. The exogenous technological change in the world market in telecommunications and IT and the crisis-driven economic reforms of 1991 took place around the same time for India to take advantage of its dormant comparative advantage in the skill endowments.

The growth of the software and services and telecommunications industries in India resulted in several positive institutional changes. One was the improvement in the Copyright Act making intellectual property rights more secure, directly relevant to the industry. The other is that the application of IT to several services such as banking, railways, and governance, reduced information (search) and transaction costs to the general public. Second, the emergence of e-commerce-based e-choupals has made a big difference to small farmers in several rural areas by reducing the transaction and search costs in the product and input markets, and consequently allowing small farmers to realize economic prices. An even more important outcome is the demonstration effect of the global practices of the software industry on the rest of the industries, previously dominated by feudal and traditional mindsets.

The interesting aspect of the success stories of companies such as Infosys in the software industry is that it achieved growth through exports by adopting the principle of 'islands of competitiveness' as a means of reducing dependence on inefficient local institutions and infrastructure. The main input that is drawn from the local institutions is skilled labor. This required the firm to invest in self-generation of infrastructure and public goods, which is an additional expenditure when compared to a similar firm in a developed economy. Apart from this, Infosys is the first company to adopt employee stock options and the GAAP model of high standards of corporate governance. Perhaps Infosys became successful by adopting honest business practices because it is a new industry and grew through exports, rather than through domestic markets that are beset with high transaction costs and entry barriers imposed by both government agencies and powerful incumbents. In the equity markets, foreign institutional investors were the ones who discovered the value of Infosys in the first place. In essence, the company's success was possible because of globalization. It overcame India's institutional constraints by adopting the organization of an 'island of competitiveness', a concept which has become a catalyst for institutional change in certain spheres in India.

One of the structural outcomes of the reforms is that most of the growth is concentrated in the western and southern part of India, while the largest northern states, Bihar and Uttar Pradesh, remain stagnant and feudal. A even more notable feature is that the western and southern states increased their relative growth rate to a higher level compared to the pre-reform period, which supports my argument that the initial market and institutional endowments of the regions work greatly in their favor in taking advantage of the reforms and increasing global integration. One of the institutional outcomes of the increasing regional disparities in economic growth is a marginal increase in the migration of labor from low-income to high-income states, facilitated by the emergence of contract labor organizations that reduce transaction and search costs, especially to unskilled and illiterate workers.

Even after fifteen years of the reforms, still close to 300 million people remain illiterate and below the poverty line. Income-inequality has shown a tendency to increase, obviously because people with human and physical capital endowments at the onset of the economic reforms benefited more from them. Some studies have shown that poverty levels declined in the post-reforms era, providing evidence for the trickle-down theory of the effect of an increased aggregate growth rate. If we give values of greater than 0 and less than or equal to 1 to that section of society that is below the poverty line, the trickle-down effect may help people who fall in the range of greater than 0.9 and less than 1. However, it is unlikely that the increased aggregate growth rate trickles down to people below the value of 0.9, who basically do not possess any productive durable assets, including literacy. To solve poverty at that level requires significant institutional change on both the public and private order institutional front. It calls for government investment in food and social security, and the provision of universal primary and secondary education. As is well known, the problem here is not just allocating resources, but building the institutional conditions that enable the services to reach the targeted groups with low transaction costs. While the governments of a few states in the south, west, and east have made some progress in implementing midday-meals schemes for schoolchildren and food-for-work programs through decentralization of governance, the governments of the largest states in the north have shown no interest in such undertakings.

An institutional change in some parts of India is the emergence of private order institutions such as self-help groups, micro-finance, and cooperative arrangements as means of overcoming the dismal failure of the state in solving poverty and illiteracy. One interesting outcome of economic growth is the demonstration effect on the poor with respect to the opportunity-set associated with education and skills. There is qualitative evidence of the poor investing in education for their children in private schools to redress the failure of the government-run schools, and of the emergence of private schools targeting the poor. These institutional changes are some of the means of reducing the segmentation of institutions and markets in India through private order institutional arrangements.

Some of these private institutions are welcome solutions. But not all of them represent the best arrangement. Some of them simply reflect the desperation of the public at the lack of a corresponding public institution, and though they bring some relief, the social resource cost is far greater than if a well-managed public institution provides them. When a private firm produces its own infrastructure, it solves the problem of the infrastructure bottleneck at a much larger social cost. In other words, long-term efficiency-enhancing institutional change has to come from improvements in the public order institutions on several fronts.

The analysis of the competitive dynamics of firms revolved around the proposition of convergence of best practices under comparative economic logic. The underlying differences for benchmarking are viewed from technological and organizational aspects. The competition for the benchmarking of best practices is simplified as between local firms and new-entrant TNCs, because TNCs from developed economies bring in the latest technologies and organizational practices, depending on local market opportunities and the institutional conditions of the protection of property rights and the transaction costs of business. If the superior technologies and practices of TNCs spread to local firms, this will have important implications for the local market and for institutional evolution.

Competition from new-entrant TNCs drove several local firms to undertake technological and organizational restructuring in a significant way, which caused several Indian firms to become globally competitive in terms of undertaking exports, setting up green-field ventures overseas, and also acquiring firms in developed economies. The process of restructuring generated new markets and the expansion of existing ones, and saw the creation of intermediate-product markets, inter-firm linkages and markets for information, as well as further opening-up of the economy to the world and institutional change internal to firms.

The increase in the number of firms, both local and TNCs, in several industries resulted in an increase in demand and competition for skilled labor and wage rates. This led to three responses in the labor markets. First, firms increased their internal technological and organizational efforts at improving productivity. Second, the labor market responded by increasing the number of young people acquiring industry-specific skills, thereby increasing the pool of skilled people. There was an emergence of private educational institutions in response to the increase in demand for skilled labor, especially in the software industry, and specialized employment agencies and organizations for reducing the transaction and search costs of the labor market. Finally, competitive dynamics also necessitated the professionalization of management, moving away from the feudally based norms of the family business of the pre-reforms era, which, in turn, deepened and expanded the markets for managerial talent.

The labor market institutions increasingly tilted in favor of skilled workers and managers, while the semi-skilled and unskilled workers were pushed towards the informal markets. While formal employment agencies have started to play an important role in reducing the transaction costs of the labor market for skilled labor and managers, the institutional arrangement of contract-labor suppliers has started to play an important role for semi-skilled and unskilled labor. Although these institutions reduce the transaction costs of labor markets, semi- and unskilled labor still faces high transaction costs because institutions for the formal certification of semi-skilled labor such as carpenters, plumbers, etc. do not exist in India. This, in turn, makes the bargaining power of the workers low with respect to the intermediary contractors. A consequence of this is that the workers end up with a wage rate lower than their productivity, owing to the transaction costs of the intermediaries.

Another important example of competitive dynamics between TNCs and local firms resulting in the emergence or expansion of new markets and institutional change is the case of subcontracting practice in the automobile industry. Prior to the entry of Suzuki in the industry, subcontracting activity between large and small firms was based on asymmetrical bargaining relations. Suzuki contributed to change for the better in the institutional arrangement in a significant way by developing vendor firms through long-term contracts and technology-transfer. These practices spread to other firms through imitation and spillovers. This resulted in the development of the intermediate-product market, and first-tier vendor firms realized world-standard technology and a high degree of export-competitiveness.

The functioning of capital markets is one of the critical institutions of capitalism for channeling capital into productive investments. Property rights and agency relations are two key institutions in determining the efficient utilization of capital. One of the common causes of the institutional failure of capitalism in both advanced capitalist economies and even more in developing economies is agency costs of capital markets at different levels.

In India's case, one of the dominant features of capital markets in the Fabian socialist years was the relation between the government-funded public financial institutions and the politically powerful family-run businesses. The political capturing of industrial licensing and the DFIs by powerful groups helped them not only to build diversified family empires but also to divert capital for personal objectives. Although this institutional arrangement resulted in a diversified industrial base in India, it also meant underutilization and diversion of accumulated capital for unproductive activities. On the equity market front, the Bombay Stock Exchange, dominated by a few stockbrokers belonging to an ethnic community, monopolized the markets, generating marked informational asymmetries and agency costs. There have been significant institutional changes in capital markets in the post-reform era.

The series of stock market scandals in the immediate aftermath of the reforms, which destroyed billions of rupees' worth of the public savings, prompted the government to implement the institutional reforms of setting up the National Stock Exchange and the regulatory body, the SEBI. The NSE, by implementing screen-based trading all over the country, curtailed the monopoly power of the Bombay Stock Exchange and reduced the informational imperfections and transaction costs of equity trading to the public. The government reforms of allowing foreign institutional investors also contributed to improvements in capital market institutions by forcing corporations to improve disclosure practices, and generated markets for information. The interesting side of the globalization effect on capital markets is shown by Infosys in the software industry, which adopted global standards of corporate governance (GAAP) even in the absence of a legal obligation in the home market. This provided a benchmark for the regulatory body, the SEBI, to learn and spread it among other companies.

The importance of DFIs started to decline in the post-reform era. Some of these institutions have started to reform themselves so as to become merchant bankers and venture capitalists. The large incumbents and family businesses can no longer take long-term capital financing from these institutions for granted. Consequently, capital costs for local firms increased. Several large firms overcame this disadvantage, especially when competing with TNCs, by tapping into the ADR and GDR markets and listing in overseas stock exchanges, which requires them to adopt efficient disclosure and corporate governance practices. The outcome of these institutional changes is improvements in the utilization of capital and a reduction in non-performing assets.[4]

One of the outcomes of the reforms is significant technological and organizational restructuring of the incumbent diversified business groups and the emergence of dynamic stand-alone companies. The restructuring of family businesses resulted in institutional changes both within the firms and external to firms. In order to compete with new-entrant TNCs and more agile younger firms, firms adapted new, imported technologies. The adaptation of new technologies with tacit and codified elements required changes in internal institutions, such as reducing excess hierarchy, and the adoption of decentralized organizational coordination and of incentive-compatible practices by workers and managers.

In the globalising Indian economy, there have been organizational innovations by private entrepreneurs on several dimensions. For example, Indian software companies mastered the global software delivery model, which has become a worldwide benchmark. In Bangalore city, which is the most globally linked city in India, specialized intermediary firms have emerged which can build world-class facilities for high-technology firms within five to six months. Even more interesting is that specialized firms have emerged to help TNCs and local firms to overcome the high transaction costs of entry into the market by applying the BOT (build, operate and transfer) concept to the software and BPO industries. In other words, organizational innovations and specialized intermediaries operated by private players have started to emerge in the post-reform era for utilizing the market opportunities of globalization in an economy still beset with inefficient institutions and high transaction costs.[5]

However, there has been a mismatch between market growth and institutional change in several dimensions. A simple example is that the devaluation of the rupee in 1991 led to the rapid growth of exports of labor-intensive industries such as leather goods, garments, dyes, etc., which are also pollution-intensive and tend to be regionally concentrated, especially on river belts. This caused severe pollution of rivers and agricultural lands because the regulatory institutions were ineffective. This resulted in high costs, mainly to the weak and disfranchised poor, who are unable to incur the transaction costs of forming countervailing private order institutions. A similar example is the growth of Bangalore city, not matched by a corresponding growth of public infrastructure and provision of public goods, which is controlled by inefficient government bodies characterized by corruption and mismanagement. The mismatch of market growth and institutional change in the country, mostly a result of the inefficiency of government bodies at different levels, will put brakes on India's growth in the future. Just as changing perceptions of economic opportunity-sets is a positive institutional change, the general acceptance of corruption in all walks of life by the public is a major institutional hindrance with significant economic costs.

The above issue refers to the prevailing drawbacks of the governance of public order institutions in the context of a large developing economy under democratic political institutions. Until the early part of the 1990s, in several academic and journalistic circles, India's poor economic growth was attributed to its functioning of democracy, especially by comparing it with the success stories of South Korea during the 1970s and 1980s and China since 1979, under totalitarian political systems. One of the interesting areas of research is comparing the evolution of capitalist institutions in democratic India and politically communist China to understand the relation between democracy and capitalism.

Once India was able to initiate economic reforms through economic crisis in 1991, it accelerated its growth. By early 2000, the reforms resulted in the emergence of a few world-class industries and indigenously born companies, because private entrepreneurs enjoy property rights in democratic India, while China denied property rights to its people until 1998.

The other link between democracy and institutions is free speech and a free press. In China, the press is highly controlled, while in India there is a free press. As a result of the reforms, a large number of privately owned television channels for entertainment and news coverage have come into existence at both the national and regional levels. The television channels have become a means for alterations in the perceptions and expectations of people, and also changes in the governance of the public order institutions. To give an example of the latter, in the state of Andhra Pradesh in 2005, there are four regional news channels trasmitting twenty-four-hour news in the local language (Telugu). There is intense competition between the channels for viewers, and they have started to go aggressively after stories of the political and economic corruption of government agents at both the capital and very local levels. One should expect that this should lead to improvements in the governance of government agencies with time.

# Appendices

## Appendix 1: industry data

*Table 16* The industry list

| SITC | Industry | SITC | Industry |
|------|----------|------|----------|
| 3873 | Clocks and watches | 3143 | Footwear |
| 3861 | Photographic films | 3089 | Plastic packaging goods |
| 3795 | Metal tanks and fabrications | 3085 | Plastic tubes and pipes |
| 3751 | Two-wheelers | 3052 | Rubber and rubber products |
| 3751 | Bicycles | 3011 | Tyres and tubes |
| 3714 | Automobile ancillaries | 2895 | Carbon black |
| 3713 | Commercial vehicles | 2892 | Explosives |
| 3711 | Passenger cars and vehicles | 2879 | Pesticides |
| 3692 | Dry cells | 2874 | Phosphatic fertilizers |
| 3691 | Storage batteries | 2873 | Nitrogenous fertilizers |
| 3679 | Electronic components | 2851 | Paints and varnishes |
| 3669 | Communication equipment | 2844 | Cosmetics and toiletries |
| 3651 | Consumer electronics | 2843 | Caustic soda |
| 3643 | Wires and cables | 2841 | Soaps |
| 3634 | Domestic appliances | 2834 | Pharmaceuticals |
| 3632 | Pumps | 2823 | Plastic films |
| 3632 | Air-conditioners and refrigerators | 2821 | Plastic resins |
| 3621 | Motors and generators | 2816 | Dyes and pigments |
| 3613 | Switching apparatus | 2813 | Industrial gases |
| 3612 | Transformers | 2621 | Paper and paper products |
| 3577 | Computer software | 2448 | Wood |
| 3571 | Computer hardware and peripherals | 2281 | Synthetic yarn |
| | | 2231 | Woolen textiles |
| 3569 | General purpose machinery | 2221 | Synthetic fabrics |
| 3562 | Ball bearings | 2211 | Cotton and blended yarn |
| 3561 | Compressors | 2111 | Tobacco products |
| 3552 | Textiles machinery | 2085 | Liquor |
| 3536 | Prime movers | 2082 | Beer |
| 3462 | Castings and forgings | 2079 | Vanaspati |
| 3441 | Structurals | 2076 | Vegetable oils |
| 3354 | Aluminum products | 2066 | Cocoa products and confectionery |
| 3334 | Aluminum | | |
| 3321 | Ferro alloys | 2061 | Sugar |
| 3317 | Steel tubes and pipes | 2041 | Starches |
| 2822 | Plastic sheets | 322 | Glass and glass ware |
| 3315 | Steel wires | 286 | Organic chemicals |
| 3291 | Abrasives | 281 | Inorganic chemicals |
| 3255 | Refractories | 205 | Bakery and milling |
| 3253 | Cement | 202 | Dairy |
| | | – | Jute products |
| | | – | Soda ash |

The data in Table 16 was collected from the publications of the Center for Monitoring the Indian Economy (CMIE) for the period of 1989 to 2003. The CMIE does not classify industries on the basis of Standard International Trade Classification (SITC). The classification by the US industry department is matched with the industry list to arrive at the SITC classification for the data. The CMIE industry data includes all the publicly listed companies in India, which are drawn from the company balance sheets reported by firms. The industry aggregate figures provided by the CMIE are derived by adding up the data for all firms belonging to each industry. One of the drawbacks of this is that the CMIE data does not include unorganized small firms. This drawback especially applies to industries such as textiles, footwear, and dyes and pigments.

*Econometric analysis of inventory behavior*

The econometric analysis is based on the panel data for seventy-eight industries for the fifteen-year period from 1989 to 2003. I have undertaken panel data econometric analysis, which utilizes information on both inter-temporal dynamics and the individuality of entities being investigated and controls for the effects of missing or unobserved variables (Cheng, 1986). The panel data estimates allow controlling for unobservable (omitted) variables by using fixed effects, and also capture market dynamics through the time-series element. With panel data, one can treat some of the variables as exogenous without violating the theory. The role of omitted variables can be treated as either a fixed constant effect over time for each industry, or as a purely random effect. I present the results for the fixed-effects model.

Variables:
*INGS* Inventories of finished and semi-finished goods to sales
*INRS* Inventories of raw materials to sales
*T* Time
*ADS* Selling costs (advertising+distribution+marketing) to sales
*EX* Exports to sales
*IM* Imports of capital and intermediate goods to sales
*DEPS* Depreciation to sales
*RDS* Research and development expenditure to sales
*VI* Vertical integration (value-added/sales)

$$INGS = -636 + 0.63\ T - 0.00016\ T^2 + 0.12\ ADS - 0.30\ RDS - 0.05\ EX + 0.02\ IM$$
$$(3.19)^* (3.19)^* \quad (3.2)^* \quad (1.9)^{**} \quad (1.5)^{**} \quad (3.16)^* \quad (1.15)$$

$$-0.12\ VI + 0.66\ DEPS \tag{1}$$
$$(6.9)^* \quad (7.6)^*$$

$R^2 = 0.13$, $F = 20$, $N = 1,168$

$$INRS = 148 - 0.002\ T - 0.0000002\ T^2 + 0.05\ ADS - 0.52\ RDS - 0.018\ EX$$
$$\quad\quad (0.05)\quad (0.02)\quad\quad (0.01)\quad\quad\quad (1.2)\quad\quad (3.2)*\quad (1.46)**$$

$$\quad\quad + 0.10\ IM - 0.02\ VI + 0.37\ DEPS \quad\quad\quad\quad\quad\quad\quad\quad (2)$$
$$\quad\quad\quad (7.8)*\quad (1.71)**\quad (5.7)*$$

$R^2 = 0.42,\ F = 100$

Notes:
Figures in parentheses are t-values: * significant at 0.01 level; ** significant at 0.05 levels.

I have introduced the time variable into the equation to examine the time-trend dimension of inventory behavior. Introducing time as the explanatory variable implies that the changes in inventory behavior are exogenous. However, the main argument is that inventory levels change in response to changes in markets and institutional factors (transaction costs) in response to the reforms. Therefore, I take these to provide empirical regularities, rather than the testing of hypotheses. Equation 1 refers to raw materials inventories to sales, and equation 2 to finished and semi-finished goods inventories to sales as dependent variables.

The consistently significant result for all the estimations is that the time path of changes in the inventories to sales exhibits an inverted 'U' shape, which implies that inventories at the beginning of the reforms increased and, after a time period, started to decline. At the initial stages of the reforms, firms' inventories increase if the capacities expand faster than the expected increase in demand owing to exuberant expectations. As the effect of the reforms deepens and the growth rate becomes sustainable with growth in markets and improvements in institutional conditions, inventories start to decline. In the case of the second equation, in which inventories of raw materials to sales is the dependent variable, the estimated coefficients of the time variable are statistically insignificant.

I introduced exports and imports to sales as the explanatory variables following the argument that increasing exposure to international trade reduces transaction costs and thereby leads to lower inventories. The interesting aspect of the results is that an increase in export orientation significantly contributes to lowering inventories. On the other hand, the estimated coefficients of imports variable is statistically significant only in the case of equation 2, and is positive. One reason could be that there are still high transaction costs of importing, and firms or industries that depend on imports maintain high inventories.

The *RDS* variable represents technology – the extent of the investment made by industries in purchasing overseas technology. The estimated coefficient of this variable is negative and statistically significant in explaining inventories of finished and semi-finished goods and raw materials to sales, which implies that industries that adopt modern technologies are able to reduce the transaction costs of markets and hence lower inventories. Vertical integration is an organizational choice to overcome high market transaction costs. The estimated coefficients of the variable are statistically significant and negative in both the equations, which implies that the higher the vertical integration, the lower the inventories. If the institutional conditions persist, firms adopt higher vertical integration for efficiency.

The depreciation to sales variable is introduced as an explanatory variable to control for the implications of physical capital intensity on inventories. Interestingly, the estimated coefficient of the variable is positive and statistically significant in both the equations. This variable also captures the intangible intensity of the assets – firms with higher intangible assets show lower levels of depreciation to sales. The results imply that firms that are able to develop intangible assets are able to reduce inventory levels and associated costs.

## Appendix 2: firm-level data

Extensive firm-level panel data is collected from Prowess, the computerized database of the CMIE referring to the time period of 1989 to 2003 for fourteen industries. Table 17 provides a summary of the information.

*Table 17* Firm-level data

| Industry | Number of firms | Industry | Number of firms |
|---|---|---|---|
| Air-conditioners (AC) | 5 | Motorcycles (MC) | 4 |
| Auto components (ATC) | 24 | Paper and paper products (PP) | 20 |
| Commercial vehicles (CV) | 6 | Pharmaceuticals (PCP) | 38 |
| Cotton blended yarn (CB) | 20 | Refrigerator (RG) | ?? |
| Communications equipment (CE) | 22 | Software (SI) | 34 |
| Dyes and pigments (DP) | 20 | Textile machinery (TM) | 21 |
| Electronic goods (EG) | 32 | Tyres and tubes (TT) | 25 |

*Measurement of technical efficiency (TE)*

I estimate firm-level relative productivity indices on the basis of Farrell's (1957) production frontier approach. Farrell's method shows relative technical (in)efficiency (*TE*) as the extent of deviation of output realized by a firm (for a given level of inputs employed) from the best practice in an industry. Measuring *TE* on the basis of panel data overcomes the shortcomings of the estimates based on cross-sectional data (Pitt and Lee, 1981). The panel data capture cross-sectional information of firms in an industry and also repeated observations over time for a given firm. This, in turn, overcomes the shortcomings of strong distributional assumptions about composed error terms. Apart from this, the method does not impose the assumption that technical efficiency is independent of factor inputs. The stochastic production frontier is utilized in estimating firm relative technical inefficiency (efficiency) indices which take values above 0 and less than 1.

By taking the Cobb-Douglas functional form, we can represent the technology as follows:

$$Y_{it} = \alpha + \beta \, X_{it} + v_{it} - u_i \tag{1}$$

where $Y_{it}$ is the observed output, $X_{it}$ is a vector of inputs: i index firm (i = 1....N): t index time (1....t). $\alpha$ and $\beta$ are the unknown parameters to be estimated. $v_{it}$ represents symmetrically distributed random errors. $u_i$ represents technical inefficiency with one-sided distribution, which means that output must lie on or below the frontier. The random error $v_{it}$ is assumed to be identically and independently distributed across firms and time with identical zero mean and constant variance. It is also assumed to be uncorrelated with factor inputs. u, which represents *TE*, is modeled as a half-normal or exponential distribution. The model allows *TE* to vary across firms and in time.

The Cobb-Douglas production functional form is utilized. Value-added is taken as output and *K* (rental value of capital) and *L* (salaries and wages) as inputs. Value-added and capital values are normalized by the wholesale producer price indices, and salaries and wages are normalized by the consumer wholesale price indices. The base year of the prices is 1994. The production function is estimated separately for each industry by adopting the fixed effects model.

*SC* is selling costs (which includes distribution, direct advertising and marketing expenditures) to sale. This variable is used as both a flow and

*Table 18* Econometric explanation of market shares

| Industry | Constant | TE | SC | SC*FE | $R^2$ | F | N |
|---|---|---|---|---|---|---|---|
| AC | −0.18 (1.9)* | 1.1 (4.6)* | −1.3 (1.8)** | 0.6 (2.1)* | 0.42 | 12 | 79 |
| CV | 0.12 (8.3)* | 0.09 (3.1)* | 0.05 (0.24) | 0.22 (1.0) | 0.12 | 3.8 | 89 |
| EG | −0.04 (11.3)* | 0.62 (37.5)* | 0.0009 (0.02) | −0.005 (2.5)* | 0.75 | 470 | 471 |
| MC | 0.08 (3.9)* | 0.47 (8.9)* | −3.7 (9.5)* | 3.6 (6.5)* | 0.77 | 58 | 59 |
| RG | −0.21 (1.95)* | 1.4 (5.3)* | −1.9 (1.8)** | −0.01 (0.78) | 0.4 | 11 | 59 |
| TT | −0.007 (3.4)* | 0.22 (30)* | −0.0073 (0.54) | 0.001 (1.5)* | 0.79 | 370 | 316 |

Notes
Figures in parentheses are t-values.
*   Significant at 0.01 level.
** Significant at 0.05 level.

stock variable with four-year additions. The results are similar in both the cases. The results in Table 18 refer to the estimations with this variable as a flow. *FE* is foreign equity embedded in firms to capture the multinational dimension of firms.

One common result across all the industries is the statistically significant positive association between market share and the relative production efficiency of firms. The interactive variable of *SC\*FE* captures whether TNCs are able to increase their market share by increasing their expenditure on distribution and advertising more than local firms. The results in general, except in the case of the electronic goods industry, indicate that TNCs are able to increase their market share more by investing in selling costs than local firms.

## Appendix 3: a conceptual methodology of convergence

Suppose $S_t$ and $s_t$ respectively denote a vector of state variables for a TNC and a local firm in period $t$, and $R_t$ and $r_t$ the vector of response variables. Assume that the choice of response variables depends only on the state variable of the firm, given that of its competitor.

Then the response vector for the TNC is:

$$R_t = g(S_t; s_t) \tag{1}$$

and, likewise, that for the local firm is:

$$r_t = g(s_t; S_t) \tag{2}$$

The hypothesis of catching up by the local firm implies a process:

$$s_{t+1} - s_t = f(S_t - s_t), \text{ with } f' > 0$$

We augment this latter hypothesis by assuming $f' \geq 0$, to include the possibility that there may not be any catching-up during the sample period, e.g. if the local firm chooses to compete entirely using its response variables. The augmented equation can be written as:

$$s_{t+1} - s_t = f(S_t - s_t), \text{ with } f' \geq 0 \tag{3}$$

Note that if $f' > 0$, not only the gap $(S_t - s_t)$, but also $(R_t - r_t)$ narrows down over time. Initialize time by setting the period of entry of the TNC as 0. If $S_0 > s_0$, then, from equations 1, 2, and 3 one of two possibilities is expected over the sample period:
(i) If $f' = 0$, then $S_t > s_t$, and $R_t \neq r_t$ for all $t$.
(ii) If $f' > 0$, then $s_t$ increases with $t$ over the sample period. In this case, $(S_t - s_t)$ and $|(R_t - r_t)|$ fall over time. This may lead to a situation where

they may become statistically insignificant, and then $S_t > s_t$, and $R_t \neq r_t$ may or may not hold in a statistically significant sense over the sample period.

For the empirical exercises, $S$ and $s$ are scalars, and will stand for variables such as *TE*, distribution to sales ratio, administrative expenditures for capturing internal organizational efficiency of the TNC and the local firm respectively.

(1) Regarding the first part of the proposition, i.e. TNCs, at the time of entry, are superior to local firms in some attributes, we can have the following cases:

(i) If $S_t > s_t$, and $R_t \neq r_t$, the proposition is not rejected.

(ii) If $(S_t - s_t)$ and $|(R_t - r_t)|$ are not significantly different from zero, but $s_t$ increases over the sample period, we can not reject the possibility of initial differences among TNCs and local firms.

(iii) If $S_t < s_t$, the proposition is rejected.

(iv) If $S_t$ and $s_t$ are not significantly different, while $R_t \neq r_t$, we infer that a difference exists between TNCs and local firms, but cannot establish the superiority of either. This is because, while a difference in *TE* results in different responses, we cannot have unambiguous prior expectation about the sign of the difference.

(2) Regarding the second part of the proposition, i.e. that there is a convergence process, we can have the following relevant cases:

(i) If $S_t > s_t$ and/or $R_t \neq r_t$, and $s_t$ increases in time, we may infer that there is a convergence process.

(ii) If $S_t > s_t$ does not hold, but $s_t$ increases over time, we cannot reject the possibility of a convergence process. In this case the initial superiority of TNCs can be argued to have been eroded through spillover, and thus be absent in the sample.

(iii) If $S_t < s_t$ and $s_t$ increases through time, the increase cannot be attributed to spillover. It is, however, possible to suggest (or rather not reject) that the increase of $s_t$ is the result of competition with TNCs rather than a spillover process.

(iv) If $S_t > s_t$, while $s_t$ is invariant in time, we conclude that TNCs have superiority but it has not spilled over during the sample period.

(v) If $s_t$ decreases over time, there is no case for a convergence.

## Appendix 4: econometric evidence of productivity gains in the Indian industry

I have estimated the Cobb-Douglas production function in which the time variable is introduced to test for productivity increase or decrease in post-reform Indian industry. I present the results for both the industry-level panel data of seventy-eight industries, and also the firm-level data. The results presented are for fixed-effects model controlling for industry/firm-specific factors and omitted variable bias. The random effects estimations provided similar results, which are not presented. The variables are as follows: $V$ is value-added as output normalized by wholesale price index, salaries and wages are for labor input ($L$) normalized by consumer prices and $K$ is the capital input in terms of rental value of capital [(plant and machinery* interest rate) + depreciation] normalized by wholesale prices. $T$ refers to time (years). Equation 1 refers to the results of the industry-level data, and equation 2 to the firm-level data.

$$\log V = 90,909 - 91\ T + 0.022\ T^2 + 5 \log L + 0.86\ K \qquad (1)$$
$$\quad (3.9)^* \quad (3.9)^* \quad (3.9)^* \quad\quad (41)^* \quad (2)^*$$

$R^2 = 0.71$, $F = 679$, $N = 1,168$

$$\log V = -11.12 + 0.006\ T + 0.70 \log L + 0.17 \log K \qquad (2)$$
$$\quad\ (3.9)^* \quad (4.27)^* \quad (23.9)^* \quad\quad (7.5)^*$$

$R^2 = 0.68$, $F = 965$, $N = 1,456$

Figures in parentheses are t-values: * significant at 0.001 level.

As mentioned before, the time variable $T$ is introduced to capture the productivity change over the years.[1] In the case of equation 1, the time trend in the productivity growth shows a 'U' shape – it decreases initially and, after a stage, starts increasing. The equation refers to firm-level data with all the industries (see Table 7) pooled into one sample. In the case of equation 2, concerning the firm-level data, the regression dropped $T^2$ variable and the estimated coefficient of $T$ is positive and statistically significant.[2] The neoclassical theory of diminishing returns is the maintained hypothesis, which is embodied in the Cobb-Douglas form itself. The concave time function says something about the nature of technological progress but not about returns to factors. Owing to the logarithmic form of the function, the linear trend in the second estimation implies an exponential rate of technological progress.

## Appendix 5: econometrics explanation of vertical integration

The following paragraphs detail the econometric explanation of vertical integration with industry-level panel data. The time variable is introduced explicitly, along with other explanatory variables, to examine time-trend changes in vertical integration in the post-reforms era.

Variables:
$VI$       vertical integration (value-added/value of output)
$T$        time in years

*DPS*   depreciation/sales
*RDS*   R&D expenditure/sales
*IMS*   imports of intermediate and capital goods/sales
SCS   total selling costs to sales

$$VI = -1,185 + 1.18\ T - 0.0002\ T^2 + 1.12\ DPS + 0.19\ RDS - 0.05\ IMS + 0.37\ SCS$$
$$\quad\ (3.6)^*\quad (3.6)^*\quad\ (3.6)^*\quad\quad (8.8)^{**}\quad (0.5)\quad\quad (1.9)^*\quad\quad (3.6)^*$$

$R^2 = 0.13$, $F = 24$, $N = 1,168$

Figures in parentheses are t-values: * significant at 0.01 level, ** significant at 0.05 level.

The above results refer to the fixed-effects model and the random effects estimations provide similar results, but these are not presented. The time-trend changes in vertical integration show an inverted 'U' shape, which implies that vertical integration declines at a decreasing rate – it increases initially, and declines later on providing support for Stigler's hypothesis. Once the markets and institutions start to improve, the vertical integration levels of industries decline, especially for an Indian economy beset with high transaction costs before the reforms. The *DPS* variable captures the physical/intangible assets capital-intensity of industries. The higher the value of this variable, the higher the physical capital-intensity, and the lower is the intangible asset-intensity. The estimated coefficient of this variable is positive and statistically significant, implying that industries with higher physical capital-intensity show higher vertical integration. As discussed before, Physical-capital-intensive commodity industries increased their vertical integration to realize economies of scale for both local and export markets. The negative sign of the coefficient of the imports variable has obvious implications, in that industries that import raw materials and intermediate goods show lower vertical integration. As far as the results associated with the selling cost variable are concerned, industries that spend more on distribution and advertising may find vertical integration a more efficient organizational choice in order to realize economies of scale in reputation effects. These results should in essence be taken to provide empirical regularities, rather than strict tests of hypotheses, because of the explicit introduction of time as a variable into the equations, which implies that changes in *VI* are governed by exogenous factors.

*Table 19* Industries with decline in annual average growth rate in vertical integration, 1990–9

| Industry | GVI | VI 90 | VI 99 | GPTS | GVA | GRS | GADS | GIMSI | GES | GNF |
|---|---|---|---|---|---|---|---|---|---|---|
| Starches | −0.018 | 0.45 | 0.32 | 0.15 | 0.22 | 1.8 | 0.09 | 0.22 | 1.22 | 0.12 |
| Textile machinery | −0.016 | 0.51 | 0.39 | 0.10 | 0.19 | 0.75 | 0.023 | 0.077 | 0.10 | 0.043 |
| Phosphate fertilizers | −0.013 | 0.50 | 0.45 | 0.34 | 0.10 | 1.5 | 0.037 | 0.129 | 0.22 | −0.003 |
| Cold rolled coils | −0.009 | 0.49 | 0.47 | −0.03 | 0.15 | 0.50 | 0.009 | 0.02 | 0.08 | 0.077 |
| Domestic appliances | −0.008 | 0.369 | 0.32 | 0.66 | 0.16 | 0.21 | 0.093 | 0.076 | 0.14 | 0.053 |
| Cotton, blended yarn | −0.008 | 0.465 | 0.400 | 0.257 | 0.167 | 0.83 | 0.047 | 0.13 | 0.18 | 0.060 |
| Air conditioners | −0.008 | 0.330 | 0.336 | 0.227 | 0.190 | 0.05 | 0.139 | 0.26 | 0.37 | 0.113 |
| Plastic resins | −0.008 | 0.413 | 0.382 | 0.067 | 0.203 | 0.40 | 0.029 | 0.035 | 0.082 | 0.007 |
| Organic chemicals | −0.008 | 0.377 | 0.346 | 0.016 | 0.147 | 0.26 | 0.057 | 0.071 | 0.053 | 0.0001 |
| Synthetic yarn | −0.007 | 0.467 | 0.4187 | −0.004 | 0.178 | 0.33 | 0.038 | 0.050 | 0.205 | 0.0393 |
| Ferro alloys | −0.005 | 0.613 | 0.590 | −0.082 | 0.126 | 0.576 | 0.006 | 0.069 | 0.073 | 0.095 |
| Abrasives | −0.004 | 0.472 | 0.413 | 0.288 | 0.164 | 0.438 | 0.030 | −0.002 | 0.050 | −0.045 |
| Nitrogenous fertilizers | −0.004 | 0.536 | 0.522 | 0.002 | 0.095 | 0.229 | −0.029 | 0.060 | 0.134 | 0.025 |
| Paints, varnishes | −0.001 | 0.405 | 0.404 | 0.229 | 0.113 | 0.268 | 0.036 | 0.065 | 0.050 | 0.028 |
| Passenger cars, jeeps | −0.001 | 0.309 | 0.299 | 0.775 | 0.174 | 0.0743 | 0.063 | 0.072 | 0.104 | 0.098 |
| Average | −0.011 | 0.448 | 0.405 | 0.200 | 0.160 | 0.556 | 0.045 | 0.09 | 0.207 | 0.048 |
| Standard deviation | 0.009 | 0.08 | 0.079 | 0.248 | 0.037 | 0.514 | 0.443 | 0.071 | 0.296 | 0.048 |
| Average of total sample | 0.011 | 0.415 | 0.446 | 0.109 | 0.1901 | 0.644 | 0.078 | 0.095 | 0.136 | 0.047 |
| Standard deviation | 0.018 | 0.096 | 0.09 | 1.42 | 0.069 | 1.53 | 0.067 | 0.107 | 0.169 | 0.04 |

Note
The definitions of variables are shown in Table 20.

*Table 20* Industries with increase in annual average growth rate in vertical integration, 1990–9

| | GVI | VI 90 | VI 99 | GPTS | GVA | GRS | GADS | GIMS | GES | GNF |
|---|---|---|---|---|---|---|---|---|---|---|
| Transformers | 0.019 | 0.409 | 0.455 | 0.083 | 0.152 | −0.067 | 0.067 | −0.006 | 0.141 | −0.002 |
| Two-wheelers | 0.02 | 0.33 | 0.377 | 0.060 | 0.241 | 0.103 | 0.07 | 0.023 | 0.053 | −0.012 |
| Vegetable oils | 0.02 | 0.28 | 0.314 | 0.023 | 0.256 | 0.54 | 0.117 | 0.16 | 0.066 | 0.029 |
| Switching apparatus | 0.021 | 0.449 | 0.533 | 0.100 | 0.172 | −0.08 | 0.078 | 0.004 | 0.133 | 0.021 |
| Bakery and milling | 0.023 | 0.296 | 0.337 | 0.0708 | 0.165 | 3.71 | 0.080 | 0.411 | 0.007 | 0.0433 |
| Explosives | 0.027 | 0.321 | 0.322 | 0.266 | 0.197 | 0.825 | 0.220 | 0.028 | 0.086 | 0.008 |
| Vanaspati | 0.029 | 0.26 | 0.309 | 0.110 | 0.251 | 0.967 | 0.103 | 0.153 | 0.087 | 0.011 |
| Tobacco products | 0.029 | 0.367 | 0.532 | 0.137 | 0.221 | 0.186 | 0.097 | 0.248 | 0.131 | 0.043 |
| Refrigerators | 0.030 | 0.339 | 0.435 | 8.5 | 0.25 | 0.11 | 0.249 | 0.026 | 0.066 | 0.088 |
| Metal tanks | 0.035 | 0.177 | 0.213 | 0.006 | 0.189 | 0.203 | 0.194 | 0.120 | −0.015 | 0.073 |
| Storage batteries | 0.037 | 0.391 | 0.496 | 0.186 | 0.587 | 0 | 0.142 | 0.623 | 0.841 | 0.130 |
| Dry cells | 0.048 | 0.335 | 0.520 | −0.335 | 0.207 | 0.551 | 0.108 | 0.004 | 0.457 | 0.203 |
| Bicycles | 0.048 | 0.228 | 0.302 | 1.04 | 0.256 | 1.20 | 0.027 | 0.171 | 0.034 | 0.024 |
| Computer software | 0.052 | 0.463 | 0.510 | 2.38 | 0.465 | 0.430 | −0.01 | 0.129 | 0.188 | 0.007 |
| Plastic tubes, pipes | 0.104 | 0.227 | 0.595 | 0.634 | 0.348 | 8.57 | 0.305 | −0.007 | −0.030 | 0.058 |
| Average | 0.036 | 0.322 | 0.415 | 0.883 | 0.263 | 1.14 | 0.122 | 0.135 | 0.148 | 0.048 |
| Standard deviation | 0.020 | 0.083 | 0.114 | 2.14 | 0.117 | 2.18 | 0.086 | 0.172 | 0.216 | 0.067 |
| Average of total sample | 0.011 | 0.415 | 0.446 | 0.109 | 0.190 | 0.644 | 0.078 | 0.095 | 0.136 | 0.047 |
| Standard deviation | 0.018 | 0.096 | 0.093 | 1.42 | 0.069 | 1.53 | 0.067 | 0.107 | 0.169 | 0.044 |

Notes
GVI      annual average growth rate of vertical integration.
VI 90    degree of vertical integration in 1990.
VI 99    degree of vertical integration in 1999.
GPT      annual average growth rate of net profits to sales.
GRS      annual average growth rate of royalties and technical fees paid, normalized by sales.
GADS     annual average growth rate of selling expenditure, normalized by sales (selling expenditure includes direct advertising, distribution, and marketing).
GIM      annual average growth rate of imports of intermediate and capital goods, normalized by sales.
GEX      annual average growth rate of exports to sales.
GNS      annual average growth rate of net fixed assets to sales.
GVA      growth in valued-added.

# Notes

## 1 Introduction

1  In 2005, the international oil prices hit an all time high of $60 a barrel because of rapid increase in demand for oil from China and India. In other words, the swift growth of these economies not only presents significant growth in markets and structural changes in the worldwide organization of manufacturing and services, but also increasing demand on world resources.

2  In the 1980s and 1990s, while the South and South East Asian countries had been able to take advantage of globalization and grow economically, most African countries declined, despite following the free market and operating open trade and invesment policies.

3  One can criticise this assumption of initial endowments as ad hoc. Nevertheless, every theory, however complete it may be, takes some factor as exogenously given. If one takes the Marxian theory of the dialectic interpretation of the evolution of economic systems as a complete explanation in historical terms, even in this case the starting point is the primitive communism of collective ownership of resources. How the primitive communism came about has to be taken to be exogenous. Douglas North's (1990) historical analysis of the evolution of market institutions in the United States observes that initial capitalist institutions came about in the US through British colonial rule.

4  In other words, this book does not undertake the study of a situation similar to the extreme example of Russia, in which the shift from communism to capitalism was made in the absence of critical capitalist institutions.

5  The importance of the observation can be seen from the Russian experience. The sudden move of Russia to a capitalist system after years of communism without any minimum endowment of capitalist institutions resulted in disastrous consequences. Even now Russia struggles to bring an order. The press reports in the early part of 2000s show that close to 50 percent of the Russian people would want communism to come back.

6  Government failures are seen in terms of economic policies being captured by a small powerful vested interest groups at the cost of the welfare of the majority and thereby causing overall economic inefficiency.

7  Ahlstrom *et al.* (2000) observe that these transaction costs take the form of practicing different forms of guanxi which include co-opting strategies in terms of offering shares to local officials, hiring people within government, entertaining the government officials, etc. The traditional Chinese patterns of social relations are called guanxi.

## 2 The conceptual framework

1 This behavioural assumption can be seen in terms of building blocks of institutions that mitigate costs of myopic self-interest of individual behaviour.
2 The social choice theory of Arrow can be seen as an outcome of observing the majority fascism under Hitler, arising out of democracy. One of the ways of overcoming it is a decentralized structure of democracy with checks and balances at different levels.
3 On the other hand, it is also possible that these agents could organize collective action to bargain with government and redistribute income in their favour, which reduces overall efficiency. For example it is argued that large farmers and producers of fertilizers appropriated the major part of the benefits of the Green Revolution in India.
4 There are several examples of similar outcomes, especially in the post-reform period, when controls on capital are removed without proper regulatory rules and proper definition and enforcement of property rights. If the negative externalities of growth are properly accounted for, the economic growth rate will be lower than it is officially shown.
5 This information is gathered from my discussions with software professionals in Bangalore.
6 The essential point is that if improvements in property rights and contracts laws are followed by improvements in the capital markets, it generates not only productivity gains but also entrepreneurial dynamics. This is also the case with the stock markets. If government enacts rules driving firms to adopt full disclosures, it reduces informational asymmetry between the principals and agents and thereby improves the control rights of investors. This contributes to improvements in corporate governance and better utilization of capital, thereby increasing investment avenues for the public.

## 3 Initial conditions and policy reforms

1 To cite an example, on one of my return trips from overseas, the customs officials at Hyderabad city airport demanded customs duty for the goods I was carrying. When I protested by citing the new customs rules, he muttered "You educated people . . ." and let me go.
2 Capitalist institutions and global trade existed in India long before the entry of Europeans. During the early sixteenth century, India traded extensively with East Africa, Turkey, Persia, China, Sumatra, and Malacca. The ports on the Coromandel coast in the east and west coasts were hubs of intense commercial activities and trading zones. The wide-ranging and sophisticated network had existed since the ninth century. Historical evidence shows that kings such Chola in the south created an administrative and financial infrastructure for international trade (Arasaratnam, 1986).
3 When this was abolished in independent India, the family-owned or controlled companies formed identifiable business groups over time (Khanna and Melito, 1997).
4 For example, Indira Gandhi, who suspended democracy and imposed the Emergency in 1975, had to abandon it within two years and lost power in the following general election.
5 For example, as discussed before, in 2004 the NDA government lost the elections and the Congress party in coalition with the left formed the central government. One of the reasons given was that the previous government left the rural poor behind. The ruling Congress party announced the common minimum program in 2004 to benefit the rural poor, but the institutional con-

ditions for delivering the social benefits to the poor were missing owing to lack of decentralization, and ill-defined center and state government political equations. As an illustration, in the state of West Bengal, which implemented land reforms and decentralization at the village level, rural poverty went down, while the feudal institutions of Bihar and UP keep rural poverty levels high.

6 The values range from greater than 0 to less than or equal to 1. If it takes a value of one, it means that a firm is fully vertically integrated.

7 However, there is a qualification for this observation. Just because several studies documented a negative correlation between firm size and export orientation for Indian industries (Patibandla, 1988, 1995), this does not imply that the smaller firms had the technology $MC_2$ with larger economies of scale. This relationship is applicable to industries with a long-tailed market structure in which capital-intensive and labor-intensive technologies coexist and exports of small firms were a result of comparative advantage in the low labor costs and high transaction costs of the domestic market.

8 It is generally observed that many TNCs that win Indian government approval to invest never actually proceed. In 2001, about $10 billion a year in approvals were granted, but the actual investment rate was about $2.5 billion.

## 4 The direction of structural changes

1 Business and investment are no longer perceived as something undertaken by the less educated and money-minded class, but as worthy pursuits that complement education, status, and culture.

2 To give an example, in 2002 the government of India streamlined the income tax rules and simplified the past oppressive tax rates to a flat rate of 30 percent. This, in turn, increased the tax payment compliance of the rich to a certain degree. Increased public compliance reduces the predatory and bribe-extracting powers of the income tax officials. In the early part of the 2000s, the revenue department instructed all the banks in the country to report (depositor) transactions above Rs 50,000 to the local income tax department. In 2004 one can see this notice in every bank branch in India. This was meant to track black money in the economy. Logically, when income tax is paid at the source, this rule is meaningless. This stipulation significantly increases transaction costs for the banks and the harassment of the public.

3 In the early 2000s, one finds even low-income groups carrying mobile phones. I have often seen three-wheeler drivers in the cities of Bangalore and Hyderabad using mobile phones to organize their business service.

4 The industries that showed a decline in inventories to sales comprise commodity industries, such as textile yarn and chemicals, but also the fastest-growing manufacturing industries, such as two wheelers, communication equipment, and domestic appliances, and the modern, high-tech industries, such as pharmaceuticals and computer software. It is important to note that these industries have a higher average export and import orientation than the total sample of seventy-eight industries.

5 It is rather consistent with the previous observation, based on calculations of Nagaraj, that the salaried staff and supervisors are the ones who experienced the highest growth in income in the post-reforms period.

6 For example, a large number of senior managers in India's software companies, both local and TNCs, were ex-employees of public sector firms, such as C-DOT in telecommunications and ISRO in space research.

7 I ran a simple regression with the panel data set of seventy-eight industries, as described before, in which budget share (total sales) of industries in GDP is

regressed against a set of industry characteristics variables. The budget share of industries captures the changing relative importance of different industries in GDP. The results show that industries with international orientation through exports and imports, and the increasing presence of multinational firms have been able to increase their relative shares in GDP in the post-reform era.

8 However, the import substitution and licensing policies resulted in most large industrial houses enjoying a long-run monopoly, and they consequently under-utilized this skilled labor, which was one reason for the large amount of brain-drain from India.

9 At this time the idea of software technology parks was formulated to provide the satellite and other infrastructure facilities to software exporting firms.

10 On other hand, India's movie industry is the second-largest in the world. However, the piracy of movies is rampant in India. A probable reason could be that the industry is not able to organize itself as effectively as the software industry. Only in 2005 has the movie industry in the south of India begun to convince some state governments to curtail the piracy, as a large number of movies have started to lose revenue from theater screenings.

11 A 'choupal' is a meeting-place in the villages of India.

12 Companies that belong to the Pharmaceutical Research and Manufacturers of America spent about $19 billion on R&D in 1997.

13 The imposition of IPRs in developing economies through the WTO benefits global TNCs by blocking firms in India from exporting to other developing economies at low prices.

14 Power-looms are weaving factories with an average of ten to twenty looms each. They manufacture woven cloth, but are different from the integrated mills that not only weave, but also perform spinning and processing in the same premises. Apart from power-looms and mills, there are a few other types of cloth producers in India, such as handlooms, factories that weave man-made fibres, and silk-weaving factories (Roy, 1996).

15 A good example of this is Arvind Mills, which entered collaboration with Lauf-fenmuehle of Germany for marketing. The other major Indian firms that have tied up with reputable international textile companies are Mafatlal Industries and Moraji Mills. Several large Indian firms began to collaborate with inter-national brand names, such as, Van Heusen, Benetton (Italy), Cluett Peabody (USA), La Perla (Italy), Marzotto (Italy), and Lacoste, etc., for international marketing.

16 On the contrary, in Bombay city, one finds people in queues at bus stations and movie theaters moving in a civilized manner.

## 5 Competitive dynamics

1 A competitive capital market can be viewed as one in which an economic agent with a good project proposal can raise capital without collateral and with low transaction costs.

2 Hotelling's location model of product differentiation is a classic theory of convergence in microeconomics. When firms compete for consumers with diverse preferences by differentiating their products, in the end all products converge to similarity in characteristics. For someone living in India, like me, Coca Cola and Pepsi Cola look and taste alike, except for the fact that two different popular movie stars advertise the products. Another example could be that on several occasions the political manifestos of competing political parties appear identical. In this model, competition leads to degeneration towards populism, in which consumers with extreme preferences will be worse off. I concentrate

on the issue of convergence of best practices, which augments the efficiency of industries, rather than Hotelling's type of outcome.

3  The mainstream strategic management literature conceptualizes the competitive advantage of firms in terms of each firm's ability to differentiate itself from others and sustain the difference. The notion of a competitive advantage is a relative concept and implies that firms must seek to distance themselves from their competitors along key competitive dimensions in order to ensure superior performance for themselves. Convergence in this view would represent a threat to the competitive advantage and profit positions of firms. In Porter's (1990) diamond model of the competitive advantage of nations, firms derive competitive advantages in response to the demands of their home market environments, which they may be able to leverage across national borders. Porter's framework was inspired by the Japanese example, in which the competitive advantage of Japanese firms was characterized in comparison to the American and west European counterparts. On the other hand, the resource-based view of the firm concentrates on the micro firm-level foundations of competitive superiority. In other words, a firm's competitive advantage rests on its idiosyncratic and difficult to imitate resources, acquired through its history (Penrose, 1959).

4  Under Cournot-Nash strategic rivalry, each firm takes the other firm's choice (output) as given and maximizes its profits. A firm can achieve the competitive advantage of capturing a higher market share and profits by generating asymmetric advantages on the demand and production side. In consumer welfare terms, in both cases, either through an increase in the number of firms or an increase in the relative efficiency of firms, the market price approaches the marginal cost of production.

5  One can question this argument if one takes the pure Cournot-Nash game in which each agent takes the other's actions as given and maximizes their payoffs through not knowing that the other is doing the same. If both agents know that the other is doing the same, competition turns into collusion.

6  One can cite a couple of examples for this type of behaviour of local firms from Indian industries. Bajaj Auto in the two-wheeler industry and TELCO in the light commercial vehicle industries are well-established local firms. After the policy reforms, they did not take up a joint equity venture with any transnational firm but bought technology from overseas firms through licensing agreements.

7  Thus, replicating a local distribution network and building a long-term relationship with vendor firms may take years for a new entrant.

8  As the relative advantage of incumbents in terms of accumulated knowledge of the local market and institutional conditions would be with managers, new entrants attempt to attract them away from incumbents. A simple proof of this behavior is that, since the early nineties, quite a few organizations specializing in head-hunting have appeared in India. Apart from this, recent press reports show that some of the new entrants in the automobile industry attempted to capture vendor firms cultivated by local firms by providing incentives for opportunistic behavior.

9  In my informal interview, one of the executives of a leading domestic scooter manufacturer observed that managers used to visit dealers once a year before the reforms. After the reforms, the visits increased to four times a year.

10  Similar arguments with regard to product differentiation choices of incumbents and new entrants can be made. In the pre-reforms period, the behavior of local firms was akin to monopolists or cartelized oligopolies selling sub standard goods at high prices with a 'take it or leave it' attitude. Despite enjoying a

large domestic market, they did not generate significant brand loyalty that could be used against new entrants TNCs in the post-reform era. This, in turn, gives an asymmetric advantage to new entrant TNCs. In the post-reform period, an incumbent has to grapple with significant sunk costs in existing product lines for changing product specification. On the other hand, a TNC contemplating entry looks at the range of qualities in the product market as an ex ante choice without any sunk costs constraining it. Apart from this, new entrants TNCs have information about the choices already made by incumbents and the expected changes in the income levels of the consumers. Incumbents can buy some time by exploiting their relative advantage in their well established distribution networks in the short and medium run but in the long run they have to replace the choices made in relation to the pre-reforms conditions with the efficient choices in response to new competition (Patibandla, 2002c).

11 Also see Patibandla (2002a) for similar results.

12 The qualitative analysis of the case studies is based on press reports and field interviews with executives of a few of the companies.

13 To emphasize the effect of Maruti on the organization of production, Tewari (2005) observes that it created, for the first time, "greater flexibility in supply despite being located within a rigid policy environment and demonstrated that unionization, which has been used by critics as a scapegoat for poor performance, need not hinder, and can, in fact, help productivity gains at the firm level."

14 In India, whatever local entrepreneurial activity is taking place is mostly in terms of copying technologies and practices from the developed economies, rather than coming out with totally new technologies. This is because there are a lot of opportunities to make wealth by imitative rather than innovative activity in India, similar to what was witnessed in Japan between 1960 and 1990. Once India is able to develop conditions for an effective national innovative system, it may then stimulate innovative activities, a point that is discussed in the following chapter.

## 6  Technological change

1 For example, the Japanese producers in the automobile and electronics industries imitated technologies from the West and were able to realize higher productivity than the producers in the West by adopting different organizational practices, such as quality control, human resource management, and vendor development.

2 As shown by Romer (1990), non-rivalry has two important implications for the theory of growth. First, non-rival goods can be accumulated without limits on a per capita basis, whereas a piece of human capital such as the ability to add cannot. Each person has only a finite number of years that can be spent acquiring skills. Second, a non-rival good engenders knowledge spillovers, that is incomplete excludability. These two features of knowledge cause long-run sustained economic growth.

3 The literature on Schumpeter's (1947) technological innovation makes the distinction between invention and innovation. Invention is generation of a new idea or theory, and innovation is turning it into a commercial product.

4 Apart from this, high tax rates also took away a part of potential savings to augment the government budget.

5 The percentage of non-performing loans in the portfolio of Indian banks is about a third of those held by China's banks.

6  The limitation of this example in the present context is that it does not refer to incentives for adoption of technology, as Hollywood movies are made for the US and the western European market, where the copyrights are well protected. Developing the market for these movies in countries like India is a matter of spreading the fixed costs that are already invested. Interestingly Indian movies are widely pirated in the US and in western Europe by the immigrant community from Asia, a fact that local governments ignore.

7  The extension of this is developing distribution, after sales service, and product warranties. This requires firms to generate distribution and information markets and develop contractual relations with distribution companies with appropriate incentives that minimize informational imperfections and agency costs.

8  In other words, if Indian firms did not have to invest in the self-generation of infrastructure, they could achieve even higher productivity.

9  For example, I paid Rs 21,000 for a 20 inch color TV in 1994. In 2004, I bought a 29 inch flat-screen TV of the latest type for Rs 14,000 (about $250), which, after accounting for inflation, shows a steep decline in real prices within ten years.

10  *Economic Times*, 23 June 2005.

11  Okada (2004) shows that quite a few Indian firms with joint ventures with TNCs in the auto industry sent their workers to foreign plants to provide their employees with exposure and training in technology. She gives an example of a firm in wiring harness manufacturing which sent fifty employees a year and several supervisors and engineers to its Japanese joint-venture partner for three months' on-the-job training, which accelerated technology transfer.

12  Furthermore, several TNCs in the software industry built linkages with local universities and engineering colleges to generate sufficient numbers of engineering graduates (Patibandla and Petersen, 2002).

13  This observation is based on my field interview with software professionals in Bangalore in 2004.

14  Schumpeter called the innovative activities of private agents under capitalism 'creative destruction'. Innovations resulting from defence research are literally creations coming out of means of destruction; the first inventions of prehistoric men were tools for hunting, which were later used for wars among the tribes. In modern times, the tools of war are improvised into commercial products. The creation of the Nobel prize is a classic example of rewarding excellence in research through the funds generated by the invention of dynamite.

15  We project the successful stories of the NIS of different countries from historical examples of the past. It belongs to the era of the supremacy of nation-states. In future, the social 'innovation systems' may no longer be 'national'. They will have structures that we cannot possibly imagine at the moment.

16  One of the small firms that HP supported in Bangalore has developed a product for Internet technology and has become very successful.

17  I am grateful to my students Nikhil Rajendra, Suvojit Mukherjee, Vikas Revankar and S. Vishwanath at the Indian Institute of Management, Bangalore (2004) for helping me to derive this figure. All of them are software professionals working for leading technology companies in Bangalore.

18  Interestingly, one of the leading biotechnology companies, Biocon, was set up as early as 1976 to produce industrial enzymes. However, its rapid growth took place only after the mid-1990s as it diversified into fermentation technology and the production of insulin.

19  One of the frequently shown advertisements on TV in 2005 is by an employment agency called 'The Monster.Com', which shows a professional who, when

mistreated by his boss, throws a cake at him, as he is confident that The Monster.Com will find him his next job with ease.

20 To give an example, an MBA graduate from the leading management schools gets a salary that is four times that of an assistant professor with a doctorate degree employed in the universities.

21 This should remind us of Mahatma Gandhi: "I do not want my doors closed and windows stuffed. I want the breezes of all lands to blow through my house. But I refuse to be blown off my feet by any of them."

22 Three of my ex-students who graduated from the Indian Institute of Management, Bangalore started an intellectual property rights consultancy service in 2004. My Web search in January 2005 has shown quite a few of these service agencies registered in India to provide technical and legal guidance on registering patents and copyrights, and protecting them.

## 7 Organizational change

1 A popular joke about these developments was that Dhirubhai Ambani, a poor, uneducated man, built the business from scratch with entrepreneurial talent, while his sons, who obtained MBAs from the prestigious Wharton and Stanford business schools, were ready to break it up.

2 Please note that in all economies, households are net savers and business is a net borrower. Financial institutions are supposed to channel household saving for business investment. That happened in India too. In fact there was less intermediation in India because of the weakness of India's financial institutions. The main criticism of the institutional arrangements is the cheap terms at which business in India got household savings via public financial institutions, thus denying households a fair return on their savings.

3 The groups appear to have benefited from pecuniary scope economies, such as in accessing cheap capital or other favors from official sources (and in paying bribes). Note that the governmental policies spurred diversification by non-family groups, such as Hindustan Lever and the Indian Tobacco Company (ITC), as well as the family groups. ITC, for instance, which pays more tax than any other company in India, contemplated building a power plant for precisely that reason.

4 This observation is based on the field study research of one of my colleagues, whose name is kept confidential.

5 An example is the firm Nirma in the detergents industry, which gave tough competition to the multinational Hindustan Lever. It adopted a production technique of low net assets and high variable inputs and got different households to process the chemicals on a subcontract basis. The final product was assembled at the factory. By adopting this practice it remained registered as a small firm for quite some time throughout the 1980s, although it realized a high sales turnover running into millions of rupees.

6 A colleague joked that his father had to pay a bribe to pay his income tax.

7 According to this view, first propounded by Williamson (1970) and Alchian (1969), the corporate headquarters is a more informed provider of capital and it can effectively monitor and ensure efficient use of capital by different units of the firm. The external capital market in which there are many small debt and equity investors may fail to invest in information and monitoring costs towards minimizing the moral hazard behavior of managers (the agency problem).

8 High rates of taxation of corporate profits magnified the benefits of diversification into tax shelters.

9 This observation shows the contradiction in the argument of Rajan and Zingales.

10 One more relevant feature is that the industries in Table 20, that increased their *VI* also show a much higher growth rate in selling costs to sales (*GADS*), or reputation effects and forward integration into distribution and customer service. The industries that showed decline in *VI* show higher growth in exports (20.7 percent) than the industries that increased export orientation (14.0 percent), despite having the most export-oriented software industry in this group.

11 In 2005, it started to sell tickets at petrol stations in major cities.

12 I am grateful to Mr Gopinath for giving me access to the figure.

13 Readers who are interested in the details can look at the journal article.

14 The results also show that FIIs prefer to invest in younger and more outward-oriented firms.

15 His study shows that such interlocks positively impact a company's performance. A colleague who worked for a public sector telecommunications company said that most of the strategic reports of the company reached the CEO of a competing private company before they reached the CEO of the public sector company. Under these kinds of institutional conditions, interlocked companies obviously perform better than stand-alone companies.

16 Goswami gives an example of a leading knowledge-based company that had no knowledge whatsoever regarding international board practices and the nuances of corporate governance. The desire to become a global player prompted it to adopt high standards of corporate governance.

17 The recommendations of the Birla Committee with regard to the board of directors are that the board should have an optimum combination of executive and non-executive directors. Companies with a non-executive chairman should have at least one third of the board members as independent directors. The board should meet at least four times a year. Financial institutions should appoint nominees only on a selective basis. A director should not be a member in more than ten committees across all the companies in which he is a director. Qualified and independent audit committees should be set up, with independent members.

18 On the other hand, the stock market scam in the US in the late 1990s was partly attributed to the stock options given to managers, who developed a strong interest in keeping the stock prices high by manipulating information and accounts and engaging in insider dealings.

19 A rigorous mathematical model of this argument is in Patibandla and Sinha (2005).

20 My paper with Sinha (2005) shows an econometric explanation of four firm concentration ratios for the seventy-nine industries during the period 1989 to 1999. The results show that changes in concentration for the time period under consideration demonstrate a convex trend. Concentration increases at a decreasing rate over time. An increase in the export-orientation of industries reduces industrial concentration. We interpreted the results to mean that general improvements in productivity through technological and organizational changes result in a decline in prices, especially those of capital and intermediate goods, which in turn reduces entry barriers for new entrants. The increased outward international orientation of industries can also be a source of decline in entry costs to new players.

21 The leading Indian software firm Wipro pioneered this model of governance.

22 One of the issues relating to fully owned subsidiaries is the extent of decentralization from the parent firm. Low levels of decentralization and assigning

low-end tasks to managers and skilled people in India results in high attrition, which leads to high costs. In a few TNC operations that I visited in Hyderabad and Bangalore, the skilled personnel complained of the jobs assigned to them being unchallenging and of low-end nature.

23 I am grateful to my students Nishit Kumar, Nitin Rastogi, and Ramakrishna Potti at the Indian Institute of Management, Bangalore (2004) for bringing this organizational choice in BPO industry to my notice.

24 The first appearance of the BOT model goes back to the nineteenth century, during the building of the Suez Canal. The construction of the canal was financed by European capital (the French) and the Egyptian ruler Pasha Muhammad Ali, who had the concession to operate it (Levy, 1996).

## 8 The evolution of public and private order institutions

1 Press reports show that, in several instances, property disputes are settled by resorting to the mafia in Bomaby because of the high costs and delays of the courts.

2 Interestingly, the neoclassical economists formalized Adam Smith's idea of the invisible hand into perfectly competitive markets in which collusion or cooperation is irrelevant because of the large number of autonomous producers and consumers. However, Adam Smith pointed out the possibility of producer collusion in his famous statement, "People of the same trade seldom meet together, even for merriment and diversion, but the conversation ends in a conspiracy against the public, or in some contrivance to raise prices."

3 The passage of the Sherman Act in the US in 1890 by the Congress gave federal judges extraordinary powers in regulating commerce by drawing fine lines between cooperation and illegal collusion, between competition and monopolization.

4 There are trade-offs between the rigidity and flexibility of the rules, and their effectiveness differs in different countries depending on the organization of the government and private parties. Rigidity may give a signal of credible commitments and thereby elicit investment. At the same time, in order to promote investment, some degree of flexibility is required in the regulations in the context of changing technologies and the increasing complexity of economic activity. This is especially necessary when contracts are highly incomplete in high-technology areas.

5 In 1992, the constitution of India was amended to increase decentralization to village-level (Panchayat) Local Governance Institutions (LGI) by recognizing local governance as a part of the governance system of the country. The constitutional amendment states that LGIs should involve the local community in taking decisions. It provides broad guidelines for the devolution of functions and financial resources. Although the constitutional reform increased the democratic base of the country, several state governments have been reluctant to decentralize in the true sense.

6 A widely prevalent private order institution of social security was the joint family system of parents being taken care of by children when old. Even this institutional arrangement is on the decline as the mobility of labor increases across regions and across the globe, and the material aspirations of the middle class go up, resulting in the splitting-up of joint families.

7 An explanation can be drawn from a model of semi-feudalism, where the feudal owner is not interested in land improvement because that would increase the tenant's share and make the tenant less dependent on the feudal landlord.

8 Although the government of India established the Competition Commission of India under the Competition Act 2002, so far, it has remained only a nominal body.

9 The father of the nation, Mahatma Gandhi, said, "A customer is the most important visitor on our premises. He is not dependent on us. We are dependent on him. He is not an interruption of our work, he is the purpose of it. He is not an outsider to our business, he is a part of it. We are not doing him a favour by serving him. He is doing us a favor by giving us an opportunity to do so." What prompted Mahatma Gandhi to say this could be the fact that the widely prevalent practices were actually the opposite of what he advocated. In the pre-reforms era, sellers always behaved as if they were doing a favor to consumers by selling their products.

10 Fosters' brewing company had to endure the process of obtaining government investment and brewing licenses for eleven years in India. Once the investment took place, the company grew very rapidly owing to increasing domestic demand for beer.

11 The minister announced that the Indian government would not default on its contractual obligations with DPC with the statement, "We will pay DPC all unpaid electricity bills of MSEB which contractually fall on us. The Government of India has never failed in fulfilling any of its obligations. We will never default on our contractual commitments to anyone." (Patibandla, 2005b).

12 For example, DPC charges unit prices ranging between Rs 3.01 and Rs 4.25 per kWh of electricity, while a local firm, the Tata Electric Company, offers it at Rs 1.40.

13 In Bangalore city, when a big construction project contract was given to a large firm (L&T), it built a flyover in record time. Since then, it is alleged that the firm was denied subsequent contracts because there were no pay-offs from the firm to local government agents.

14 One of the grand-scale incidences of corruption in India in the 1980s was the Bofors scandal, when a Swedish armaments company bribed top-level politicians and bureaucrats to sell arms to India. Sweden is supposed to be one of the least corrupt countries in the world.

15 In his lecture at the Indian Institute of Management, Bangalore (2004), the eminent journalist Mark Tully commented that people in the villages of India hate civil servants more than politicians, because politicians come to the people at least once every five years during the elections, while the bureaucrats with tenures do not have to.

16 However, under democracy the free press can play an effective monitoring role and reduce these hazards.

17 Similar behavior can be noticed in the case of the Communist Party in 2005. The party promotes economic reforms in those states in which it is in power, and blocks it in the center.

18 Under centralization, political interest calculations trap economic policies more on the rent-seeking and distribution of rents, rather than efficiency. However, it is possible that the group who gets the bigger piece of the pie is the one which is worse off on efficiency grounds in the long run. The loser in the distributional conflict may realize that his or her chance lies in increasing his or her efficiency. The qualitative evidence for this argument is that the fastest-growing states in India at present have been politically the least-powerful states in the center, and the most stagnant states are the ones which had the highest representation in the center.

19 In an interview to *Newsweek*, Ratan Tata has recently complained that some

business pressure groups are slowing down specific reforms (*Financial Express,* 27 June 2005).
20 NASSCOM, the software industry association, has been effectively protecting and pushing for deregulation as the association has grown in membership in recent years. Certain other industry associations which were previously dominated by big houses have become broad-based and representative of the industry.
21 As I discussed in Chapter 4, the other institutional innovation in reducing poverty is the e-choupals system in the rural areas.
22 It is important to note that the leaders of the organization (Kurien) kept the government out of the picture to ensure its management by members alone.

## 9 Conclusion

1 In the context of India, the example is the state of West Bengal, which has been ruled by the Communist Party since the late 1970s. On the positive side, Communist rule empowered the villages through land reforms and decentralization, but on the other hand, the democratic institutions degenerated into the strong-arm tactics of the Communist Party, which block other parties in contesting elections and challenging the Communist Party rule.
2 A few examples are N. R. Murthy and his associate founding members of Infosys, Ramlinga Raju of Satyam Computers, Kiran Majumadar of Biocon, Krishna Ella of Bharat Biotech, and Gopinath of Air Deccan.
3 In the case of telecommunications, also, previous investments by the government helped the private sector to grow rapidly in the post-reform era. For example C-DOT, which is a public sector undertaking, spread telephones all over India, including remote rural areas, in the mid-1980s.
4 As I discussed in Chapter 5, Sutton's study of India's and China's auto-component industry shows that the productivity of capital in India is higher. Moreover, China's financial institutions have three times more non-performing assets than India.
5 These markets were there in the pre-reforms era also at a very low end of the market. For example, when I used to go the railway station to make a reservation, generally there were long queues. There were also middlemen who for a small amount of money, would stand in the queue and get the ticket for you, which is not a bribe. It would, on the other hand, be a bribe in the case of middlemen who had contacts with the ticket sellers, and some middlemen, especially in movie theaters, buy the tickets in bulk in advance and sell them in the black market in collusion with the ticket sellers.

## Appendices

1 These results are taken to provide empirical regularities rather than a test of a theory, because when we introduce $T$ into the production function, technological change is treated as exogenous. In my approach, policy changes are exogenous and technological change is a result of the market dynamics in response to policy reforms.
2 The equation is estimated with firm-level panel data for each industry separately. The results for these are similar to those in equation 2.

# References

Adler, P. S., 1999, *Hybridisation in the Japanese Firm*, New York: Oxford University Press.

Aggarwal, A., 2004, 'Strategic Approach to Strengthening the International Competitiveness in Knowledge Based Industries: The Indian Pharmaceutical Industry', RIS Discussion Papers, New Delhi.

Ahlstrom, D., Bruton, G. D., and Lui, S. S. Y., 2000, 'Navigating China's Changing Economy: Strategies for Private Firms', *Business Horizons*, January.

Ahluwalia, M. S., 1999, 'India's Economic Reforms: An Appraisal', in J. Sachs, A. Varshney, N. Bajpai (eds), *India in the Era of Economic Reform*, Delhi: Oxford University Press.

Ahluwalia, M. S., 2002, 'State Level Performance under Economic Reforms in India', in A. Krueger (ed.), *Economic Policy Reforms and the Indian Economy*, New Delhi: Oxford University Press.

Akerlof, G., 1970, 'The Market for Lemons: Qualitative Uncertainty and the Market Mechanism', *Quarterly Journal of Economics* 84, 488–500.

Alchian, A. A., 1969, 'Corporate Management Property Rights', in H. Maine (ed.), *Economic Policy and the Regulation of Corporate Securities*, Washington, DC: American Enterprise Institute.

Alchian, A. A. and Demsetz, H., 1972, 'Production, Information Costs and Economic Organization', *American Economic Review* 62, 777–95.

Aliber, R. Z., 1970, 'A Theory of Direct Foreign Investment', in C. P. Kindleberger (ed.), *The International Corporation*, New Haven: Yale University Press.

Amsden, A., 1989, *Asia's Next Giant: South Korea and Late Industrialization*, New York: Oxford University Press.

Anant, T. C. A. and Goswami, O., 1997, 'Getting Everything Wrong', in Dilip Mookherjee (ed.), *Indian Industry: Policies and Performance*, New Delhi: Oxford University Press.

Aoki, M., 1990, 'Towards an Economic Model of the Japanese Firm', *Journal of Economic Literature* 28, 1–27.

Arasaratnam, S., 1986, *Merchants, Companies and Commerce on the Coromandel Coast 1650–1740*, New Delhi: Oxford University Press.

Aron, R. and Singh, J., 2002, 'IT Enabled Strategic Outsourcing: Knowledge Intensive Firms, Information Work and the Extended Organizational Form', Wharton School of Business, University of Pennsylvania.

Arrow, K. J., 1951, *Social Choice and Individual Values*, New York: Wiley.

Arrow, K. J., 1964, 'On the Role of Securities in the Optimal Allocation of Risk Bearing', *Review of Economic Studies*, April, 91–6.

Arrow, K. J., 1974, *The Limits of Organization*, New York: Norton and Company.

Banerjee, Abhijit V., 1997, 'A Theory of Misgovernance', *Quarterly Journal of Economics*, 112(4), 1289–332.

Banerjee, A., 2004, 'Who is Getting the Public Goods in India? Some Evidence and Speculation', in K. Basu (ed.), *India's Emerging Economy*, Cambridge, Mass.: MIT Press.

Banerjee, A., Mookherjee, D., Munshi, K., and Ray, D., 2001, 'Inequality, Control Rights, and Rent Seeking: Sugar Cooperatives in Maharastra', *Journal of Political Economy* 109(1), 138–90.

Banerjee, A. and Munshi, K., 2002, 'How Efficiently is Capital Allocated? Evidence from the Knitted Garment Industry in Tirupur', Dept of Economics, MIT, Cambridge.

Bardhan, P., 1984, *The Political Economy of Development in India*, New Delhi: Oxford University Press.

Bardhan, P., 1997, 'Corruption and Development: A Review of Issues', *Journal of Economic Literature* 35, 1320–46.

Bardhan, P. and Mookherjee, D., 2004, 'Decentralization in West Bengal: Origins, Functioning and Impact', working paper, Department of Economics, University of California, Berkeley.

Basant, R., Chandra, P., and Mytelka, L. K., 1998, 'Strategic Partnering in Telecom Software: Northern Telecom's Technology Network in India', working paper no. 98-07-01, Indian Institute of Management, Ahmedabad.

Basant, R. and Rani, U., 2004, 'Labor Market Deepening in the Indian Information Technology Industry: An Explorative Analysis', paper presented at workshop on Cross-Border Dynamics in India's IT Sector, Indian Institute of Management, Bangalore, June.

Basu, S. and Lie, D., 1996, 'Corruption and Reform', working paper 55, William Davidson Institute, Michigan.

Beck, T. L. and Loayza, R. N., 2000, 'Finance and the Sources of Growth', *Journal of Financial Economics* 58, 261–300.

Becker, G., 1968, 'Crime and Punishment: An Economic Approach', *Journal of Political Economy* 76(2), 169–217.

Beena, P. L., 2000, 'An Analysis of Mergers in the Private Corporate Sector in India', working paper no. 301, Centre for Development Studies, Trivandrum.

Bhagwati, J., 1993, *India in Transition: Freeing the Economy*, Oxford: Oxford University Press.

Bhagawati, J. N. and Desai, P., 1970, *India: Planning for Industrialisation*, Delhi: Oxford University Press.

Bhagawati, J. N. and Srinivasan, T. N., 1975, *Foreign Trade Regimes in Economic Development: India*, New York: Columbia University Press.

Bhagawati, J. N. and Srinivasan, T. N., 1983, *Lectures in International Trade*, Cambridge, Mass.: MIT Press.

Bhagawati, J. N. and Srinivasan, T. N., 1993, *India's Economic Reforms*, New Delhi: Ministry of Finance.

Bhalla, S. S., 2003, 'Crying Wolf on Poverty', *Economic and Political Weekly*, 5 July.

Bhattacharya, Sugata and Patel, Urjit R., 2003, 'Markets, Regulatory Institutions, Competitiveness and Reforms', paper prepared for the workshop on 'Understanding Reforms' organised by the Global Development Network, Cairo, Egypt.

Bhattacharya, S. and Patel, U. R., 2003, 'Reform Strategies in the Indian Financial

Sector', paper for conference on India's and China's experience with reform and growth, IMF and NCAER, New Delhi, 15–16 November.

Bhide, A., 2000, *The Origin and Evolution of New Businesses*, New York: Oxford University Press.

Bhide, A., 2004, 'What holds back Bangalore Business? Preliminary: On-going Study', Columbia Business School, NY.

Bhole, L. M., 1995, 'The Indian Capital Markets at the Cross Roads', *Vikalpa* 20, 29–41.

Bhudiraja, S., Piramal, G., Ghoshal S., and Bauman, R. P., 2003, 'Bajaj Auto', in S. Ghoshal, *World Class in India*, New Delhi: Penguin.

Bolton, P. and Scharfstein, D. S., 1998, 'Corporate Finance, the Theory of the Firm, and Organization', *Journal of Economic Perspectives* 12, 95–114.

Bowonder, B. and Richardson, P. K., 2000, 'Liberalization and the Growth of Business-led R&D: the Case of India', *R & D Management* 30, 4.

Bruch, M. and Hiemenz, U., 1983, 'Small and Medium Scale Manufacturing Establishments in Asian Countries: Perspectives and Policy Issues', report no. 9, Economics Office Report Series, Asian Development Bank.

Business Today, 1999, 'Fathers, Sons and CEOS', cover story, June.

Bussolo, M. and Whalley, J., 2002, 'Globalization in Developing Countries: the Role of Transaction Costs in Explaining Economic Performance in India', OECD, Paris.

Cairncross, F., 1997, *The Death of Distance*, London: Orion House.

Caniels, M. C. J. and Romijn, H. A., 2003, 'Dynamic Clusters in Developing Countries: Collective Efficiency and Beyond', *Oxford Development Studies* 31(3), 275–92.

Caves, R. E., (1996), *Multinational Enterprise and Economic Analysis*, Cambridge: Cambridge University Press.

Cawthorne, P. M., 1995, 'Of Networks and Markets: The Rise and Rise of a South Indian Town, the Example of Tiruppur's Cotton Knitwear Industry', *World Development* 23(1), 43–56.

Chandler, A., 1977, *The Visible Hand: The Management Revolution in American Business*, Cambridge, Mass.: Harvard University Press.

Chandra, P. and Tirupati, D., 2003, 'Successful Business Strategies for Firms in Large Emerging Economies: The Story of Amul', Indian Institute of Management, Ahmedabad.

Chandrashekar, S. and Basvarajappa, K. P., 2001, 'Technological Innovation and Economic Development: Choices and Challenges for India', *Economic and Political Weekly*, 25 August.

Cheng, H., 1986, *Analysis of Panel Data*, Cambridge: Cambridge University Press.

Clark, G. and Wolcott. S., 2001, 'One Polity, Many Countries: Economic Growth in India, 1857–2000', working paper, University of Mississippi.

Coase, R. H., 1937, 'The Nature of the Firm', *Economica* 4, 386–405.

Coase, R. H., 1960, 'The Problem of Social Costs', *Journal of Law and Economics* 3, 1–40.

Coase, R. H., 1964, 'The Regulated Industries: Discussion', *American Economic Review* 54, 194–7.

Coase, R. H., 1992, 'The Institutional Structure of Production', *American Economic Review* 82, 713–19.

Collins, W. J., 1999, 'Labor Mobility, Market Integration, and Wage Convergence in Late 19th Century India', *Exploration in Economic History* 36, 246–77.

Cornwell, C., Schmidt, P., and Sickles, R., 1990, 'Production Frontiers with Cross-sectional and Time-series Variation in Efficiency Levels', *Journal of Econometrics* 46, 185–200.

Crémer, J., 1995, 'Arms Length Relationships', *Quarterly Journal of Economics* 110, 275–96.

*Cuts*, 2004, 'Policy Watch', 5, 2–3.

Dalal, S., 2002, 'Tax Traitors: Comparisons and Contrasts', *Indian Express*, 16 September.

Das-Gupta, A., 2004, entry on 'Corruption', *The Oxford Companion to Economics in India*, New Delhi: Oxford University Press.

Das-Gupta, A., 2005, 'An Assessment of Revenue Structure and Performance of Indian States', background study for the World Bank Report on State Fiscal Reforms in India 'Progress and Prospects', Delhi: McMillan, Goa Institute of Management.

Das-Gupta, A. and Mookherjee, D., 1998, *Incentives and Institutional Reforms in Tax Enforcement*, New Delhi: Oxford University Press.

Das Gurucharan, 1999, 'The Problem', www.India-seminar.com.

D'Costa, A. P., 1995, 'The Restructuring of the Indian Automobile Industry: Indian State and Japanese Capital', *World Development* 23(3), 485–502.

De, B., 2003, 'The Incidence and Performance Effects of Interlocking Directorates in Emerging Market Business Groups: Evidence from India', Indira Gandhi Institute for Development Research, working paper WP-001, Mumbai.

Deaton, A. and Dreze, J., 2002, 'Poverty and Inequality in India: A Reexamination', *Economic and Political Weekly*, 7 September.

Delong, B. J., 2001, 'India Since Independence: An Analytic Growth Narrative', Dept of Economics, University of California, Berkeley.

Desai, A. V. (ed.), 1988, *Technology Absorption in Indian Industry*, London: Wiley.

Desai, A. V., 2005, 'India', in S. Commander (ed.), *The Software Industry in Emerging Markets*, Northampton: Edward Elgar.

Desai, L. M., 2002, 'Democracy and Development: India 1947–2002', Australian South Asia Research Centre, Research School of Pacific and Asian Studies, Australian National University.

Desai, L. M., 2003, 'India and China: An Essay in Comparative Political Economy', paper for IMF conference.

Dholakia, B. and Dholakia, R., 1993, 'Growth of Total Factor Productivity in Indian Agriculture', *Indian Economic Review*, 25–40.

Dixit, A., 1980, 'The Role of Investment in Entry Deterrence', *Economic Journal* 90, 95–106.

Dixit, A., 1999, 'Some Lessons from Transaction-Cost Politics for Less Developed Countries', Dept of Economics, Princeton University.

Djankov, S., Glaeser, E., Porta, R. L., Lopez, F., and Shleifer, A., 2003, 'The New Comparative Economics', *Journal of Comparative Economics* 31, 595–619.

Dossani, R., 1999, 'Assessing Venture Capital in India', Asia/Pacific Research Center, Stanford University.

Dossani, R. and Kenny, M., 2004, 'The Next Wave of Globalization: Exploring Relocation of Service Provision to India', paper submitted for the 'Globalization, Employment, and Economic Development' Workshop, Sloan Workshop Series in Industry Studies, Rockport, Mass., 14–16 June.

Dreze, J. and Sen, A. K., 1996, *India: Economic Development and Social Opportunity*, New Delhi: Oxford University Press.

Dunning, J. H., 1981, *International Production and the Multinational Enterprise*, London: George Allen and Unwin.

*Economist*, 2001, 'Unlocking of India's Growth,' 2–8 June.

*Economist*, 2004, 'Can India Work?', 12–18 June.

Evans, P., 1995, *Embedded Autonomy: States and Industrial Transformation*, Princeton: Princeton University Press.

Farrell, M., 1957, 'The Measurement of Production Efficiency', *Journal of the Royal Statistical Society* A 120(3), 253–81.

Fernald, J., 2003, 'Roads to Prosperity? Assessing the Link Between Public Capital and Productivity', *American Economic Review* 89, 619–38.

Ferrantino, M., 1992, 'Technology Expenditures, Factor Intensity, and Efficiency in Indian Manufacturing', *Review of Economics and Statistics* 74, 689–700.

Fisman, R. and Khanna, T., 2004, 'Facilitating Development: the Role of Business Groups', *World Development* 32(4), 609–28.

Forbes, N., 2002, 'Doing Business in India: What has Liberalization Changed?', in A. Krueger (ed.), *Economic Policy Reforms and the Indian Economy*, New Delhi: Oxford University Press.

Forbes, N. and Wield, D., 2002, *From Followers to Leaders: Managing Technology and Innovation in Newly Industrializing Countries*, New York: Routledge.

Freeman, C., 1997, 'The "National System of Innovation" in Historical Perspective', in D. Archibugi and J. Michie (eds), *Technology, Globalization and Economic Performance*, Cambridge: Cambridge University Press.

Ghemawat, P. and Khanna, T., 1998, 'The Nature of Diversified Groups: A Research Design and Two Cases Studies', *Journal of Industrial Economics* 46(1), 35–61.

Ghemawat, P. and Patibandla, M., 1999, 'India's Exports Since the Reforms: Three Analytic Industry Studies', in J. Sachs, A. Varshney, and N. Bajpai (eds), *India in the Era of Economic Reform*, Delhi: Oxford University Press.

Glaeser, Edward and Goldin, Claudia, 2004, 'Corruption and Reform: Introduction', Dept of Economics, Harvard University.

Glaeser, E. L. and Shleifer, A., 2003, 'The Rise of the Regulatory State', *Journal of Economic Literature* 41(2), 401–25.

Goldar, B. S., 1986, *Productivity Growth In Indian Industry*, New Delhi: Allied Publishers.

Gordon, J. and Gupta, P., 2003, 'A Tale of Two Giants: India's and China's Experience with Reform', IMF–NCAER Conference, New Delhi.

Gordon, J. and Gupta, P., 2003, 'Understanding India's Service Revolution', IMF, Washington, DC.

Goswami, O., 2001, 'The Tide Rises, Gradually: Corporate Governance in India', OECD Development Centre, Paris.

Grossman, S. and Hart, O., 1986, 'The Costs and Benefits of Ownership: A Theory of Vertical and Lateral Integration', *Journal of Political Economy* 94(4), 691–719.

Gulati, A., 1990, 'Fertilizer Subsidy: Is the Cultivator Net Subsidized', *Indian Journal of Agricultural Economics*, January–March.

Gulyani, S., 2001, 'Innovation with Infrastructure: How India's Largest Carmaker Copes with Poor Electricity Supply', *World Development* 27(10), 1749–68.

Gupta, S., 2003, 'Reforms via Bathinda', *Indian Express*, September.

Hannan, M. T. and Freeman, J., 1984, *Organizational Ecology*, Harvard University Press.

Harris, B., 2002, 'India's Informal Economy – Facing the 21st Century', paper for the Indian Economy Conference, Cornell University, 19 and 20 April.

Harris-White, Barbara, 2003, *India Working: Essays on Society and Economy*, Cambridge: Cambridge University Press.

Hart, O. and Moore, J., 1990, 'Property Rights and the Nature of the Firm,' *Journal of Political Economy* 6, 1119–58.

Hart, O. and Moore, J., 1998, 'Cooperatives and Outside Ownership', NBER working paper, W 6421.

Hayek, F., 1945, 'The Use of Knowledge in Society', *American Economic Review* 35, 519–30.

Hazari, R. K., 1966, *The Structure of the Corporate Private Sector: A Study of Concentration, Ownership and Control*, Bombay: Asia Publishing House.

Hazari, R. K., 1986, *Industrial Policy in Perspective: Essays in Industrial Policy*, New Delhi: Naurang Rai Concept Publishing House.

Heeks, R., 1996, *India's Software Industry*, New Delhi: Sage Publications.

Heston, A., and Kumar, V., 2005, 'Institutional Flaws and Corruption Incentives', Indian Institute of Management, Bangalore.

Hirschman, A. O., 1958, *The Strategy of Economic Development*, New Haven: Yale University Press.

Holmstrom, B., 1979, 'Moral Hazard and Observability', *Bell Journal of Economics* 10, 74–91.

Huang, Y., 2001, 'Why More is Actually Less: Interpretations of China's Labor-Intensive FDI', working paper no. 375, William Davidson Institute, University of Michigan.

Huang, Y., 2002, *Selling China: Foreign Direct Investment During the Reform Era*, New York: Cambridge University Press.

Huang, Y., Jr. and Hogan, K., 2002, 'India's Intellectual Property Rights Regime and the Pharmaceutical Industry', Harvard Business School.

Huang, Y. and Khanna, T., 2003, 'Can India overtake China?', *Foreign Policy*, July.

Hymer, S. H., 1960, *The International Operations of National Firms: A Study of Direct Foreign Investment*, Ph.D. dissertation, MIT, published by MIT Press (1976), Cambridge, Mass.

Intarakumnerd, P., Chairatana, P., and Tangchitpiboon, T., 2002, 'National Innovation System in Less Successful Developing Countries: The Case of Thailand', *Research Policy* 31, 1445–57.

Jacobsson, S. and Alam, G., 1994, *Liberalization and Industrial Development in the Third World*, New Delhi: Sage Publications.

Jalan, Bimal, 1996, *India's Economic Policy: Preparing for the Twenty-First Century*, New Delhi: Viking.

Jayaraman, N., 2002, 'Coca-Cola Parches Agricultural Land in India', www.globalpolicy.org.

Jensen, M. C. and Meckling, W., 1976, 'Theory of the Firm: Managerial Behavior, Agency Costs, and Ownership Structure', *Journal of Financial Economics* 3, 305–60.

Jha, N., 1998, 'Initiatives of Government of India on Regulatory Reform in the Context of the Action Plan for Effective and Responsive Government', paper presented at OECD, Paris.

Joshi, Vijay and Little, I. M. D., 1994, *India: Macroeconomics and Political Economy 1964–1991*, Washington, DC: World Bank and Oxford University Press.

Kaldor, N., 1966, *Causes of the Slow Rate of Economic Growth: of the United Kingdom*, Cambridge: Cambridge University Press.

Kambhampati, U. S., 2003, 'Trade Reforms and the Efficiency of Firms in India', *Oxford Development Studies* 31(2), 219–33.

Kapur, D. and Ramamurti, R., 2001, 'India's Emerging Competitive Advantage in Services', *Academy of Management Executive* 15(2), 20–33.

Katrak, H., 1997, 'The Private Use of Publicly Funded Industrial Technologies in Developing Countries: Empirical Tests for an Industrial Research Institute in India', *World Development* 25(9), 1541–50.

Katrak, H., 2002, 'Does Economic Liberalization Endanger Indigenous Technological Developments? An Analysis of the Indian Experience', *Research Policy* 31, 19–30.

Kazmi, Amy Louise, 2002, 'Why India's Poor Pay for Private Schools', letter published on Internet.

Kazmin, A. M., 2000, 'Why India's Poor Pay for Private Schools', *Business Week*, April.

Khanna, T., 2004, 'Facilitating Development: The Role of Business Groups', *World Development* 32(4), 609–28.

Khanna, T. and Melito, D., 1997, 'Modern India', HBS case 797-108, Harvard Business School.

Khanna, T. and Palepu, K., 1997, 'Why Focused Strategies May Be Wrong for Emerging Markets', *Harvard Business Review*, July–August.

Khanna, T. and Palepu, K., 1999, 'Emerging Market Business Groups, Foreign Investors, and Corporate Governance', NBER working paper W. 6955.

Khanna, T. and Palepu, K., 2000, 'Is Group Affiliation Profitable in Emerging Markets? An Analysis of Diversified Indian Business Groups', *Journal of Finance* 55(2), 86.

Khanna, T. and Palepu, K., 2004, 'Globalization and Convergence in Corporate Governance: Evidence from Infosys and Indian Software Industry', forthcoming in *Journal of International Business Studies*.

Kidron, M., 1965, *Foreign Investment in India*, London: Oxford University Press.

Kremer, M., 2002, 'Pharmaceuticals and the Developing World', *Journal of Economic Perspectives* 16(4), 67–90.

Kremer, M., Muralidharan, K., Chaudhury, N., Hammer, J. and Rogers, H., 2004, 'Teacher Absence in India', Dept of Economics, Harvard University.

Krishnan, R. T., 2003, 'The Evolution of a Developing Country Innovation System During Economic Liberalization: The Case of India', paper presented at the first Globerics conference, 3–6 November.

Krishnan R. T. and Prabhu, G. N., 1999, 'Creating Successful New Products: Challenges for Indian Industry', *Economic and Political Weekly*, 31 July.

Krueger, A. O., 1974, 'The Political Economy of Rent Seeking Society', *American Economic Review* 64, 291–303.

Krueger, A. O., 2004, 'Economic Policy Reforms and the Indian Economy', *Journal of Asian Economics* 14, 971–3.

Krueger, A. and Chinoy, S., 2002, 'The Indian Economy in Global Context', in A. Krueger (ed.), *Economic Policy Reforms and the Indian Economy*, New Delhi: Oxford University Press.

Krugman, P., 1994, 'The Myth of Asia's Miracle', *Foreign Affairs* 73, November–December, 62–78.

Kundu, A. and Gupta, S., 1996, 'Migration, Urbanization and Regional Inequality', *Economic and Political Weekly*, 28 December.

Kuznet, S., 1966, *Modern Economic Growth: Rate, Structure and Spread*, New Haven: Yale University Press.

La Porta, R., Lopez-de-Silanes, F., Shleifer, A., and Vishny, R., 1997, 'Legal Determinants of External Finance', *Journal of Finance* 57, 1147–57.

Lall, S., 1987, *Learning to Industrialize*, London: Macmillan Press.

Lall, S., 1992, 'Technological Capabilities and Industrialization', *World Development* 20(2), 165–86.

Lebenstein, H., 1966, 'Allocative Efficiency vs. X-efficiency', *American Economic Review* 56, 392–401.

Lema, R., 2005, 'The Role of Collective Efficiency in Banglore's Software-Export Success', presented at DRUID Academy winter conference.

Lema, R. and Hesbjerg, B., 2003, *The Virtual Extension, International Development Studies*, Roskilde University, Denmark.

Levi, Y. and Pellegrin-Rescia, M. L., 1997, 'A New Look at the Embeddedness/ Disembeddedness Issue: Cooperatives as Terms of Reference', *Journal of Socio-Economics* 26(2), 159–79.

Levy, B. and Spiller, P., 1996, *Regulations, Institutions and Commitment*, Cambridge: Cambridge University Press.

Levy, S. M., 1996, *Build, Operate and Transfer: Paving the Way for Tomorrow's Infrastructure*, New York: John Wiley & Sons, Inc.

Li, David, 1996, 'A Theory of Ambiguous Property Rights in Transition Economies: The Case of the Chinese Non-State Sector', *Journal of Comparative Economics* 23(1), 1–19.

Li, S., Li, S., and Zhang, W., 2000, 'The Road to Capitalism: Competition and Institutional Change in China', *Journal of Comparative Economics* 28, 269–93.

Little, M. D., Majumdar, D., and Page, J. M., 1987, *Small Manufacturing Enterprises: A Comparative Study of India and Other Economies*, Oxford: Oxford University Press.

Lucas, R. E., 1988, 'On the Mechanics of Economic Development', *Journal of Monetary Economics* 22, 3–42.

McConaughy, D., 1994, 'Founding-family-controlled Corporations: An Agency Theoretic Analysis of Corporate Ownership and its Impact on Performance, Operating Efficiency and Capital Structure', Doctoral thesis, University of Cincinnati.

Majumdar, S. K., 2004, 'The Hidden Hand and the License Raj: An Evaluation of the Relationship Between Age and the Growth of the Firm in India', *Journal of Business Venturing* 19, 107–25.

Manikutty, S., 2000, 'Family Business Groups in India: A Resource-Based View of the Emerging Trends', *Family Business Review* 13(4), 279–92.

Menon, S., 2001, 'The Great Indian Betrayal', *The Week*, 15–18 July.

Meyer, J. and Rowen, B. P., 1977, 'Institutionalized Organizations: Formal Structures as Myth and Ceremony', *American Journal of Sociology* 83, 340–63.

Milgrom, P. and Roberts, J., 1992, *Economics, Organization, and Management*, Englewood Cliffs, NJ: Prentice-Hall.

Modigliani, F. and Miller, M., 1958, 'The Cost of Capital, Corporate Finance, and the Theory of Investment', *American Economic Review* 48, 261–97.

Mohan, R. and Aggarwal, V., 1990, 'Commands and Controls: Planning for Industrial Development', *Journal of Comparative Economics* 14(4), 681–712.

Mookherjee, D. (ed.), 1997 *Indian Industry Policies and Performance*, New Delhi: Oxford University Press.

Mukherjee Reed, A., 2002, 'Corporate Governance Reforms in India', *Journal of Business Ethics* 37, 249–68.

Myrdal, G., 1968, *Asian Drama: An Inquiry into the Poverty of Nations*, Clinton, Mass.: Penguin Books.

Nagaraj, R., 1984, 'Sub-contracting in Indian Manufacturing Industries: Analysis, Evidence and Issues', *Economic and Political Weekly* 19, 1435–52.

Nagaraj, R., 2004, 'Fall in Organized Manufacturing Employment: A Brief Note', *Economic and Political Weekly*, 24 July.

NCAER, 2002, India Market Demographic Report, New Delhi.

Nelson, R. R., 1987, *Understanding Technical Progress as an Evolutionary Process*, Amsterdam: Elsevier.

Nelson, R. R. and Winter, S. J., 1982, *An Evolutionary Theory of Economic Change*, Cambridge: Harvard University Press.

Nenadic, S., 1993, 'The Small Family Business in Victorian Britain', *Business History* 29, 86.

North, D. C., 1989, 'Institutions and Economic Growth: A Historical Introduction', *World Development* 17(9), 1319–32.

North, D. C., 1990, *Institutions, Institutional Change and Economic Performance*, Cambridge: Cambridge University Press.

North, D., 1993, 'Institutional Change: A Framework of Analysis', lecture at WIDER, Helsinki.

North, D. and Weingast, B., 1989, 'Constitutions and Commitment: The Evolution of Institutions Governing Public Choice in 17th Century England', *Journal of Economic History* 49, 903–32.

Nurkse, R., 1953, *Problems of Capital Formation in Underdeveloped Countries and Patterns of Trade and Development*, Oxford: Oxford University Press.

Okada, A., 2004, 'Skills Development and Inter Firm Learning Linkage under Globalization: Lessons from the Indian Automobile Industry', *World Development* 32(2), 1265–88.

Olson, Mancur, 1965, *The Logic of Collective Action*, Cambridge, Mass.: Harvard University Press.

Olson, Mancur, 1982, *The Rise and Decline of Nations: Economic Growth, Stagflation, and Social Rigidities*, New Haven: Yale University Press.

Pack, H. and Westphal, L., 1986, 'Industrial Change and Technological Strategy', *Journal of Development Economics* 22, 87–128.

Patibandla, M., 1988, 'Role of Large and Small Firms in India's Engineering Exports', *Economic and Political Weekly*, 28 May.

Patibandla, M., 1994, 'Firm Size and Export Behaviour', doctoral thesis, Jawaharlal Nehru University, New Delhi.

Patibandla, M., 1995, 'Firm Size and Export Behaviour: An Indian Case Study', *Journal of Development Studies* 31(6), 868–82.

Patibandla, M., 1997, 'Economic Reforms and Institutions', *Economic and Political Weekly*, 24 May.

Patibandla, M., 1998, 'Structure, Organizational Behavior and Technical Efficiency', *Journal of Economic Behavior and Organization* 34(3), 431–42.

Patibandla, M., 2002a, 'Policy Reforms, Evolution of Market Structure: A Study of an Emerging Economy', *Journal of Development Studies* 38(3), 95–118.

Patibandla, M., 2002b, 'Foreign Direct Investment in China: A New Perspective', *Economic and Political Weekly*, 23 November.

Patibandla, M., 2002c, 'Product Differentiation and Market Demand for TNCs in an Emerging Economy', *Indian Economic Journal*, January–March.

Patibandla, M., 2005a, 'Equity Pattern, Corporate Governance and Performance: A Study of India's Corporate Sector', forthcoming article in *Journal of Economic Behavior and Organization.*

Patibandla, M., 2005b, 'Pattern of Foreign Direct Investment in Developing Economies: A Comparative Analysis of China and India', forthcoming article in *International Journal of Management and Decision Making.*

Patibandla, M., 2005c, 'Emerging Landscape and New Value Propositions in the Civil Aviation Sector: In Conversation with Captain Gopinath, MD, Air Deccan', *IIMB Management Review*, March, 31–40.

Patibandla, M. and Amarnath, H. K., 1994, 'An Analysis of Short Run Price Instability of Cotton Harn', *Economic and Political Weekly*, 27 August.

Patibandla, M. and Chandra, P., 1998, 'Organizational Practices and Employee Performance', *Journal of Economic Behavior and Organization* 37(4), 432–42.

Patibandla, M., Kapur, D., and Petersen, B., 2000, 'Import Substitution with Free Trade: The Case of India's Software Industry', *Economic and Political Weekly*, 8 April.

Patibandla, M. and Petersen, B., 2002, 'Role of Transnational Corporations in the Evolution of a High-tech Industry: the Case of India's Software Industry', *World Development* 30(9), 1561–77.

Patibandla, M. and Petersen, B., 2004, 'Role of Transnational Corporations in the Evolution of a High-tech Industry: the Case of India's Software Industry – A Reply', World Development 32(3), 561–66.

Patibandla, M. and Prusti, R., 1998, 'East Asian Crisis as a Result of Institutional Failures: Lessons for India', *Economic and Political Weekly*, 28 February–6 March.

Patibandla, M. and Sanyal, A., 2005a, 'Corruption: Market Reform and Technology', Indian Institute of Management, Bangalore.

Patibandla, M. and Sanyal, A., 2005b, 'Foreign Investment and Productivity: A Study of Post-Reform Indian Industry', *Review of Applied Economics* 1(1), 21–35.

Patibandla, M. and Sastry, T., 2004, 'Capitalism and Cooperation', *Economic and Political Weekly*, 3 July.

Patibandla, M. and Sinha, D., 2005, 'Economic Reforms, Evolution of Industrial Structure: A Study of Indian Industry', Indian Institute of Management, Bangalore.

Parente, S. L. and Prescott, E. C., 1994, 'Barriers to Technology Adoption and Development', *Journal of Political Economy* 102(2), 298–321.

Parente, S. L. and Prescott, E. C., 1999, 'Monopoly Rights: A Barrier to Riches', *American Economic Review* 89(5), 1216–33.

Payne, P. L., 1978, 'Industrial Entrepreneurship and Management in Great Britain', in *Cambridge Economic History of Europe*, vol. VII, Cambridge: Cambridge University Press.

Penrose, E., 1959, *The Theory of the Growth of the Firm*, New York: Wiley.

Pfeffer, J., 1996, 'Understanding Organization: Concepts and Controversies', in *Handbook of Social Psychology* (fourth edn), New York: McGraw-Hill.

Piramal, G., 1996, *Business Maharajas*, New Delhi: Penguin.

Piramal, G. A., 1999, 'Crisis of Leadership', <www.india-seminar.com>.

Pirenne, H., 1937, *Economic and Social History of Mediaeval Europe*, New York: Harcourt, Brace and World.

Pitt, M. and Lee, L., 1981, 'The Measurement and Sources of Technical Efficiency in the Indonesian Weaving Industry', *Journal of Development Economics* 9, 43–63.

Porter, M., 1990, *The Competitive Advantage of Nations*, New York: Free Press.

Posner, R. A., 1998, 'Creating a Legal Framework for Economic Development', *World Bank Research Observer* 13(1), 1–11.

Prahalad, C. K. and Hamel, G., 1990, 'The Core Competence of the Corporation', *Harvard Business Review*, May–June, 79–91.

Pretty, J and Ward, H., 2001, 'Social Capital and the Environment', *World Development* 29(2), 209–27.

Rajan, R. G. and Shah, A., 2003, 'New Directions in Indian Financial Sector Policy', project, NCAER for Ministry of Finance.

Rajan, R. G. and Zingales, L., 1998, 'The Governance of the New Enterprise', Graduate School of Business, University of Chicago.

Rajan, R. G. and Zingales, L., 2001, 'The Firm as a Dedicated Hierarchy: A Theory of the Origins and Growth of Firms', *Quarterly Journal of Economics* 116(3), 805–51.

Rajan, G. R. and Zingales, L., 2003, *Saving Capitalism from Capitalists: Unleashing the Power of Financial Markets to Create Wealth and Spread Opportunity*, New York: Crown Business.

Rakshit, M., 2004, 'Some Macroeconomics of India's Reforms Experience', in Kaushik Basu (ed.), *India's Emerging Economy*, Cambridge: MIT Press.

Rao, D. N. and Gupta, S., 2004, 'Recent Developments on the Regulatory Framework for the Private Sector in Infrastructure', Indian Institute of Management, Bangalore.

Rao, M. G. and Singh, N., 2002, 'Fiscal Transfers in a Developing Economy – The Case of India', paper presented at the seminar in Comparative Federalism, University of Birmingham, 19 January.

Reddy, Y. V., 2002, *Lectures on Economic and Financial Sector Reforms in India*, New Delhi: Oxford University Press.

Romer, P. M., 1990, 'Endogenous Technological Change', *Journal of Political Economy* 98, S71–102.

Rosario, S. L., 1999, 'Emerging Patterns of Transnational Activity in India: A Study of Foreign Collaboration Intentions in the 1990s', unpublished Ph.D. thesis, Indian Institute of Management, Ahmedabad.

Rosenberg, N., 1972, *Technology and American Economic Growth*, New York: Harper and Row.

Roy, S., 2004, 'Technology Transfer from National R&D Laboratories and the Development of Regional Industrial Clusters in India', *Industry and Higher Education*, February.

Roy, T., 1996, 'Market Resurgence, Deregulation, and Industrial Response: Indian Cotton Textiles in the 1990s,' *Economic and Political Weekly*, 25 May.

Roy, T., 2001, *The Economic History of India, 1857–1947*, New Delhi: Oxford University Press.

Sachs, J. D., Varshney, A., and Bajpai, N. (eds), 1999, *India in the Era of Economic Reforms*, Delhi: Oxford University Press.

Sanyal, A., 1984, 'Accumulating Changes in the Nature of Controls in the Indian Economy', *Social Scientist*, May, 33–41.

Sanyal, A., 1986, 'Borrowing From the Rich', *Economic and Political Weekly*, 9 July.

Sanyal, A., 2000, 'Audit Hierachy in a Corrupt Tax Administration', *Journal of Comparative Economics* 28(2), 364–78.

Sanyal, A., 2004, 'Bribes in a Supply Line', *Economica* 71, 155–68.

Sarma, A., 1997, 'Performance of Public Enterprises in India', in Dilip Mookherjee (ed.), *Indian Industry: Policies and Performance*, New Delhi: Oxford University Press.

Saxenian, A., 1994, *Regional Advantage: Culture and Competition in Silicon Valley and Route 128*, Cambridge: Harvard University Press.

Schmidt, P. and Sickles, R., 1984, 'Production Frontiers and Panel Data', *Journal of Business and Economic Statistics* 2, 367–74.

Schumpeter, J. A., 1947, 'The Creative Response in Economic History', *Journal of Economic History* 7, 149–59.

Sen, K. and Vaidya, R. R., 1997, *The Process of Financial Liberalization in India*, New Delhi: Oxford University Press.

Shah, A., 1998, 'Institutional Change in India's Capital Markets', Indira Gandhi Institute of Development Research, Mumbai.

Shah, A., 1998, 'The Institutional Development of India's Securities Markets', in T. Waghmare (ed.), *The Future of India's Stock Markets*, New Delhi: Tata McGraw-Hill.

Shaw, A. and Thomas, S., 2002, 'The Evolution of the Securities Markets in India', Indira Gandhi Institute of Development Research, Mumbai.

Shleifer, A. and Vishny, R., 1997, 'A Survey of Corporate Governance', *Journal of Finance* 52, 737–83.

Simon, H., 1957, *Models of Man*, New York: Wiley.

Singh, N. and Srinivasan, T. N., 2002, 'Indian Federalism, Economic Reform and Globalization', Dept of Economics, Yale University.

Smith, S. E., 2000, 'Opening Up to the World: India's Pharmaceutical Companies Prepare for 2005', Asia Pacific Research Center, Institute for International Studies, Stanford University.

Solow, R., 1988, 'Growth Theory and After', *American Economic Review* 78, 307–17.

Spence, M., 1976, 'Informational Aspects of Market Structure: An Introduction', *Quarterly Journal of Economics* 90(4), 591–7.

Srinivasan, T. N., 2000, *Eight Lectures on India's Economic Reforms*, New Delhi: Oxford University Press.

Srivistava, A., 2004, 'Coke with yet Another New Twist: Toxic Cola', www.Indiaresource.org.

Srivastava, R. and Sasikumar, S. K., 2003, 'An Overview of Migration in India, its Impact and Key Issues', Dept for International Development, UK.

Stigler, G., 1951, 'The Division of Labor is Limited by the Extent of the Market', *Journal of Political Economy* 59, 185–93.

Stiglitz, J. E., 1987, 'Learning to Learn, Localized Learning and Technological Progress', in P. Das Gupta and P. Stoneman (eds), *Economic Policy and Technological Performance*, Cambridge: Cambridge University Press.

Stiglitz, J. E. and Weiss, A., 1981, 'Credit Rationing in Markets with Imperfect Information', *American Economic Review* 71(3), 393–410.

Sundaram, K. and Tendulkar, S. D., 2003, 'Poverty in India in the 1990s', *Economic and Political Weekly*, 15 November.

Sutton, J., 2004, 'The Auto-Component Supply Chain in China and India: A Bench Mark Study', London School of Economics and Political Science.

Tewari, M., 2005, 'Foreign Direct Investment and the Transformation of Tamil

Nadu's Automotive Supply Base', in Yves-André Fauré, Loraine Kennedy and Pascal Labazée (eds), *Productions locales et marché mondial dans les pays émergents: Brésil, Inde, Mexique*, Paris: IRD, Karthala.

Tewari, M. and Pillai, P., 2003, 'Negotiated Collective Action and Adjustment in Tamil Nadu's Leather Industry', working paper, Chapel Hill: University of North Carolina.

Tooley, J., 2000, 'Private Schools for the Poor in India', *Economic Affairs*, June.

Tripathi, D., 2004, *The Oxford History of Indian Business*, New Delhi: Oxford.

UNCTAD, 2002, *The World Investment Report: Promoting Linkages*, New York: United Nations.

Varshney, A., 1999, 'Mass Politics or Elite Politics? India's Economic Reforms in Comparative Perspective', in J. Sachs, A. Varshney and N. Bajpai (eds), *India in the Era of Economic Reform*, Delhi: Oxford University Press.

Verma, J. R., 1997, 'Corporate Governance in India: Disciplining the Dominant Shareholder', *Management Review*, October–December, 5–18.

Virmani, A., 2004, 'Telecommunication Reforms in India', ICRIER, New Delhi.

Waldman, A., 2003, 'India's Poor Bet Precious Sums on Private Schools', *New York Times*, 15 November.

Waldman, A., 2004, 'Indian Soyabean Farmers Join the Global Village', <www.nytimes.com>, accessed 15 November 2004.

Weiner, M., 1999, 'The Regionalization of Indian Politics and Its Implications for Economic Reforms', in J. Sachs, A. Varshney, and N. Bajpai (eds), *India in the Era of Economic Reform*, Delhi: Oxford University Press.

Weingast, B. R., 1998, 'The Political Impediments to Economic Reforms: Political Risk and Enduring Gridlock', Institute for Policy Research, Stanford University.

Williamson, J. and Zagha, R., 2002, 'From Slow Growth to Slow Reform', Centre for Research on Economic Development and Policy Reform, working paper, Stanford University.

Williamson, O. E., 1970, *Corporate Control and Business Behavior*, New Jersey: Prentice Hall.

Williamson, O. E., 1975, *Markets and Hierarchies: Analysis and Antitrust Implications*, New York: Free Press.

Williamson, O. E, 1981, 'The Modern Corporation: Origins, Evolution, Attributes', *Journal of Economic Literature* 19, 1537–68.

Williamson, O. E., 1983, 'Credible Commitments: Using Hostages to Support Exchange', *American Economic Review* 73, 519–40.

Williamson, O. E., 1985, *The Economic Institutions of Capitalism*, New York: Free Press.

Williamson, O. E., 1998, 'Economic Institutions and Development: A View from the Bottom', in Mancur Olson and Satu Kahkonen (eds), *A Not So Dismal Science*, New York: Oxford University Press.

Williamson, O. E., 2002, 'The Theory of the Firm as Governance Structure: From Choice to Contracts', *Journal of Economic Perspectives* 16, 171–95.

World Bank, 2004, 'Doing Business in 2005', Washington, DC.

Yergin, D., 1998, *The Commanding Heights*, New York: Simon and Schuster.

Yunus, M., 1998, *Banker to the Poor: The Autobiography of Muhammad Yunus, Founder of the Grameen Bank*, London: Aurum Press.

Zagha, R., 1999, 'Labor and India's Economic Reform', in J. Sachs, A. Varshney, and N. Bajpai (eds), *India in the Era of Economic Reform*, Delhi: Oxford University Press.

# Index